RONALD D. BONNELL

RONALD D. BONNELL

RONALD D. BONNELL

Relational Information Systems

Relational Information Systems

T.H. Merrett

McGill University, Montreal

Reston Publishing Co.
A Prentice-Hall Company
Reston, Virginia

Library of Congress Cataloging in Publication Data

Merrett, Timothy Howard
   Relational information systems.

   Bibliography: p.
   1. Data base management.   2. Information storage
and retrieval systems.   I. Title.
QA76.9.D3M45 1983   001.64   82-25036
ISBN   0-8359-6642-9

© 1984 by Reston Publishing Company, Inc.
A Prentice-Hall Company
Reston, Virginia 22090

10 9 8 7 6 5 4 3 2 1

Printed in the United States of America

To
Hazel Howard
and
John Campbell Merrett

TABLE OF CONTENTS

PREFACE

Relational Information Systems applies the result of database research to information systems design. The approach that has given the greatest insight into the nature of data and the requirements on databases is the relational approach, which is taken here. As a book on databases, **Relational Information Systems** is concerned with applicability. As a book on information systems, it is concerned with computer techniques.

As a technical book on the application of database research to information systems, it is directed at several classes of reader. First, the student or researcher of databases in a university computer science department will find a range of material from explanations, illustrated with examples, of basic database concepts to advanced treatments of the recent research literature. Second, the professional programmer or systems analyst will find a thorough treatment of the most efficient and general implementation algorithms and file structures. Third, the student of information systems in a university school of management studies will find simple discussions of powerful ways to conceive and describe applications problems, amplified by two fully worked out commercial applications. Finally, the technical manager, say of an information systems department, who wants to bring his knowledge up to date, so as to be able to guide his departmental activities more professionally, will find an understandable overview of database and information systems techniques.

Not all of these classes of reader will need or want to read the whole book. The chart below is a guide to the structure of the book. This structure is two-dimensional and permits various paths through the material. There are six parts, four on relational techniques and two on applications. Each part is divided into three to four chapters (with the omissions as indicated) with corresponding chapters in each part having the same orientation.

The "Basics" chapters introduce the fundamental concepts, using plenty of examples, and are for all the above classes of reader. The "Implementation" chapters emphasize data structures and algorithms, and are for programmer/ analyst and computer science student. The "Cost Analysis" chapters give mathematical analyses (at the level of college freshman mathematics) of the implementation techniques, and serve both to introduce analysis methods and to give further understanding of the algorithms. The "Advanced Topics" chapters review database research literature, either to give a historical perspective or to survey important applicable areas that still pose open research problems. The "Cost Analysis" and "Advanced Topics" chapters are intended for the computer science student and database researcher.

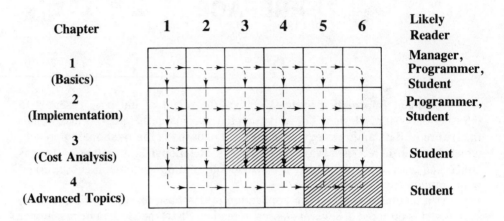

Exhibit P-1. The Prerequisite Structure of the Chapters of this Book.
(▨ indicates omitted chapters in Parts 3, 4, 5 and 6)

The paths through the book are indicated by the dashed lines in Exhibit P-1. To read a chapter requires first grasping the material on *all* paths which lead to it. Thus to understand Chapter 2.2, you must have followed Chapters 1.1, 2.1 and 1.2. The general prerequisite for the book is an ability to think precisely, as might be developed by mathematics courses up to the college freshman level. In addition, readers of the "Implementation" chapters are assumed to know how to write computer programs and in particular how to deal with data on secondary storage such as magnetic disks. Readers of the "Cost Analysis" chapters should know freshman calculus and statistics and be prepared to refer to cited texts if necessary. The appendix gives a quick review of the graph theory terminology that is needed. Readers of the "Advanced Topics" chapters are expected to read the cited research articles that interest them, although the overviews attempt to be comprehensible on their own and to serve as useful guides to deeper reading.

Notwithstanding these minimum requirements, the book will require some dedication to absorb wholly, and, for computer science courses, is best suited at the senior undergraduate and first-year graduate levels. For instance, a one-semester course at this level might cover Chapters 1.1, 2.1, 3.1, 4.1, 1.2 and 2.2, with excursions into other parts of the book according to the interests of the students and the discretion of the instructor.

A part-by-part description of the contents of **Relational Information Systems** follows. When you have read the book, or the levels of the book that interest you,

you should have a better idea of how to understand, design or implement either a specific information system or a general database system.

$$\bullet \quad \bullet \quad \bullet$$

1. RELATIONS.   This part explains what relations are and how they represent data. It examines all the common and some uncommon ways of storing relational data on available and potential media. It gives the basic tools for cost analysis of these data organizations.
2. OPERATIONS on RELATIONS.   The relational algebra and its analogy with common operations on files are studied, illustrated by applications. The basic ways of performing these operations are also described and analyzed.
3. OPERATIONS on ATTRIBUTES.   To find sums, subtotals, averages, etc., readers need to operate on the columns, or attributes, of relations. This part gives the basic processes that are needed and describes their implementation.
4. QUERIES and QUANTIFIERS.   A great deal of database research has concentrated on query processing and query languages. Information systems applications often need such a capability. Part 4 discusses the categories of queries that can arise and some implementations.
5. MANUFACTURING PROFIT.   This part describes the first of two applications, which illustrate the relational and domain algebras (see Parts 2 and 3). A full, if universalized, application to compute manufacturing costs from labor, equipment and materials data, and to compute profits from costs and price data, is given. This leads to some general principles of implementation and a discussion of the problem of computing the closure of a relation.
6. ACCOUNTING.   Part 6 shows a broad view of the whole manufacturing firm, first in terms of its funds flow and then in terms of a parallel set of operating data, including the manufacturing costs of Part 5. The relations and operations required to generate financial statements (e.g., Income Statement, Balance Sheet) are spelled out. The discussion of how to implement the system introduces the concept of chronological relations.

$$\bullet$$

It is premature here to attempt to define "database" or "information system." The book answers the questions "What is a database?" and "What is an information system?" Here it is only possible to make some initial characterizations, to set the tone for the rest of the book.

Databases are characterized by large amounts of data, permanently stored. Information systems are characterized by updating this data, retrieving selected portions of it and manipulating these to produce relevant results. Databases thus require secondary storage, which is both capable of preserving data beyond the duration of any one program run, and is able to hold far more data than can fit at any one time in the main memory of a computer.

Both the permanence and quantity of data in database pose problems that do not arise in ordinary computing with data that is manipulated entirely by one program and only during the time the program is running on the computer. Information systems thus require special techniques for manipulating this data, and safeguards against changing it erroneously. It is characteristic of the data in the database of an information system, however, that it is composed of many different units of data all of the same form. Thus, the transfer of data from secondary to primary memory, and its manipulation, is a highly repetitive process. The relational approach adopted in this book allows us to transcend the repetitive similarities of data items and concentrate on the relevant differences among the different forms of data.

All this will be easier to understand once you have read Chapters 1.1 and 2.1. But we will make one more general point now. FORTRAN is a successful, if inelegant, programming language. It was the first "high level" programming language, which means that it allows programmers to manipulate the objects they are interested in rather than the objects the computer uses, such as registers and bits. The objects of interest in the case of FORTRAN are numbers—integers, real and complex—which the FORTRAN programmer can add, subtract, multiply and generally operate on with all the familiar operations of arithmetic and algebra. In the case of information systems, the objects to be manipulated are the sets of units of data with the same form.

To operate on the individual units is repetitive, like a numerical program which has to operate on bits instead of numbers. The basic objects must contain the repetition, rather than force the programmer to worry about it. Thus, the objects which are manipulated by the operations of the information system must be *sets* of data units. It is currently difficult to discuss these objects, and the operations on them, a difficulty which does not affect the programmer dealing with numbers and the familiar operations of arithmetic: database objects have only been with us for a decade or so; arithmetic has evolved over millennia.

This book speaks of database objects—relations—and their operations—the relational algebra. These are new topics, but they have already been the subject of hundreds of research articles, explanations and applications. Much of what is discussed is strange at first, and much has not yet been widely used in practice. But the pace of evolution of databases and information systems is much more rapid than the development of arithmetic, and even in the months during which this book was being written, relations and relational operations have made large advances in the practicing community of computer users. Even microcomputers have algebraic relational databases, and the operations discussed in this book have been implemented on a tiny machine. Relations are the Arabic numerals of information systems and their simplicity and systematic power is gaining them ascendency over the anaolgues of Roman numbers.

• • •

An author who sets out to write a book—probably without really knowing what he is up against—thinks that it will just be a matter of putting down what he knows, with perhaps some checking of details and surveying some weak areas. But the combinatorial complexity of correlating that knowledge (which anyway turns out to be quite inadequate), those details, and those surveys, is greater in a book than in an article of one tenth the length, and the author accumulates debts to others at a rapid rate. Many people have reviewed and commented on all or parts of the manuscript of this book. They have complained, questioned and clarified. They have contributed greatly to the quality of the result which, since I have not always followed their advice, remains tarnished through my fault alone. They include L.R. Amey, W.W. Armstrong, N.B. Dale, F.A. Daneliuk, M. Gilman, H.C. Ho, H.R. Howson, H.L. Morgan, J.A. Orenstein, E. J. Otoo, W. Page, J.H. Reneau, P.G. Sorenson, M. Uretsky, many anonymous reviewers, and numerous students in my graduate courses on Databases and Information Systems who have lived through the development of material on the following pages.

I am grateful to Academic Press Inc. for permission to reproduce much of Merrett and Otoo [1982] in Secton 1.2-3. I am grateful to Philips Research Laboratory, Brussels, for permisson to reproduce the example queries of Lacroix and Pirotte [1976a] in Chapter 4.1. I am indebted to McGill University and my collegues in the School of Computer Science for facilities provided, congenial associates and a sabbatical leave during which this book was commenced.

Luc Devroye has enthusiastically solved numerous statistical problems. Yahiko Kambayashi's visit in 1979 and Tomasz Imielinski's from 1982-84 provided stimulating and fruitful discussion. Bill Armstrong has been a constant inspiration and his proximity at Université de Montréal until 1982 has been invaluable. Diane Chan, with remarkable competence and more remarkable cheerfulness, did all the typing. Mary Ann Mongeau and Jack Orenstein each proofread the whole text. Ben Wentzell and Dan McCauley are the editors at Reston who, respectively, saw some worth in the book and bore the brunt of preparing it for publication, with the help of an incisive copy editor and professional staff.

Mary Ann Mongeau, my wife, and my children, Andrea and Patrick, bore with my absence, spiritual if not physical, for long periods. The children play a role in the text, along with their cousins—the least I could do to make up for lost playtimes over a span of half their lives. Mary Ann, I love you.

This book is dedicated to my parents, to whom I owe everything.

Relational Information Systems

1

RELATIONS

BASICS: About Data

1.1-1   Instances of Relations

Consider the data in Exhibit 1.1-1.

Exhibit 1.1-1. An Instance of the Relation ORDERBOOK (ORD#, CUSTOMER, SALESMAN, ASSEMBLY, QTY)

ORD #	CUSTOMER	SALESMAN	ASSEMBLY	QTY
4	Pennsylvania Railroad	Hannah Trainman	Car	37
3	London & Southwestern	Eric Brakeman	Car	23
2	New York Central	Natacha Engineer	Locomotive	1
7	Grand Trunk Railway of Canada	Natacha Engineer	Locomotive	47
3	London & Southwestern	Eric Brakeman	Caboose	3
5	New York Central	Hannah Trainman	Locomotive	13
7	Grand Trunk Railway of Canada	Natacha Engineer	Caboose	43
8	Great North of Scotland	Eric Brakeman	Toy Train	37
1	Great North of Scotland	Eric Brakeman	Locomotive	2
5	New York Central	Hannah Trainman	Car	31
6	Baltimore & Ohio	Hannah Trainman	Car	17
4	Pennsylvania Railroad	Hannah Trainman	Toy Train	11
3	London & Southwestern	Eric Brakeman	Locomotive	5
1	Great North of Scotland	Eric Brakeman	Toy Train	7
7	Grand Trunk Railway of Canada	Natacha Engineer	Car	139

A considerable amount of information is represented in Exhibit 1.1-1, and it is not difficult to see what it means: a salesman called Hannah Trainman has obtained an order from the Pennsylvania Railroad for 37 Cars, which has been recorded on Order Number 4; and so on. More inspection will reveal that Order Number 4 also includes 11 Toy Trains sold by the same salesman to the same customer; that Hannah Trainman is involved with two other customers via two other orders concerning 13 Locomotives and 48 additional Cars; that a total of 55 Toy Trains have been ordered, etc.

Notice that we are hampered in making these additional observations because the data is not ordered in any convenient way. For instance, it might be handy if all rows for a given Order Number were together and the groups arranged by ascending Order Number. We also might get rid of some of the duplicated information, such as the fact that each Order Number involves exactly one customer and exactly one salesman. If all the Order Number 4's were together, for example, we need not repeat Pennsylvania Railroad or Hannah Trainman. The result of these changes would appear as follows.

ORD#	CUSTOMER	SALESMAN	ASSEMBLY	QTY
1	Great North of Scotland	Eric Brakeman	Toy Train	7
			Locomotive	2
2	New York Central	Natacha Engineer	Locomotive	1
3	London & Southwestern	Eric Brakeman	Car	23
			Locomotive	5
			Caboose	3
•	•	•	•	•
•	•	•	•	•

Note that the representation of the data is now more complicated in that we have added horizontal lines to distinguish the items pertaining to different orders. These lines correspond to various implementation devices, such as trailer records, repeating groups, pointers, etc.

We could take the process further by grouping together all information for each customer.

CUSTOMER	ORD#	SALESMAN	ASSEMBLY	QTY
Baltimore & Ohio	6	Hannah Trainman	Car	17
Great North of Scotland	1	Eric Brakeman	Toy Train	7
			Locomotive	2
	8	Eric Brakeman	Toy Train	37
•	•	•	•	•
•	•	•	•	•

Here there is a second type of horizontal line, separating subgroups for different order numbers within the group for each customer. This further breakdown is not unique: we could also group by salesman.

SALESMAN	ORD#	CUSTOMER	ASSEMBLY	QTY
Hannah Trainman	4	Pennsylvania Railroad	Toy Train	11
			Car	37
	5	New York Central	Locomotive	13
			Car	31
	6	Baltimore & Ohio	Car	17
•	•	•	•	•
•	•	•	•	•

Which of these modifications of the data of Exhibit 1.1-1 we might choose depends on the application we have in mind. The information would probably be *recorded* in sequence of order number, since each salesman would file his orders as he acquires a customer, and order numbers would be allocated in sequence. A summary of *customer interests* might require grouping by customer, and an analysis of *salesman activity* could use a grouping by salesman. None of the above would improve on Exhibit 1.1-1 for an examination of what *assemblies* were selling well, and depending on the physical layout of the records on tape or disk, might well perform relatively poorly.

Exercise   1.1-1:   Complete the three above-grouped versions of Exhibit 1.1-1. Show a version grouped by assemblies.

What is important is that none of the alternative representations adds information that is not already present in Exhibit 1.1-1, and Exhibit 1.1-1 is the simplest representation in that it uses no extraneous constructs (e.g., horizontal lines). The alternative representations give us handy ways of viewing the data for particular uses, but they do not augment the essential information of Exhibit 1.1-1. In fact, they can cloud the issue for some applications by emphasizing inappropriate groupings and orderings.

Thus we take Exhibit 1.1-1 to be the essential and simplest form of the data, and will represent all data in this or analogous forms. Exhibit 1.1-1 is an *instance of an m-ary relation* satisfying the following properties. (In Exhibit 1.1-1, m is 5.)

1) All rows are distinct.
2) The ordering of the rows is immaterial.
3) Each column is labelled making the ordering of columns insignificant.
4) The value in each row under a given column is simple, e.g., it does not have components such as (6, Hannah Trainman, Car, 17) nor has it multiple values such as {Toy Train, Locomotive}. The precise meaning of "simple" depends on the operations to be performed on the relation, as discussed in Section 2.1-5.

The rows of Exhibit 1.1-1 are called the *tuples* or the "n-tuples" of the instance of the relation, which is defined to be a set of tuples. An instance of a relation is thus an abstraction of which Exhibit 1.1-1 is only a representation. We will soon see other useful representations of instances of relations. The notion of a *relation* is a further abstraction which takes into account the propensity of database users to change their data from time to time. It is discussed in Section 1.1-2.

The columns of Exhibit 1.1-1 are labelled by *attributes*. An attribute is associated with a set of values called a *domain*. That is, Hannah Trainman, Eric Brakeman, and Natacha Engineer are all elements of the domain associated with the attribute SALESMAN. A domain may have several attributes associated with it, in different relations or in one relation.

It is legitimate to consider a set of attributes as a single group and even to give it a name. Thus in Exhibit 1.1-1, the set {CUSTOMER, SALESMAN} might be called the attribute PARTIES if it were convenient to consider the parties to the order together.

It should be noted that the terms used here do not quite conform to the definitions given in the original papers and most of the literature on relations, although the differences are negligible in practice. What we call an instance of a relation is usually called a *normalized relation* or a relation in *first normal form*. We will consider no other kind of relation in this book, so we include normalization (property 4, above) in the concept. What we will call a relation in Section 1.1-2 has no counterpart in the literature except, vaguely, "time-varying relation."

• • •

You may still be bothered by Exhibit 1.1-1 because it seems an awkward and verbose way to describe the information. If you agree that the various ways of grouping and sequencing the tuples force the data into particular forms and obscure its general nature, you may nevertheless feel that these groupings and orderings express some aspects of the "meaning" of the data. I agree with you. But the advantages of the very simple and symmetrical[1] form of Exhibit 1.1-1 should not be thrown away. Let us see what we can do to capture the meaning of Exhibit 1.1-1 better within the framework of properties 1 to 4.

We have observed that each order number involves one customer and one salesman. This is, in a sense, a unit of meaning in its own right: an order might be defined as the result of a deal between a customer and a salesman. Since this might be considered an independent fact, we might represent it separately, say in an instance of a 3-ary (ternary) relation ORDERS (ORD#, CUSTOMER, SALESMAN).

This leaves the attributes ASSEMBLY and QTY to be dealt with. The "meaning" that is significant here is that an assembly is part of an order—each order may be for several assemblies—and the quantity is a descriptive item associated with the assembly and the order. Thus ORD# must be linked with ASSEMBLY and QTY, say in another instance of a 3-ary relation, ORDLINE (ORD#, ASSEMBLY, QTY). The attributes CUSTOMER and SALESMAN are not directly relevant—or, if we need to know their connection with ASSEMBLY, we have lost no information by splitting up Exhibit 1.1-1 as long as we can somehow use ORD# as a link between ORDERS and ORDLINE (see Part 2). The result of the split is shown fully in Exhibit 1.1-2.

---

[1] In the sense that no one attribute, such as ORD#, is favored by the arrangement of tuples.

Exhibit   1.1-2.   Instances of Relations ORDERS and ORDLINE.

ORD#	CUSTOMER	SALESMAN	ORD#	ASSEMBLY	QTY
4	Pennsylvania Rail-road	Hannah Trainman			
			4	Car	37
3	London & South-western	Eric Brakeman	3	Car	23
			2	Locomotive	1
2	New York Central	Natacha Engineer	7	Locomotive	47
			3	Caboose	3
7	Grand Trunk Rail-way of Canada	Natacha Engineer	5	Locomotive	13
			7	Caboose	43
5	New York Central	Hannah Trainman	8	Toy Train	37
			1	Locomotive	2
8	Great North of Scotland	Eric Brakeman	5	Car	31
			6	Car	17
			4	Toy Train	11
1	Great North of Scotland	Eric Brakeman	3	Locomotive	5
			1	Toy Train	7
6	Baltimore & Ohio	Hannah Trainman	7	Car	139

a) ORDERS (ORD#, CUSTOMER,
SALESMAN)

b) ORDLINE (ORD#, ASSEMBLY,
QTY)

It would be possible to split ORDERS further, say into OC (ORD#, CUS-TOMER) and OS (ORD#, SALESMAN), but the motivation is less strong. It would, however, be wrong to split ORDERS into OC and say CS (CUSTOMER, SALESMAN). This is because CUSTOMER cannot correctly provide the link between the two components. For instance, OC contains the tuples

ORD#	CUSTOMER
2	New York Central
5	New York Central
•	•
•	•

and CS contains

CUSTOMER	SALESMAN
New York Central	Natacha Engineer
New York Central	Hannah Trainman
•	•
•	•

In trying to reconstruct the original information, we would have no choice but to form four tuples,

ORD#	CUSTOMER	SALESMAN
2	New York Central	Natacha Engineer
2	New York Central	Hannah Trainman
5	New York Central	Natacha Engineer

ORD#	CUSTOMER	SALESMAN
5	New York Central	Hannah Trainman
•	•	•
•	•	•

since we have no way of knowing from OC and CS that only the first and the last of the four are meant to be there.

Exercise 1.1-2:   Which other values of CUSTOMER give trouble of this sort in splitting ORDERS into OS and CS?

Exercise 1.1-3:   Which values of SALESMAN give similar trouble if ORDERS are split into OS (ORD#, SALESMAN) and CS?

It is not possible to split ORDLINE at all: any attempt will lead to reconstruction difficulties. The precise treatment of splits has grown into an extensive theory. Some of this is discussed in Chapter 1.4, but the theory has limited application and may be inherently incomplete. For our purposes it is usually adequate to rely on an appreciation of the meaning of the data, as we have done. Exhibit 1.1-2 gives an adequate representation of ORDERBOOK (Exhibit 1.1-1) without the aid of theory, and similar decompositions can be reached easily for most relations found in practice.

We will discuss here only one important theoretical term, which is used more precisely in the relational context than in most discussions of data. A *key* of a relation is a minimal subset of its attributes, which can be used to identify each tuple uniquely. That is, if we know a value for each attribute in the key, we can find in the relation at most one tuple matching these values. The word "minimal" implies that if K is a key of a relation R, then K together with X (K ∪ X) for some disjoint set X of attributes of R cannot be called a key, even though K ∪ X obviously has the property of uniquely identifying each tuple. For instance, ORD# is a key of ORDERS, because there are 8 values in the attribute ORD# and only 8 tuples in the relation. The set {ORD#, CUSTOMER} is not a key, even though a pair of values of ORD# and CUSTOMER will pinpoint any given tuple of ORDERS. Such a set is sometimes called a *superkey*. The relation ORDLINE has a two-attribute key, {ORD#, ASSEMBLY}.

Exercise 1.1-4:   What is the key of the relation ORDERBOOK in Exhibit 1.1-1?

The key is related to the possibility of splitting a relation: a relation may always be split into two components linked by its key. Thus ORDERS splits into OC and OS. The components of a split can also be linked by a non-key, as witnessed by the successful split of ORDERBOOK using ORD# as link. The failure to split ORDLINE is related to the fact that ORDLINE is a ternary relation with a two-attribute key.

Note that in most information processing circles the term "key" is applied to any attribute that happens to be of interest, as in "search key." Sometimes a "key" in this usage identifies a single tuple, but more often it identifies only a group of tuples.

• • •

We have said that the form of an instance of a relation shown in Exhibits 1.1-1 and 1.1-2 is one possible representation of a more abstract concept. Two other representations are helpful: the graph form and the matrix form. They are applicable to m-ary relations but most easily discussed for 2-ary (binary) relations such as OS. Exhibit 1.1-3 shows these three forms, using obvious abbreviations for Hannah Trainman, Eric Brakeman and Natacha Engineer. The ordering of values is in principle arbitrary for each form, but has been made in Exhibit 1.1-3, with readability in mind. In the graph form, the tuples are represented by edges. For a binary relation, these edges have two ends; for an m-ary relation the "edge" would have m "ends" and the graph would become a special form of "hypergraph." In the matrix form, each tuple is represented by the entry 1. For a binary relation, the space is two-dimensional; for an m-ary relation it would be m-dimensional.

These alternative representations are sometimes much handier than the table form, when m is small enough that they are not unwieldy. For instance, the graph form makes plain the fact that ORD# is a key by the way that edges converge on each salesman from different order numbers. In the matrix form this is again clear, since each row has only one entry.

Instances of relations with m > 2 can often be represented by conventional graphs and matrices. For instance, the proper form of ORDERS is given in Exhibit 1.1-4a, (note the "three-ended edges"), but because ORD# is a key, we can get away with using Exhibit 1.1-4b, corresponding to the split into OC and OS. With

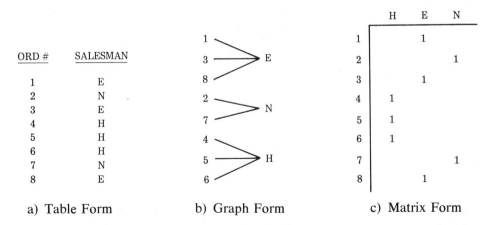

ORD #	SALESMAN
1	E
2	N
3	E
4	H
5	H
6	H
7	N
8	E

a) Table Form

b) Graph Form

	H	E	N
1		1	
2			1
3		1	
4	1		
5	1		
6	1		
7			1
8		1	

c) Matrix Form

Exhibit 1.1-3: Table, Graph and Matrix Forms of OS (ORD#, SALESMAN).

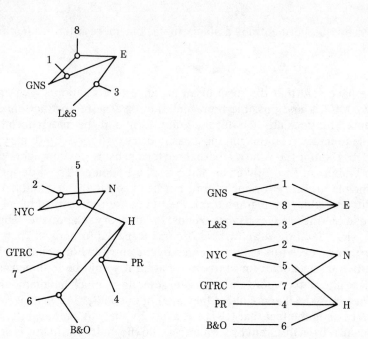

a) As a Hypergraph   b) As a Graph

Exhibit 1.1-4. Two graph forms for ORDERS (ORD#, CUSTOMER, SALESMAN)

ORDLINE we can use another trick to simplify the hypergraph to a graph, and the three-dimensional array to a matrix, based on the fact that the key, {ORD#, ASSEMBLY}, is binary and a value of QTY is associated with each ORD# — ASSEMBLY pair. Exhibit 1.1-5 shows the result, using abbreviations for the assemblies (Q is Caboose). In the graph, the edges are drawn between order number and assembly, then labelled with the quantity: the graph is now really a network. In the matrix, the 1 entries are replaced by the values for QTY.

These tricks enable us to extend the graph, and sometimes the matrix forms, to cope with most practical kinds of relation instances, with advantages for clarity of visualization. We make use of all three forms throughout this book.

Exercise 1.1-5:   Represent ORDERBOOK of Exhibit 1.1-1 in graph form.

● ● ●

The attributes of the relations discussed so far are drawn from distinct domains. Exhibit 5.1-2 shows the graph form of an instance of a relation, BOM (ASSEMBLY, SUBASSEMBLY, QTY), with attributes ASSEMBLY and SUB-ASSEMBLY drawn from the same domain. This relation describes the component

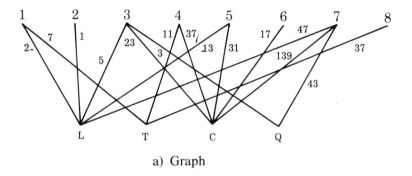

a) Graph

	T	L	C	Q
1	7	2		
2		1		
3		5	23	3
4	11		37	
5		13	31	
6			17	
7		47	139	43
8	37			

b) Matrix

Exhibit   1.1-5.   Graph and matrix forms for ORDLINE (ORD#, ASSEMBLY, QTY)

parts of assemblies such as Toy Train. These components in turn have components, as shown in the graph. The relationship between an assembly and all its components, their components, and so on, as depicted in the graph, is a partial ordering. The mathematically-inclined reader may want to produce relational examples of trees, lattices, equivalence relations and the like.

Another type of relation, which is of theoretical importance, is the *Cartesian product*. We could call it the *independence relation*. Suppose that each salesman is permitted to deal with all customers: there is no predefined territory. Exhibit 1.1-6a shows the matrix form of this relation between salesmen and customers: the Cartesian product of two sets consists of all possible pairs that can be made by taking the first element from the first set and the second element from the second set. It is a trivial relation: it asserts that customers and salesmen are independent of each other. It is interesting, however, in the context of other instances of a relation. Exhibit 1.1-6b shows the relation CS, which gives the actual liaisons between customers and salesmen which have culminated in orders. The set of tuples of CS is a subset of the Cartesian product. This is the basis of a definition of an instance of a relation:

Definition   1.1-1:   Given sets $D_1, D_2, \ldots, D_m$, not necessarily distinct, and consisting of simple elements, *an instance of a relation* on these sets is a subset of the extended Cartesian product, $D_1 \times D_2 \times \ldots \times D_m$. D_i is called the ith *domain* of the relation.

This definition contains one notion, extended Cartesian product, that is a simple extension to more than two sets of the Cartesian product, and another notion, simple elements, that depends on the kind of operations that can be performed (discussed in Part 2).

	H	E	N
B&O	1	1	1
GNS	1	1	1
GTRC	1	1	1
L&S	1	1	1
NYC	1	1	1
PR	1	1	1

a) Cartesian product

	H	E	N
B&O	1		
GNS		1	
GTRC			1
L&S		1	
NYC	1		1
PR	1		

b) CS

Exhibit 1.1-6.   Binary Instances of Relations between CUSTOMER and SALESMAN.

A relation can be *implicit* or *explicit*. An example of an implicit relation is DOUBLE (J,K) defined $K = 2 \times J$, where J and K are attributes on the domain I, the set of integers. Most relations of interest for information systems are explicitly defined by a set of tuples, such as ORDERBOOK and the other relations of this section.

1.1-2   Changing Data

Most data stored on a computer is not static. We change it to reflect changes in situations, in policy, or in status. The relation CS in Exhibit 1.1-6b could be an example. Salesmen are dynamic people with a vocation of finding new customers. Even if the universe of customers were restricted to the six shown, the picture would change constantly as new deals were made. For the sake of harmony, the company might want to impose territories on the salesmen, such as those indicated by Exhibit 1.1-7. We can interpret these two examples to mean that no salesman may be credited with an order for a customer outside his allotted territory. *Any instance of relation CS would have to be a subset of the territorial restriction selected by the company*. For example, the instance shown in Exhibit 1.1-6b would be a violation of the mutually exclusive territorial restriction shown in Exhibit 1.1-7a (because of Hannah Trainman's deal with New York Central), but would be a valid instance of a relation based on the overlapping restriction of Exhibit 1.1-7b.

	E	H	N
GNS	1		
L&S	1		
B&O		1	
PR		1	
NYC			1
GTRC			1

a) Mutually Exclusive

	E	H	N
GNS	1		
L&S	1		
B&O	1	1	
PR		1	1
NYC		1	1
GTRC			1

b) Overlapping

Exhibit   1.1-7.   Two Possible Territorial Restrictions on Relation CS.

When we add the dimension of time to data, it is useful to be able to say which data is legal and which is not as we change from one instance to another. The best way to do this is to specify the whole set of legal instances. Thus, we could say that the legal instances of CS are the subsets of the overlapping territories of Exhibit 1.1-7b. We say a *relation* R (X) on a set X of attributes is the set of legal instances (according to some external specification), R_1 (X), R_2 (X), ...

The object called a "relation" above is normally tremendously big, in terms of the number of individual values involved. An instance of a relation will usually contain enough data to exceed the primary memory capacity of a computer. A *set* of such instances could be unthinkably large. Thus, while instances of relations must be capable of explicit representation on the secondary storage of a computer, a set of instances, namely a relation, cannot be listed explicitly.

For the mathematically-inclined, who know the concept of a *power set,* we define

Definition   1.1-2:   A *relation* is a subset of the power set of the extended Cartesian product of its attributes.

The problem of specifying *which* set of instances a relation is must be solved by implicit rather than explicit means. We must be able to give a *rule* characterizing the legal instances of a relation. Such a rule is known as an *integrity constraint* or a *semantic invariant*. The territorial restrictions of Exhibit 1.1-7 are quasi-explicit examples: the associated rule is that an instance of CS must be a subset of the tuples shown in the territorial restriction.

Another example is a *functional dependence,* A → B imposed on two attribute sets, X and Y, of a relation R:

Definition   1.1-3:   X → Y (X *functionally determines* Y: Y is *functionally dependent* on X) in R (X,Y, . . .) if for any two tuples $(x_1, y_1, . . .)$ and $(x_2, y_2, . . .)$, $(x_1, x_2 \in X; y_1, y_2 \in Y)$, $x_1 = x_2$ implies $y_1 = y_2$.

The matrix form shows most clearly how a functional dependence restricts a relation to a set of instances. If values of X head the rows and values of Y head

	H	E	N
1	1		
2	1		
3	1		
4	1		
5	1		
6	1		
7	1		
8	1		

a

	H	E	N
1	1		
2	1		
3	1		
4	1		
5	1		
6	1		
7	1		
8		1	

b

	H	E	N
1	1		
2	1		
3	1		
4	1		
5	1		
6	1		
7	1		
8			1

c

	H	E	N
1	1		
2	1		
3	1		
4	1		
5	1		
6	1		
7		1	
8	1		

d

	H	E	N
1			1
2			1
3			1
4			1
5			1
6			1
7			1
8			1

e

Exhibit 1.1-8. Instances of OS (ORD#, SALESMAN) satisfying ORD# → SALESMAN.

the columns, then X → Y if and only if each row has at most one entry. Exhibit 1.1-3 gives an example: ORD# → SALESMAN in OS. The relation OS with this restriction has $3^8 = 6561$ valid instances, some of which are shown in Exhibit 1.1-8.

A generalization of functional dependence is *mapping cardinality*, $X \xrightarrow{\ell}_{s} Y$, which says that each value of X is associated with at least s and at most ℓ values of Y in a relation. X → Y is the special case s = 1 and ℓ = 1. For example, the territorial restriction of Exhibit 1.1-7 could be replaced or augmented by the requirement that each salesman handle between 2 and 3 customers, SALESMAN $\xrightarrow{3}_{2}$ CUSTOMER. Another constraint that limits the set of instances is *constancy* of an attribute, such as a person's birthdate. Further types of semantic invariant can be imagined, but only functional dependence has been extensively studied.[2]

Not all constraints on data can be expressed by specifying permissible instances. *Intra-relation* constraints are exemplified by requiring a particular

---

[2] The so called multivalued dependence will be discussed as decompositions in Part 2. This important notion and its generalizations are not constraints in quite the same sense as those discussed here although they have semantic significance.

sequence of instances, such as constraints imposed by the sequence restriction on marital status:

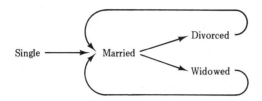

Inter-relation constraints, such as a requirement that ORDERBOOK be equivalent to ORDERS and ORDLINE in the sense of Section 1.1-1, could be considered part of the relational algebra, to be developed in Part 2. These further types of constraints can themselves be described by *second-order* relations, which have relations as values. Second-order relations can also have attributes or domains as values. Exhibit 1.1-9 shows a relation describing the functional dependence among a set of attributes. Another case is the requirement that an attribute be *mandatory* or *total* for its domain: e.g. in OFFSPRING (PARENT, CHILD) with CHILD, PARENT c PERSON, CHILD is mandatory for PERSON because every person must be somebody's child.

Exhibit   1.1-9. The functional dependences of ORDERBOOK,
FD (DETERMINES, DEPENDS).

	ORD#	CUSTOMER	SALESMAN	ASSEMBLY	QTY
{ORD#}	1		1		
{ORD#, ASSEMBLY}					1

A second-order relation, such as instantiated in Exhibit 1.1-9, appears to violate the requirement of simplicity of attribute values, since the values of DETERMINES are the sets {ORD#} and {ORD# , ASSEMBLY}. Simplicity depends on the operations allowed on the values, which will be discussed in Chapter 2.1: if the operations are restricted to set operations and exclude operations on the elements of the set, then a set is considered simple. A second-order relation is usually static, although there is no reason in principle why it should not change in time and have further integrity constraints, perhaps expressed by a third-order relation.

Exercise   1.1-6:   Confirm that the dependences shown in FD, Exhibit 1.1-9, hold for ORDERBOOK. What further functional dependences are consequences? Do still more dependences hold for the instance of ORDERBOOK shown in Exhibit 1.1-1?

Review Questions and Exercises, Chapter 1.1

1.1-7   What properties must be satisfied by an instance of a relation?

1.1-8   Given the following information, what relations would you find it appropriate to form on the attributes (given in capitals)? Each EMPloyee receives a WAGE and works in one or more TEAMs. Each TEAM spends a certain number of HOURS on each of one or more pieces of EQUIPment making each of one or more ASSEMBLYs. Show some example data.

1.1-9   What is a key of a relation?

1.1-10   Represent the following data as a relation:

x	0	$\pi/4$	$\pi/2$	$3\pi/4$	π	$5\pi/4$	$3\pi/2$	$7\pi/4$	2π
sin(x)	0	$1/\sqrt{2}$	1	$1/\sqrt{2}$	0	$-1/\sqrt{2}$	-1	$-1/\sqrt{2}$	0

1.1-11   Represent the following network as a relation. What is the matrix form?

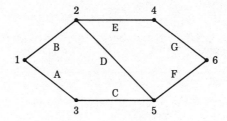

1.1-12   Represent the following tree as a relation. What is the graph form?

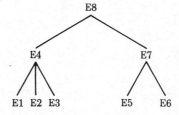

1.1-13   How many ways can the following relations be split into two without losing information?

a) (STUDENT   OFFICE   TELEPHONE)

STUDENT	OFFICE	TELEPHONE
S1	O1	T1
S2	O1	T1
S3	O2	T2
S4	O2	T2
S5	O3	T2

b) (STUDENT OFFICE BLACKBOARD)

S1	O1	B1
S2	O1	B1
S3	O2	B2
S4	O2	B2
S5	O3	B2
S3	O2	B3
S4	O2	B3
S5	O3	B3

c) (A   B   C)

A1	B1	C1
A2	B1	C2
A3	B2	C3

1.1-14 The DBTG Data model [CODASYL, 1971] consists basically of a construct called a "set" (not to be confused with the mathematical term) which is an association of a unique "owner" tuple on attributes $O_1, \ldots, O_k$ with a set (the mathematical term) of "member" tuples on attributes $M_1, \ldots, M_l$ such that no member tuple is associated with more than one owner tuple. How would you describe this construct using terms defined in Section 1.1-2?

1.1-15 How would the mathematical concept of a function, $F: X \rightarrow Y$, be expressed in relational terms?

1.1-16   a. Given the attributes COURSE, PROFESSOR, ROOM, WHEN, STUDENT and GRADE, formulate meaningful statements which will break down the data belonging to these attributes into at least three relations.

b. Stating your assumptions clearly, and giving sample data if necessary, show all functional dependences, and hence keys, for each of the relations in Exercise 1.1-16a. Are there any functional dependences which involve attributes of more than one of these relations?

1.1-17   a. Given the following statement and the attributes embedded in it (words that are capitalized), formulate some meaningful statements which will break down the data belonging to these attributes into smaller relations:

an AGENT represents a PRODUCT with a given PRICE,

produced by a COMPANY.

b. Stating your assumptions clearly, and giving example data if necessary, show all functional dependences, and hence keys, for each of the relations in Exercise 1.1-17a.

1.1-18   a. Given the attributes BANK, ACCOUNT, LOAN, CUSTOMER, ADDRESS (of customer), BALANCE (of account) and AMOUNT (of loan), formulate some meaningful statements which will break down the data belonging to these attributes into at least three relations. (ACCOUNT and LOAN identify accounts and loans, respectively.)

b. Stating your assumptions clearly, and giving sample data if necessary, show all functional dependences, and hence keys, for each of the relations in Exercise 1.1-18a. Are there any functional dependences which involve attributes of more than one of these relations?

1.1-19   a. Given the following statement and the attributes embedded in it (words that are capitalized), formulate some meaningful statements which will break down the data belonging to these attributes into smaller relations:

a SUPPLIER is in a CITY and supplies a PRODUCT costing PRICE.

b. Stating your assumptions clearly, and giving example data if necessary, show all functional dependences, and hence keys, for each of the relations in Exercise 1.1-19a. Can you think of any constraint that might apply which is not limited to just one of your relations?

IMPLEMENTATION: Data Structures

All implementations in this book will use secondary memory. The primary memory of a computer is "random access memory" (RAM): the time to find an item of data in RAM is comparable to the time to transfer it to the processing unit of the computer. Secondary memory, on the other hand, sacrifices access time to save money: the time to find an item of data is usually orders of magnitude greater than the time to transfer it to primary memory. (This transfer time for secondary memory, however, is often nearly the same as that for RAM.) In terms of 1980's technology, Exhibit 1.2-1 shows the tradeoff between these two characteristics for various types of devices. We see a progressive increase in access/transfer ratio as the cost decreases from RAM to magnetic tape. (The positioning of the newer technologies in Exhibit 1.2-1 is uncertain: magnetic bubble memories may decrease in cost relative to other methods, and video disks are the subject of conflicting claims.)

Another important characteristic of secondary memory is "non-volatility": information is not lost when power is shut off. This makes it possible to store information permanently without paying for energy and supporting equipment. In the last four categories in Exhibit 1.2-1, floppy and hard magnetic disk, video disk and magnetic tape, the medium can be removed from the recording equipment, so that the potential storage capacity is unlimited.

Secondary memory thus gives us the facility for large (because cheap) permanent data bases. Despite the rapid improvements in technology and the plummeting cost of RAM, it is reasonable to suppose that there will always be a demand for secondary memory. It is also the assumption in this book that the price to be paid for cheapness and permanence is a high access/transfer ratio. This ratio is central to our treatment of data on secondary memory. Because access is expensive while transfer is cheap, data must be transferred from secondary to primary memory in *blocks* of hundreds or thousands of bytes, and it must be organized so that each block is used as fully as possible while in RAM. Transferring a block in order to learn the contents of only a few bytes is not economical if a great deal of information is to be examined in this way. Thus, much of the processing that we discuss in the book will require data to be *clustered* so that the data can be read and written with a minimum number of accesses to each block.

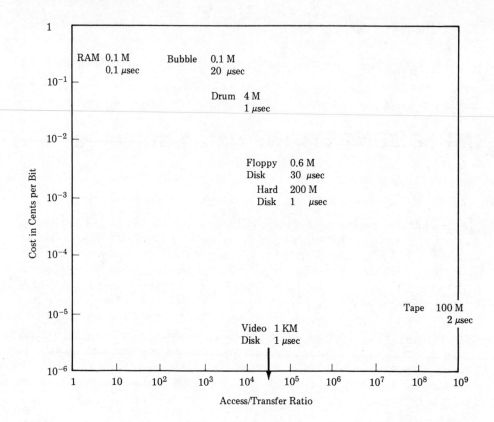

Exhibit 1.2-1. Cost *vs.* Access/Transfer Speed Ratio for 1980's Memory Technology, Showing Typical Unit Capacities and Transfer Times per Byte.

We next examine in more detail the characteristics of available types of secondary memory. Then we discuss the logical organization of data into files. Finally we devote a section to each of some basic data structures.

1.2-1   Secondary Storage

Exhibit 1.2-1 shows the types of memory we will consider in this book. There are three categories: RAM, which we are not concerned with; tape; and circulating memories. This last includes the disk memories (floppy, hard, and video), drum, and magnetic bubbles. It is a category which will be of major concern for many years.

• • •

Circulating memories each have a characteristic rate of revolution, which may be a visible revolution as for the disks (300–3600 r.p.m.) or a circulating current of magnetic "bubbles" (~ 7500 r.p.m.). They therefore have a *latency time,* which is how long one must wait before the data comes round. The *mean latency time* is the time for half a revolution (100–8.3 msec for disks, ~ 4 msec for bubbles).

Bubbles and drums have no further delay: they are "head per track" devices in which many revolving loops of data are examined in parallel. The disk devices, on the other hand, rely on a single head to handle many tracks: each *track* is a circular band on the spinning disk, and the *head* is a reading/writing device on a mechanical arm that can move in and out between the concentric tracks. For disks there is thus a delay associated with the motion of the arm from one track to another. The average arm delay for disks can be from .03 to .1 sec. Hard magnetic disks usually have a more complicated structure than floppy or video disks, with several disk surfaces on a common spindle, and a rake of arms moving simultaneously from one set of tracks (one track per surface) to another. Thus the natural grouping of tracks is not in terms of the few hundred on each surface, but in terms of tracks of common diameter on the twenty-odd surfaces. This group of tracks is called a *cylinder,* and the mechanical arms are considered to move from cylinder to cylinder.

The track is thus a notion common to all circulating memories, namely the loop of data that can be read or written by one head in the period of revolution. The *track length* limits the size of the blocks of data that can be transferred to and from primary memory. This can run from a few hundred bits in bubble memory, to 3K-20K bytes on magnetic or video disk. In most cases, this capacity is so great that other considerations limit the block size. One such consideration is *sectoring* of the track capacity into smaller units, as is usually done with floppy disks and other media for small computers. Blocks of data are normally transferred to and from a *buffer* in main memory, and main memory capacity is a limiting factor on the blocksize. The most important consideration is the tradeoff between the amount of data transferred with each block and the number of accesses required. This tradeoff depends on the application and will be the subject of a number of optimization analyses later in the book.

To fix our ideas for the discussions and calculations of this book, we will describe two magnetic disk devices whose specifications, given in Exhibit 1.2-2, are about state-of-the-art for the 1980's. One is a removable hard disk, RISDISK, and the other is a two-sided $5\frac{1}{4}''$ floppy, RISFLOPPY. Note that they are equivalent in terms of the access/transfer ratio of 14100 (which is selected to equal the access/transfer ratio of another fictitious disk unit, MIXTEC (Knuth [1973] §5.4.9)). This enables us to do a single calculation for both units in many of the cost analyses to follow.

Exhibit 1.2-2. Specifications for Magnetic Disk Units to be Used in This Book

	τ TRANSFER TIME/BYTE	ρ ACCESS/ TRANSFER RATIO	σ ROTATION SPEED	λ AVERAGE LATENCY	μ AVERAGE ARM DELAY	β BYTES/ TRACK	γ TRACKS/ CYLINDER	ν CYLINDERS /UNIT
RISDISK	2 μ sec	14100	3000 rpm	10 ms	18.2 ms	10000	20	500
RISFLOPPY	30 μ sec	14100	300 rpm	100 ms	323 ms	6666	2	45

Exercise   1.2-1:   Confirm that the following relationships hold in Exhibit 1.2-2:
$\lambda = 1000 \times 60/(2 \times \sigma)$; $\tau = 60 \times 10^6/(\gamma \times \beta)$; $\rho = 1000 \times (\lambda + \mu)/\tau$. What is their significance?

Exercise   1.2-2:   What are the total capacities of RISDISK and RISFLOPPY?

Video disks are different from the other devices discussed in that they are a "write-once" medium. The holes burned in the disk by laser cannot be erased.

● ● ●

Magnetic tape is in a category of its own. Circulating memories are sometimes called "direct access storage devices," implying that data can be accessed directly by going to its track and waiting for it to come round. (They are often abused by being treated as RAM.) Tape does not have this direct access capability; the average wait to access data somewhere on a 2400-foot reel of tape at 200 inches per second is half the tape, or 72 seconds. It is a sequential memory and characterized by a very high access/transfer ratio. Once the data has been found, however, the transfer rate is very good and can compete with any of the circulating memories. With a recording density of 6250 bits per inch, a nine-track tape (which transmits 9 bits in parallel to give a full byte plus a parity bit) at 200 inches per second transmits at 1.25 megabytes a second, a transfer time of 0.8 μsec per byte. Tapes are simple and cheap, which, together with their data transfer rate, makes it likely that they will continue to be used whenever sequential processing is appropriate.

Tape imposes no limits on the block size of data written on it, except that between each block on the tape there is a gap of empty tape required to accommodate the deceleration and acceleration of the tape when it stops between blocks. Such an inter-block gap is typically 0.6 inches, or the equivalent of 3750 bytes. Thus, a blocksize of less than this many bytes will result in a half-empty tape. The longer the block, the more economical the usage of tape.

Tape is also suitable for *variable-length* data, in a way that is awkward for circulating storage. Such data might correspond to nonnormalized forms of relations such as the groupings of ORDERBOOK by ORD#, CUSTOMER or SALESMAN in Section 1.1-1, and as such we would not be interested in it. Most current use of header and trailer records, repeating groups, etc. can be traced to early practice with magnetic tapes. Variable-length data might also, however, correspond to *compacted storage* of (normalized) instances of relations, and this is of considerable interest.

As with RISDISK and RISFLOPPY, we invent a tape unit, RISTAPE, for the discussion of this book. Exhibit 1.2-3 describes a device which is slightly ahead of the 1980's commercial market, but not ahead of the technology. (The average latency here is half the time to read the entire tape.)

Exhibit 1.2-3. Specifications for Magnetic Tape Unit to be Used in This Book.

	τ TRANSFER TIME/BYTE	ρ ACCESS/ TRANSFER RATIO	σ TAPE SPEED	λ AVERAGE LATENCY	REWIND TIME	δ RECORDING DENSITY	ι INTER-BLOCK GAP	ϕ TAPE LENGTH
RISTAPE	2.1 μ sec	90 M	75 ips	192 sec	144 sec	6250 bpi	0.6 in	2400 ft

Exercise   1.2-3:   Confirm that the following relationships hold in Exhibit 1.2-3:
$\lambda = 12 \times \phi/(2 \times \sigma)$; $\tau = 10^6/(\delta \times \rho)$; $\rho = 10^6 \times \lambda/\tau = 12 \times \phi \times \delta/2$. What is their significance?

Exercise   1.2-4:   What is the total capacity of RISTAPE?

• • •

Data is transferred to and from secondary storage in blocks, whose sizes depend on economic considerations determined by the application. Such considerations do not necessarily take into account the *record length* for the application: this is the number of bytes required to store each tuple of the relation. Usually the block is big enough to hold several records. If each record has the same length (fixed length records), it is usually further stipulated that the block length is a multiple of the record length, so that records are not split between blocks.

Exercise   1.2-5:   How many RISDISK and RISFLOPPY tracks would be required to store a file of 1250 80-byte records with 41 records per block?

Exercise   1.2-6:   It is convenient to measure delays such as average latency and average arm delay in terms of *equivalent bytes,* the number of bytes that could be transferred during the delay. Give expressions for the average latencies of disk and tape, and for the average arm delay of disk, in equivalent bytes.

1.2-2   Files

For our purposes, files are relations considered with implementation in mind. When we speak of files, we are more concerned with questions of how they are accessed, how they are sorted, and where they are stored than we are when we speak of relations.

The *record* is the basis of the logical organization of data, as the block is the basis of its physical organization on secondary storage. A record is *first* if we can store enough information in primary memory to locate the record directly without a prior access to secondary memory. Otherwise a record is *next*. A *file* is a set of records, and we can identify two extreme types of file. An *immediate file* contains only first records. A *serial file* contains all next records, except for one which is called the first record, such that each record uniquely determines the record, if any, which will be accessed next. All files are a blend of serial and direct file, with the serial subfiles usually known as *access paths*. We will discuss sequential files, which are purely serial; direct and hashed files, which are almost purely immediate; and logarithmic or tree files, in which the length of each access path is proportional to the logarithm of the number of records.

A record is located in terms of a specified value for part of the record. This part is called a *search key*. It is often abbreviated to "key," but we will always say "search key" to distinguish it from the precisely defined term "key" of Section 1.1-1. If a record represents a tuple, as it often does, the search key corresponds to one or more attributes. A search key may not uniquely identify a record; several records may have the same value for the part specified as search key.

The process of locating and transferring a first record to RAM is called *immediate access,* and the same process for a next record is called *serial access*. Serial access can be accomplished by storing the records adjacent to each other physically, e.g., in the same block; or by storing the address of the next record—a *pointer*—with the preceding record. Immediate access is achieved by using a table—an *inverted file*—to associate record addresses with search key values, or by using a *hash function* (or "key-to-address transformation") to compute the address for any given search key value.

The use of an inverted file for immediate access is limited by the capacity of primary memory to store the table. This consideration gives rise to logarithmic or tree files, in which several levels of inverted files are maintained, with all but the first level occupying more space than is available in primary memory. The first level gives the addresses of records, or blocks of records, in the second level, which are then used to locate records in the next level, and so on. Each level locates some factor, f, times as many records on the next level, so that the total number, N, of records is a power of f, and the length of the access path is roughly $\log_f N$. An *indexed file* is such a logarithmic file, in which all data is on the last level, and the earlier levels, called *indexes,* contain only search key values and pointers. A logarithmic file with data at all levels is called a *tree*.

We illustrate these terms with ORDERS from Section 1-1, which we give again here in abbreviated form (Exhibit 1.2-4). Each record holds a tuple and, we suppose, requires 80 bytes (6 for ORD#, 40 for CUSTOMER, 34 for SALESMAN). In a serial file, the records might be sorted on ORD# as shown in Exhibit 1.2-4, with tuple (1, GNS, E) occupying the first record. In an immediate file, the record addresses might correspond with ORD# so that the tuple corresponding to an order can be found directly.

Suppose that ORD# is the search key. Since it is also the key of ORDERS, it uniquely identifies a record. The search for ORD# = 6, say, would proceed as

Exhibit 1.2-4. ORDERS

ORD#	CUST	SALES
1	GNS	E
2	NYC	N
3	L&S	E
4	PR	H
5	NYC	H
6	B&O	H
7	GTRC	N
8	GNS	E

follows. On the serial file, the first record would be accessed and ORD# found to be 1, not 6. Then each next record would be accessed in turn until ORD# = 6, when the search would be successful. On the immediate file, a calculation using only RAM would ascertain that ORD# = 6 corresponds to the sixth record, and this would be accessed directly.

Exhibit 1.2-5 shows an indexed version of ORDERS suitable for searching on ORD#. The index blocks hold two entries each and the index is organized in two levels. The data is stored on the third level, two records per block. Here the search for ORD# = 6 requires three accesses (i.e., $\log_2 8$). The first index block is accessed and, since 6 is greater than 4 but ≤ 8, the second pointer is followed and the second block of the second level of index accessed. Here 6 ≤ 6, so we know that ORD# = 6 is matched by the last record on the third data block: we access this block.

Suppose that the search key is {CUSTOMER, SALESMAN}. This is not a key, and some values for the pair will specify more than one record, e.g., (CUSTOMER, SALESMAN) = ('GNS', 'E'). On the serial file, all records must be inspected; we do not have the benefit of records sorted on the search key to tell us when we can stop. On the immediate file, we need either a table or a hash function.

A table might be compounded of two inverted files, as shown in Exhibit 1.2-6. The search for (CUSTOMER, SALESMAN) = ('GNS', 'E') becomes the search for CUSTOMER = 'GNS' **and** SALESMAN = 'E'. The inverted file for CUSTOMER tells us that records 1 and 8 satisfy CUSTOMER = 'GNS' and that for SALESMAN gives records 1, 3 and 8 for SALESMAN = 'E'. Thus, records 1 and 8 are accessed directly.

A possible hash function for ORDERS on {CUSTOMER, SALESMAN} is

$$h(CUSTOMER, SALESMAN) \stackrel{\Delta}{=}$$
$$(f(CUSTOMER) + 27 \times f(SALESMAN)) \bmod 4 \qquad (1.2\text{-}1)$$

where $f(X)$ is the position in the alphabet (from 1 to 26) of the first letter of the character string X and a **mod** b is the remainder of integer a after division by integer b. Exhibit 1.2-7a shows the effect of storing ORDERS according to this hash function. Note that one of the four addresses (2) attempts to hold four records, while its capacity is two. We resolve the collisions at address 2 by causing the later records to migrate down until they find a free location, to which a pointer is set up, as shown in Exhibit 1.2-7b. In this table, the records are also grouped two per block. Thus, a search for (CUSTOMER, SALESMAN) = ('B&O', 'H') causes a direct access to address h('B&O', 'H') = (f('B&O') + 27 × f('H')) **mod** 4 = (2 + 27 × 8) **mod** 4 = 2. The records at this location do not match, so the pointer is followed to location 1. The records here do not match either, so the next pointer is followed to location 3, where we are successful.

The index of Exhibit 1.2-5 is of no use for searches on {CUSTOMER, SALESMAN}. Exhibit 1.2-8 shows a suitable logarithmic organization, this time a "B-tree." Each block holds two records, but only one block is more than half

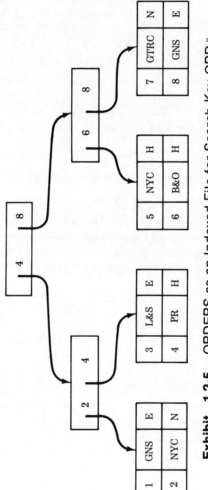

Exhibit 1.2-5. ORDERS as an Indexed File for Search Key ORD#

Exhibit 1.2-6. Inverted files for ORDERS

E 1, 3, 8	B&O 6 L&S 3
H 4, 5, 6	GNS 1, 8 NYC 2, 5
N 2, 7	GTRC 7 PR 4
a) Inverted on SALESMAN	b) Inverted on CUSTOMER

full. The search for (CUSTOMER, SALESMAN) = ('GNS', 'E') needs four accesses. In the root block, GTRC comes after GNS in alphabetical order. So we follow the left pointer to the first matching record. Then, since the search key is not a key of ORDERS, we must check out all successors of this record. The left pointer leads to a nonmatch, but the right pointer leads to the other matching record.

• • •

These examples illustrate the basic concepts of immediate access, serial access, search key, inverted file, hashing, index, and tree, as well as record and block. You can also get from them an impression of the difference between searching for keys and non-keys, and for single and multiple attributes. Detailed discussion of specific file organizations follows in subsequent sections. First, however, we must introduce some important problems: updating, batching of requests, and secondary search keys.

Exhibit 1.2-7. Applying Hashing and Collision Resolution to ORDERS

ORD#	CUST	SALES	h(C,S)		ORD#	CUST	SALES
4	PR	H	0	0	4	PR	H
2	NYC	N	0		2	NYC	N
7	GRTC	N	1				
1	GNS	E	2	1	7	GRTC	N
8	GNS	E	2		5	NYC	H
5	NYC	H	2				
6	B&O	H	2	2	3	L&S	E
3	L&S	E	3		6	B&O	H
				3	1	GNS	E
					8	GNS	E

a) Before Collision Resolution   b) With Blocking and Chaining

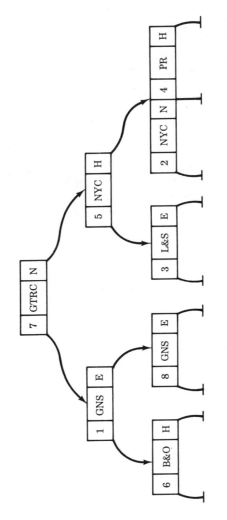

Exhibit 1.2-8. ORDERS as a B-tree of Order 3 for Search Key {CUSTOMER, SALESMAN}

The examples do not investigate deleting, adding, or changing records. A file that is growing or changing rapidly requires flexible data structures. We call such a file *volatile,* although volatility is a hard concept to quantify in general. Direct and sequential files, with fixed key-to-address functions or fixed orders of records, are inflexible and break down at quite low volatility. Indexed files can similarly cause problems, but trees can be made very flexible. One way to achieve flexibility is to discover a systematic way of *splitting* blocks as the file grows. Another way is to reorganize periodically and to provide, between reorganizations, a buffering data structure called a *differential file*.

The examples are limited to searches which retrieve only one or two records from the file. Much information processing is concerned with a high proportion or even all of the file. We define the *activity* of a particular process on a file as the proportion of the records actually needed to all the records in the file; it is a numerical value ranging from 0 to 1. Immediate access is suitable for low-activity processes, but involves an overhead that soon destroys its superiority to serial access of physically contiguous records as activity increases. (The breakeven activity turns out to be surprisingly low, usually less than 1%, as we shall see.) Thus sequential files, even on magnetic tape, must still be seriously considered. Grouping of searches together in a batch is one way to increase activity and is justified whenever the user is content to wait while the batch is formed and processed. *Clustering* of data is very important in high-activity processing, to prevent repeated accesses to the same block. File organizations which preserve natural ordering of data are one way to achieve clustering and efficient high-activity processing.

Finally, the examples make it plain that a file organization suitable for one search key is likely to be unsuitable for another. When we were searching ORDERS on ORD# we sorted the file or arranged the record addresses or constructed an index in ways that were wholly unsuited for a search on {CUSTOMER, SALESMAN}, and vice-versa. Relations, on the other hand, appear completely *symmetrical* among their attributes. Frequently this symmetry is spurious; many attributes will never be search keys or do more than tag along in processing. On the other hand, a single attribute or a single set of attributes is often inadequate as a basis for file organization; we may need two or more search keys for the same file in an application. To solve this problem, a file may be organized according to one set of attributes, called its primary search key, and supporting data structures provided for the so-called secondary search keys. We shall also see implementations which preserve symmetry among some of the attributes or sets of attributes.

This discussion gives us three additional aspects that we must watch for in considering file organizations, as well as their basic access speeds: their behavior under requirements for high and low *volatility, activity,* and *symmetry*. We go on now to a more detailed discussion of various types of direct, logarithmic, and sequential file organizations. It is handy to start this discussion with a rough summary of how well these basic types of organization cope with these aspects. Exhibit 1.2-9 gives such a summary, assuming that auxiliary methods (Section 1.2-6) are not used and that periodic reorganizations are not allowed.

	VOLATILITY		ACTIVITY		SYMMETRY	
	LOW	HIGH	LOW	HIGH	LOW	HIGH
DIRECT	√√	(√)	√√	(√)	√√	(√)
LOGARITHMIC	√	(√√)	√	(√)	√	(√)
SEQUENTIAL	√	×	×	√√	√	√√

Symbols: √√   Very Well (Direct Access Requires Low Symmetry, Activity and Volatility)

√   Well

×   Poorly

(√√)   B-trees Perform Very Well

(√)   File Organization can be Adapted to Give Good Performance

Exhibit   1.2-9. How Well File Organizations Perform Under Various Requirements

1.2-3   Direct Files

1.2-3a Hashing

Hashing requires two procedures: a key-to-address transformation, supplied by the *hash function,* and a method for *collision resolution.* As Exhibit 1.2-6 and the associated text imply, hashing is as near as we can get to direct access, since we can hope for no more than one access to secondary memory for each record. How many more accesses there are than one per record depends on the number of collisions and how they are resolved.

The number of collisions depends on the hash function, on how fully the storage space allocated to the file is occupied, and on the distribution of keys in the file. Since we should discuss hashing in general, not for a particular file, the latter is effectively beyond our control. The occupancy of the storage space is taken as a parameter, α, between 0 and 1: the *load factor,* α, is the ratio of occupied to available record locations. The choice of hash function requires a blend of theoretical considerations and experience with actual files. Functions for hashing within primary memory have been extensively studied (see Knuth [1973] § 6.4) and combine speed of evaluation with randomizing of addresses so that collisions are reduced. We will discuss only two of the most successful of these methods, division hashing and multiplicative hashing. In hashing to secondary memory, other requirements may become important. Speed is of less concern, since most computations involving only RAM are faster than an access to secondary storage. Indeed, we might even tolerate looking up a large table, such as part of an index, to determine the record location; thus we could consider indexed files as a form of hashing. Requirements of volatility, activity, or symmetry may lead us to such involved hash functions.

Division hashing assumes the hash key, k, is an integer, and defines

$$h(k) = k \bmod n,$$

the remainder of k divided by a prime number n chosen to be just larger than the minimum storage requirements of the file. The address, h(k), takes on the values $0, 1, \ldots, n-1$. A prime number is chosen because a number with factors, especially if some are small factors, tends to preserve the regularities that are found in most data, which can cause collisions. Exhibit 1.2-6a illustrates division hashing where n = 8 is not prime, but happens to work well for this particular file. This example also shows one way to get an integer from a hash key, {CUSTOMER, SALESMAN}, which is alphabetical: treat names as integers of base 26 (27 happened to be a little better for the example). A faster way would be to exclusive-or the individual bytes of the hash key.

Multiplicative hashing is useful when n is not prime and especially if it is a power of 2. If $n = 2^m$, we define

$$h(k) = ((Ak) \bmod w)| \, m \overset{\Delta}{=} \text{ the first m bits of } (Ak) \bmod w$$

where w is the word size of the computer (assumed to be a power of 2, e.g., 2^{16}) and A is an integer which is relatively prime to w, (i.e., A and w have no common factors, A $\bmod 2 \neq 0$). A value of A near $(\sqrt{5} - 1) w/2$ is recommended (see Knuth [1973] §6.4).

When we are hashing to secondary storage, we do not usually assign an address to each record location (although we did so in Exhibit 1.2-6), but to each block. Thus, n is the number of blocks in the file, and the load factor is $\alpha = N/nb$, where b is the blocksize (number of records per block) and N is the number of records in the file. This in itself greatly reduces collisions, because potential clusters of records are spread out among the record locations at each address. Something of this effect can be seen in Exhibit 1.2-6b, where each block has the address h(CUSTOMER, SALESMAN)/2; only one overflow pointer is required, whereas two would have been needed if there were one record per block.

We will discuss two methods of collision resolution. The simplest, *linear probing,* is also statistically the best if the block size is large enough: if address h(k) causes a collision, try $h(k) - 1, h(k) - 2, \ldots$ until an empty location is found where the new record can be inserted. For a search, try $h(k), h(k) - 1, \ldots$ until the record is found or an empty location indicates that the record is not present. (NB. The address reduction is done cyclically: $h(k), \ldots, 1, 0, n-1, n-2, \ldots, h(k) + 1$ gives the sequence to be tried.)

Exercise   1.2-7:   Formulate Algorithm LI (Hash Insert with Linear Probing) for a file with n blocks of b record locations each.

Exercise   1.2-8:   Formulate Algorithm LS (Hash Search with Linear Probing) for the same file.

The disadvantage of linear probing is that a crowded file often requires accessing every block in the file. *Separate chaining* to an independent overflow area overcomes this and has the best average behavior at small block sizes. This requires that each address have a pointer to a sequence of records in the overflow area, chained together by pointers. Where applicable, it is prudent to associate an overflow area with each cylinder of secondary storage, to eliminate arm motion during a search. Separate chaining has the aesthetic drawback that pointers are required and that overflow records are treated differently from the rest. This distinction between overflow and normal records, however, often makes possible the more elaborate hashing functions that will be discussed.

Exercise   1.2-9:   Formulate Algorithm SS (Hash Search with Separate Chaining) for a file with n blocks of b record locations each.

Volatility

Deletions are straightforward, with separate chaining. If the record to be deleted is an overflow record, remove it and reconnect the chain of pointers without it. (We must also link the newly-available record location to a list of free spaces so that it can be used again.) If the record is not an overflow record, we must replace it by the first record in the overflow chain, if any, and reduce the overflow chain accordingly.

Exercise   1.2-10:   Formulate Algorithm SD (Hash Delete with Separate Chaining) for a file with n blocks of b record locations each.

With linear probing we must do a similar reorganization of the file when we delete, as specified in

Algorithm LD: (Hash Delete with Linear Probing.) Delete a record hashed by linear probing to location $i = ab + \ell$ i.e., location ℓ of block a.

LD1   (Remove record.) Mark location empty and set $j \leftarrow i$.
LD2   (Decrease i cyclically.) $i \leftarrow i - 1$. If $i < 0$ then $i \leftarrow i + bn$.
LD3   (Check overflows.) If location i is empty, terminate.
        $r \leftarrow h(\text{key of record at location } i)$.
        If $\lfloor i/b \rfloor = \lfloor j/b \rfloor$ goto LD2.
        If r lies cyclically between $\lfloor i/b \rfloor$ and $\lfloor j/b \rfloor$ (i.e., $\lfloor i/b \rfloor \leq r < \lfloor j/b \rfloor$ or

$\lfloor i/b \rfloor < \lfloor i/b \rfloor$ and $(r < \lfloor j/b \rfloor$ or $\lfloor i/b \rfloor \leq r))$ then goto LD2.

LD4   (Rearrange overflows.) Move the record at location i to location j and goto LD1.

This algorithm leaves the file as it would be if the deleted record had never been inserted by Algorithm LI.

● ● ●

Insertions pose more of a problem than deletions. Eventually we can add only so many records to a hashed file before the storage space becomes full. After that it would seem that we must choose a new hash function to fit a larger storage area and rehash the entire file. However, by loosening our requirements on the hash function, we can enable it to handle an indefinitely large number of keys. One technique is called *virtual hashing* by its author (Litwin [1980]).

Virtual Hashing

The basic requirement for a dynamic method of storing records on blocks is to be able to *split* blocks when they become full. A way of doing this is to have a sequence of related hash functions, $h_0(k) = k \bmod \nu, \ldots, h_j(k) = k \bmod 2^j\nu$, where ν is the number of blocks originally in the file; each function maps to a storage area twice the size of its predecessor.

Since $2^j\nu$ is not prime, multiplicative hashing is preferable to division hashing, and we would let ν be a power of 2, e.g., $\nu = 1$.[1] We could use this sequence in the following way. When a block overflows, rehash *only* that block, using the next hash function in the sequence; if the new address is not yet allocated, allocate it by doubling the storage area. A bit map of one bit per block can tell us which hash function to use in subsequent searches of the file. This method has the double drawback of requiring a bit map, which may not fit in RAM, and of a load factor, α, which oscillates between a maximum value and half that value due to the periodic doubling of the storage space. Instead we examine a refinement called *linear* hashing.

Linear hashing uses the same sequence of hash functions, repeatedly doubling the storage capacity, but we allocate new storage only one block at a time. This restriction dictates which block to split at any given time and prevents us in general from splitting the block that actually caused the overflow. The sequence of splits must be block 0, then block 1, and so on up to block $\nu - 1$, when the storage space is doubled. After this we split block 0, then block 1, and so on up

---

[1] Orenstein has observed, however, that since $k \bmod 2^j$ is the last j bits of k in binary representation, we can get an *order-preserving* key-to-address transformation by taking the *first* j bits of k. The dynamic hashing methods discussed in this section thus lead to a dynamic order-preserving data structure as well.

to block $2\nu - 1$, when the space is doubled again. This means that we must cope with overflow records on blocks that are waiting to be split.

In the following algorithm, we use a pointer $p = 0, \ldots, 2^{j-1}\nu$ to indicate the next block to be split, and we control the splitting with a threshold load factor, α_0. If $\alpha_0 = 0$, we split every time there is a collision. Otherwise we try to keep the load factor $\alpha \geq \alpha_0$.

Algorithm LHI: (Linear Hash Insert). Insert record r with key k. Initially $j = 0 = p$, $n = \nu$ and for any k, $h_{-1}(k) = -1$.

LHI1   (Hash.) a ← if $h_{j-1}(k) < p$ then $h_j(k)$ else $h_{j-1}(k)$. If a is not full, store r in block a and terminate.

LHI2   (Split Control.) If $\alpha \leq \sigma_0$, store r as an overflow from block a and terminate.

LHI3   (Allocate.) If $p = 0$, $j \leftarrow j + 1$. Allocate block $p + 2^{j-1}\nu$. $n \leftarrow n + 1$.

LHI4   (Overflow.) Store r as an overflow from block a.

LHI5   (Split.) Rehash block p (including overflows) using h_j.

LHI6   (Move pointer.) $p \leftarrow p + 1$. If $p \geq 2^{j-1}\nu$, $p \leftarrow 0$.

Exercise   1.2-11:   Illustrate Algorithm LH1 with $\alpha_0 = 0$ and $\nu = 1$ by allocating integers k = 0, 1, 2, 4, 5, 6, 8, 9, 10, 12, . . . to a storage space of 2-record blocks (b = 2). Use division hashing and linear probing for overflows.

Linearly hashed records can be deleted, using

Algorithm LHD: (Linear Hash Delete.) Delete record r with hash address a, given j and p from state of insertion algorithm, LHI, and $\alpha' = (N - 1)/(n - 1)$ b, the load factor after deleting a record and freeing a block.

LHD1   (Split control.) If $\alpha' > 1$, delete r as in ordinary hashing and terminate.

LHD2   (Set pointers to the halves of the last split.) $p \leftarrow$ if $p = 0$ then $2^{j-1}\nu - 1$ else $p - 1$. $p' \leftarrow p + 2^{j-1}\nu$.

LHD3   (Delete and rehash.) If $a = p$ or $a = p'$, rehash blocks p,p' without r, using h_{j-1}. Otherwise delete r as in ordinary hashing and rehash blocks p,p' using h_{j-1}.

LHD4   (Deallocate.) Free block p' (relocating any overflow records that may be in it). $n \leftarrow n - 1$. If $p = 0$, $j \leftarrow j - 1$.

Exercise   1.2-12:   Test algorithm LHD by deleting keys from the hash file built up in Exercise 1.2-11.

A refinement of linear hashing which grows more smoothly involves *partial expansions* (Larson [1980]). Suppose the initial number of blocks is a multiple of some integer K, say K = 3. The process of doubling the number of blocks is achieved by a series of K partial expansions, $v, 4v/3, 5v/3, 6v/3 = 2v$. This is done by rehashing triplets of blocks to quadruplets of blocks, quadruplets to quintuplets, and quintuplets to sextuplets. Once the doubling is complete, we repeat the cycle until another doubling is achieved—$2v, 4 \times 2v/3, 5 \times 2v/3, 6 \times 2v/3 = 4v$—and so on. This leads to a finer control over the load factor, which can now be kept above a quite high threshold value.

Activity and Symmetry

It would seem that a batch of r search requests on a hashed file needs r times as much work, on the average, as a single request; we do one search after another. If r is very large, i.e., $r > n$, then we access each block more than once.

Exercise   1.2-13:   Suggest a way to improve high-activity searches on hashed files. What about overflows?

In the next subsection, we will consider *order-preserving* direct access methods, which are useful for high activity and indispensible for such particular cases as range queries (e.g., find records for order numbers 3 thru 7).

$$\bullet \quad \bullet \quad \bullet$$

Hashing seems to work for strictly one search key, since the hash address dictates the order of the stored records. Suppose we have a second or even a third attribute on which to search the file. Clearly, we cannot achieve an organization of the data which gives an essentially one-probe access for each search key. We ask here how well we can do with a *multidimensional hash function*.

For instance, we might need to search ORDERS on ORD# as one search key or {CUSTOMER, SALESMAN} as another. We could use a two-dimensional hash function, the vector

h (ORD#, {CUSTOMER, SALESMAN}) = (ORD# **mod** 2, (f (CUSTOMER) + 27 × f (SALESMAN) **mod** 2)

using f from Equation 1.2-1. This has possible values (0,0), (0,1), (1,0) or (1,1), and the assignment of records of ORDERS to each block is

BLOCK	RECORDS (IDENTIFIED BY ORD#)
(0,0)	2, 4, 6, 8
(0,1)	—
(1,0)	1, 5
(1,1)	3, 7

This averages two records per block, but the distribution is unequal. To access a given value of ORD# (say ORD# = 2) requires retrieving two blocks (e.g., (0,0), (0,1)). Note that this result is independent of the fact that ORD# is a key of the relation ORDERS.

Exercise   1.2-14:   For a file of n blocks hashed on m attributes (i.e., an m-dimensional hash vector), what is the cost of a search which specifies k of the m attributes?

If we go to the trouble of specifying multidimensional hash functions, it is worthwhile to take the additional step of investigating *order-preserving* multidimensional key-to-address transformations because of the great additional variety of multidimensional queries thus made possible.

1.2-3b Tidying

In order to avoid an unwieldy acronym to abbreviate "order-preserving direct access functions," we call them "tidy functions," in contrast to hash functions. In the 1936 edition of *Roget's Thesaurus of English Words and Phrases,* tidy falls under the category "Reduction to Order." Tidy functions, like hash functions, *reduce* the space of all possible values of the search key to a storage space just containing the records actually present. Unlike hash functions, tidy functions preserve *order*.

Tidy functions are plainly *distribution-dependent*. The aim of hashing is to scatter records uniformly in the storage space, for any distribution of search keys. Tidying must preserve order, and thus is forced to condense thinly-distributed search keys more than closely-distributed search keys. We can quantify this by defining the *cumulative distribution function* for an attribute A

$$D_A (a) \stackrel{\Delta}{=} \text{probability } (A \le a) \qquad (1.2\text{-}2)$$

Then the tidy function, $t_A (a)$, mapping this attribute onto a storage space of n blocks, is an approximation to

$$\lceil n \, D_A (a) \rceil \qquad (1.2\text{-}3)$$

For example, the attribute CUSTOMER of ORDERS has the alphabetical distribution shown in Exhibit 1.2-10. The distribution is shown resolved to the first letter of the CUSTOMER name, and the tidy function given is for n = 8 blocks, i.e., one per tuple. A customer beginning with 'A' would be sought at address 0 (no such block), a customer beginning with 'B' thru 'F' at address 1, and so forth. The uniform distribution, by contrast, would have a D(a) which increases linearly from 0 at a = 'A' to 1 at a = 'Z'. (Note that ORDERS contains two tuples for GNS and NYC and one tuple for each other value of CUSTOMER.)

The notion of distribution can be extended to more than one dimension. Exhibit 1.2-11 shows the *tuple distribution* for the relation TOYMAKERS (TOY, MAKER) and its associated (cumulative) *axial distributions,* D_{TOY} (t) and D_{MAKER} (m). Note that the whole alphabet is not displayed in this example; the table and distributions can easily be transformed into ones which place the TOY and MAKER values in the right locations on alphabetic axes.

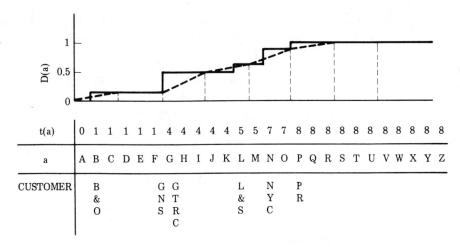

t(a)	0	1	1	1	1	1	4	4	4	4	4	5	5	7	7	8	8	8	8	8	8	8	8	8	8	8
a	A	B	C	D	E	F	G	H	I	J	K	L	M	N	O	P	Q	R	S	T	U	V	W	X	Y	Z
CUSTOMER		B & O					G N S	G T R C				L & S		N Y C		P R										

Exhibit 1.2-10. Distribution of Tuples of ORDERS by CUSTOMER

MAKER \ TOY	Caboose	Calico Cat	Car	Locomotive	Toy Train	Tractor	Tricycle	Truck	Ukulele	D_{MAKER} (m)	
Amloco Toys				1						1	0.03
Canloco Ltd.				1						1	0.06
Dink Inc.			1	1						2	0.13
Extrafun		1	1	1						3	0.22
Fischerman	1		1	1	1					4	0.34
General Toy Corp.	1	1	1	1	1	1	1	1	1	9	0.63
Mettal Toys	1		1	1	1		1	1		6	0.81
Noisy Toys		1	1	1	1	1				5	0.97
Playloco				1						1	1.0
	3	3	6	9	4	2	2	2	1		
$D_{TOY}(t)$	0.09	0.19	0.38	0.66	0.78	0.84	0.91	0.97	1.0		

Exhibit 1.2-11. Tuple and Axial Distributions in Two Dimensions

The partition lines in Exhibit 1.2-11 show how we would define the tidy function to partition TOYMAKER into 4×4 blocks. It is clear that equation 1.2-3, which was used to place partition boundaries at $D_{TOY}(t) = .25$, $D_{TOY}(t) = .5$, $D_{TOY}(t) = .75$, $D_{MAKER}(m) = .25$, $D_{MAKER}(m) = .5$ and $D_{MAKER}(m) = .75$, does not serve multidimensional data as well as for data in one dimension. Suppose the block size were $\lceil 32/(4 \times 4) \rceil = 2$ tuples. Then four of the sixteen blocks overflow on up to three tuples each, for a total of 9 tuples overflowing. To avoid overflows, we would have to extend the block size to 5 and the storage space to $5 \times 16 = 80$ tuples.

Exercise   1.2-15:   What is a better partitioning of TOYMAKERS into 4×4 blocks?

$\bullet \quad \bullet \quad \bullet$

Knowing the exact distribution function, $D_A(a)$, for an axis A, requires storing considerable data. In fact, about N parameters are required in one dimension, and about $m \times N \uparrow (1/m)$ in m dimensions. This is comparable to the size of the file itself, and so does not serve well as a technique to search the file. The answer, of course, is to approximate $D_A(a)$ by a function involving fewer parameters. One such approximation is piece-wise linear, dividing the search key range into p equal intervals of width w values and using

$$D_A(a) \simeq \frac{1}{N} L_i(a), \qquad i = \left\lfloor \frac{a - a_0}{w} \right\rfloor \qquad (1.2\text{-}4)$$

where

$$L_i(a) = \begin{cases} \dfrac{a - a_0}{w} N_0 & i = 0 \\[3ex] \displaystyle\sum_{j=0}^{i-1} N_j + \dfrac{a - a_i}{w} N_i & i = 1, \ldots, p\text{-}1. \end{cases} \qquad (1.2\text{-}5)$$

This has 2p parameters: $a_i = a_0 + w$ is the first value of interval i and N_i is the number of tuples actually found in interval i. The first term in $L_i(a)$, for $i > 0$, is just the cumulative sum $N_0 + \ldots + N_{i-1}$. The tidy function, $t_A(a) = \lceil n D_A(a) \rceil$, produces a smoothed-out distribution of the tuples on the storage space. If the new distribution is not smooth enough, its (nonlinear) distribution function could be approximated by a further piece-wise linear function on the same intervals, at the expense of 2p more parameters, and so on. The choice of the number of intervals is left to the user. Alternatively, the intervals for the piece-wise linear approximation may be split to adapt the approximating function to the variations of the distribution.

A simple piece-wise linear approximation to the distribution of tuples of ORDERS is shown as a dotted line in Exhibit 1.2-10. Eight intervals of width w = 3 values (except the last interval has w = 5) were chosen, and the parameters are

i	0	1	2	3	4	5	6	7
a_i	'A'	'D'	'G'	'J'	'M'	'P'	'S'	'V'
N_i	1	0	3	1	2	1	0	0

(Of course, the alphabet must be translated into numbers to do the arithmetic, e.g., 1 for 'A' to 26 for 'Z'.) Interval 2 ('G'-'I') would be a good candidate for interval splitting. Note that w need not be a whole number; we could have used w = 3.67.

Another adaptive parameterized approach, which gives the user explicit control of the storage utilization and the number of overflows, produces a tidy function called a *condensed directory* by Held (1975),

$$t(a) = b_i + \left\lfloor \frac{a - a_i}{w_i} \right\rfloor \qquad a_i \le a < a_{i+1} \qquad i = 1, \ldots, p. \qquad (1.2\text{-}6)$$

This has 3p parameters, where p is the number of partitions; each part has a lowest value, a_i of the search key, stored on block b_i, and has a width, w_i values per block. For instance, using the ordinal number of the first digit in the customer's name as the search key, f (CUSTOMER), the one-partition tidy function

$$t_{\text{CUSTOMER}}(c) = \left\lfloor \frac{c - 2}{4} \right\rfloor \qquad (1.2\text{-}7)$$

gives only two overflows as shown in the bottom row

block	0		1		2		3	
CUSTOMER	B & O	G N S	G N S	G T R C	L & S	N Y C	N Y C	P R
f(CUSTOMER)	2	7	7	7	12	14	14	16
t_{CUSTOMER}	0	1	1	1	2	3	3	3

A conventional index would correspond to four partitions, and would have the same overflows because CUSTOMER is not a key.

Exercise 1.2-16: What are the values of α and π (see Exercise 1.2-15) for the above example on CUSTOMER?

Exercise 1.2-17: Formulate Algorithm H, embodying the following procedure to establish the condensed directory (Equation 1.2-6) by making distribution-dependent guesses at the widths w. For some predetermined integer, g, (g $\le$ 5 is usually adequate) of guesses, look ahead b $\times$ 2^{g-1} records from a_i, the first record of the current partition. Set g trial values of

w_i, $w_i^{(j)} = (a_{i+2^j b} - a_i)/2^j$, $j = 0, \ldots$, g-1, where b is the block size. With predetermined limits, α_0, π_0 for the load and probe factors respectively (see Exercise 1.2-6), inspect the file from record a_i on, allocating addresses according to g tidy functions of the form (Equation 1.2-6) while $\alpha \geq \alpha_0$ and $\pi \leq \pi_0$. When either $\alpha < \alpha_0$ or $\pi > \pi_0$ for all g guesses, terminate the partition and assign to it the best of the g tidy functions. Then start a new partition and repeat.

Exercise   1.2-18:   What would be a good collision resolution method to handle overflows in Algorithm H?

Exercise   1.2-19:   What can you say about unsuccessful searches using a tidy function?

Multipaging

The technique of multidimensional paging, or *multipaging,* searches for optimal tidy functions in more than one dimension. Optimality is measured in terms of the *load factor,* $\alpha \overset{\Delta}{=}$ (number of tuples)/(capacity of storage), which should be as high as possible, and the *probe factor,* $\pi \overset{\Delta}{=} 1 +$ (number of tuples which overflow)/(total number of tuples), which should be as low as possible.

The fact that we seek a tidy function constrains the partitions of each axis to cross the whole space perpendicular to that axis. Thus, the partition between Car and Locomotive on the TOY axis of Exhibit 1.2-11 separates tuples for Cars from Tuples for Locomotives across the whole space, independently of the value of MAKER; it is a straight line at right angles to the TOY axis. This constraint has the disadvantage that a densely populated area of the tuple distribution (e.g., the region around (General Toy Corp, Locomotive) in Exhibit 1.2-11) can have many overflows, while another part of the same distribution can be very sparse (e.g., the upper right corner). It has, however, the very great advantage that the whole space can be addressed via the axes. If there are n blocks of data in an m-dimensional space, there will be only about $\sqrt[m]{n}$ partitions on each axis and thus only m $\times$ $\sqrt[m]{n}$ (or 2 $\times$ m $\times$ $\sqrt[m]{n}$ or 3 $\times$ m $\times$ $\sqrt[m]{n}$) parameters instead of n (or 2n or 3n). For instance, 100 blocks in two dimensions will need two indexes of only 10 entries each if the space is partitioned 10 $\times$ 10. This expected saving is what enables us to speak of tidy *functions* rather than multidimensional directories; we can anticipate the indexes will fit into RAM in many cases.

Exercise   1.2-20:   a) Make calculations which show that axial indexes of very large files can fit entirely in RAM in the best case of equal numbers of partitions for each axis.

b) What, on the other hand, are the worst cases?

Exercise   1.2-21:   How do we locate each of the n blocks representing an m-dimensional partition during a search? For instance, if the $n = 4 \times 4$ blocks of Exhibit 1.2-11 have addresses $0, 1, \ldots, 15$, how do we associate these addresses with the block coordinates $(0,0), (0,1), \ldots, (3,3)$?

Exercise   1.2-22:   Use the relationship $\alpha = N/nb$ and the constraints $\lceil N/n \rceil = b_0 \leq b \leq \lfloor N/\alpha_0 n \rfloor$ and $\alpha_0 \leq \alpha \leq N/nb_0$ (where α is the load factor, required to exceed a minimum value, α_0, b is the blocksize with a minimum value b_0 for a given n, n is the number of blocks and N is the number of records) to solve the following problem. Given $N = 10000$, $\alpha_0 = 0.8$, b should be about 55 records per block. We want to multipage the file with about equal numbers of partitions on each of three axes. Find n and its three factors $f_1 \times f_2 \times f_3 = n$, the range of acceptable values for α, and the range of corresponding values for b.

Assuming that we know the factors f_j, $j = 1 .. m$ (see Exercise 1.2-22) such that the jth axis is partitioned into f_j segments and $n = \Pi f_j$, we can use the *axial distribution,* i.e., the number of tuples for each different value on the jth axis, to generate the tidy function for that axis as in Equation 1.2-3. The set of m axial tidy functions constitutes the tidy function for the m-dimensional space.

Since we expect the axis to contain relatively few values, we are less concerned about approximating the axial distribution. In fact, it is best to know it completely because, unlike the one-dimensional case, there can be many more than one tuple per value, with the result that the axial distribution can take sudden large jumps. This leads to ambiguity about the placement of the partition boundaries. (If the attribute corresponding to the axis is a key, the axial distribution will have N values and no sudden jumps. In this case, approximating may be acceptable.)

For example, to make a 4×4 partitioning of TOYMAKERS in Exhibit 1.2-11, we seek to place boundaries at $D_{TOY} = .25, .5$ and .75 and the same for D_{MAKER}. These values do not exist, and the boundaries shown are only one of the possible sets. In fact, Exercise 1.2-15 discovers a better set of boundaries from the point of view of optimizing α and π. In general, each boundary has two potential locations. For instance, the boundary corresponding to $D_{TOY} = .25$ can be placed just before or just after $D_{TOY} = .38$ (i.e., TOY = Car). Thus, axis j has $2 \uparrow (f_j - 1)$ different sets of boundaries to be investigated for optimality. Of course, this total is reduced in practice by interactions between the boundaries: if the $D_{TOY} = .25$ boundary is placed after TOY = Car, then the $D_{TOY} = .5$ boundary cannot go there.

In fact, the best of the $\sim 2 \uparrow (f_j - 1)$ sets of boundaries, from the point of view of minimizing overflows *between* segments on the jth axis, can be found in only two scans of the axial distribution, one forward and one backward. Before showing this, we consider the effect of minimizing overflow between segments. First, this does not necessarily minimize total overflow, since tuples can overflow between blocks *within* a segment. In Exhibit 1.2-11, each of the four segments along the TOY axis consists of four blocks. If the block size is two tuples, the segment containing Locomotive has only one overflow (9 tuples in 4 blocks $\times$ 2 tuples each). But within the segment, two more tuples overflow. Second, however, we are limited to working with the axial distributions and to doing this kind of inter-segment minimization, because any other approach would require repeated scans of the entire file. It is desirable to limit processing of the data file to one pass, after the axial distributions are found, and we certainly could not afford an exponential number of passes of even a small file. Thus we choose to sacrifice true optimality for what we hope is a good approximation.

To see how to minimize inter-segment overflows among the f segments by linear scans of the axial distribution, consider placing the first boundary. (The "zeroth" boundary is already placed at $D_A = 0$.) There are, in general, two choices, and so, depending on the width of the first segment, there are two possible total inter-segment overflows. Now we proceed by induction: consider placing the kth boundary. We assume that the two choices for the k-1st boundary have already given us two possible total inter-segment overflows and show that the kth boundary does the same. In general, there are four possible combinations of k-1st and k^{th} boundary locations: $(before_{k-1}, before_k)$, $(before_{k-1}, after_k)$, $(after_{k-1}, before_k)$, and $(after_{k-1}, after_k)$, where $before_i$ means place boundary i before $D_A = i/f$ and $after_i$ means place it after $D_A = i/f$, scanning in ascending order of D_A. We have, by assumption, the total inter-segment overflows for $before_{k-1}$ and $after_{k-1}$, and it is easy to find out if the new total inter-segment overflow for $before_k$ is less if $before_{k-1}$ or if $after_{k-1}$ is used; and the same for the total for $after_k$. Thus we can move along from one boundary to the next, recording the least total cost for each position of the boundary and a pointer from each position to the position of the preceding boundary that gave rise to that cost.

The reverse scan, done later, follows the pointers to pick up the path, or set of boundary positions, giving the least overall cost.

This method is complicated a little by the possibility of boundaries coinciding. It unfortunately seems to be limited to the one-dimensional problem of scanning a single axial distribution, and not extendible to placing the multidimensional partition boundaries. It is best represented as a graph, and Exhibits 1.2-12 and 1.2-13 show graphs for the two axes of TOYMAKERS. In Exhibit 1.2-12, the boundary for the first segment ($D_{TOY} = .25$) can fall on either side of $D_{TOY} = .38$. The cost for $before_1$ is 0 and that for $after_1$ is 4 overflows. The boundary for the second segment ($D_{TOY} = .5$) can fall on either side of $D_{TOY} = .66$; the $before_2$ case coincides with $after_1$, so that they cannot co-exist. The $(before_1, before_2)$ combination costs 0 overflows, so the total cost for $before_2$ is 0 overflows. The $(before_1, after_3)$ case costs 7 overflows while the $(after_1, after_2)$ case costs 1. The minimum of $7 + 0$ and $4 + 1$ is $4 + 1 = 5$, so the pointer associated with $after_2$ points to $after_1$. (The pointer is represented by a short arrow; ignore the long arrow for the mo-

| | 3 | 3 | | 6 | | 9 | | 4 | | 2 | 2 | 2 | 1 | |

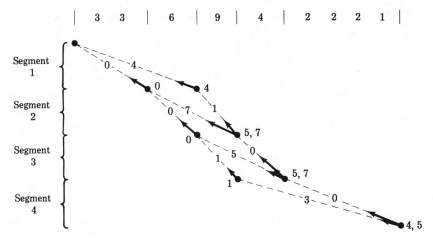

Exhibit 1.2-12. Partitioning Network for Toys Axis.

| | 1 | 1 | 2 | 3 | | 4 | | 9 | | 6 | | 5 | 1 | |

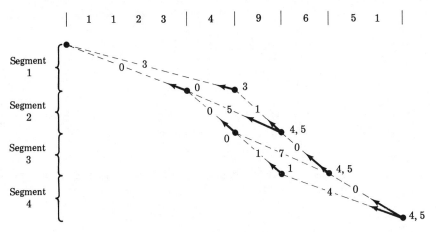

Exhibit 1.2-13. Partitioning Network for Manufacturers Axis.

ment.) The final best cost is 4 overflows, given by the following set of choices: $before_1$, $before_2$, $before_3$. The next best cost is 5 overflows, given by two combinations of long and short arrows: $before_1$, $before_2$, $after_3$ and $after_1$, $after_2$, $after_3$. Note that the boundaries for TOYMAKERS preferred by Exhibits 1.2-12 and 1.2-13 still are not the best, as determined in Exercise 1.2-15, although they are an improvement over Exhibit 1.2-11. The tradeoff between π and α is

α	.5	.67	1
π	1.06	1.13	1.25

However, the choice provided by the *combination* of best and next best costs in Exhibits 1.2-12 and 1.2-13 includes the optimum case discovered in Exercise

1.2-15. Having the choice is the reason for considering next best and even next-next best costs in the analysis. This is discussed later.

• • •

Exhibit 1.2-14 gives a detailed algorithm for placing candidate boundaries and for constructing the overflow graph to find the least overflows. (Extending this to find the next best cost and so on is simple.) The next three paragraphs, explaining the flowchart, may be skipped by the reader interested only in the above overview.

The algorithm uses integer count of tuples (*entry*) instead of the cumulative axial probability distribution, D_A, at each value of the axis. It considers the right boundary of each segment and therefore introduces segment 0, whose right boundary is the leftmost boundary of the axis. The above terminology "before" and "after" becomes *first* and *second* respectively because both candidate boundaries are always placed, even in the degenerate case where they coincide (e.g., if D_{TOY} = .25 somewhere in the distribution). Initially, *segment* = 1 and the boundary for segment 0 is assumed placed before the first entry. For each entry, we accumulate $A \leftarrow A + entry$; $a \leftarrow A/(N/f)$; $\Delta \leftarrow$ increase in $\lfloor a \rfloor$. When boundaries are placed, we increase *segment* by 1.

We must consider three sets of conditions:

1) $\Delta = 0, \Delta = 1$ or $\Delta > 1$
2) $a = \lfloor a \rfloor$ or $a > \lfloor a \rfloor$
3) the boundary location before the entry has/has not already been occupied by a boundary for the previous segment.

If we abbreviate (1) by {0 , 1, >}, (2) by {=, ≠}, and (3) by {Y, N}, we have the following outline of the boundary placement part of the algorithm (* means 'any condition', 'c.b.' means 'candidate boundary/boundaries').

Condition	1	2	3	Action
	0	*	*	no c.b.
	1	=	*	first, second c.b. after
	1	≠	Y	first, second c.b. after
	1	≠	N	first c.b. before, second c.b. after
	>	*	Y	first, second c.b. after
	>	*	N	first, second c.b. before

In addition, if $\Delta > 1$, we have a *backlog* of Δ-1 boundaries to be placed, which we do so that Δ segments all coincide at the one value of the attribute, sharing the tuples equally among the segments. Boundary locations are stored in *bdy (segment, first/second)*.

As well as placing the boundaries, the algorithm constructs the graph and calculates the minimum path length. The graph is represented by pointers from each candidate boundary to the candidate boundary of the previous segment which

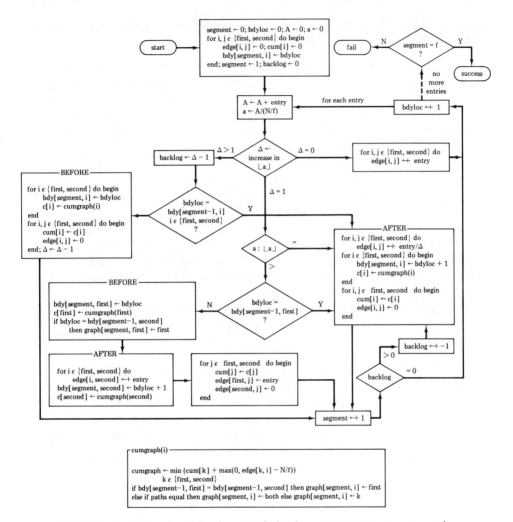

Exhibit   1.2-14.   Partitioning an Axis. (x←+y means x ← x + y)

gives rise to the least cumulative overflow *(graph (segment, first/second)* with the values *first/second/both).* The minimum path length is held in accumulators, *cum (first/second),* which keep track of the least cost from the left-most boundary to the right boundary candidates of the current segment—and finally to the rightmost boundary of the axis. For each segment, up to four edges of the graph must be considered at any one time: *edge* (i, j) for i, j ϵ *{first, second}.*

So far, apart from finding the axial distributions, we have not used the file of data at all. When we have a small set of possible partitionings for each axis, we can inspect the file to determine the best combination of partitionings. For instance, Exhibits 1.2-12 and 1.2-13 give the following

	PARTITIONING	COST	SET OF BOUNDARIES
TOY axis	A	4	$before_1$, $before_2$, $before_3$
	B	5	$before_1$, $before_2$, $after_3$
	C	5	$after_1$, $after_2$, $after_3$
MAKER axis	a	4	$after_1$, $after_2$, $after_3$
	b	5	$before_1$, $after_2$, $after_3$
	c	5	$before_1$, $before_2$, $before_3$

Each of these sets corresponds to four distinct boundary candidates for its axis: those shown in Exhibit 1.2-11 plus an extra TOY candidate boundary after Toy Train, and an extra MAKER candidate boundary after Metal Toys. Since four boundary candidates divide each axis into five pieces, a 5 × 5 histogram suffices to decide among the nine possible combinations of {a, b, c} with {A, B, C}. Exhibit 1.2-15 gives this histogram; the numbers in the cells are the counts of tuples in the corresponding region of the file. The histogram is filled by a single pass of the data file.

Exhibit 1.2-16 shows explicitly the results for the nine possible combinations of partitioning: bB is the best, as found in Exercise 1.2-15. The complexity of this search can be controlled by the amount of choice allowed by the algorithm to place candidate boundaries.

For the histogram building process to be feasible in one pass of the file we must be able to fit the histogram entirely in RAM. The number of tuples counted per cell is of the order of the block size, and can be supposed to be < 256. Thus, one byte per cell suffices for the histogram, which has about n cells—not many more (the file has n blocks). In many cases this many bytes of RAM are available.

Exhibit **1.2-15.** Tuple Histogram for TOYMAKERS

aA

2	3	5	1
2	1	1	5
1	1	1	3
1	1	2	2

α	0.67	1
π	1.13	1.25

aB

2	3	6	0
2	1	2	4
1	1	2	2
1	1	3	1

α	0.67	1
π	1.13	1.25

aC

5	5	1	0
3	1	1	4
2	1	1	2
2	2	1	1

α	0.67	1
π	1.16	1.28

bA

1	2	4	0
3	2	2	6
1	1	1	3
1	1	2	2

α	0.67	1
π	1.13	1.25

bB

1	2	4	0
3	2	4	4
1	1	2	2
1	1	3	1

α	0.67	1
π	1.09	1.25

bC

3	4	0	0
5	2	2	4
2	1	1	2
2	2	1	1

α	0.67	1
π	1.13	1.25

cA

1	2	4	0
1	1	1	1
2	1	1	5
2	2	3	5

α	0.67	1
π	1.16	1.28

cB

1	2	4	0
1	1	2	0
2	1	2	4
2	2	5	3

α	0.67	1
π	1.13	1.25

cC

3	4	0	0
2	1	1	0
3	1	1	4
4	3	2	3

α	0.67	1
π	1.09	1.31

Exhibit   1.2-16. π-α for Candidate Partitionings. Note Diagonal Symmetry.

Exercise 1.2-23 gives an upper limit to the number of cells required to be held in RAM—a bound which is not at all tight.

Exercise   1.2-23:   With at most two positions per boundary, the histogram needs at most 2^m entries for each block in the final multipage structure, i.e. $n \times 2^m$ entries. However the file could be sorted on one axis and processed one value at a time on that axis. Then $1/n \uparrow (1/m)$ of the histogram needs to be in RAM at any time, and less if we sensibly choose the largest axis to sort on. What is the upper bound on the number of histogram cells that must fit into RAM?

• • •

In summary, we present in outline an algorithm for multipaging a file.

Algorithm MP: Multipaging a file. Predetermined values: minimum load factor, α_0; number, $\#_0$, of different values to be considered of total segment overflows. Minimum blocksize, $b_0 = \lceil N/n \rceil$.

MP1   Find the axial distributions for each axis.
MP2   Choose partitioning factors f_i, $i = 1, \ldots, m$
MP3   For each axis
      Scan Forward (for candidate boundaries and total overflows)
      For each value of total overflow, $1, \ldots, \#_0$
          Scan Backward (for partitionings)
MP4   Build histogram in RAM using candidate boundaries
MP5   For each partitioning of axis 1
    •
      •
        •
        For each partitioning of axis m
          For each blocksize $b \leftarrow b_0, b_0 + 1, \ldots$ while $\alpha = N/nb > \alpha_0$
             Evaluate π and choose partitioning with largest α among those of smallest π so far.

Steps MP1 and MP4 access the file and cost about $n \log n$ and n accesses respectively, if the file has n blocks. Step MP3, Scan Forward, is specified in Exhibit 1.2-14. Scan Backward is a simple depth-first search.

Exercise   1.2-24:   How would you implement the variable number of nested loops in step MP5?

Exercise   1.2-25:   Given an m-dimensional tuple distribution histogram in RAM with f_i segments on axis i, $i = 1, \ldots, m$, and two candidate boundaries between each segment, how many configurations are there to be examined by an exhaustive search to find the cheapest of all these configurations?

Multipaging may not work if the tuples are badly distributed. As a procedure we recommend: try Algorithm MP and if the π-α trade-off is unsatisfactory, use a method other than multipaging. The cost of trying is only order n log n and if it works, multipaging is hard to beat for speed and versatility.

Exercise 1.2-26: Multipage ORDERBOOK (Exhibit 1.1-1) on ORD# and ASSEMBLY in n = 4 × 2 blocks.

Dynamic Multipaging

Multipaging can be used for volatile files, at the sacrifice of guaranteed limits on π and α. We look at the case of a growing file.

The method has the same basis as all procedures for dynamically modifying a secondary storage structure. When a block overflows, split it and allocate new storage. The constraint imposed by multipaging is that segment boundaries must cross the whole space, and not remain confined to one block. Thus when we split a block we must split all blocks in the same plane as the block, where a "plane" of blocks is a space of one dimension less than the multipage space, and is perpendicular to one of the axes. (In two dimensions, this means all blocks in a line at right angles to an axis.) Thus one of the axes gets an extra segment each time a split is made. If there are n blocks to start with in m dimensions, a split adds only $n \uparrow (1 - 1/m)$ blocks, roughly speaking, or, to be more precise, n/f new blocks where f was the original number of segments along the axis. About 2n/f blocks are accessed to do the split. For practical values of n and m, this work is reasonably small, and the load factor, α, is not badly reduced by the split.

Before a split is done, it is possible to see if one of the boundaries of the overfilled block can be shifted to advantage. A "boundary" is a segment boundary, i.e., a plane perpendicular to an axis, and, again, shifting the boundary for one block means shifting it for all n/f blocks which it bounds. If shifting a boundary reduces overflow to an acceptable amount, a split need not be done.

With m axes, the overfilled block in question belongs to m different planes and has m sets of two boundaries each. The axis can be chosen to optimize performance. For instance, if shifting is possible, choose the shift which most reduces the overflows. If splitting is necessary, the choice can be made using several criteria. First, the ratio V/f for each axis, where V is the number of different values and f the number of segments for the axis (after the insertion but before the split), should remain as nearly constant as possible over all axes. (This is a rule of thumb and could be changed, but some such consideration must appear in the choice of axes or else the following criteria will tend to cause one axis to be segmented repeatedly and the other axes to have few, if any, segments.) Second, the probe factor, π, should be reduced as much as possible by the split. Third, the load factor, α, should be reduced as little as possible.

This discussion can be summarized in the following outline for an algorithm.

Algorithm MSI: Multipage Search and Insert.

MSI1. (Search) Find block for new tuple. If tuple there, report and terminate.

If inserting the tuple does not increase the probe factor above a prespecified threshold, π_0, insert and terminate.

MSI2. (Shift)　　For each axis

For each of the two boundaries of the block that are perpendicular to the axis.

Compare the increase of overflows over all blocks in the plane between the boundaries if the boundary is shifted after inserting *versus* if not shifted.

If some shifts give a probe factor $\leq \pi_0$, make the shift which reduces the overflows the most and terminate.

MSI3. (Split)　　For each axis

Calculate V/f, π and α, where V, π and α are the number of values on the axis, the probe factor and the load factor after insertion and splitting, and f is the number of segments of the axis before splitting.

Choose the axis with the largest ratio V/f and, if several, choose the axis with the largest π and, if several, choose the axis which will reduce α the least. Split the plane of blocks perpendicular to this axis, placing the new boundary so that π is minimized. Insert and terminate.

● ● ●

Algorithm MSI and the preceeding discussion do not specify how the resulting multipaging space is to be addressed. We need to know how to assign block locations from 0 to n − 1, so that splitting a plane affects the contents of the blocks in the plane only and assigns the n/f new block numbers in a systematic fashion.

We can break this problem into two parts. First we deal with splitting only the outside planes ("faces") of the space, which is, for each axis, the perpendicular plane corresponding to the largest values of the axis. Later we consider how to extend the method for faces, to split internal planes as well.

Exhibit 1.2-17a shows a multipaged arrangement of the TOYMAKERS relation, which has been built up dynamically by insertion of the tuples in random order. The entries are abbreviated: "G L" stands for "General Toy Corp., Locomotive", etc. Tuples which have overflowed their blocks are shown outside—D Car, P L, etc. The threshold value of the probe factor is assumed to be $\pi_0 = 1.25$, so that six overflows are allowed for the 26 tuples present. In this state of the file, $\pi = 1.23$ and $\alpha = 1$. (The block size is 2 tuples: 26 tuples appear to be stored in a space with room for 24. We do not worry now about where the overflows are placed, and we calculate our α in terms of primary storage only, except that $\alpha \leq 1$.)

The integers in the top left corners of each block are the block locations, from 0 to 11. The specific sequence of the blocks is a function of how the multipage space was built up dynamically. We are about to add another face to the space, which will illustrate this process.

Suppose that we now want to add N Tr (Noisy Toys, Tractor). This belongs in block 8 but does not fit. Insertion will increase π to $1 + 7/27 = 1.26$, which is not acceptable. We cannot shift the MAKER boundary from G (General Toy Corp) to M (Mettal Toys) because this will cause a net increase to 9 overflows. Nor can we shift the TOY boundary from Tr (Tractor) to T (Toy Train) to any advantage: the number of overflows increases to an unacceptable 8. Shifting the other TOY boundary L (Locomotive) is clearly impossible. So we must split block 8.

Two choices are open to us. We can split the MAKER plane, blocks 4, 5, 8, 11. This will decrease V_{MAKER}/f_{MAKER} from $9/3 = 3$ to $9/4 = 2.25$, will decrease π from $1 + 7/27$ to $1 + 4/27 = 1.15$, and will decrease α from 1 to .84. Or, we can split the TOY plane, blocks 6, 7, 8: V_{TOY}/f_{TOY} goes from $9/4 = 2.25$ to $9/5 = 1.8$, π goes to $1 + 6/27 = 1.22$, and α goes to $27/(5 \times 3 \times 2) = .9$. Since our primary criterion is to reduce the largest V/f, we merely need to compare 3 (MAKER) with 2.25 (TOY) to decide to split the MAKER plane.

Exhibit 1.2-17b shows the result. (The remaining five tuples of TOY-MAKERS have been inserted in Exhibit 1.2-17b, giving $\alpha = 1, \pi = 1.25$.) The new blocks are 12, 13, 14 and 15, which we see have been added as a MAKER plane, forming a new face for MAKER.

In this example, blocks are always added one face at a time. We can use this to see from the location numbers in Exhibit 1.2-17a how the space was built up. First there was block 0, then TOY was split to add block 1. Then MAKER split twice, first adding blocks 2, 3 then adding blocks 4, 5. Next TOY split again, giving 6, 7, 8, and again, giving 9, 10, 11 and the arrangement of Exhibit 1.2-17a. Each split affects only the old and new face of blocks, leaving the others unchanged.

Exercise 1.2-27:   Using the sequence numbers shown, build up the multipage space for TOYMAKERS with Algorithm MSI and confirm that Exhibit 1.2-17 is the end result. Use $\pi_0 = 1.25$ and when the axis to be split is not uniquely identified by the algorithm, split TOY.

	C	Cal	Car	L	T	Tr	Tri	Tru	U
A				5					
C				15					
D			8	19					
E		2	31	24					
F	28		3	18	12				
G	27	25	7	4	14	17	29	22	1
M	0		6	16	9		20	23	
N		30	10	11	13	26			
P				21					

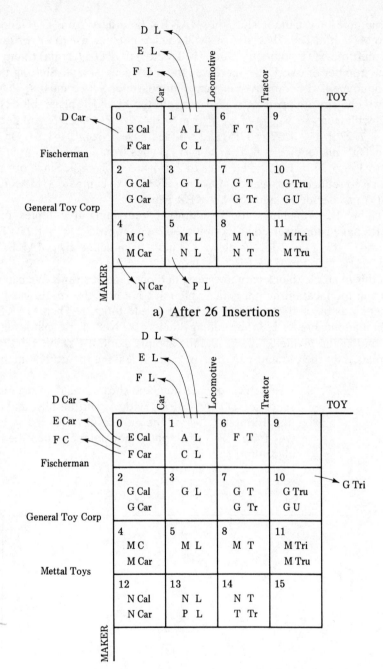

a) After 26 Insertions

b) After 32 Insertions. Split by Insertion of N Tr.

Exhibit 1.2-17. Dynamic Multipaging of TOYMAKERS.

Exercise 1.2-28: Compare the results of dynamic and static multipaging of TOYMAKERS.

The next question we tackle is how to find the right block in a query. For instance, we know where F T is in the space, but how do we know if its block number is 6, 4 or 2? It would be 2 if TOY had been split at least twice at the beginning of the file buildup, instead of only once. It would be 4 if MAKER had been split only once immediately after the first split of TOY, then followed by a second split of TOY.

To keep track of which of these possible evolutions of TOYMAKERS actually occurred, we will use *axial directories*. These are auxiliary storage structures for the multipage space, one for each axis. Such structures are needed in any case, as in static multipaging, as indexes to the segments. We here add one integer for each segment. In keeping with the multipaging approach, these directories are considered short, needing typically only n $\uparrow$ (1/m) entries each.

The axial directory for the new face in Exhibit 1.2-17b, blocks 12-15, must inform us that the starting location is 12 and the face contains 4 blocks. This is equivalent to knowing that the file occupied a 3×4 space before the split which created the new face: $3 \times 4 = 12$ blocks were already present, so the new face must start at location 12; since the new face results from a MAKER split, it must contain as many blocks as $f_{TOY} = 4$, the number of segments in TOY. Of this pair of numbers, 3 is already known from the fact that the new face is segment 3 (the fourth segment, but numbering from 0) of the MAKER axis, and thus is described in entry 3 of the axial directory. So all we need to store is 4, the number of segments on the TOY axis at the time of creating the new face. Thus, 4 is recorded at location 3 of the MAKER axial array.

The directories for TOYMAKERS are shown in Exhibit 1.2-18. This gives all the information needed to locate any block correctly, except that, for simplicity, the index entries (Fischerman, Car, etc.) are not shown. The entries of the axial array are created when the corresponding plane is added to the multipage space. The ith entry of the axial array is the size of the plane, and the product of the entry and i is the starting block number for the plane.

Exercise 1.2-29: Extend the rule for forming axial arrays to an m-dimensional multipage space.

To see how we use the axial arrays to locate a block, consider again the problem of finding F T. Since F $\leq$ Fischerman, the upper limit of the first row of blocks in Exhibit 1.2-17 and since Locomotive < T $\leq$ Tractor, the bounds of the third column, ordinary axial indexing tells us that the coordinates of the block for F T are (0,2)—remember we count from 0. We must decide whether block (0,2) was created in the 0th MAKER plane or in the 2nd TOY plane. This is easy: calculate the starting block numbers for each plane and choose the larger, since that will be the most recently formed plane. Thus, $0 \times 0 = 0$ is less than $2 \times 3 =$

	TOY	0	1	2	3
		1	1	3	3

MAKER

MAKER					
0	1	0	1	6	9
1	2	2	3	7	10
2	2	4	5	8	11
3	4	12	13	14	15

Exhibit   1.2-18.   Block Location Numbers and Axial Arrays for TOYMAKERS

6, so (0,2) belongs to the TOY plane starting at location 6. It is the 0th element of this plane, so its location number is 6. (Block (1,2) is block one of the same plane, and so has block number $6 + 1 = 7$, and so on.)

Exercise   1.2-30:   Give the algorithm to find the location number of block (m,t) using axial entries row(m) and col(t) for a two-dimensional array.

Exercise   1.2-31:   Generalize Exercise 1.2-30 to an m-dimensional array.

Using these methods and incorporating index entries into the axial arrays, we have the final form for TOYMAKERS shown in Exhibit 1.2-19. The axial arrays for a larger file could be stored in various ways, such as B-trees (see Section 1.2-4). Since we assume that they are likely to fit into RAM, we do not pursue this further.

Exhibit 1.2-20 shows TOYMAKERS after dynamic multipaging under different conditions, namely the constraint $\pi = 1$. This gives much less leeway and we note that the result, $\alpha = .44$, is hardly satisfactory. We are reminded by this that dynamic multipaging does not guarantee the results, and that judicious choice of constraints by the designer is important. This version of TOYMAKERS also shows us how dynamic multipaging splits planes that are not faces, i.e., internal planes. The newly created plane simply forms a face, and a pointer from the axial index is used to straighten out the resulting departure from strict order of the values. This loss of the order-preserving property of the data space does not affect clustering, and hence retrieval efficiency, because it involves a permutation only of the segments.

Exercise   1.2-32:   Apply Algorithm MSI and the addressing techniques discussed above to derive Exhibit 1.2-20 from the tuples of TOYMAKERS presented in the sequence of Exercise 1.2-27, with the probe factor, π, not permitted to exceed 1.

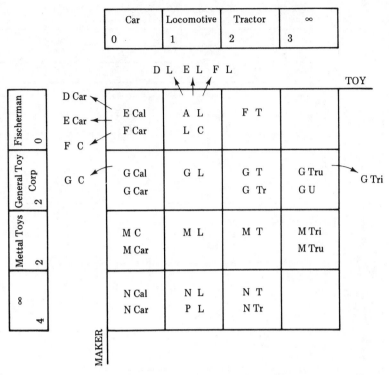

	Car	Locomotive	Tractor	∞
0		1	2	3

Exhibit 1.2-19. Multipaged TOYMAKERS with Axial Arrays

Exercise 1.2-33: How would you delete tuples from a file stored with dynamic multipaging?

1.2-3c Summary of Direct Access

Direct access is the best possible access method on the average, with a cost that is independent of the number of records to be searched and usually only one access. With ill luck in the distribution of the data, however, and some overflow methods, the cost can be as bad as accessing every block of the file.

Volatility. Virtual hashing is one technique which allows the file to grow arbitrarily large, and has graceful behavior under frequent changes without losing the one-access average performance of direct access. Dynamic multipaging is a further method, with the additional benefits of preserving order (high activity) and allowing secondary search keys (high symmetry).

Activity. To cope with high activity we introduced the tidy functions for order-preserving direct access, so that batches of requests and requests involving many adjacent tuples can be processed.

Symmetry. We extended tidy functions to multidimensional paging, which has the property of requiring directories only for the axes of the multidimensional

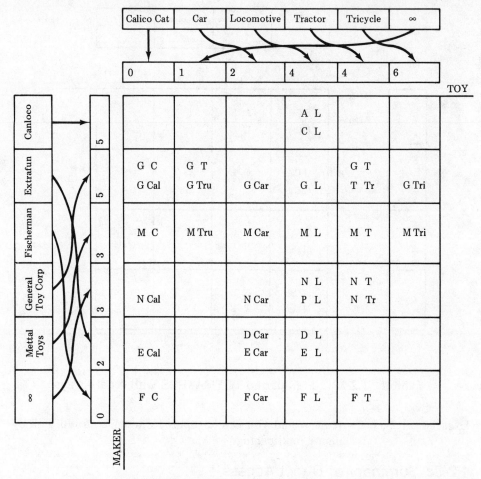

Exhibit   1.2-20.   TOYMAKERS Multipaged Under $\pi = 1$, Showing Permuted Index

space. Since such directories often are small enough to fit into RAM, this method is a direct access technique. Multipaging is sensitive to the distribution of tuples in the space, and may not always give the desired tradeoff between load factor α and probe factor π. If unsatisfactory, a logarithmic method must be used (see next section).

1.2-4   Logarithmic Files

The average number of probes required to access a record on a hashed file on secondary storage is very small. The maximum number of probes, however, for hashed and other direct access organizations encountered in the last section, can be as much as one per block, searching for a single record that has overflowed. If we want a guaranteed fast access, we had better avoid direct files.

Direct files also require a specific arrangement of the data, and an organization that is good for one purpose may be bad for another. For instance, there are conflicts among hashing, virtual hashing, c-directories and multipaging in the way records are distributed in the storage space. Thus, for any given direct file organization we may need *supplementary data structures* as interfaces with processes for which the direct file is not optimally arranged.

Logarithmic files are based on trees, whose height is logarithmically proportional to the number of nodes (see Appendix). The maximum number of accesses, if each node is a block of data, is the height of the tree. The base of the logarithm depends on the fanout (the number of descendants of a node) and the best tree is that with the greatest average fanout. Fanout is determined by the number of search keys we can get on a block, which depends on how much data is associated with each key. This fact, plus the consideration that the data is usually best arranged for some suitable direct access method, leads us to consider *indexes* first in this section.

An index of a file is a supplementary file for a given search key. It contains values of the search key and pointers to the relevant blocks of the main file. Searching an index is done by comparison of search keys and depends on their being ordered within the index. If the main file is also ordered on the search key, only one search key per block of main file need be stored on the index—either the first or the last. This is the organization called *indexed sequential* and is the limiting case of c-directories. If, on the other hand, the main file is arranged in some other way, the index must contain an entry, and a pointer, for every value of the search key. It is usually then called a *secondary index* or *inverted file*.

Indexed sequential organization has no advantages over c-directories, except possibly in occasional long searches for the latter if overflows are not well handled, and except that it is often designed to match the cylinder-track configuration of particular hardware. The most versatile secondary index structure is the *B-tree*, which we now discuss.

B-trees as Secondary Indexes

A B-tree for {CUSTOMER, SALESMAN} is shown in Exhibit 1.2-8. A better one is shown in Exhibit 1.2-21. (One is for ORDERS and the other is for ORDERBOOK, but this is a minor distinction.) The first B-tree is not an index but contains one or two whole tuples in each node. The second is an index, with leaf nodes containing pointers to the blocks of the main file (which happens to be multipaged) holding the relevant tuples. The first is uniform, in that all nodes are similar (except that all pointers from the leaf nodes are null). The second has two types of node—leaf nodes, which contain full search keys and pointers to the main file, and internal nodes which contain only abbreviated versions of the search keys, called *separators*, and pointers to the descendant nodes.

ASSEMBLY	ORD # 1	2	3	4	5	6	7	8
Caboose	page (0,0)	(PR,H,37)	L&S,E,3	page (0,1)	page (0,2)		GTRC,N,43	page (0,3)
Car		(NCY,N,1)	L&S,E,23		NYC,H,31	B&O,H,17	GTRC,N,139	
Locomotive	GNS,E,2		L&S,E,5	page (1,1)	NYC,H,13	page (1,2)	GTRC,N,47	page (1,3)
Toy Train	GNS,E,7	page (1,0)		PR,H,11				GNS,E,37

a) Multipaged on ORD# and ASSEMBLY (see Exercise 1.2-24) with Page Addresses.

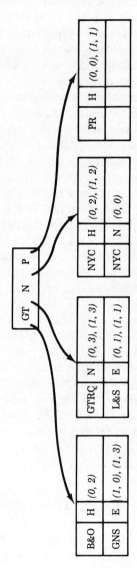

b) Prefix B*-tree Index for {CUSTOMER, SALESMAN}.

Exhibit 1.2-21. ORDERBOOK (see Exhibit 1.1-1) Multipaged with Secondary Index.

The search procedure on the internal nodes of trees of the type shown in Exhibit 1.2-21 is the same as that for the tree in Exhibit 1.2-8 except that in the latter case the search can stop before a leaf node is reached, while in the former, all searches must proceed to the leaf node, and from there to the main file. The advantage of the tree of Exhibit 1.2-21 is that the individual entries are smaller and so more of them can be stored in a node, thus increasing the fanout and decreasing the height of the tree. This is true for the leaf nodes in general, and is especially true for internal nodes where the separators can be very short.

Exercise   1.2-34:   The internal nodes of trees of the type of Exhibit 1.2-21 (and all nodes of the tree of Exhibit 1.2-8) have the format p_0 k_1 p_1 . . . k_{f-1} p_{f-1} where f is the fanout for the node, p_i is a pointer to a descendant node, and k_i is a separator (or a key plus data). Give the search procedure, Algorithm BS, for trees of this type.

Exercise   1.2-35:   How must Algorithm BS be modified for a search on the tree of Exhibit 1.2-8?

Volatility

The discussion so far does not say exactly what B-trees are. They were proposed (Bayer and McCreight [1970]) as a secondary storage method for dynamically changing data. The problem is keeping the tree *balanced*. Consider the following search and insertion procedure for a binary tree in primary memory.

Algorithm IS2P: (Binary tree search and insert.) Node p of form ℓ_p, k_p, r_p: left pointer, key, right pointer. Search key to be found is sk.

IS2P1   (Start) Set p ← root of tree. If tree empty, make new node q, root ← ℓ, goto IS2P5.

IS2P2   (Match) If sk = k_p, terminate successfully.

IS2P3   (Left subtree) If sk < k_p,
if ℓ_p ≠ null then p ← ℓ_p, goto IS2P2.
else make new node q, ℓ_p ← q, goto IS2P5.

IS2P4   (Right subtree) If sk > k_p,
if r_p ≠ null then p ← r_p, goto IS2P2.
else make new node q, r_p ← q, goto IS2P5.

IS2P5   (Insert) Set ℓ_q ← null, k_q ← sk, r_q ← null.

Exercise   1.2-36:   Apply Algorithm IS2P to the following sequences of keys, in the order given, and construct the resulting binary trees: A,B,C,D,E,F,G; D,B,F,A,C,E,G; A,G,B,F,C,E,D; D,F,B,E,C,G,A.

The result of Exercise 1.2-36 is that two of the trees are *degenerate,* i.e., simple linear lists of n = 7 levels, while two are *balanced,* i.e., all leaf nodes are at the same level, $[\log_2 n] = 3$. The probability of getting a degenerate tree out of the n! possible input sequences of keys is very small, but so is the probability of getting a perfectly balanced tree. However, well-balanced trees are common; see Knuth III [1973], § 6.2.2.

The B-tree preserves balance while it is built by requiring that each node have a certain minimum number of subtrees. The original definition, corresponding to Exhibit 1.2-8, of a *B-tree of order f* required each node to be at least half-full:

B1.   The root has at least two subtrees (unless it is a leaf).
B2.   Every node, apart from root or leaf, has s subtrees with $f/2 \le s \le f$.
B3.   All leaves appear on the same level.

The node structure $p_0, k_1, p_1, \ldots, k_{s-1}, p_{s-1}$ and rule B2 imply that a node can contain at most f-1 entries. If the B-tree stores fixed-length records, as in Exhibit 1.2-8, this gives the blocksize. We see that the storage utilization (load factor) can be as low as 50%: in Exhibit 1.2-8, $\alpha = 8/14 = 57\%$.

The conditions B1, B2 and B3 dictate the design of the insertion algorithm. In particular, we need to know how to split a block (node) when it becomes full.

Algorithm BI: (Insert search key sk into B-tree.)
    BI1.   (Search.) If sk found, terminate successfully. (If the search key is not a key, the match must occur on sufficient attributes to form a key or all matching records must be found.)
    BI2.   (Subtree pointers.) Set p, q ← null.
    BI3.   (Empty.) If s = null (see search algorithm BS), create root node q, sk, p. Terminate.
    BI4.   (Full?) If node s not full, insert entry sk, p. Terminate.
    BI5.   (Split.) Split node s (including sk). Set p ← new node, q ← s, s ← parent of s, sk ← $k_{\lceil f/2 \rceil}$. Goto B13.

Step BI5 specifies the split procedure: the full node is split in two, with the key $k_{\lceil f/2 \rceil}$ moving up into the parent node and the entries after it moving to a new block (Exhibit 1.2-22). If the parent node is also full, the process repeats until, if necessary, a new root node is created, in which case the height of the tree increases by one.

Exercise   1.2-37:   Verify that conditions B1, B2 and B3 follow from Algorithm BI.

Exercise   1.2-38:   Derive Exhibit 1.2-8 by applying Algorithm BI to an alphabetical sequence of the tuples of ORDERS, sorted on CUSTOMER, SALESMAN and ORD#.

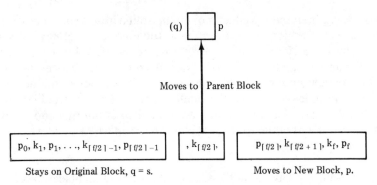

Exhibit 1.2-22. Splitting a Node of a B-tree

We immediately seek to improve the storage utilization. It is clearly not necessary that α be as low as 50% overall, since we split only one block at a time. However, in pathological cases such as Exhibit 1.2-8, splits may occur with maximum possible frequency with no filling up of existing nodes. One way to avoid this is to attempt to *overflow* before splitting a node. We can check the left (or right) neighbor or sibling node and place the new entry there instead of splitting; the entry in the parent node can be "rotated" appropriately so that no search degradation results. If both nodes are full, we split two for three, thus guaranteeing $\alpha \geq 2/3$. We could get $\alpha \geq 3/4$ by checking both neighbor nodes and splitting three for four only if all three are full. The single-neighbor version is called a *B*-tree* (Knuth [1973], § 6.2.4).

The second improvement that can be made is in the fanout. Exhibit 1.2-21 limits full keys and data to the leaves and stores only separators in the internal nodes, as mentioned. A *separator* between one key, k, and a previous key is those initial letters (digits) of k which are sufficient to distinguish it from the previous key. Because separators are made up of the first letters of keys, or prefixes, the tree of Exhibit 1.2-21 is called a *prefix* B*-tree (Bayer & Unterauer [1977]). The modification to the algorithm needed here is to cope with variable-length keys: we simply modify the requirement that the node have at least f/2 subtrees to state that the node must be at least half-full (for B*-trees, two-thirds full).

Exercise 1.2-39: Assume that each leaf node of the prefix B*-tree holds f-1 fixed-length entries and pointers to the main file and that internal nodes hold variable-length prefixes and pointers up to b bytes each. Give simple splitting rules for leaf and internal nodes.

When leaf nodes are split in Exercise 1.2-39, separators must be generated to be passed up to the parent internal nodes. These separators can vary considerably in length, and it may be that a generated separator is much longer than one which would be generated if we had moved the split a little to one side or the other. This introduces the notion of a *split interval*, the number, ϵ, of keys or separators that we can move to either side of the split point specified for leaves in Exercise 1.2-39. This number can be kept small. Indeed, too big an ϵ wastes storage space.

A similar flexibility can be allowed for overflows: adjust the new boundary between the pair of leaves so that the smallest separator is inserted into the parent node, within a range ϵ. Finally, all this can be applied to internal nodes, so that the smallest separator within the split interval is moved up when an internal node splits or overflows.

Exercise   1.2-40:   Give a method, Algorithm P*I, which searches and inserts new entries into a Prefix B*-tree, incorporating all the above discussion.

Exhibit 1.2-23 shows the result of applying Algorithm P*I to the following names of some of the participants in the 1980 Very Large Data Bases conference, entered in order of their appearance in the initial sessions. Session 0: Armstrong, Hsiao, Gotlieb. Session 1: Schmidt, Kent, Date, Shneiderman, Thomas, Ting, Walker, Demolombe, Rosenkrantz, Hunt. Session 2: Bochmann, Le Bihan, Esculier, Le Lann, Litwin, Gardarin, Sedillot, Treille, Mohan, Adiba, Lindsay, Epstein, Stonebraker, Brodie, Schmidt, Rowe, Mylopoulos, Smith, McLeod. Session 3: McLeod, Wilson. All blocks are thirty bytes long. Leaf nodes contain two names and session numbers. Internal nodes contain as many separators and two-byte pointers as possible. We do not store the lengths of separators but assume they are distinguished from pointers by suitable flags (e.g., pointers are negative integers and so always have the first bit set).

Exercise   1.2-41:   Show that Algorithm P*I eventually produces Exhibit 1.2-23.

Exercise   1.2-42:   Formulate Algorithm P*D to delete the entry corresponding to search key sk from a Prefix B*-tree.

Exercise   1.2-43:   How would you arrange the variable-length separators in the internal nodes for ease of searching?

Activity

If we use B-trees to index data arranged in some independent way on a data file, we cannot expect much fewer data-file accesses for a set of s searches than s × (the average number of accesses for a single search). This is because we must suppose a completely random mapping between the search keys in the index and the blocks of the data file holding the corresponding records. (If there is some correlation between neighboring search keys in the index and neighboring records in the blocks—"clustering"—performance will improve, but we cannot assume a

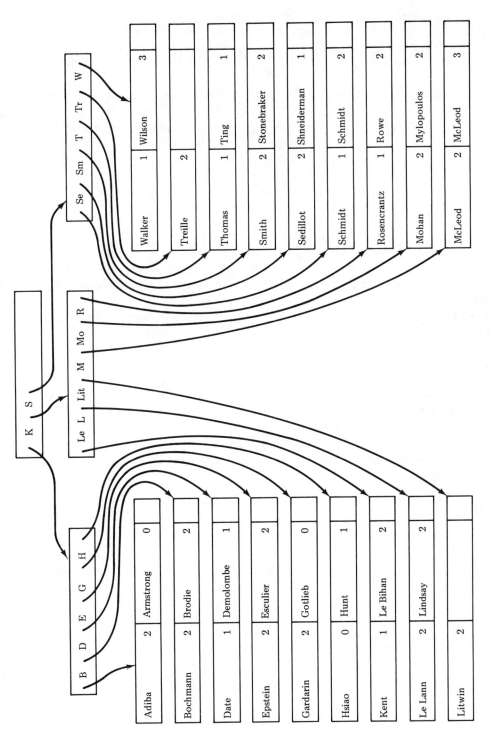

Exhibit 1.2-23. Constructing Prefix B*-tree

correlation in general.) The following exercise shows that a search for two consecutive search keys in these circumstances is overwhelmingly likely to require two
accesses to the main file.

Exercise   1.2-44:   A sequence of N records is placed in n blocks, of capacity
                      b records each, at random with equal probability that an
                      item goes into any of the $\leq$ nb locations available to it.
                      Show that the expected number of consecutive pairs that
                      land in the same block is about 1/n of all pairs. In general,
                      the expected number of consecutive p-plets (pair, triplet,
                      quadruplet, . . .) that land in the same block is about n $\uparrow$
                      $(1 - p)$ of all p-plets.

Since the B-tree index is ordered, however, we can save accesses to the
B-tree by making S searches in a single batch rather than doing them all separately.
This requires sorting the batch so that its order corresponds to that of the index:
sorting a subset of the search keys need not be expensive. The best response to
a batch of queries is attained if there is room in RAM for a buffer for each level
of the B-tree. The first request causes the buffers to be filled, following the path
from the root to the leaf node on which the first search key is (or is not) found. The
second request may be for the same leaf node, in which case no new accesses are
needed. Or it may be for a subsequent leaf node, and a new path must be read into
the buffers: most of this path is likely to be already in RAM and only the buffers
for the levels of the tree near the leaves would need to be replaced. This process
continues with the third and subsequent requests. Updates can also be handled,
provided they do not cause splits, concatenation, overflow, or underflow: just
rewrite any buffer that has been changed before replacing its contents. Splits and
other activities involving neighboring blocks require at least two more buffers in
RAM.

Exercise   1.2-45:   Formulate algorithms for batched search, insertion, and
                      deletion on prefix B*-trees.

If the leaf nodes of the B-tree store the records, not just complete search
keys, then the data is clustered optimally for this search key, and batch searching
is at its best. Otherwise, we can avoid repeated accesses to each block at the
expense of a second sort. When the B-tree has been used to obtain the block
addresses of the data, sort these and then access the blocks in sequence. This sort
would also be relatively cheap.

Symmetry

It is not difficult to extend tree-structured files and indexes to cope with
multi-attribute searches on multidimensional data. Exhibit 1.2-24a shows the

3-way tree grown by inserting ORDLINE (ORD#, ASSEMBLY, QTY) (Exhibit 1.1-5) in ascending order of QTY. The attributes ASSEMBLY and ORD# take turns being the "discriminator," i.e., being the basis of comparison and decision which subtree to investigate. At the root node (level 0) ASSEMBLY is the discriminating attribute; a search for, say, ORD# = 8 and ASSEMBLY = 'T' would take the rightmost branch because 'L' < 'T'. At the next level, ORD# is the discriminator; the search will branch right again because 3 < 8. At level 2, ASSEMBLY is again discriminator. In the example, we get a match, 'T' = 'T', on the discriminator, so we compare the rest of the search key; since 4 < 8, we again take the right branch, arriving at the desired record. Exhibit 1.2-24b shows the data space of Exhibit 1.1-3b partitioned by the tree. Note the pattern of horizontal partitions containing vertical partitions containing horizontal partitions and so on. The details of the diagram obscure this—some of the partitions are empty and the boundaries zigzag at the discriminating tuple—so we show an abstraction in Exhibit 1.2-25.

Two things are apparent from this diagram and the above discussion. First, the storage method is more adaptable than multipaging, and it is dynamic. A partition can be defined anywhere we want within another partition, depending on the record to be inserted, without concern about joining boundaries together to make straight lines across the whole data space. This enables the structure to cope with volatile data but makes it harder to answer the kind of geometrical queries handled by multipaging. (Many queries are still possible—see Bentley [1975].) Second, the tree is not balanced. It grows at the leaves, not at the root like a B-tree, and partitioning can be nested to different depths in different parts of the tree.

A major advantage of tree structures over direct access is that, if balanced, they have predictable worst cases (while direct access has much better average performance). So there is only limited reason for using a multidimensional tree instead of multipaging, if we cannot balance the tree.

We now look at a multidimensional variant of the B-tree which was proposed by Robinson [1981]. This grows at the root, and thus preserves its balance by allowing the discriminator to vary not only within a level but even within a node. Like the prefix B-tree, leaves differ from internal nodes by containing data or pointers to the main data file. The internal nodes contain prefixes, discriminators and pointers to other nodes. Exhibit 1.2-26 shows a "K-D-B-Tree" for ORDLINE, where the data was inserted in ascending order of QTY. It should be emphasized that this is only one of many (possibly about 1000 different trees for this data inserted in this order); a large choice of discriminating attribute and value is allowed each time a node is split.

The parentheses in the internal nodes of Exhibit 1.2-26a indicate the order of comparison. Suppose we wanted to find the record with (ORD#, ASSEMBLY) = (3, Caboose (Q)). Starting at the root node and the outermost level of parentheses, we inspect ORD#. Since 3 ≥ 3, we look at the entries to the right of ORD#3. The next level of parenthesis is ASSY Q: Q ≥ Q, so we look at the entry to the right of ASSY Q. This is a pointer to the next node. The next node gives us two

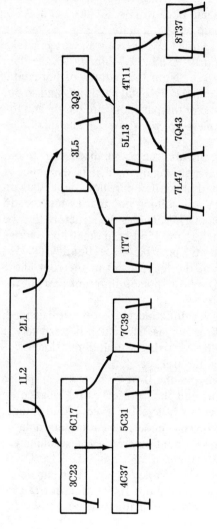

a) As an Unbalanced Tree.

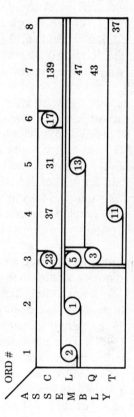

b) As a Partitioning of the Data Space.

Exhibit 1.2-24. Multidimensional Tree on ORD#, ASSEMBLY for ORD-LINE.

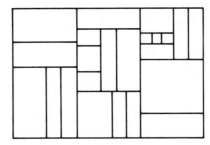

Exhibit   1.2-25.   A Three-Way Partitioning.

comparisons {ORD# 4 then ORD# 7) but we get $3 \leq 4$ on the first comparison and so proceed to the leaf node without comparing 3 to 7. There we find the entry (3, Caboose, 3).

Exhibit 1.2-26 is incomplete. The final tuple, (7, Car, 139) must be added. Exhibit 1.2-27 shows the result. We now describe the insertion process. First a search for (ORD#, ASSEMBLY) = (7, Car), as above, brings us to the leaf node containing entries (5, Car, 31) and (6, Car, 17). We will suppose that a leaf node may hold up to two tuples and so this leaf is full. We will also suppose that an internal node is limited to three sets of discriminator attribute and value, so that the parent node of this leaf is also full. To add the new tuple, we must split the leaf. We have two choices: split at ORD# 6, giving one tuple (5C31) on the new "left node" and two tuples (6C17, 7C139) on the new "right node", or at ORD# 7, giving (5C31, 6C17) and (7C139). (If the new tuple had been, say (7L139), we would have the further alternative of splitting at ASSY L.) We choose the first, arbitrarily. This puts the new discriminator pair, ORD# 6, into the parent node, which already has three entries; it must split. Again we choose ORD# 6 to split the node (the alternative is ASSY L), and go up into the root node in a new innermost parenthesis to the left of ASSY Q. The splitting of the internal node is illustrated in Exhibits 1.2-26b and 1.2-27b. The dotted line in the former shows the new split of the leaf node. Since this discriminator, ORD# 6, was chosen to split the internal node, the splitting line is continued right across the region, and two new ("left" and "right") regions are produced.

Exercise   1.2-46:   Formulate Algorithm KDBI to search and insert a new tuple into a K-D-B-Tree. You need a subsidiary Algorithm KDBS to split nodes.

Exercise   1.2-47:   Apply Algorithm KDBI to the data of ORDLINE, presented in ascending order of QTY.

Deletions from K-D-B-Trees are relatively straightforward, except that merging underfilled nodes together may be a problem when the union of the

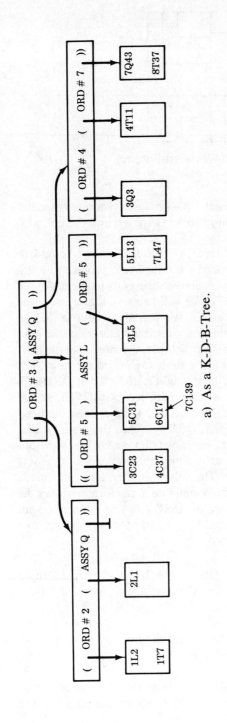

a) As a K-D-B-Tree.

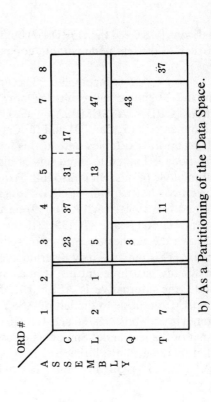

b) As a Partitioning of the Data Space.

Exhibit 1.2-26. K-D-B-Tree on ORD#, ASSEMBLY for ORDLINE (Missing 7C139)

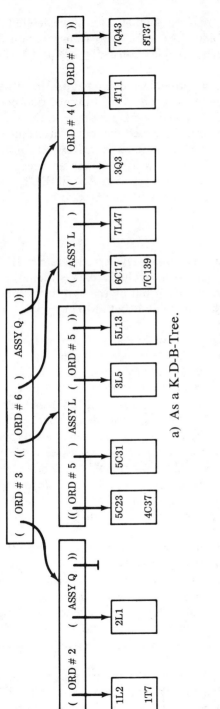

a) As a K-D-B-Tree.

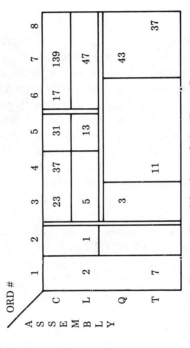

b) As a Partitioning of the Data Space.

Exhibit 1.2-27. K-D-B-Tree on ORD#, ASSEMBLY for ORDLINE.

71

rectangular regions they represent is not itself rectangular. Thus if we deleted 1T7 from Exhibit 1.2-27, we could not recombine 1L2 and 2L1 into a single region. We could, however, combine the three adjacent regions consisting of ORD# 1 and ORD# 2 in this case.

This incidentally points out that some possible recombinations have been missed in Exhibit 1.2-27, which arise just as a result of splitting internal nodes without any deletions. Tuples 3L5 and 5L13 could occupy a single leaf, and, for reasons due to an earlier split similar to the one discussed above, the discriminator ASSY Q is no longer needed to separate the two regions for ORD# 2. Furthermore, tuples 3Q3 and 4T11 could be combined on a leaf after an acceptable rearrangement of the parentheses for the region (ORD# $\geq$ 3, ASSEMBLY $\geq$ Q). These improvements would increase the load factor α from 68% to 83%.

Tries

The digital tree or *trie* (pronounced "try" but derived from "re*trie*val" by Fredkin [1960]) is an alternative approach to logarithmic data structures. In this structure, an entry is not represented by a leaf but by the *path* from root to leaf. If we assume an entry is written using some alphabet of $|\alpha|$ symbols, each node of the trie is an $|\alpha|$-way branch point.

This is illustrated in Exhibit 1.2-28b for a binary alphabet. Each internal node (circles: ignore for the moment any symbols inside these circles or any squares touching them) is a two-way branch, left for 0 and right for 1 in the binary alphabet. Thus the path *0* 0 *0* 1 *1* 0 *1* 0 *0* 0 *0* leads to the leaf (square node) with 23 in it. (We will come to the significance of italicized symbols later.) The trie has been built up by inserting the entries in Exhibit 1.2-29. The bit sequences determine the paths in the trie from root to the leaf corresponding to the entry. In principle, all paths should have 16 edges (17 nodes including the leaf) in this example, since the sequences of Exhibit 1.2-29 are 16 bits long, making the trie a fixed-height tree of 17 levels. In fact, however, we do not continue any path once its leaf node has been uniquely determined. Thus, for instance, the last bit in each path never appears and the trie has only 16 levels. And the path, already given, leading to the leaf with 23 in it, has only 11 edges.

Since each path in the trie defines the bit sequence of its entry by the left and right branches it takes, we do not need to store this sequence at the leaf (except from the point where we have truncated the path), which is a principal advantage of the trie. Moreover, it clearly does not matter in which order the trie is built up: all N! permutations of an input set of N entries will give the same trie. The trie is thus always balanced, in the sense that if a sequence of at most h-1 symbols of the alphabet is needed to record the search key of an entry, the trie will have at most h levels.

If the trie is built up dynamically, however, the order of input makes a difference to the intermediate states of the trie. We show this in Exhibit 1.2-28b for the order of data in Exhibit 1.2-29, using the squares touching internal nodes.

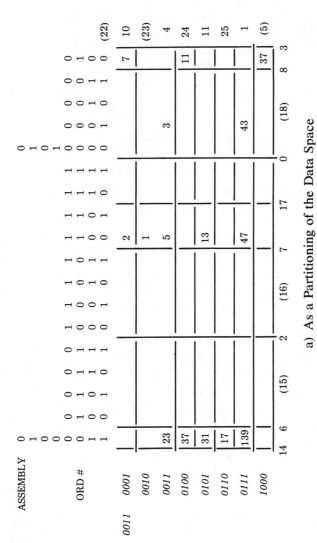

a) As a Partitioning of the Data Space

Exhibit 1.2-28. K-d trie for an ORD#, ASSEMBLY for ORDLINE.

b) As a k-d Trie   continued

Exhibit 1.2-28   continued

Exhibit 1.2-29. ORD# Interleaved with ASSEMBLY, and QTY from ORDLINE.

0	0	*0*	1	*1*	0	*1*	0	*0*	0	*1*	0	*0*	1	*0*	1	37
0	0	*0*	1	*1*	0	*1*	0	*0*	0	*0*	0	*1*	1	*1*	1	23
0	0	*0*	1	*1*	0	*1*	0	*0*	1	*0*	1	*1*	0	*0*	0	1
0	0	*0*	1	*1*	0	*1*	0	*0*	1	*1*	1	*1*	0	*1*	0	47
0	0	*0*	1	*1*	0	*1*	1	*0*	0	*0*	0	*1*	0	*1*	1	3
0	0	*0*	1	*1*	0	*1*	0	*0*	1	*1*	1	*0*	0	*1*	0	13
0	0	*0*	1	*1*	0	*1*	1	*0*	0	*1*	0	*1*	0	*1*	1	43
0	0	*0*	1	*1*	0	*1*	1	*1*	0	*0*	1	*0*	0	*0*	0	37
0	0	*0*	1	*1*	0	*1*	0	*0*	1	*0*	1	*0*	0	*1*	0	2
0	0	*0*	1	*1*	0	*1*	0	*0*	0	*1*	0	*0*	1	*1*	1	31
0	0	*0*	1	*1*	0	*1*	0	*0*	0	*1*	0	*1*	1	*0*	1	17
0	0	*0*	1	*1*	0	*1*	1	*0*	0	*1*	1	*0*	0	*0*	0	11
0	0	*0*	1	*1*	0	*1*	0	*0*	1	*0*	1	*1*	0	*1*	0	5
0	0	*0*	1	*1*	0	*1*	1	*0*	0	*0*	1	*0*	0	*1*	0	7
0	0	*0*	1	*1*	0	*1*	0	*0*	0	*1*	0	*1*	1	*1*	1	139

These represent leaves of the various intermediate tries. Thus the first entry is stored as a leaf, which is the root of the trie, since no distinction among leaves needs to be made in this first trie of only one entry. When the second entry is inserted, however, it coincides with the first for the first 10 bits and differs for the first time only in the 11th. Thus we get a second trie of 12 levels, which zigzags with no branches until it reaches the node before the two leaves containing 23 and 37, respectively. This process continues, illustrating how dynamic insertions can be made until the full trie has grown. Note that in this trie, no discrimination is made at all by the first 8 levels: this is characteristic of tries, which can be pruned (from the root!) in practice.

Exercise 1.2-48: Formulate Algorithm TSI (Trie Search and Insert) for binary tries.

Exercise 1.2-49: How would you extend Algorithm TSI to tries on arbitrary alphabets?

Exercise 1.2-50: How would you delete an entry from a binary trie?

Exercise 1.2-51: Compare the trie of Exhibit 1.2-28 with the best and worst cases of a binary tree for the same data. How is the trie superior?

Now we come to Exhibit 1.2-28a, the italicized bits and the numbers in the internal nodes of Exhibit 1.2-28b. We wish to show that tries can be used for multidimensional data as readily as trees, and to introduce the *k-d trie* (Orenstein [1982]. Exhibit 1.2-28a shows the same data space as Exhibits 1.2-24b, 1.2-26b and 1.2-27b only the digits of ORD# and the characters representing ASSEMBLY have been replaced by their ASCII bit-codes. The entries of Exhibit 1.2-29 have been produced by interleaving the bit-codes ORD# and ASSEMBLY. Thus the tuple (3, C, 23) becomes (*00110011,* 01000011, 23) and interleaves to give the entry (*0001101000100101*, 23). This interleaving just produces the effect of the alternating discriminator of the multidimensional tree in Exhibit 1.2-24: it could be done in different ways if the number of different values or if the probability of access of one attribute were significantly different from the other (see Chang & Fu [1980]).

The discriminating nodes of Exhibit 1.2-28b correspond to partitions of the data space as shown by the numbers. Thus node 0 divides the space in two, between ASSEMBLY = 01001111 and ASSEMBLY = 01010000, node 1 divides the space between ORD# = *00110111* and ORD# = *00111000*, and so on. Note that these partitions cross the whole space in straight lines, like multipaging rather than like multidimensional trees, and so suggest easier and more versatile query algorithms. (See Section 2.2-2 for a review of queries that can be implemented easily with multipaging.) For this reason, we give one partition number to the whole set of nodes in Exhibit 1.2-28b that corresponds to each straight line.

Exercise   1.2-52:   What are the portions of the space in Exhibit 1.2-28a corresponding to the three nodes labelled "4" in Exhibit 1.2-28b.

Clearly the k-d trie can be used for data with any number of dimensions, simply by introducing an appropriate interleaving of the bits (or of the symbols of any alphabet). We notice an important fact about k-d tries in any number of dimensions: the partitions divide the *space* independently of the data that is present. Thus, different data in Exhibit 1.2-28a would still give the same partitions (although different ones may be used). The advantage of this is that the trie and its height are determined by the space rather than by the data, so that, in particular, the trie can never become degenerate in the sense that access cost is linear in N, the number of nodes, for arbitrarily large N. The disadvantage is that the maximum height of the trie can be unacceptably large, and excessive clustering of the tuples in the data space can force long paths to appear in the trie. This is illustrated by Exhibit 1.2-28, in that all tuples fall in a small subspace (ORD#, ASSEMBLY) = (*00110001*, 01000011) to (*00111000*, 01010100) of the full space of $2^8 \times 2^8$ values, and the trie therefore has a long stem before branches begin.

The tree-trie comparison of Exercise 1.2-51 applies in any number of dimensions, and shows that if a balanced tree can be used it is probably better than a trie except for the possibility of extremely compact representations of tries. However, we have seen that balancing a multidimensional tree is hard. The k-d trie is "balanced" in any number of dimensions in the sense that its height is limited. However, this is not so useful to us as the fact that the k-d trie defines a *linear ordering* on data of arbitrary dimensions. This ordering enables us to use conventional trees, such as B-trees which can be balanced, to store multidimensional data, and it has properties which make it useful in doing multidimensional searches on this data while it is stored in one-dimensional ("linear") trees.

This linear ordering was called "Z-ordering" by Orenstein [Orenstein and Merrett, 1982], and corresponds to an inorder traversal of the k-d trie. More simply, and without having to build the k-d trie, the Z-ordering results from the ordering we get when we interleave the bit sequences for the attributes in each tuple, as we have already illustrated in Exhibit 1.2-29, and interpret the result as an integer. Exhibit 1.2-30 shows the resulting ordering imposed on a square two-dimensional space. Not every point in the space need be occupied by a tuple, of course, but the tuples that are present are ordered according to their locations in the space. The graphical presentation in Exhibit 1.2-30a shows how adjacent tuples in the space tend to be close in the Z-ordering, except for occasional gaps. These gaps are quantified in Exhibit 1.2-30b: we call the number shown for each location of the space the *Z-order address* of that location. The difference between Z-order addresses of two locations, which are adjacent in one attribute, is independent of the other attributes. Thus the difference between Z-order addresses for (Attrib. 0) = 0 and (Attrib. 0) = 1 is 2 for all values of (Attrib. 1). These differences are called *gaps,* and we can see that they repeat systematically. In fact, the gap between values α and $\alpha + 1$ of some attribute depends only on a quantity t, which is the size of the sequence of 1's terminating the binary representation of α. Thus we have

α	0	1	2	3	4	5	6	7	
α in binary	0	1	10	11	100	101	110	111	. . .
t	0	1	0	2	0	1	0	3	

For an m-dimensional square, with bits chosen cyclically from each attribute for interleaving, the gap for attribute i, $0 \le i < m$, is

$$G(i,t) = \frac{2^{m-1-i}}{2^m - 1} [(2^m - 2) 2^{mt} + 1] \qquad (1.2\text{-}8)$$

where t depends on the value α of attribute i as given above.

Exercise   1.2-53:   Verify Equation 1.2-8 for the case m=2, i=0, 1, t=0, 1, 2 from Exhibit 1.2-30b.

Exercise   1.2-54:   Derive Equation 1.2-8.

Orenstein [Orenstein and Merrett, 1982] has argued that this arrangement of gaps establishes a sufficient correspondence between closeness of tuples in a multidimensional space and their closeness in the linear Z-ordering, that multidimensional searches may be done efficiently while the tuples are stored in a one-dimensional data structure. Thus we have the benefits of using a one-dimensional structure to store the tuples in Z-order, namely that balance can be preserved and, indeed, that the algorithms and utilities for dealing with the structure have already been coded by somebody else.

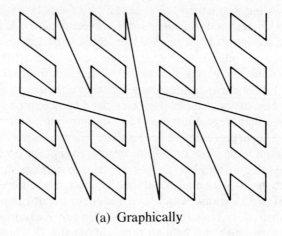

(a) Graphically

Attrib. 1							
21	23	29	31	53	55	61	63
20	22	28	30	52	54	60	62
17	19	25	27	49	51	57	59
16	18	24	26	48	50	56	58
5	7	13	15	37	39	45	47
4	6	12	14	36	38	44	46
1	3	9	11	33	35	41	43
0	2	8	10	32	34	40	42

Gaps on Attrib. 1 axis (top to bottom): 1, 3, 1, 11, 1, 3, 1

Gaps on Attrib. 0 axis (left to right): 2, 6, 2, 22, 2, 6, 2

Attrib. 0

(b) Numerically, Showing Gaps

Exhibit   1.2-30.   Z-ordering in a two-dimensional square

Summary of Logarithmic Files

Logarithmic files are based on tree structures and are so named because their costs are proportional to the logarithm of the number of records. Direct access is better on the average but can be much poorer in the worst cases.

Volatility. Tree-structured files, in the form of B-trees, are very appropriate for frequently changing data, since the automatic rebalancing implemented with insertions and deletions ensures that the access path is always logarithmic in the number of records to be searched.

Activity. Since trees are order-preserving, they are good for batch searching with many search keys at once. If the tree is only an index to a main file, some of this advantage is lost, since an extra cost of sorting the record addresses is required.

Symmetry. Only one relatively recent technique, that of K-D-B-Trees, is available which preserves the above advantages in the multidimensional case. This method cannot guarantee good utilization of storage.

Tries are a form of tree in which the data values are given by the path rather than stored explicitly. They partition the data space in a way similar (in multiple dimensions) to multipaging, but are independent of the number and values of the tuples themselves. Tries solve the problem of how to guarantee a good worst-case search performance in multidimensional space by suggesting a linear ordering for multidimensional data that enables well-known one-dimensional logarithmic files to be used.

1.2-5   Sequential Files

Records can be maintained in a sequence in two ways: by a linear chain of pointers or by physical contiguity in a linear memory. We will not consider the first way further, because it does not take into account the high access to transfer ratio of secondary memory. It does not, in general, cluster records into blocks, but provides access to the same block many times as the pointer chain twines through memory. Pointer chains are used as access paths in direct and logarithmic files, but are not of interest in purely sequential files.

We will take "sequential file" to mean physically sequential, with adjacent records grouped into blocks which are stored in sequence in secondary memory. All the types of secondary memory discussed in this book are linear, in that data is transferred to primary memory in a sequence of primitive units. (These units may be bits, or bytes transferred bit-parallel, or some larger unit whose components are transmitted in parallel; data consisting of many units is nonetheless transferred in sequence.) This accounts for the importance of having a physical sequence of records whenever their logical structure permits.

Since the possible variety of physical sequential files is limited, we can greatly condense our discussion of their behavior under conditions of varying volatility, activity, and symmetry. There are only two types of sequential file, *ordered* and *unordered*. This distinction presupposes that some aspect of the record, usually a search key comprised of one or more fields, imposes a logical sequence on the set of records, usually alphabetic or lexicographic order. In an ordered sequential file, the physical sequence corresponds to the logical sequence. An unordered sequential file has no such correspondence.

Consider the search for a single record using the search key. If the record is present in the file, it will be found on the average after half the records in the file are inspected, whether the file is ordered or not. If the record is not there, the ordered file will still require half a pass to detect its absence, since once we pass the point in the logical sequence where it should be we need look no further. The unordered file, on the other hand, needs to be searched in its entirety to be sure a record is not there. For this type of search, ordering is preferable—but not greatly preferable—to not ordering.

If there is high volatility, in particular if the file is growing rapidly, an ordered file must be repeatedly sorted to maintain its order. No maintenance is needed for an unordered file. If there are deletions, both types of file must be compressed, unless they are built to tolerate blank spaces. (Here the file of chained pointers is superior since pointers can be joined to bypass deletions or broken to allow insertions. These techniques work well in RAM.)

If there is high activity, with many records being sought at a time, the ordered file can be searched in a single pass by sorting the search requests into a corresponding order. The unordered file requires, in principle, a pass for each request, although in practice we can make use of RAM to reduce the work.

The ordered file lacks symmetry, since it is sorted on one set of attributes, leaving the others unordered. The unordered file is completely symmetrical, in that no attribute is favored. The processing of requests involving many attributes or complex logical conditions is the same for each: search the whole file.

Sequential files are thus of little use for quickly processing requests involving only a few records within a large amount of data. If the request is sufficiently complex, however, there may be no alternative to scanning the entire file, or even sorting it. Then a sequential file is the obvious form if only because it is the simplest. It is less apparent that sequential files become the best possible way of processing data as activity increases. Section 1.3-5 shows that at only one or two percent activity the ordered sequential file is superior to direct access even for very simple queries. With secondary storage devices capable of scanning megabytes of data in a few seconds, many "real-time" applications are adequately served by collecting requests for, say, five seconds then processing them as a batch against a sequential file. This allows great complexity of request with great simplicity of software and may make the most efficient use of the machine.

Sorting

Evidently sorting is of central importance in the processing of sequential files. It is also important in setting up logarithmic files and even direct files. Sorting is the subject of whole books and we shall look at it here only very superficially, without pretending to specify the details of a sorting utility.

The obvious method of sorting N items costs about N^2 comparisons: compare every item with every other item and position it accordingly. For example, find the smallest of the N items and place it first; find the smallest of the remaining N-1 items and place it next, and so on. However, it is apparent that if we divide the set into two sets of about N/2 items each and somehow sort these, they can be combined by a 2-way merge in only order N steps. The cost is now two sorts of order $(N/2)^2$ each and a merge of order N—cheaper than the single sort. Thus encouraged, we divide the two halves into quarters, these into eighths and so on until each set contains only one element. Merging these sets in pairs, the resulting sets in pairs, and so on, a final sorted set of N items is achieved giving a binary tree of merges, whose height is of order $\log_2 N$. Each level of the tree specifies merges totalling N elements, so the overall cost of sorting is order $N \log_2 N$. This exemplifies the algorithmic principle of "divide and conquer," which is applicable to any problem where it is cheaper to combine the solution of subproblems than to solve it directly.

This discussion draws our attention to merging as a crucial part of sorting. This is particularly true of sorting on secondary memory when only small parts of the file can fit at one time into RAM. What we do is to use an f-way merge instead of a 2-way merge, thus reducing the height of the merge tree to $\log_f r$, where r is the number of "initial runs," or sorted subsets of the file that we start with. This assumes that there is room in RAM for f blocks of records, which are merged by picking the smallest of the first records in each block and so on. The choice of f depends on optimization considerations given in Section 1.3-5: the results of that section suggest that, using RISDISK or RISFLOPPY and speaking crudely, f should be 20, 6, and 3, for mainframe, mini, and micro computers respectively.

The method of finding initial runs is interesting. We could, of course, have N of them, of one record each. However, it is possible to use multiway merging to create much longer and therefore fewer initial runs. This is called *replacement selection* and involves a k-way merge of the input file with itself, where k is the number of records (not blocks) that can fit into RAM.

We illustrate the whole merge-sort process with the data used to build up the B-tree of Exhibit 1.2-23. In abbreviated form, without duplicates and in input order, it is: Ar, H, Go, S, K, D, Sh, T, Ti, W, De, R, Hu, B, L, Es, Le L, Lit, G, Se, Tr, Mo, A, Li, E, St, Br, Row, My, Sm, M, Wi. We assume that there is room in RAM for eight records (which are taken to be fixed-length), apart from input and output buffers. When we come to the final merge, we will assume a blocksize of two records, so that f is 4.

Exhibit 1.2-31 shows the process of generating the initial runs. The input and output are given in order and the contents of the eight locations of RAM are shown. The eight-way merge selects the smallest of the eight entries in RAM and replaces it with the next item from the input. An entry in parentheses is one which alphabetically precedes the last item output: it has missed the current initial run and must wait for a new one to start. The initial runs have 11, 17, and 4 items, respectively. Neglecting the third, which is the tail end of the input, these runs are each seen to exceed RAM capacity in size. Their average length is almost twice the RAM capacity of eight records.

A nice argument involving a snowplough on a circular road in a snowstorm shows that the average length of the initial runs is exactly twice the RAM capacity (Knuth [1973], § 5.4.1). The incoming records are the falling snowflakes, distributed uniformly over the road. The smallest record currently in RAM (i.e., the output) is the position of the plough. The number of records in RAM is the amount of snow on the road, whose height decreases linearly from a maximum just in front

INPUT	1	2	3	4	5	6	7	8	OUTPUT
Ar	Ar	H	Go	S	K	D	Sh	T	Ar
H	Ti					W			D
Go			(De)						Go
S		R							H
K	R				(Hu)				K
D	(B)								R
Sh		(B)		(L)			(Es)		S
T									Sh
Ti									T
W	(Lit)							(Le L)	Ti
De	Lit	B	De	L	Hu	G	Es	Le L	W
R	Se	Se	Tr						B
Hu							Mo		De
B						(A)			Es
L					Li				G
Es								St	Hu
Le L									L
Lit				(E)					Le L
G									Li
Se					(Br)				Lit
Tr	Row								Mo
Mo							My		My
A							Sm		Row
Li	(M)								Se
E		Wi							Sm
St									St
Br									Tr
Row									Wi
My	M			E	Br	A			A
Sm									Br
M									E
Wi									M

Exhibit 1.2-31. Selection replacement giving three initial runs.

of the plough to zero just behind it. The expected size of the initial run is the total snow removed by the plough in one trip around the circle—which is just twice the amount of snow on the road at any one time because the plough is always pushing away an accumulation of a fixed height.

We now move to the merge phase. We are allowed a four-way merge given a blocksize of 2 and a RAM capacity of 8 records, but we have only three initial runs; only $[\log_4 3] = 1$ level is needed in the merge tree for this example. Exhibit 1.2-32 shows schematically the initial runs and the final result.

Exhibit 1.2-32. Merging the initial runs to give the sorted sequence.

Ar, D,		Go, H, K,				R,	S, Sh,		T, Ti, W,	
B, De, Es, G,		Hu, L, Le L, Li, Lit, Mo, My,	Row, Se,	Sm, St,		Tr, Wi	
A, Br, E,			M,							

Merge sorting on secondary storage is thus straightforward. Most of the subtlety, which we do not discuss, lies in the arrangement of the initial runs on the various storage devices, and depends on whether we have four or more tape units, one or two disk drives, etc. Devising merge patterns which minimize tape rewinds or disk arm motion has produced a great variety of external sorting methods (Knuth [1973], § 5.4).

Exercise   1.2-55:   Given the merge degree, f, what is the best way to arrange the r initial runs for merging?

1.2-6   Auxiliary Methods

The preceding three sections have examined the three basic categories of file organization and discussed variations of them which are effective under various requirements of volatility, activity, and symmetry. Often a file organization which has been selected for its performance under one set of requirements is not entirely appropriate for other conditions which also arise. Thus a sequential file, selected because of a frequent need for high-activity processing, is too slow for an occasional low-activity request. Or a static multipaged organization is chosen for an environment which is moderately active on several attributes, but is hard-put to cope with the volatility of a growing file. Or a B-tree is used in a dynamic application but must be supplemented to handle queries on attributes other than the primary one.

To adapt the basic file organizations to requirements that go beyond their principal capacity requires *auxiliary methods.* Some of these have been mentioned, such as secondary indexes for high symmetry. The main ones are *differential files* and *file reorganization* for high volatility; *batching* and *sort-merge techniques* for high activity; *indexing* for low activity and for high symmetry.

Differential Files

A differential file is a means of giving a dynamic capability to any file organization that does not cope well with volatility. It is a small file that records all the changes to the main file and is interrogated before the main file in any query. If the main file has one of the direct-access organizations, the extra access (or accesses) to the differential file may be a significant proportion of the total accesses for a request; this can be dealt with in a couple of ways. First, we can simply ignore the differential file. This will give quite adequate results for queries in the many applications where it is not crucial to have up-to-the-minute information. Second, if we are doing an update or need the latest data, we can use a *Bloom filter.* This is a direct access table stored in RAM in which each record maps to a bit, which is set on if there is an entry for the record in the differential file. On a request, if the Bloom filter bit is set for a record, we check the differential file before the main file. Since several records may map to the same bit (there is no provision for collision resolution), the Bloom filter will occasionally suggest unnecessarily that we should look first in the differential file, but we will never fail to look there for a record that actually is in the differential file.

Periodically the differential file is integrated into the main file by a *reorganization*. This can be done efficiently as a high-activity merge in a night-time run. Only when the data must be available at all times is it hard to schedule this periodic reorganization, although even then a copy could be reorganized and switched into service at the end, or a "differential differential file" could be made for the differential file.

As an example, consider Exhibit 1.2-33a, a multipaged instance of the relation

Parents' Ages (Mother's Age, Father's Age, Offspring).

The differential file which updates this is shown in Exhibit 1.2-33b: "d" means delete and "a" means add. Incorporation of the updates produces Exhibit 1.2-34, which needs different partition boundaries for minimal π than those shown in Exhibit 1.2-33. A reorganization would have to respecify the boundaries. Before reorganization takes place, however, we could access the data via the following Bloom filter, computed using the hash function $h(M, F) = (M \bmod 2, F \bmod 2)$.

	F 0	1
M		
0	1	0
1	0	1

Exercise   1.2-56:   a) What would the average number of probes be per record if $h(M, F) = (M + F) \bmod 4$?

b) If $h(M, F)$ in (a) were recorded as

M	F 0	1
	0	1
	2	3

consistency with the hash function in the text and used *together* with $h(M, F)$ of the text, what would the average number of probes be per record?

In the filter, bit $(0, 0)$ corresponds to the update tuple (d, 34, 40, Mac) and so is set. Bit $(1, 1)$ corresponds to the three other update tuples. It also corresponds to the tuple (23, 23, Sam), which is not on the differential file. Bit $(0, 0)$ similarly corresponds to (28, 26, Sue) and (40, 40, Sal), so that these will also be searched for first on the differential file even though they are not there. Thus the total cost to access

a) Main File

M \ F	23	24	26	29	35	40	42
19		Joe	Tom				
22				Jan			
23	Sam						
24	Ann						
28			Sue				
29	Nan	Win					Bob
34					Jim	Mac	
40						Sal	

b) Differential File

	M	F	O
d	29	23	Nan
a	23	29	Nan
d	34	40	Mac
a	29	35	Pat

Exhibit 1.2-33. Parents' Ages (compare Exhibit 1.2-34)

M \ F	23	24	26	29	35	40	42
19		Joe	Tom				
22				Jan			
23	Sam			Nan			
24	Ann						
28			Sue				
29		Win			Pat		Bob
34					Jim		
40						Sal	

Exhibit 1.2-34. Parents' Ages.

every record on the combined file before reorganization, assuming an extreme case of at most one access to each file per record, will be 12+3. The three superfluous accesses are to check the differential file for the three records that are not there but not discriminated by the Bloom filter. This is an average of 1.25 probes per record instead of 1, which is not bad since 1/3 of the file has been changed.

Sorted Batches

With an ordered sequential file, the natural way to cope with high activity is to sort the requests into the same sequence as the file and merge the two. The cost, apart from sorting, is never more than a single pass of the file. Given that the time to do this is used in transferring data (which is more efficient than searching for it), this is not as bad as it might seem. Similar methods can be used for high activities on files whose organizations do not seem at first sight amenable to high activity processing. For instance, requests on a hashed file can be sorted in order of the *hash values* of their search keys, and then merged with the data file in the usual linear way. Similarly, a batch of r requests can be sought in a logarithmic index more quickly than r independent searches for individual requests. The resulting addresses in the data file can then be sorted and merged with the data file. We illustrate these two cases.

Consider the following set of requests on the hash table shown in Exhibit 1.2-7b:

CUSTOMER	SALESMAN
'GTRC'	'N'
'NYC'	'H'
'GNS'	'E'
'NYC'	'N'

The values of h(CUSTOMER, SALESMAN) as specified in Section 1.2-2 are, respectively 1, 2, 2, 0. Moreover, there is an overflow pointer from block 2 to block 1 in that table, so that the requests ('NYC', 'H') and ('GNS', 'E') would require two accesses each: a total of six accesses for the four requests if carried out independently. If we sorted the hash addresses (0, 1, 2), a modestly clever search algorithm could combine overflow with searches for other records in the batch and reduce the total to three accesses. Such savings would be much more significant for a file with a realistic blocksize.

Exercise   1.2-57:   Devise the "modestly clever" algorithm for a batched search of a file with collision resolution by linear probing.

Consider the same set of requests, this time on the indexed multipaged data of Exhibit 1.2-21. The results of independent searches of the prefix B*-tree index are (assuming the root node remains in RAM after the first search)

REQUEST		# ACCESSES	
CUSTOMER	SALESMAN	TO INDEX	LIST OF DATA PAGES
'GTRC'	'N'	2	$(0,3)$, $(1,3)$
'NYC'	'H'	1	$(0,2)$, $(1,2)$
'GNS'	'E'	1	$(1,0)$, $(1,3)$
'NYC'	'N'	1	$(0,0)$

By sorting the requests first, we could have found the data page addresses for the two 'NYC' queries in a single access instead of two. If we further process the requests independently against the data file, we need seven more accesses, one for each page in each list. If, however, we sort the data page addresses first, we avoid the duplicated access to page $(1,3)$. The total saving of two out of twelve accesses would probably not justify the two sorts in this example, but sorting may be worthwhile for realistically large blocksizes.

Indexing

We have already discussed indexing in some detail in Section 1.2-4, where we considered logarithmic files as indexes rather than as tree-structured data files. The index is an auxiliary file while the underlying main file usually has a direct or a sequential organization. If the main file organization is sequential or multipaged, its low-activity performance could be improved by access via an index. If it is hashed or otherwise has low symmetry, indexes can be constructed for each attribute on which search capability is required.

This latter use of indexes, to increase symmetry, is limited by cost considerations. For a file of m attributes, $2^m - 1$ indexes would be necessary to achieve complete symmetry of access: one for each non-empty subset of the m attributes[3]. (This does not take into account the attribute or sets of attributes accommodated by the main file organization.) In practice the requirement for symmetry is relatively modest, but in principle the problem is highly complex. Section 1.3-6 discusses the problem of deciding which attributes to build secondary indexes for.

---

[3] This ignores the possibility of using the index or, say, attributes XY as an index for X to $0\left(\lfloor \frac{m}{m/2} \rfloor\right)$ are required.

Review Questions and Exercises, Chapter 1.2

1.2-58 What are two distinctive differences between secondary memory and RAM?

1.2-59 What is the consequence of the high access/transfer ratio of secondary memory?

1.2-60 What is the unit for measuring the access/transfer ratio and why?

1.2-61 Explain the terms *latency time, arm delay, track, cylinder, track length* and give typical numbers associated with each.

1.2-62 Define the terms *first* and *next* record, *immediate* and *serial* file. Describe direct, logarithmic and sequential files using these terms.

1.2-63 Define the terms *volatile, activity* and *symmetry* in the context of files.

1.2-64 Define the *load factor*.

1.2-65 If we have 1000 blocks' worth of data to store using division hashing, how many blocks should we allocate?

1.2-66 If we used multiplicative hashing for the 1000 blocks of data, how many blocks should we allocate and what would h(k) be?

1.2-67 Describe the collision resolution methods, *linear probing* and *separate chaining*.

1.2-68 What is the central problem in designing an access method for a growing file?

1.2-69 When a block is split in linear hashing, its local load factor is cut by a factor of 2. How can this cut be reduced?

1.2-70 How does a tidy function differ from a hash function?

1.2-71 What are the 2p parameters of the piecewise linear approximation P to $D_A(a)$?

1.2-72 How can the creation of a C-directory be limited to one pass of the data?

1.2-73 What is a simple geometrical interpretation of the ratios $n \uparrow (1 - 1/m) : n$ and $2mn \uparrow (1 - 1/m) : n$?

1.2-74 What is the advantage of dividing a multidimensional space into blocks using boundaries that are hyperplanes, each perpendicular to one of the axes?

1.2-75 What are advantages and disadvantages of the way of partitioning a two-dimensional space into 3 × 4 blocks shown in the diagram?

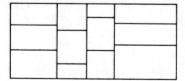

1.2-76 What are the axial distributions of the following relation (shown as a set of tuples)?

{(b,x,1), (a,y,1), (c,x,2), (c,y,1), (a,z,2), (b,y,2), (a,z,3), (d,y,3), (e,z,1), (c,w,4), (c,w,5), (a,y,4)}

1.2-77 What are the best partitions of the axial distributions of Exercise 19 into a) two segments each b) three segments each?

1.2-78 a) If the relation of Exercise 19 were to be multipaged on three attributes using $n = 6$ blocks, how many cells would be in the histogram to choose the best of the partitions suggested in Exercise 20? How many different combinations of boundaries would have to be tried? b) What if we imposed the condition $V/f \simeq$ constant?

1.2-79 What is the best multipage organization for the relation of Exercise 19, using $n = 6$ blocks and $V/f \simeq$ constant?

1.2-80 If the tuple (b,z,2) were added to the multipage space of Exercise 22, using the dynamic algorithm, MSI, with the constraint $\pi \leq 1.1$, what would the resulting π-α tradeoff be?

1.2-81 Show the two possible page numberings for the multipage space of Exercise 22 and show what they become after the insertion of Exercise 23.

1.2-82 What are the advantages and disadvantages of storing data in sorted order if it is to be indexed by a logarithmic access method?

1.2-83 What are the requirements which define a B-tree?

1.2-84 How would you define a B-tree structure with a load factor guaranteed to exceed $\ell/(\ell + 1)$ for $\ell \leq f/2$?

1.2-85 Explain the term "discriminator."

1.2-86 What are sequential files good for?

1.2-87 What is the principle of "divide and conquer"?

1.2-88 Which would be the cheaper way to find four separate items in the file of Section 1.2-5: to search the unordered file four times (once for each item) or to sort it as described and then find all four items in a single pass?

1.2-89 What is a differential file?

1.2-90 Compare the relative advantages of direct, logarithmic and sequential files.

1.2-91 Multipage the relation shown:

a. For a blocksize b= 2, 3 or 4 find the partitioning factors f_s and f_p which most nearly equalize V_s/f_s and V_p/f_p while keeping $\alpha \geq 0.8$.

P S	1	2	3	4	5	6	7
a	1	1				1	
b			1	1	1	1	
c			1		1		
d	1		1			1	1
e		1					1

b. Show the axial distributions and the graphs for finding the partition boundaries using f_s and f_p from (Question 1.2-91a.). Find all boundaries that give the least number of overflows.

c. Use the full data of the relation on S and P to find the best multipaging of the candidate boundaries from (Question 1.2-91b.). What are π, α?

1.2-92 Multipage the relation shown:

a. For a blocksize b= 2, 3 or 4 find the partitioning factors f_s and f_p which most nearly equalize V_s/f_s and V_p/f_p while keeping $\alpha \geq 0.8$.

P S	1	2	3	4	5	6	7
b		1	1	1		1	
c			1		1		
d	1		1			1	1

b. Show the axial distributions and the graphs for finding the partition boundaries using f_s and f_p from (Question 1.2-92a.). Find all boundaries that give the least number of overflows between segments.

c. Use the full data of the relation on S and P to find the best multipaging of the candidate boundaries from (Question 1.2-92b.). What are π, α?

1.2-93 A videodisk has 40000 tracks with 128 1Kbit sectors on each. It rotates at 16 revolutions per second and the mean arm movement time is 100ms. Calculate $\tau, \rho, \sigma, \lambda, \mu, \beta, \gamma$ and ν and compare with Exhibit 1.2-2. What is the total capacity of the disk (both sides) and, if a disk costs $25.00, what is the cost per bit?

COST ANALYSIS

1.3-1   Computational Complexity

The most direct way to gain insight into an algorithm or a problem is to discover its *computational complexity*. We have already made use of this by describing logarithmic access as an order log N process, serial access as order N and so on. Some of the algorithms discussed in this book and their (time) computational complexity are shown below

Exhibit   1.3-1.   Some Polynomial-Time Processes

PROCESS	TIME	
Direct access	$O(1)$	(on the average)
Logarithmic access	$O(\log N)$	N records in file
Sequential access	$O(N)$	"
Topological sorting	$O(E)$	E edges in graph
Sorting	$O(N \log N)$	N records in file
Transitive closure	$O(V^3)$	V vertices in graph

The notation $O(f(n))$ has a precise definition for any function f: a process $P(n)$ has complexity $O(f(n))$ if there are two constants c and n_0 such that the cost of $P(n)$ is not greater than $c|f(n)|$ for all $n \geq n_0$.

To help your intuition about how much can be accomplished in a given time by algorithms of various complexity, here is a table of the number of records that can be processed, assuming a time of 3 ms per record processed. (This time corresponds to 10 100-byte records per block on RISDISK, since 1000 bytes costs 30 ms to access and transfer on the average.) The $\log_2 N$ row shows the $\log_{10}$ of the answer in parentheses: e.g., in 1 sec 2.2×10^{100} records can be searched.

Note that an $O(1)$ process takes a time independent of the number of records, so that a record can be, say, found in an arbitrary file in a fixed period of time. An $O(\log N)$ process also covers a lot of ground: a second is more than enough time to search a tree containing the most enormous file. In the $O(N \log N)$ row, we use base 20 because this is the recommended order of merge for a merge-sorting on a mainframe computer (see Section 1.3-5); the row gives the number of records that can be sorted by a very crude merge-sort. Note how little we gain by allowing 20, 30 or 60 times more time in the exponential processes.

Exhibit   1.3-2.   The Size of File that can be Processed in Various Times for Various Complexities.

# RECORDS PROCESSED	IN 1 SEC	IN 1 MIN	IN 1 HOUR	IN 1 DAY	IN 1 MONTH	IN 1 YEAR
1	∞	∞	∞	∞	∞	∞
$\log_2 N$	(10^2)	$(6.0_{10}3)$	$(3.6_{10}5)$	$(8.7_{10}6)$	$(2.6_{10}8)$	$(3.2_{10}9)$
N	$3.3_{10}2$	$2.0_{10}4$	$1.2_{10}6$	$2.9_{10}7$	$8.6_{10}8$	$1.1_{10}10$
$N \log_{20} N$	190	$6.8_{10}3$	$2.9_{10}5$	$5.9_{10}6$	$1.4_{10}8$	$1.5_{10}9$
N^2	18	140	770	$3.8_{10}3$	$2.1_{10}4$	$7.3_{10}4$
N^3	6.4	27	110	310	950	$2.2_{10}3$
2^N	8.4	14	20	25	30	33
10^N	2.5	4.3	6.1	7.5	8.9	$1.0_{10}1$

Exercise   1.3-1:   Recalculate Exhibit 1.3-2 for RISFLOPPY, assuming 100-byte records.

It has become traditional in computer science to place a dividing line between algorithms of *polynomial* and *exponential* complexity. All the processes in Exhibit 1.3-1 are of polynomial complexity. Finding all the subsets of a set of m elements costs $O(2^m)$ and is of exponential complexity. So is processing all elements in an m-dimensional space with v values on each axis (considered as a function of m): the cost is $O(v^m)$. (Problems with polynomial time complexity are called *P-complete*. An important class of problems that are suspected to be exponential is called *NP-complete*. These problems can be run on a "nondeterministic Turing machine" in polynomial time. Since a nondeterministic Turing machine can execute an arbitrary and usually growing number of computations in parallel, it seems to be able to do things that an ordinary (deterministic) computer can do only in exponential time—but nobody knows.)

For our purpose, however, which is the processing of potentially large files on relatively slow secondary storage, this distinction is not very useful. On one hand, a polynomial-time process, say $O(N^2)$, on a file of $N = 10^6$, records at a rate of 3 milliseconds per record, will cost 3×10^9 seconds or 96 years. About the highest complexity we are likely to be able to tolerate for large files on secondary storage is $O(N \log N)$, and then with quite a large base for the logarithm. On the other hand, finding all the keys given a set of functional dependencies on m attributes can cost $O(2^m)$ (see Exercise 1.1-6: potential keys are rows of the table entirely filled with 1s). If m is about 20 (and it is unlikely to be more), this is only a million operations, which are all performed in primary memory and are likely done once for all at the time of designing the database; we would not hesitate to do this exponential computation if we really needed to know the answer.

1.3-2   Practical Cost Analyses

Analysis of processes involving secondary storage is essentially counting the number of *accesses* that are made to the secondary memory or alternatively counting the number of *passes* of a file. We make the simplifying assumption that processing done in RAM, say on the data once it is in a buffer, is infinitely fast. While this assumption is quite crude, the circumstances of practical cost analyses make it justifiable. In fact, data transfer rates from secondary storage are comparable with data processing in RAM, and it is only if we use secondary storage very ineffectively that the access times make processing on secondary storage two or more orders of magnitude slower than processing in RAM. However, for a given type of operation on a file, the amount of processing done on each record in RAM is usually more or less constant, and the number of accesses is still a good measure of the processing cost.

The main variation on counting accesses takes into account the effective ratio of access time to transfer time for a particular process on a particular secondary device. This could be used simply to give the processing time in milliseconds, but such a measure is entirely device-dependent and becomes inapplicable if another device is used, and obsolete as technology improves. Instead, we give the result in *effective accesses* or *effective passes,* which is the number of accesses or passes that would be required if the entire processing time were used just to transfer data. This measure is somewhat device dependent, but it is an empirical fact that the access/transfer ratio of various categories of secondary storage (e.g., magnetic disks: see Section 1.2-1 and Exhibit 1.2-1) are pretty much the same and only somewhat affected by technological advances such as increased recording density. (For seven major removable hard disks covering a couple of generations of technology, the ratio ranges from 14×10^3 to 67×10^3.)

We often cannot produce simple formulas for the cost of a process, so we now define a spectrum of machine and file sizes for which we will be able to compute explicit numbers of passes or accesses. Since the relative size of RAM capacity to file size is usually significant, by suitably specifying three machines and three files we can cover nine combinations of machine and file. Our machines and files are

Machines

Machine	RAM Capacity
Main	10^6 bytes
Mini	10^5 bytes
Micro	10^4 bytes

Files

File Size	Medium	Example
10^5 bytes	Floppy	Payroll of large factory
10^8 bytes	Hard	Telephone book of large city
10^{11} bytes	Video	Social security of large country

We will suppose that the specified RAM capacity of each machine is entirely available for data buffers and processing, and is not needed for programs or operating software. We suggest above the kind of media on which the files might be found. Combining files and machines gives us the following ratios of file to RAM: .1, 1, 10, 10^2, 10^3, 10^4, 10^5, 10^6, 10^7. Many of the cost analyses to follow will be summarized in a 3 by 3 table of all these combinations.

All the cost analyses that we do must be placed in their practical perspective. The practical environment of most information systems is one in which salaries of users and programmers, overhead, etc., are more significant than run-time computer costs. This book as a whole is dedicated to providing more effective programming techniques for more flexible information systems, thus reducing programmer and user costs. The cost analysis sections of the book, however, concentrate on the problem of how long it takes to run the algorithms and procedures discussed in the implementation sections. With the practical perspective in mind, we will be satisfied with quite approximate analyses wherever it is necessary to make simplifying assumptions. The main purpose of doing cost analyses is to provide further insight into the computational processes. In a number of cases, however, we try to discover which of various alternate methods is best, and for this reason we try to make our distinctions more fine than that between polynomial-time and NP-complete algorithms.

1.3-3   Direct Files

A direct file costs, by definition, O(1) accesses to find a record on the average. Let the cost be π probes per record and let us estimate the number of effective passes, P, to access the whole file one record at a time. This can be converted to seconds by multiplying by $N R \tau 10^{-6}$, where N is the number of records, R is the number of bytes per record and τ (Exhibit 1.2-2) is the transfer time per byte for the device. The time to access one record is just $P R \tau 10^{-3}$ milliseconds.

The cost of reaching all records is $N\pi$ accesses. Each access requires the transfer of Rb bytes (b is the blocksize—number of record locations per block) and a seek time of ρ equivalent bytes (ρ is the access/transfer ratio—Exhibit 1.2-2). A pass of the file, on the other hand, transfers NR bytes. Thus

$$P = (\rho + Rb)N\pi/NR = (\rho/R + b)\pi \text{ effective passes} \qquad (1.3\text{-}1)$$

The number of probes, π, depends on the load factor, α, and the blocksize, b. When α is small, π is 1, independently of b. In this case, the minimum value of P is $\rho/R + 1$ effective passes, for b = 1. For various record sizes, on RISDISK or RISFLOPPY:

Exhibit 1.3-3. Ideal Minimum Cost of Direct Access

R (bytes)	10	100	1000
P (effective passes)	1411	142	15

The result of this simple analysis is to underline the disadvantage of direct access when used to access more than a very few records of the file at a time. We will return to this topic later in this section when we discuss usage distributions, and particularly in Section 1.3-5 when we apply usage distributions to compare sequential with direct access files under conditions of high activity.

Hashing

For the moment, we will give a more precise analysis of π versus α and b in the cases of hashing with separate chaining and linear probing overflow methods. We will also apply the analysis to virtual hashing. We do not give an analysis of the behavior of tidy functions because these are too distribution-dependent to be discussed analytically, and because the algorithms we have constructed for order-preserving direct access all incorporate some kind of mechanism to check the tradeoff between π and α.

Although we now go into a certain amount of mathematical detail, a main emphasis of this discussion is to find an easily-computed way to approximate $\pi(\alpha, b)$. To anticipate, this approximation is $\pi(\alpha, b) \simeq 1 + \omega(\alpha, b)$ where ω is given by Equation 1.3-8 and $1 + \omega$ is plotted in Exhibit 1.3-7. To understand the limitations of this crude approximation, you must, of course, read the details.

Exhibit 1.3-3 might give a rough approximation if we plan to use a direct access file as a temporary workspace (e.g., Section 5.3-1) but if we want to store the file permanently we should consider $\alpha \geq 0.8$. A more realistic estimate of cost depends on knowing $\pi(\alpha, b)$. This function has been the subject of elaborate studies. We will give the optimum results for the case, linear probing, that is easiest to implement. We will also look at some of the formulas for separate chaining, which is the simplest case to analyze.

Exhibit 1.3-4 for linear probing is computed using a procedure which recalculates the entries for Table 6.4.4 in Knuth [1973] §6.4. The range of blocksizes implied by Exhibit 1.3-4 (250 to 15000 bytes) is likely to be restricted by practical considerations. It is of interest to show that the value of P is not very sensitive to changes in b near the minimum for any given α. Exhibit 1.3-5 shows the ratio of P to its minimum for a given value of α as a function of b. If we are content to be within 10% of the minimum cost, a range 1000 to 10000 for the number of bytes per block is acceptable.

The number of probes, π, discussed here is for a *successful* search. The search for an absent record may investigate every block of the file. We can give formulas for the cost of successful and unsuccessful searches with linear probing in the case b = 1:

$$\text{successful search} \quad \pi_L(\alpha, 1) \simeq \frac{1}{2}\left(1 + \frac{1}{1 - \alpha}\right) \tag{1.3-2}$$

$$\text{unsuccessful search} \quad \pi_L'(\alpha, 1) \simeq \frac{1}{2}\left(1 + \frac{1}{(1 - \alpha)^2}\right) \tag{1.3-3}$$

Exhibit 1.3-4. Blocksize, b, Mean Probe Factors, $\pi(\alpha, b)$ for Minimum Effective Passes, P, with Linear Probing.

R	α	.70	.75	.80	.85	.90	.93	.95	.97
	b	25	29	36	47	63	78	100	148
10	π	1.005	1.008	1.011	1.016	1.027	1.041	1.05	1.07
	P	1443	1451	1463	1481	1514	1550	1591	1671
	b	11	12	15	18	24	29	36	48
100	π	1.035	1.049	1.058	1.081	1.113	1.156	1.19	1.27
	P	157	161	165	172	184	197	211	241
	b	4	5	5	6	8	10	12	15
1000	π	1.190	1.196	1.289	1.359	1.450	1.554	1.69	1.97
	P	21.6	22.9	24.6	27.3	32.0	37.5	44.0	57.5

An unsuccessful search is clearly worse, since probes must be made until an empty location is found; the limit is when $\alpha = 1$ and all n blocks must be accessed.

We now develop some formulas for separate chaining, which is the easiest collision resolution to analyze and gives results that can a) be used to test hash functions and b) be used to give crude cost estimates for hashing in general.

The probability that an ideal hash function places k out of n records in one of the n blocks is

$$B(k, N, n) = \binom{N}{k}\left(\frac{1}{n}\right)^k\left(1 - \frac{1}{n}\right)^{N-k} \tag{1.3-4}$$

the binomial distribution. This is made up of the probability, $(1/n) \uparrow k$, of placing k specified records in one location, the probability, $(1 - 1/n) \uparrow (N - k)$ of not placing the remaining $N - k$ records in that location, and the number of ways, $\binom{N}{k}$, of choosing the k records. We define the load factor $\alpha = N/nb$ and can use the Poisson approximation $B(k, N, m) = P(k, \alpha b) + O(1/m)$ where

$$P(k, \alpha b) = e^{-\alpha b}\frac{(\alpha b)^k}{k!} \tag{1.3-5}$$

Exhibit 1.3-5. Values of P (Effective Passes) Relative to the Minimum for Linear Probing.

α	.85				.93				.95				.97			
			R				R				R				R	
b	π	10	100	1000	π	10	100	1000	π	10	100	1000	π	10	100	1000
5	1.449	1.38	1.23	1.01	2.202	2.01	1.63	1.12	2.77	2.46	1.92	1.20	4.10	3.47	2.48	1.36
10	1.186	1.14	1.04	1.05	1.554	1.42	1.19	1.00	1.84	1.64	1.32	1.01	2.50	2.12	1.57	1.05
20	1.069	1.03	1.00	1.34	1.246	1.15	1.02	1.13	1.39	1.25	1.06	1.08	1.72	1.47	1.15	1.02
50	1.015	1.00	1.13	2.38	1.077	1.01	1.04	1.84	1.13	1.04	1.02	1.65	1.26	1.10	1.00	1.40
100	1.003	1.02	1.41	4.19	1.029	1.00	1.26	3.13	1.05	1.00	1.20	2.72	1.12	1.01	1.12	2.22
200	1.000	1.09	1.98	7.84	1.009	1.05	1.75	5.76	1.02	1.03	1.65	4.96	1.05	1.01	1.49	3.91

Exhibit 1.3-6. Successful and Unsuccessful Searches
with Linear Probing (b = 1).

α	.7	.75	.8	.85	.9	.93	.95	.97	.99
$\pi(\alpha, 1)$	2.167	2.500	3.000	3.833	5.500	7.643	10.50	17.17	50.50
$\pi'(\alpha, 1)$	6.056	8.500	13.000	22.72	50.50	102.5	200.5	556.1	5000.5

Consider b = 1. The number of accesses to find all k records at the location
is $1 + 2 + \ldots + k = \binom{k+1}{2}$ and the expected number of accesses is (Heising [1963])

$$\pi(\alpha, 1, 1) = \frac{1}{\alpha} \sum_k \binom{k+1}{2} \ B(k, N, n) = 1 + \frac{N-1}{2n} \qquad (1.3\text{-}6)$$

$$\simeq \frac{1}{\alpha} \sum_k \binom{k+1}{2} \ P(k, \alpha) = 1 + \alpha/2$$

Now suppose b > 1. The number of records overflowing each block is

$$\Omega(\alpha, b) = \sum_{k>b} \ (k-b) \ B(k, N, n) \qquad (1.3\text{-}7)$$

$$\simeq \sum_{k>b} \ (k-b) \ P(k, \alpha b)$$

and the number of overflows per record is

$$\omega(\alpha, b) = \Omega(\alpha, b)/(\alpha b) \qquad (1.3\text{-}8)$$

$$\simeq \left(\sum_{k=0}^{b} \ (b-k) \ P(k, \alpha b) - (1-\alpha)b \right) / (\alpha b)$$

Exhibit 1.3-7 shows a plot of $1 + \omega$ versus α for various b, and gives a measure
of the probe factor, π_s, for successful searches with separate chaining.

The reason we have discussed ω is because it is easier to calculate than the
expressions which follow, and these other expressions make certain assumptions
about the handling of overflows. So far, we have said nothing about where the
overflows are placed. They might very well be placed back in the blocks of the
main file, as with linear probing, although a special format is required to handle the
pointers which make up the chains. Indeed, the interpretation of α as the occupied
proportion of all the space available to the file requires this. In practice, however,
a separate overflow area is used, so that α measures the occupied proportion of
the main or primary part of the file. In fact, to interpret α the first way requires
us to wait until the entire file is hashed before looking for places in the primary

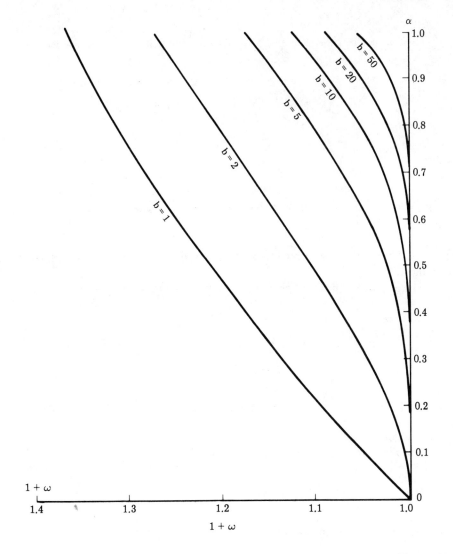

Exhibit 1.3-7. $1 + \omega\,(\alpha, b)$: $1 +$ Number of Overflows per Record
for Separate Chaining

storage area to put the overflow chains, otherwise overflows will reduce the effective sizes of the blocks and alter the formula for ω.

If we store the overflow records separately, we must choose a blocksize, say c, for the overflow area. Then the expression for the average number of probes in a successful search becomes

$$\pi_s(\alpha, b, c) = 1 + \frac{n}{N} \sum_{k>b} \left[\binom{k_1 + 1}{2} c + k_2 k_3 \right] B(k, N, n)$$

$$\simeq 1 + \frac{1}{\alpha b} \sum_{k>b} \left[\binom{k_1 + 1}{2} c + k_2 k_3 \right] P(k, \alpha b) \qquad (1.3-9)$$

where

$$k_1 = \left\lfloor \frac{k - b}{c} \right\rfloor \ , \ k_2 = (k - b) \bmod c \text{ and so } k = k_1 c + k_2 ; k_3 = \left\lceil \frac{k - b}{c} \right\rceil$$

is the total number of overflow blocks associated with a home block with k records hashing to it.

The average number of probes in an unsuccessful search with separate chaining is

$$\pi_s'(\alpha, b, c) = 1 + \sum_{k>b} k_3 B(k, N, n) \simeq 1 + \sum_{k>b} k_3 P(k, \alpha b) \qquad (1.3-10)$$

since all $k_3 = \left\lceil \dfrac{k - b}{c} \right\rceil$ overflow buckets must be inspected in an unsuccessful

search which hashes to a home block of k records.

The average amount of space allocated per block is

$$M(\alpha, b, c) = b + c \sum_{k>b} k_3 B(k, N, n) \simeq b + c \sum_{k>b} k_3 P(k, \alpha b) \qquad (1.3-11)$$

and since each block has an average of αb records, this gives

$$\mu(\alpha, b, c) \simeq 1/\alpha + c/(b\alpha) \sum_{k>b} k_3 P(k, \alpha b) \qquad (1.3-12)$$

record locations per record. The true load factor for the file is not α but $1/\mu$.

Exercise 1.3-2:   Show that $\pi_s(\alpha, b, 1) = 1 + [(\alpha b - b + 1 + \alpha/(\alpha - 1))$ $\omega(\alpha, b) - e^{-\alpha b}(\alpha b)^b/((\alpha - 1)b!)]/2 + 0(1/n)$, $\pi_s'(\alpha, b, 1)$ $= 1 + \alpha b \omega(\alpha, b)$ and $\mu(\alpha, b, 1) = 1 + c\omega(\alpha, b)$.

Exercise 1.3-3:   Show that $\pi_s(\alpha, b, \infty) = 1 + \omega(\alpha, b)$ and $\pi'(\alpha, b, \infty) = 2$.

Exercise 1.3-4: Show that, for linear probing, $\pi_L(\alpha, b) = 1 + \sum_{k \geq 1} \omega(\alpha, kb)$.

(There is no third parameter for π_L since linear probing does not use overflow buckets.)

It is apparent from Exercise 1.3-3 that $1 + \omega(\alpha, b)$ is a lower limit for the expected cost of hashing, achieved when the overflow block capacity is large enough to accommodate all overflow chains. As an estimate even for $\pi(\alpha, b, 1)$, it is never more than 25% too small, this limit being achieved when $\alpha = 1$ and $b \to \infty$. Thus $1 + \omega(\alpha, b)$ can be taken as a rough approximation to $\pi_s(\alpha, b, c)$. Some values of $(1 - (1 + \omega(\alpha, b))/\pi_s(\alpha, b, 1)) \times 100\%$, which gives the worst discrepancy between the approximation and the true value, are

b a	1	2	3	4	5	10	20	50
0.7	−5%	−5%	−5%	−5%	−4%	−3%	−1%	0%
0.8	−6%	−7%	−7%	−7%	−7%	−6%	−3%	−1%
0.9	−8%	−9%	−10%	−10%	−12%	−10%	−9%	−6%

Exhibit 1.3-8. Closeness of $1 + \omega(\alpha, b)$ to $\pi_s(\alpha, b, 1)$ (Separate Chaining).

This suggests a number of ways of dealing with overflows which would come close to achieving this lower limit: keep an overflow area of size $N\omega(\alpha, b)/\alpha'$, where α' is some secondary load factor (α' can be fairly small) and use hashing with linear probing for the overflow records; keep a cascade of overflow areas of sizes $N\omega(\alpha, b)/\alpha'$, $N\omega(\alpha, b)\,\omega(\alpha', b)/\alpha''$, ... and use hashing with separate chaining in each; or store chains of overflow records from each home block together on blocks of size b or greater for a high probability of needing only one access for all the overflows from each home block.

The ideal storage requirements would be $\mu(\alpha, b) = 1/\alpha + \omega(\alpha, b)$ locations per record in the case of deterministically handled overflows or $\mu(\alpha, b) = (1 + \omega(\alpha, b))/\alpha$ in the case of hashed overflows with linear probing and $\alpha' = \alpha$. (Compare $\mu(\alpha, b, \infty) = \infty$.)

For separate chaining, the optimum number of effective passes will not be much different from those shown in Exhibit 1.3-4 for linear probing. The ideal blocksize may be somewhat smaller because of the bad behavior of linear probing at small blocksizes (Knuth [1973], Fig. 6.44). The number of effective passes is, as with linear probing, insensitive to small changes of the blocksize near the minimum, and we do not pursue a detailed investigation.

The following exercise draws together the main results from this discussion.

Exercise   1.3-5:   Of linear probing and separate chaining, which is the better collision resolution method a) in RAM b) on secondary storage?

Virtual Hashing—Applying the Analysis

Under certain assumptions, the analysis of virtual hashing is quite straightforward (Larson [1982]). We assume a continuous expansion of storage from $p\nu_\ell$ blocks to $(p + 1)\nu_\ell$ blocks, measured by $x \in [0,1]$. That is, at a given time, $x\nu_\ell$ of the ν_ℓ groups of p blocks have been expanded to groups of p + 1 blocks, with x = 0 marking the beginning and x = 1 marking the end of the expansion. We try to keep the overall load factor at α, so we use z for the load factor of the $(1 - x)\nu_\ell$ blocks in their original state of expansion and z/q_p for the load factor of the $x\nu_\ell$ expanded blocks. Here the *expansion factor* $q_p = (p + 1)/p$ gives the increase in space required per record, and $1/q_p$ measures the relative decrease in load factor for expanded blocks.

At a given stage, x, of expansion, the expected number of accesses for a successful search, $s(z, x)$, and that for an unsuccessful search, $u(z, x)$. are

$$s(z, x, q_p) = x\, \pi(z/q_p, b, c) + (1 - x)\,\pi(z, b) \qquad (1.3\text{-}13)$$

$$u(z, x, q_p) = x\, \pi'(z/q_p, b, c) + (1 - x)\,\pi'(z, b). \qquad (1.3\text{-}14)$$

and the storage locations required per record stored is

$$m(z, x, q_p) = (x\, q_p\, M(z/q_p, b, c) + (1 - x)\, M(z, b))/ab \qquad (1.3\text{-}15)$$

since $x(p + 1)\, M(z/q, b, c) + (1 - x)\, p\, M(z, b, c)$ locations are needed per group of p blocks and all groups have zpb records on the average. In these expressions, π, π' and M can be replaced by Equations 1.3-9, 1.3-10 and 1.3-11 respectively (as Larson [1982] does) or by other expressions, such as $\pi_L(\alpha, b)$ or $1 + \omega(\alpha, b)$ for $\pi(\alpha, b)$.

Since we wish to keep a constant overall load factor of α, we set $m(z, x, q)$ = $1/\alpha$, thus giving a relationship between z and x at any stage of the expansion

$$x = g(z) \overset{\Delta}{=} (zb)\alpha - M(z, b, c)/(z\, M(z/q, b, c) - M(z, b, c)) \qquad (1.3\text{-}16)$$

or $z = g^{-1}(x)$. The inverse computation can be done numerically, but it is clear that if $z_0 = g^{-1}(0)$ satisfies Equation 1.3-16 then so does $z_0 = z_1 = g^{-1}(1)$, independently of $M(\alpha, b, c)$. Thus the number of records per primary block increases from $z_0 b$ to $q_p z_0 b = z_0 b(p + 1)/p$ during the partial expansion, After the partial expansion is complete, we have an extended set of blocks which is now taken to be the set of primary blocks, and we expand again from $z_0 b$ records per primary block, stopping at $q_{p+1} z_0 b = z_0 b(p + 2)/(p + 1)$.

The expected values of s and u are, over a full expansion from $p_0 \nu_\ell$ to $p_0 \nu_{\ell+1}$ = $2 p_0 \nu_\ell$ blocks,

$$\pi_v = (1/p_0) \sum_{p=p_0}^{2p_0} 1/(q_p z_0 - z_0) \int_{z_0}^{q_p z_0} s(z, g(z), q_p) dz \qquad (1.3\text{-}17)$$

$$\pi_v' = (1/p_0) \sum_{p=p_0}^{2p_0} 1/(q_p z_0 - z_0) \int_{z_0}^{q_p z_0} s(z, g(z), q_p) dz \qquad (1.3\text{-}18)$$

Larson [1982] calculates values for π_v and π_v' (and also for the work involved in building up the virtual hash table the size of the overflow space) using Equations 1.3-9, 1.3-10 and 1.3-11 for π, π' and M respectively in Equations 1.3-13, 1.3-14 and 1.3-15. He chooses the value of c, the overflow blocksize, which minimizes π_v in each case and gets the results shown in Exhibit 1.3-9. For minimum π_v, c is in the range $\sim$ .2b to $\sim$ .4b. Everything gets better as the number, p_0, of partial

a \ p_0	b 10			20			50		
	1	2	3	1	2	3	1	2	3
0.75	1.15	1.08	1.07	1.10	1.03	1.03	1.07	1.01	1.01
0.80	1.22	1.13	1.11	1.16	1.06	1.05	1.12	1.03	1.01
0.85	1.35	1.21	1.18	1.26	1.12	1.09	1.20	1.05	1.03
0.90	1.58	1.36	1.32	1.47	1.23	1.18	1.37	1.13	1.08
0.95	2.16	1.75	1.67	2.06	1.57	1.45	1.91	1.57	1.25

a) Expected number of probes, π_v, for successful search.

a \ p_0	b 10			20			50		
	1	2	3	1	2	3	1	2	3
0.75	1.50	1.29	1.25	1.44	1.19	1.15	1.41	1.11	1.05
0.80	1.72	1.45	1.40	1.67	1.33	1.26	1.62	1.21	1.13
0.85	2.14	1.72	1.64	2.06	1.60	1.48	1.97	1.43	1.28
0.90	2.81	2.27	2.13	2.81	2.09	1.94	2.72	1.90	1.64
0.95	4.55	3.48	3.26	4.90	3.66	3.24	4.85	3.28	2.85

b) Expected number of probes, π_v, for unsuccessful search.

Exhibit   1.3-9.   Cost of Linear Virtual Hashing with Partial Expansions (Larson [1980])

expansions increases, but the improvement is less marked after $p_0 = 2$. With $p_0 = 3$, π_v is better than linear probing in a static table, although, like linear probing, performance deteriorates badly as $\alpha \to 1$.

Activity–Usage Distributions

Suppose we have a direct-access file of N/α record locations and n blocks. We call the *usage distribution* the probability, u_L, of requiring an access to record location L. It is often convenient to write this as a probability density

$$u(L)dL = \text{probability (access is made to record in location } (L, L + dL)),$$
$$0 \leq L \leq N/\alpha \tag{1.3-19}$$

with a corresponding discrete block usage distribution

$$u_L = \int_{(\ell - 1)b}^{\ell b} u(L)dL = \text{probability (access is made to block } \ell),$$
$$1 \leq \ell \leq n. \tag{1.3-20}$$

These usage distributions help us in analyzing the cost of batches of requests for direct access and other file organizations. Suppose a batch of requests requires access to r record locations in the file. How many different blocks are accessed? If we define the random variable

$$X_\ell = \begin{cases} 0 \text{ if block } \ell \text{ is not accessed} \\ \\ 1 \text{ if block } \ell \text{ is accessed} \end{cases}$$

then X_ℓ is 0 with probability $(1 - u_\ell)^r$ and 1 with probability $1 - (1 - u_\ell)^r$. The expected number of different blocks accessed is thus

$$\overline{X}_r = \sum_{\ell = 1}^{n} 1 - (1 - u_\ell)^r. \tag{1.3-21}$$

For a uniform distribution, $u_\ell = 1/n, \ell = 1, \ldots, n$, and

$$\overline{\overline{X}}_r = n(1 - ((n - 1)/n)^r). \tag{1.3-22}$$

To attain the ideal of not more than one access to each different block requested, a batch search algorithm must, of course, gather together all requests for each block before making the access. Otherwise the batch will cost r accesses.

Often we do not know the usage distribution and must assume that it is uniform. It is useful to note that uniform usage is the worst case for direct access files, so that Equation 1.3-22 gives an upper limit for the number of "hits" or block accesses for r record requests. For small r, $\overline{\overline{X}}_r \underset{r \to 0}{\to} r$ and for large r, $\overline{\overline{X}}_r \underset{r \to \infty}{\to} n$. Exhibit 1.3-10 shows a plot of $\overline{\overline{X}}_r$.

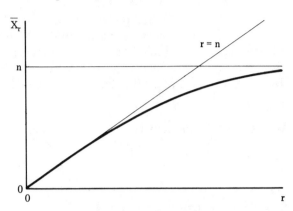

Exhibit 1.3-10. Expected Number of Different Blocks Accessed for r Record Requests with Uniform Usage

Exercise 1.3-6: Show that, under uniform usage, the probability of j of r requests being all on the same block is $P_j = \binom{b}{j} \binom{nb-b}{r-j} / \binom{nb}{r}$ and that $\lim_{b \to \infty} P_0 = (1 - 1/n)^r$, supposing that no record is requested more than once, in a file of nb record locations arranged in n blocks of size b.

Equation 1.3-22 and its relatives occur frequently in the analysis of files on secondary storage. As a second example, consider the Bloom filter of a differential file (Section 1.2-6). What is the probability of a "filtering error," i.e., that an unnecessary access will be made to the differential file? (Severance & Lohman [1976]). We consider the general case where there is not just one but H hash functions which set bits in the Bloom filter for each record that is updated. Suppose that r independent and uniformly distributed updates are made to the file of N records. Then any given bit of the F bits in the Bloom filter has probability

$$1 - ((F - 1)/F)^{rH} \qquad (1.3\text{-}23)$$

of being set, and the proportion of the N records which are expected to be updated is

$$1 - ((N - 1)/N)^r, \qquad (1.3\text{-}24)$$

i.e. the probability that a record is unchanged is $((N - 1)/N)^r$. For a given unchanged record, a filtering error occurs if all H hash functions land on one or other of the set bits of the Bloom filter, which happens with probability

$$(1 - ((F - 1)/F)^{rH})^H. \qquad (1.3\text{-}25)$$

The unconditional probability of a filtering error is thus

$$p_f = ((N - 1)/N)^r (1 - ((F - 1)/F)^{rH})^H. \tag{1.3-26}$$

If we approximate $((F - 1)/F)^{rH} \simeq \exp(-rH/F)$ for large F, we can use information theory to minimize p_f by maximizing the information in the Bloom filter. This occurs when each bit has equal probability of being on or off, i.e., $\exp(-rH/F) = 1/2$ or $H = F \ln 2/r$. This is one way of determining the number of hash functions to use on a Blood filter of F bits for r updates.

• • •

A useful class of usage distributions is the "80-20" family,

$$u_\ell = (\ell^\theta - (\ell - 1)^\theta)/(N/\alpha)^\theta \tag{1.3-27a}$$

$$u(L) = \theta/((N/\alpha)^\theta L^{1-\theta}) \tag{1.3-27b}$$

where $\theta \in [0,1]$. This class originates in the "80-20 rule," in which 80% of the activity concerns 20% of the records. We extend this rule to

$$\sum_{\ell=1}^{.2m} u_\ell / \sum_{\ell=1}^{m} u_\ell = .8 \tag{1.3-28a}$$

or

$$\int_0^{.2m} dL\, u(L) / \int_0^m dL\, u(L) = .8 \tag{1.3-28b}$$

for all $m \leq N/\alpha$: that is, not only is 80% of the activity for 20% of the records, but, within this, 64% of the activity is on 4% of the records and so on. To satisfy Equations 1.3-28a and b.

$$\sum_{\ell=1}^{m} u_\ell = cm^\theta \tag{1.3-29a}$$

or

$$\int_0^m dL\, u(L) = cm^\theta \tag{1.2-29b}$$

where $\theta = \log .8/\log .2$, and to satisfy Equations 1.3-29,

$$u_\ell = c(\ell^\theta - (\ell - 1)^\theta)$$

or   (1.3-30)

$$u(L) = c\, L^{\theta-1}.$$

Equations 1.3-27a and b follow by normalization, $1 = \sum_{\ell=1}^{N} u_\ell$ or $1 = \int_0^N dL\, u(L)$.

For the 80-20 rule, $\theta = \log .8/\log .2 = 0.1386$, but we can generalize to any θ, $0 \leq \theta \leq 1$. The extreme $\theta = 1$ is the uniform usage distribution. The discrete distribution, Equation 1.3-27a can be approximated, using the binomial theorem

$$u_\ell \simeq (H_{\lceil N/\alpha \rceil}^{(1-\theta)} \ell^{1-\theta})^{-1} \qquad (1.3-31)$$

where $H_m^{(s)} = \sum_{k=1}^{m} k^{-s}$, the generalized harmonic number of order s, is used to

normalize. Equation 1.3-30 with $\theta = 0$ gives "Zipf's law," $u_\ell = c/\ell$, formulated to fit the frequencies of word occurrence in natural languages.

Exercise 1.3-7:   Show that the expected number of blocks accessed given uniform usage (Equation 1.3-21) is greater than for any other usage distribution in the 80-20 family.

1.3-4   **Logarithmic Files**

To get an idea of the cost of using a logarithmic file, we can model it with a ϕ-ary tree (see Appendix). The ϕ-ary tree has n nodes, corresponding to blocks, each of which (except for leaf nodes, which are all at level h) has ϕ descendants; ϕ is a parameter to be fitted to actual logarithmic file and need not be an integer. To model B-trees, we have ϕ-1 records in each node, where a record may be data or, as in Secton 1.2-4, it may be index information, e.g., a separator. The real B-tree may have a variable number of descendants from each node, due to the variable length of the separators and the variable degree of occupancy of the nodes, but the model has a uniform fanout, the parameter ϕ. The number of records actually in the file is $N = n(\phi - 1)$.

The average number of accesses is essentially h, the height of the tree:

$$\sum_{i=1}^{h} i \phi^{i-1} / \sum_{i=1}^{h} \phi^{i-1} = h \phi^h/(\phi^h - 1) + 1 - \phi/(\phi - 1) \simeq h \qquad (1.3-32)$$

This can be expressed in terms of the number of nodes:

$$n = \sum_{i=1}^{h} (\phi)^{i-1} = (\phi^h - 1)/(\phi - 1) \qquad (1.3-33)$$

so

$$h = \log_\phi((\phi - 1)n - 1) \simeq \log_\phi N. \qquad (1.3-34)$$

Thus the total number of accesses to retrieve the whole file is $N \log_\phi N$. Each access requires a mean seek time of ρ and a transfer time of bR', where ρ is the access/transfer ratio (equivalent bytes) of Exhibit 1.2-2, b is the blocksize and R′ is the number of bytes per index record, including pointers to descendant nodes. If α is the load factor, $\alpha b = \phi - 1$, the number of records per block, so b = $(\phi - 1)/\alpha$. If each of the n nodes has a pointer, the number of bits needed per pointer is $\lceil \log_2 n \rceil$. There are ϕ-1 records and ϕ pointers in a node, so we can put R′ = R + $\phi \lceil \log_2 N/(\phi - 1) \rceil /8(\phi - 1)$ bytes. The number of effective passes to retrieve all records in the B-tree is thus

$$(\rho + (\phi - 1)R/\alpha + \phi \lceil \log_2 N(\phi - 1) \rceil /(8\alpha)) \, N \, \log_\phi N/(NR) \quad (1.3\text{-}35)$$

$$= (\rho/R + (\phi - 1)/\alpha + \phi \lceil \log_2 N/(\phi - 1) \rceil /(8\alpha R)) \, \log_\phi N$$

where NR is the total number of bytes to be transferred in the file.

If we minimize this with respect to ϕ, we get a good approximation to the number of effective passes

$$L \, \log_{10} N \quad (1.3\text{-}36)$$

where Exhibit 1.3-11 gives some of the values for L.

Exercise   1.3-8:   Minimize Equation 1.3-35 and derive Exhibit 1.3-11.

The number of effective passes required to retrieve all records by logarithmic search is given by Equation 1.3-36 and Exhibit 1.3-11 for the fanout, ϕ_{min}, which minimizes the cost. Exhibit 1.3-12 plots this optimum fanout versus N for some values of load factor α and record size R bytes. The cost near the minimum is very insensitive to the value of ϕ, which can vary by a factor of 2 without increasing the cost by more than 10%. More precisely, for the values of ϕ_{min} plotted in Exhibit 1.3-12, the following ranges of ϕ give a cost no greater than 1.1 times the minimum:

α / R	0.1	0.2	0.3	0.4	0.5	0.6	0.7	0.8	0.9	1
10	1164	980	895	842	804	776	753	735	719	705
20	691	571	516	482	459	441	427	415	406	397
50	364	291	258	239	226	215	208	201	196	191
100	233	181	158	145	135	129	123	119	115	112
200	155	116	99.6	90.0	83.5	78.8	75.1	72.1	69.6	67.5
500	96.9	68.5	57.1	50.6	46.3	43.1	40.7	38.8	37.3	35.9
1000	71.6	48.4	39.3	34.2	30.9	28.5	26.7	25.3	24.1	23.1
2000	55.4	35.9	28.4	24.2	21.5	19.6	18.2	17.1	16.2	15.4

Exhibit   1.3-11.   Mean Slopes: Effective Passes *vs* $\log_{10} N$

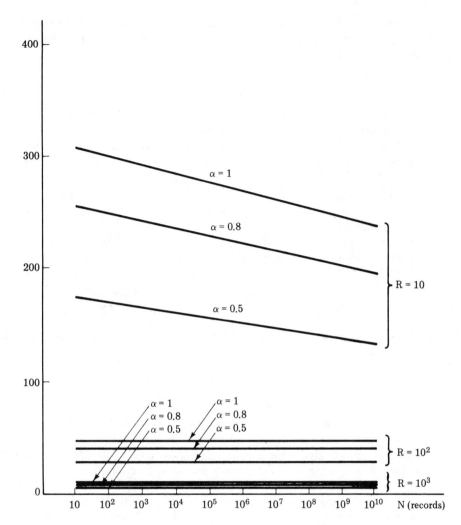

Exhibit   1.3-12.   Minimizing $[\rho/R + (\phi - 1)/\alpha + \phi \lceil \log_2 N/(\phi - 1) \rceil]/(8\,\alpha\,R)]$
$\log_\phi N$

R =	10	100	1000
ϕ/ϕ_{min}	.36 to 2.55	.43 to 2.24	.5 to 1.86

This insensitivity justifies us in using quite crude approximations for the cost of logarithmic files.

1.3-5   Sequential Files

Sorting

Sorting is very important in the processing of sequential files, and we start with an approximate analysis of that. Sorting starts with a single pass of the data to set up the initial runs. There are about r = N/2F of these, where N is the number of records in the file and F is the number of records that can fit into fast memory. This is followed by $\log_f r$ f-way merges, where f is the number of buffers that can fit into fast memory. This total data transfer is

$$2(1 + \log_f r) = 2(1 + a/\ln f) \text{ passes} \tag{1.3-37}$$

where $a = \ln r$ and the factor 2 includes both reading and writing on each pass.

To get the number of effective passes, we must add to Equation 1.3-37 the effect of seek time. This embroils us in a discussion of how and where the blocks are written out, which is a technical aspect of sorting that we skipped over in Section 1.2-5. We will make some crude assumptions for our approximate analysis, namely that data is placed on disk and that the average access time is required to fetch each block. The number of accesses is N/b per pass (b records per block), which can be expressed in terms of f, the order of the merging, if we assume that f is the number of blocks that can fit into RAM, $f = F/b : N/b = (N/F)(F/b) = fN/F$. The number of effective passes to do all these disk seeks is

$$cf = (fN/F) \times (\text{cost per access})/(\text{cost per pass})$$
$$= f\rho/F_b$$

where ρ is the access/transfer ratio of Exhibit 1.2-2 and F_b is the capacity of RAM in bytes. Thus the cost of sorting is

$$(1 + cf)(1 + a/\ln f) \text{ effective passes.} \tag{1.3-38}$$

We seek the minimum sort cost as a function of f, the order of merge. For this we need to make some assumptions about the RAM capacity of the computer, and we use the magnitudes proposed in Section 1.3-2: 10^4 bytes for a micro, 10^5 bytes for a mini and 10^6 bytes for a mainframe. The cost turns out to be quite insensitive to changes in f near the minimum and we can settle on f = 3 as a good order of merge for micros, for all file sizes, f = 6 for minis and f = 20 for mainframes. The cost in effective passes for RISDISK and RISFLOPPY is given in Exhibit 1.3-13, and the ratio of this cost to the true optimum is shown in parentheses. Exhibit 1.3-14 shows how long it would take to accomplish the sorts, assuming the transfer ratio given in Exhibit 1.2-2 respectively for RISDISK and RISFLOPPY. Clearly some of the combinations are not practical.

Exercise   1.3-9:   Optimize Equation 1.3-38 and derive Exhibit 1.3-13

The approximate analysis given here can be compared with the more painstaking discussion by Knuth [1973] § 5.4.9. For his example ($N_b = 10^7$ bytes in file, sorted using MIXTEC on a mini) the optimum is 4.61 effective passes with f = 8. We would use f = 6 and 5.88 effective passes, 28% too high.

For tape sorting, we must consider more seriously the distribution of runs on the tapes. Using Knuth's analysis of polyphase merging [1973], § 5.4.2, and our

Exhibit 1.3-13. Sort Cost in Effective Passes for f-way Merge (Parentheses give ratio: Cost/Minimum Cost).

MACHINE (F) FILE SIZE (BYTES)	Main (f = 20)	Mini (f = 6)	Micro (f = 3)
10^5			12.9 (1.04)
10^8	2.96 (1.00)	8.25 (1.00)	45.8 (1.00)
10^{11}	5.91 (1.00)	15.4 (1.00)	78.7 (1.00)

Exhibit 1.3-14 Time to Sort Using RISDISK and RISFLOPPY.

MACHINE FILE SIZE (BYTES)	Main	Mini	Micro	
10^5			2.6 sec 39 sec	RISDISK RISFLOPPY
10^8	10 min 2.5 hour	28 min 6.9 hour	2.6 hour 39 hour	RISDISK RISFLOPPY
10^{11}	2.0 week 6.9 month	1.2 month 1.5 year	6.0 month 3.0 year	RISDISK RISFLOPPY

combination of three files and three machines, we can conclude that, in terms of *number of effective passes,* polyphase merging is much worse than random disk seeks for a mainframe, comparable (with 3-4 tapes) for a mini and much better for a micro. However, for the *sort times* to be compared similarly, tape transfer rates must compare with disk transfer rates, which is plausible except for the micro. In the latter case, tape transfer rates would have to be $\frac{1}{4}$ to $\frac{1}{3}$ the disk transfer rate: it is hard to find tape drives of this performance at prices comparable to the micro-computer or to a minifloppy.

Request Distributions

We have pointed out that sequential files are very good at high activity. We now quantify this claim, relating it to the usage distributions of Section 1.3-4. We need to study the *distribution of depths,*

$$u_r(\ell)\, d\ell = \text{prob. } (\max(\ell_1, \ldots, \ell_r) \text{ is in the range } (\ell, \ell + d\ell)),$$

since a batch of r requests for records at locations $\ell_1, \ldots, \ell_r$ will at best scan the sequential file from the beginning down to the maximum of the r locations. This can be derived from the usage distribution, $u(\ell)\, d\ell = u_1(\ell)\, d\ell$, via the probability functions

$$U_r(\ell) = \int_1^\infty u_r(\ell')\, d\ell' = \text{prob. } (\max(\ell_1, \ldots, \ell_r) > \ell)$$

and

$$U(\ell) = \int_1^\infty u(\ell')\, d\ell' = \text{prob. } (\ell_i > \ell)\; \forall\, i$$

We have

$$U_r(\ell) = \text{prob. } (\ell_1 > \ell \text{ or } \ell_2 > \ell \text{ or } \ldots \text{ or } \ell_r > \ell)$$

$$= \text{prob. } (\text{not } (\ell_1 \le \ell \text{ and } \ldots \text{ and } \ell_r \le \ell))$$

(1.3-39)

$$= 1 - \prod_{i=1}^r \text{prob. } (\ell_1 \le \ell)$$

$$= 1 - (1 - U(\ell))^r$$

So now we have

$$u_r(\ell) = -\frac{d}{d\ell} U_r(\ell) = ru(\ell)(1 - U(\ell))^{r-1}$$

(1.3-40)

We can try this with the 80-20 family, $u(\ell) = \theta N^{-\theta} \ell^{\theta-1}$:

$$u_r(\ell) = r\,\theta\, \ell^{r\theta-1}\, N^{-r\theta}$$

If we discretize this to blocks of size b records each, the deepest block to be searched will be distributed as

$$d_\delta^{(r)} = \int_{(\delta-1)b}^{\delta b} u_r(\ell)\, d\ell$$

$$\simeq (\delta^{r\theta} - (\delta-1)^{r\theta})n^{-r\theta}$$

since $n = \lceil N/b \rceil \simeq N/b$.

Finally, the expected depth will be

$$\bar\delta = \sum_{\delta=1}^n \delta\, d_\delta^{(r)} \simeq (n^{r\theta+1} - \sum_{\delta=1}^{n-1} \delta^{r\theta})n^{-r\theta}$$

$$\simeq \frac{nr\theta}{r\theta+1} \text{ for large n or large } r\theta$$

(1.3-41)

In the case of *uniform usage*, $\theta = 1$ and $\bar\delta = nr/(r+1)$. This is a familiar result: for instance, searching for a single record (r = 1) takes us halfway down the file on average; searching for two takes us down $\frac{2}{3}$ of the file; and so on. As θ gets smaller (θ cannot exceed 1), $\bar\delta$ gets smaller, because the assumption we have made by using the 80-20 distribution is that the most frequently used records are at the beginning of the file.

Using Equations 1.3-41 and Equation 1.3-22 for uniform usage ($\theta = 1$), let us compare the best batch search of a sorted sequential file with that of a direct file. Equation 1.3-41 tells us the expected number of effective passes to find r sorted requests on the sequential file is $r/(r + 1)$. For the direct file, the expected number of accesses is $n(1 - ((n - 1)/n) \uparrow r)$ and so the number of effective passes is

$$\left[rR + \rho n \left(1 - \left(\frac{n - 1}{n} \right)^r \right) \right] / NR, \tag{1.3-42}$$

where ρ is the access/transfer ratio (Exhibit 1.2-2). Clearly the direct file is better for small r while the sequential file will be better for large r. The breakeven value for r satisfies

$$r/(nb) + \rho \left(1 - \left(\frac{n - 1}{n} \right)^r \right) / bR = \frac{r}{r + 1} \tag{1.3-43}$$

where $N \simeq nb$ for blocksize b. Asymptotically for large n, Equation 1.3-43 becomes

$$r/(nb) + \rho r/(nbR) = r/(r + 1)$$

or

$$r/N = R/(R + \rho) + O(1/N). \tag{1.3-44}$$

The breakeven activity, r/N, beyond which sequential files become superior to direct files is thus remarkably low, as shown in Exhibit 1.3-15. This justifies our claim in Section 1.2-2 that the breakeven activity is usually less than 1%. For small n the breakeven activity is still smaller than the asymptotic limit, which is effectively reached at about n = 1000 blocks.

Exhibit 1.3-15. Breakeven Activities, Sequential *vs.* Hashed Files

record size, R	10	100	1000
breakeven r/N	.071%	.70%	6.6%

Exercise 1.3-10: Find a very simple derivation of the asymptotic breakeven activities of Exhibit 1.3-15.

Sequential Access Time

We have discussed costs in terms of effective passes and, equivalently, number of accesses. Frequently, the actual time to do an access is important. We can treat this easily for sequential files, using a framework that is extendible to more sophisticated organizations.

If we were able to speed through the file, doing nothing but useful data transfer, the time required for one pass of a file of N records of R bytes each is

$$NR\tau$$

where τ is the transfer time per byte of the storage device, as given in Section 1.2-1. However, not all of the time is spent in useful data transfer, since we must first find the beginning of the file, we may stop to do computations from time to time, we must change cylinders on disc if the file is big enough, and tracks are not necessarily completely full. So we add a factor $\omega \geq 1$ to give the *overhead ratio* for a particular device and file, giving a time

$$NR\,\omega\tau \qquad (1.3\text{-}45)$$

to read the whole file. For sequential reading, ω is not much bigger than 1. The same format can be used for other file organizations, only ω will be rather larger because we are more likely to jump from block to block during an access. Expression 1.3-45 can even be used for files on tape, with interblock gap transits and even tape rewinds substituting for changing cylinders. To keep the disparity in the size of ω to a minimum in these different cases, we exclude the seek time to find the beginning of the file from the calculation of ω.

Exercise   1.3-11:   Give expressions for the terms of ω for a sequential file on RISDISK, using parameters from Exhibit 1.2-2.

The answers to Exercise 1.3-11 can be approximated as follows (numbers in parentheses are for a file of blocksize B = 3200 bytes and no intervening computations).

$$\omega \simeq \omega_1 + \omega_3 + \omega_4$$

Transmission time	$\omega_1 = 1$	(1)
Intercylinder delays	$\omega_3 \simeq \rho/\gamma\beta$	(0.071)
Tracks not full	$\omega_4 \simeq \beta/tB - 1$	(0.042)

1.3-6   Summary of Cost Analyses

The aim of Chapter 1.3 has been to present a set of costing techniques for implementation evaluations and some further insight. The topics have been a little disjointed and so a summary may be helpful.

In Section 1.3-3 we show that $1 + \omega\,(\alpha, b)$ gives a reasonable approximation to the probe factor for hashing with a memory utilization of α $(0 \leq \alpha \leq 1)$ and blocks of size b, where ω is the number of overflows per record for separate chaining, plotted in Exhibit 1.3-7 and fairly easily calculated. The result for separate chaining gives a reasonable guess at the results, harder to calculate but also derived in Section 1.3-3, for other collision resolution methods. Also in Section 1.3-3 we discuss the notion of a *usage distribution* and derive the well known *hit-rate* formula, $n(1 - ((n - 1)/n)^r)$, for the number out of n blocks assessed due to r requests uniformly distributed over a direct file.

In Section 1.3-4 we use a "ϕ-ary tree" to model a logarithmic file such as a B-tree, with the aim of getting an estimate of the number of passes of the file needed to retrieve it all. The results, in Exhibit 1.3-11, are useful for approximate costing of high-activity processing of trees. For low-activity processing, of course, the number of accesses per tuple retrieved is just the height of the tree, about log N if there are N tuples present. The analysis supposes that only the tree is retrieved: if the tree just contains pointers to a separate data file, the direct-access costs from "Activity-Usage Distributions" in Section 1.3-3 must be added.

In Section 1.3-5 we give an approximate analysis of sorting, leading to Exhibit 1.3-14, the set of sort costs for various configurations of file and computer that will be used in Chapter 5.3. We also introduce the notion of *distribution of depths*, derived from the usage distributions of Section 1.3-3.

The analysis of distributions of depths produces the most interesting practical result of Chapter 1.3, the breakeven comparison between sequential and direct files. This shows that for activities in excess of only about 1%, batch techniques on sequential files are superior to direct access techniques in efficiency. (We have already claimed the superiority of sequential techniques for versatility in Section 1.2-5.)

ADVANCED TOPICS

1.4-1   Relations

In the literature of the past decade or so on relational databases, the paper by Codd [1970] is acknowledged as the origin of the relational approach to data. Codd himself cites some forerunners, whom we shall look at, but he can be credited with introducing m-ary relations to database work and with formulating the first general operations on m-ary relations. Before we say more about this seminal paper, let us look at a century earlier, at the work of C.S. Peirce.

In 1870, Peirce wrote "Relative terms usually receive some slight treatment in works upon logic, but the only considerable investigation into the formal laws which govern them is contained in a valuable paper by Mr. De Morgan . . ." [Peirce 1870, referring to De Morgan, 1859].

For us, Peirce's contribution in this paper was twofold. First, he emphasized the formalism of operations on relations, although in this, like earlier writers, he concentrated on binary relations. Second, however, he introduced the general notion of m-ary relations, such as the ternary relation "giver to—of—" and the quaternary relation "winner over of—to—from—." In a later note [Peirce 1882], he introduces a matrix-like subscript notation, with $(x)_{ij}$ representing a binary relation, $(x)_{ijk}$ a ternary relation, and so on. In a postscript written nine days later he adds "I have this day had the delight of reading for the first time Professor Cayley's *Memoir on Matrices,* in the *Philosophical Transactions* for 1858. The algebra he there describes seems to me substantially identical with my long subsequent algebra for dual relatives." Thus the matrix representation of relations stems from their earliest days.

One of the predecessors Codd cites is the paper by Levein and Maron [1967], which manipulates binary relations on a disk storage. They acknowledge the need for m-ary relations, but construct these by nested "compositions" of binary relations. Ash and Sibley [1968] view these binary relations as a triple, (relation, operand1, operand2). Feldman and Rovner [1969] use triples, (attribute, object, value), and implement them using hash coding on secondary storage. Ash and

Sibley adopt these triples and hashing techniques and add operations whereby one relation may be derived from others. It is interesting to note that although Codd generalized to m-ary relations, the table form of an m-ary relation can be represented as a ternary relation—the table is, after all, a nonhomogeneous matrix—in the form (attribute, tuple, value). In this representation, the tuple from Exhibit 1.1-1

(4, Pennsylvania Railroad, Hannah Trainman, Car, 37)

would become the set of triplets

(ORD#	1	4	)
(CUSTOMER	1	Pennsylvania Railroad)	
(SALESMAN	1	Hannah Trainman	)
(ASSEMBLY	1	Car	)
(QTY	1	37	)

where 1 in each case is the identifier of the first tuple in Exhibit 1.1-1. There are obvious advantages to the m-ary relation over this form, but there are times when it is useful to be able to resort to this kind of formulation, as in relations representing data with fields that repeat or that are present or not depending on the value of some other field. Such considerations bring us to the threshold of the applicability of relations.

Codd's [1970] paper stresses the elimination from the data of structure which reflects only aspects of implementation, such as ordering, indexing and access paths. It also promotes the relational approach as a "sound basis for treating derivability, redundancy and consistency" of data. Under "derivability" Codd introduced special cases of the operators on relations which are described in Chapter 2.1. Redundancy is defined in terms of derivability, and consistency is specified for redundant sets of relations by a collection of constraint statements. Consistency in this paper is a property of the instantaneous state of a set of relations rather than of its history or changes of state. In his Turing Award lecture [Codd 1981] Codd later stressed the importance of operations and integrity rules as well as data structures in a data model.

In his 1970 paper and again in [Codd 1971a], Codd discusses the *normalization* of relations. *First normal form* (1NF) is satisfied by any relation with "simple" values in each tuple for each attribute, and is just what we have defined in Chapter 1.1 to be a relation. *Second* and *third normal forms* (2NF and 3NF) are the result of rearranging a set of relations to eliminate certain functional dependences which are undesirable because their presence allows tuples to be redundant so that inconsistencies may arise when some tuples are updated but not others. All definitions of normal forms higher than first are somewhat *ad hoc* and are subject to controversy, but a definition which contains 2NF and 3NF and is least unsatisfactory is *Boyce-Codd normal form* (BCNF):

a relation is in BCNF if every determinant is a key [Codd 1974] where a determinant is the left-hand side of any functional dependence and a key, as defined in Section 1.1-2, is the left-hand side of a functional dependence whose right-hand side is all attributes of the relation. Bernstein [1976] gives an algorithm which starts with a set of functional dependences (described somehow in L bytes) and in $O(L^2)$ time generates a minimal set of 3NF relations. Later Bernstein and Goodman [1980] use a proof that Boyce-Codd normal fails to meet its goals except in trivial cases to criticize the theory on which normalization is based.

1.4-2   Functional Dependence

Functional dependence is, of course, just a manifestation of the classical idea, in mathematics, of a function. The notion of functional dependence in relations was introduced by Codd [1971a] in his discussion of normalization. It was studied by Delobel [1972] who proposed some rules for deriving functional dependences from others. If W, X, Y and Z are sets of attributes drawn from the universe U of all attributes of a given relation, he says:

Tr	Transitivity	if $X \to Y$ and $Y \to Z$ then $X \to Z$
Rf	Reflexivity	$X \to X$
Pr	Projectivity	if $Y \subseteq X$ then $X \to Y$
Ad1	Additivity 1	if $X \to Y$ and $X \to Z$ then $X \to YZ$
		(YZ is shorthand for the union Y Z)
Ad2	Additivity 2	if $X \to Z$ and $W \to Y$ then $WX \to YZ$

Delobel and Casey [1973] added further rules:

| PS | Pseudotransitivity | if $X \to Y$ and $YW \to Z$ then $XW \to Z$ |
| Au1 | Augmentation 1 | if $X \to Y$ then $XW \to Y$ |

Exercise   1.4-1:   Use Definition 1.1-3 to prove each of the above rules.

Exercise   1.4-2:   Show that all of the above rules can be deduced from each of the following sets of rules:

{Tr, Pr, Ad1}, {Rf, Ps, Au1}, {Rf, Tr, Wk, Ad2}, {Pr, Tr, Au2}
where the new rules are

Wk	Weakening	if $W \to Z$ and $W \subseteq X$ and $Z \supseteq Y$ then $X \to Y$
		[Armstrong 1974].
Au2	Augmentation 2	if $W \to Z$ and $X \supseteq Y$ then $WX \to YZ$
		[Beeri, Fagin and Howard 1977].

Exercise 1.4-2 shows that various sets of rules are *equivalent* in the sense that all of the rules listed above can be derived from each set. The achievement of Armstrong [1974] was to show that one of these sets, namely {Rf, Tr, Wk, Ad2} is *complete,* i.e. all possible rules for functional dependences can be derived from

it (and hence from any of the equivalent sets). The converse of completeness is *consistency*, namely that the set of rules has a consistent interpretation and can lead to no contradictions: this is established in Exercise 1.4-1. We will not give Armstrong's now classical proof of the completeness of what have come to be called "Armstrong's axioms," but we will discuss some of the ideas involved.

The first is what we shall call an "Armstrong chart," which derives from the notion of the *maximal dependences*. First, a *full family* of dependences or *closure*, is just the set of all possible dependences that can be derived from a given set. Exercise 1.1-6 gives a full family for the two dependences of Exhibit 1.1-9, $O \rightarrow CS$ and $OA \rightarrow Q$, where we have abbreviated ORD#, CUSTOMER, SALESMAN, ASSEMBLY and QTY in the obvious ways. However, as we see in that exercise, the full family is cumbersome to write, needing a table of $2^m \times 2^m = 4^m$ entries for m attributes, and largely consists of *reflexive* and *projective* dependences which hold for any relation on those m attributes and so are *trivial*. The maximal dependences give a shorter way of writing the equivalent of the full family in a smaller table. This has only m columns, one for each attribute, and ℓ rows where ℓ is the number of maximal dependences. A maximal dependence is one whose left-hand side contains as few attributes as possible and whose right-hand side contains as many as possible. The Armstrong chart is obtained by eliminating from the maximal dependences those whose right-hand side is identical to the left-hand side, since these are the trivial dependences.

Exhibit 1.4-1. The Armstrong chart of ORDERBOOK

	ORD#	CUSTOMER	SALESMAN	ASSEMBLY	QTY
ORD#	*1*	1	1		
{ORD#, ASSEMBLY}	*1*	1	1	*1*	1

In the Armstrong chart, the 1s in each row pick out the subset of U which is determined by the left-hand side for that row. Thus columns corresponding to subsets of U with more than one attribute can easily be derived by additivity. Similarly, rows that can be derived by reflexive, projective and augmentation rules are omitted. This leaves only the transitive rule to be applied: Fadous and Forsythe [1975] give procedures for applying transitive rules in an Armstrong chart. In Exhibit 1.4-1, the entries are distinguished for ease of reference: 1 means the column was given originally in the right-hand side of a functional dependence; *1* means a dependence derived by projectivity and 1 gives a dependence derived by transitivity. The left-hand sides in this example were already minimal. The Armstrong chart is a much more compact representation of the full family than is the answer to Exercise 1.1-6.

The second fundamental idea in Armstrong's paper is the notion of a *saturated set*. The saturated subsets of U according to a given full family are just the right-hand sides of the maximal dependences (including the trivial ones). A saturated set of attributes is one which determines no other attributes. The notion is a kind of complement to functional dependence in that the more dependences the fewer saturated sets there are: if only trivial functional dependences are present, every subset of U is saturated; if every attribute is a key, only U is saturated. Saturated subsets form an *intersection semilattice*: U is saturated, and the intersection of any two saturated sets is also saturated. The remarkable property is that each full family of functional dependences is uniquely determined by a family of saturated sets and, of course, conversely. This provides a way of enumerating all the distinct families of dependences on a given set of attributes. Most significantly, however, it converts the study of functional dependences to a study of sets of attributes, which are more fundamental to relational database theory and more easily generalized.

Delobel and Casey [1973], Fadous and Forsyth [1975] and Bernstein [1975] consider the problem of finding all keys given a family of functional dependences. The problem is complex because there are potentially an exponential number of subsets of U which can be keys. Kim [1976] did an empirical comparison of their algorithms and found Fadous and Forsythe's algorithm to run fastest. It is easy to determine a key using the Armstrong chart: it is a row with only ones in it: e.g., {ORD#, ASSEMBLY}. The approach of Delobel and Casey is worth mentioning because they set up a formal correspondence between a dependence and a boolean implication. For OA → OCSAQ, the boolean expression is oa => ocsaq where => means implication and conjunction of two terms means to **and** them. A single boolean expression can be made for all functional dependences by oring the individual expressions together and oring this with the conjunction of the terms for all attributes: the keys correspond to the prime implicants of this expression, which can be found using a standard procedure or, for at most about six attributes, by using Karnaugh maps. Thus functional dependences can be related to boolean algebra and to a special case of switching theory. This connection has been further explored by Fagin [1976], Delobel and Parker [1978] and Nambiar [1980].

Tsao [1979] considered the interesting converse to the problem of how given functional dependences should be checked in an instance of a relation, namely the problem of finding the dependences present in a given instance of a relation. (Some of these dependences will, of course, be accidental, but this does not concern us.) Clearly we can check violations of a given dependence by sorting the data in order of the left-hand side and then looking for violations of Definition 1.1-3. To find violations of arbitrary conjectural dependences requires repeating this sort-and-scan for every possible left-hand side—an exponential number of sorts. Tsao adopts a heuristic which uses only one pass of the data, together with an analysis of the probability that the heuristic fails to detect a violation. The functional dependences claimed by this heuristic are unsure, but the violations it finds are certain. If there are N tuples and F of them can be held in RAM and thus compared each with the other, the probability that the heuristic fails to find any violations of a given functional dependence is essentially $(1 - F/N) \uparrow (2V)$ where V pairs of tuples in fact separately violate the dependence: flagrant violations will usually be detected.

Exercise   1.4-3:   Given a set of dependence violations reported by a heuristic such as Tsao's, use one of the axiom systems or the family of saturated sets to derive other violations among the dependences reported as possible by the heuristic.

1.4-3   Integrity Constraints and Data Semantics

Functional dependences are only one possible form of integrity constraint. They happen to be the only form that is simple enough to have been studied formally in depth. They are also important enough to have inspired two major data models. The first is the CODASYL DBTG model [CODASYL 1971], based on the construct of "ownership" in which one type of record has a one-to-many association with another type of record. This notion, which is fundamental to the implementation data structures of DBTG-type database systems, is just the converse of the many-to-one notion of function which appears in the relational data model as functional dependence. The second major data model is the entity-relationship proposal of Chen [1976]. This is a reaction to the semantic inadequacies of the relational model, even with functional dependences, which were criticized by Schmid and Swenson [1975]. These authors proposed semantic interpretations of relations in which some relations are seen as describing sets of *objects* or *entities* and their properties, and other relations describe *associations* or *relationships* among entities. This is a distinction which is useful in practice, but is hard to formalize because a relationship can be viewed as an entity—e.g., a marriage— and vice versa.

All models of data which are founded on specific semantic notions, such as functional dependence or entities and relationships are necessarily less general than a formalism which emphasizes abstract objects, such as relations, and operations on them. The advantage of relations is that they can have any interpretation we like. This is also their disadvantage, from the point of view of the naive user (who has been an object of great concern in database research) who should be told how to interpret what appears on his terminal screen. Our approach has been to recognize two levels: the formal level of relations and operations (Parts 1-4 of this book) and the interpreted level of applications (illustrated by Parts 5 and 6). This follows the relational view that the semantics of an application should be represented as constraints or integrity rules on the underlying formalism. Considerable research has been done on how to do this, and we now look at some of this in the light of the dichotomy between formality and interpretation.

Abrial [1974] and Hainault and Lecharlier [1974] introduced mapping cardinalities as an extension of functional dependences. Note that the mapping can be reversed, so that not only do we have SALESMAN $\xrightarrow{3}$ CUSTOMER, but we could also specify SALESMAN $\underset{1}{\overset{2}{\leftarrow}}$ CUSTOMER, i.e., CUSTOMER $\rightarrow$ SALESMAN.

If we specialize our attention to functions, we can get the classic mathematical categories of one-to-one or *monic* functions and onto or *epic* functions, illustrated in Exhibit 1.4-2. We notice that these authors focus on binary relations in their exploration of semantic properties. This restriction is adopted by a number of subsequent authors such as Weber [1976] and Roussopoulos [1977], using *semantic nets* borrowed from Artificial Intelligence, which are graphical representations of concepts and (binary) relationships among them. A useful general relationship introduced by Roussopoulos is the *isa* hierarchy among objects. This was also called *generalization* by Smith and Smith [1977b]. We will say more about this in a few paragraphs, but for the moment let us look at it formally. This binary relation is a *partial ordering* and hence is *reflexive, antisymmetric* and *transitive* in classical mathematical terms. Exhibit 1.4-3 defines these and other properties of binary relations studied by mathematics—see Parker [1960]. Since their properties are known, looking for semantic interpretations and generalizing to higher-order relations might be fruitful. This formalizing approach is in keeping with the direction set by Boole, de Morgan, Peirce and Codd.

	Many-One		One-One	
Into	PERSON $\xrightarrow{1}$ AGE	PERSON $\xleftarrow[0]{\infty}$ AGE	KING $\xrightarrow{1}$ QUEEN	KING $\xleftarrow[0]{1}$ QUEEN
Onto	CHILD $\xrightarrow[1]{1}$ MOTHER	CHILD $\xleftarrow[1]{\infty}$ MOTHER	HUSBAND $\xrightarrow[1]{1}$ WIFE	HUSBAND $\xleftarrow[1]{1}$ WIFE

Exhibit 1.4-2. Types of Function (some examples are culture-dependent— e.g., Kings and Queens must have spouses)

		E	Q	P	W	D
Reflexive	$(x,x) \in B$, all x	✓	✓	✓	✓	
Irreflexive	$(x,x) \notin B$, all x					✓
Symmetric	if $(x,y) \in B$ then $(y,x) \in B$	✓				
Antisymmetric	if $(x,y) \in B$ then $(y,x) \notin B$			✓		✓
Transitive	if $(x,y) \in B$ and $(y,z) \in B$ then $(x,z) \in B$	✓	✓	✓	✓	
Intransitive	if $(x,y) \in B$ and $(y,z) \in B$ then $(x,z) \notin B$					

E = Equivalence
Q = Quasi-Ordering
P = Partial Ordering
W = Weak Ordering
D = Dominance

Exhibit 1.4-3. Properties and Classes of Binary Relations, B.

We can discuss very specific types of constraint on *domains* as well as on *relations*. We have mentioned the **isa** hierarchy or generalization, and can add the **part-of** hierarchy or *aggregation* [Smith and Smith, 1977a]. The first specifies an inclusion relationship between domains, e.g., PARENT **isa** PERSON. The second gives a component relationship, e.g., MONTH **part-of** DATE. Brodie [1978] discusses these and an **instance-of** hierarchy and uses a language that resembles the relational algebra (called the *data type algebra*) to specify them: a **union** of domains induces an isa relationship between each operand and the result; a **cartesian product** induces a part-of relationship similarly, by giving a Pascal-like record structure. Of course, these relationships can all be described using relations— indeed, the Bill-of-Materials discussed in Chapter 5.1 is exactly a **part-of** relationship—but their application here is to the domains on which the database relations are defined. This is a different *level* of discourse, for which explicit relational representation would require second-order relations in the sense of Russell's theory of types [1908], as mentioned in Section 1.1-2. The advantage of the approach would be that constraints could be treated in the same way as data for queries and processing. Ho [1982] describes a limited attempt at doing this in a general way.

There are other types of constraint. Fagin [1981] relates attribute A of relation R to domain D by the *domain dependence* IN(A,D). Combined with the *key dependence*, of form KEY(K), stating that the attribute set K is a key of R, this is interesting from the point of view of normal forms, since Fagin can show that not only every functional dependence but also every "multivalued dependence" (see Section 2.1-2) and every "join dependence" is a consequence of keys. A relation is in *domain key normal form* (DK/NF) if all its constraints are a result of domain dependences and key dependences, and DK/NF is stronger than BCNF and the normal forms arising from multivalued and join dependences.

Other constraints arise from the consideration that domains, and notably domains underlying attributes which are primary keys for some relation, may refer to entities, i.e., objects or individuals whose existence is independent of being represented in a relation. Thus Deheneffe, Hennebert and Paulus [1974] call an attribute such as ADDRESS *obligatory* with respect to a relation such as LOCALE (PERSON, ADDRESS) if the existence of an ADDRESS requires that a PERSON lives there and that this is reflected in LOCALE. Conversely, if we have relation SUPPLIER-PART (S#, P#, QTY) and a relation SUPPLIER (S#, SNAME) then there should be an S# in SUPPLIER for every S# in SUPPLIER-PART. Abstracting from this only the fact that S# is a key of SUPPLIER and is part of the multiattribute key of SUPPLIER-PART, the same requirement becomes *referential integrity* [Codd, 1979].

Classes of integrity constraint such as mapping cardinalities or abstraction hierarchies are important but semantic and integrity issues are clearly much more general. Another approach is to use a general language to express integrity constraints: this can be an existing query language, adopted for assertions as opposed to requests, or a specially devised language. Such proposals were first made in

1975, using QUEL [Stonebraker, 1975] and SEQUEL [Eswaran and Chamberlin, 1975], and using a new language [Hammer and McLeod, 1975]. The latter two papers recognized however, that some distinctions specific to integrity constraints had to be reflected in the language: static versus dynamic[1], for instance, and relation versus domain, later elaborated by McLeod [1976]. Beta [Brodie, 1978] is a schema specification language which goes beyond these proposals and addresses the problem of consistency and verification as well as validation of some specific database. We have noted Armstrong's [1974] contribution in establishing consistency and completeness for the functional dependence axioms. For a constraint language of sufficient power to be useful, consistency is impossible to prove [Gödel, 1931]. Gödel established the undecidability of self-referencing statements. In practice, compile-time checking of a schema breaks down over semantic, much simpler issues, such as existence. Brodie does compile-time checking where he can and then resorts to validation, i.e., run-time checking the specific database.

Brodie's methods bring us into the realm of programming languages, and program methods have been useful also in the field of database semantics. There are three major approaches, *operational, axiomatic* and *denotational* [Stoy, 1977]. The operational approach considers the effect of a sequence of instructions on an abstract machine, whose states are changed in a well-defined way by each instruction: the semantics is specified by the translation of a procedure to a sequence of instructions for the machine. This is reflected in our approach of letting a programmer define the application using a simple formalism. It is not subject to proof, and it really just transfers the question of semantics from the high-level language to the machine language, but if the formalism is both powerful and simple it is probably the best practical approach. That is why in Chapter 2.1 we will be introducing a limited set of operations on relations, each of which is the equivalent of a moderately-sized program. Another version of the operational approach uses abstract data types: these are independent modules of code consisting of a set of procedures associated with a common data structure [Linden, 1976]. They associate operations with each data structure and wrap the whole up in a package.

The axiomatic approach [Hoare, 1969] gives formal rules for each statement of the language saying what is true after executing the statement and relating this to what was true before. Brodie [1978] gives, not always formally, axioms for Beta which allow him to verify (partially) specification written in Beta. Axiomatization is closely associated with data abstraction, to the extent that some writers consider the axiomatic formulation to be the abstract data type—e.g., Guttag [1976]; the "abstraction" is from any particular representation.

A recent workshop on data abstraction is edited by Brodie and Zilles [1980].

The denotational approach of Scott and Strachey [Stoy, 1977] is more mathematical. Each syntactic construct *denotes* an "object" and the syntax is mapped

---

[1] A method of treating transition rules in the same way as state rules is given in Nicolas and Yazdanian [1977].

to the domain of denoted objects by functions, which are usually recursive in keeping with the recursive formulation of most language syntax. Note that "domain" is not the relational term and consists of objects which may very well be functions themselves, as is appropriate for the "meaning" of a portion of program code. Biller, Glatthaar and Neuhold [1976] use denotational semantics for the CODASYL DBTG data manipulation language, and Vassiliou [1979] for treating null values in the relational model (see Section 2.4-3).

1.4-4   File Structures

Direct Access Files

The techniques and history of hashing are thoroughly discussed by Knuth [1973], § 6.4, and we have cited the work on dynamic hashing by Litwin [1980] and Larson [1980]. Regnier [1982] has refined Larson's method so that the locations of records in a virtually hashed file are independent of the history of insertions and deletions. Fagin *et al.* [1979] proposed a dynamic hashing technique in which a hash function maps search keys into a directory which is a *degenerate* trie—a trie with all leaves at the same level (hence containing 2^d nodes) and flattened into one level. A good hash function will create a uniform distribution of entries and so balance the trie. The directory/trie holds pointers to the data pages, usually many pointers from different directory entries to any one page: the number of pointers will be a power of 2, depending on the level of the trie the page is associated with. The number of data records on a page depends on the number of search keys that have hashed to the directory entries pointing to it. When additions cause a page to overflow, it is split and the directory pointers to it shared equally between the two new pages. If the page had only one pointer to it, the whole directory must be doubled in size. The disadvantage of this elegant method is the necessity of storing a large directory and of accessing it each time.

Some fundamental work on hash functions has been done by Carter and Wegman [1977], who show that if a hash function is chosen at random from a suitable class of functions, an expected linear time algorithm for storing a file is obtained, independently of the input data. For functions from set A to set B, the suitable classes, called *universal* classes, are such that no pair of distinct keys collide under more than $1/|B|$ of the functions: this is a new approach from the usual one of picking one hash function and analyzing all collisions under it. Such a class is $f_{m,n}(x) = h_{m,n}(x) \bmod |B|$ where $h_{m,n}(x) = (mx + n) \bmod p$ for some prime $p \geq 3$.

The order-preserving direct access functions which we have termed "tidy functions" have been reviewed by Sorenson, Tremblay and Deutscher [1978]. We have made particular use of Held's [1975] work.

Multidimensional Storage Structures

Multidimensional storage structures have only recently been developed, starting with combinatorial hashing [Rivest, 1974]—see also Knuth [1973]. Bentley [1979] reviews six methods for range searching, one kind of multidimensional query, but this includes sequential search and inverted secondary indices, which are not specifically multidimensional, and two methods that he indicates are mainly of theoretical interest. That leaves a brief discussion of "cellular" methods, which have recently been developed by Tamminen [1982], and Bentley's own work on k-d trees. A number of database and other applications are referred to.

Cellular methods require a directory to each region of the file, and therefore of size O(N) where the file contains N records. Tamminen [1982] uses the degenerate trie of extendible hashing [Fagin *et al*, 1979] as a multidimensional structure called *extendible cell*, but without the benefit of preliminary randomization. Both Tamminen and Bentley, in the paper referred to here and in earlier work referred to by themselves, discuss geometrical and geographical applications, and in the case of Tamminen [1982] this hides somewhat the general applicability of the method.

K-d trees and the theoretical methods discussed in Bentley [1979] are of course logarithmic files. So are K-D-B trees [Robinson, 1981] and k-d tries [Orenstein, 1982]. These also require directories of size O(N), and access is at least O(log N) instead of O(1) (on the average) as in the direct access methods.

Multipaging was proposed by Merrett [1978a] and the refinement of dynamic multipaging by Merrett and Otoo [1982]. I am grateful to Academic Press Inc. for permission to reproduce much of Merrett and Otoo [1982] in Section 1.2-3. Its advantage over other methods is that it is direct access and requires no directory. The method owes its inspiration to Rothnie and Lozano's multiple key hashing [1974], to the work of Held [1975] on controlling probe and load factors and to a sense of the importance of clustering related data in the same part of physical storage.

Logarithmic Files

Comer [1979] gives a tutorial survey on B-trees. He uses the term B$^+$-trees for B-trees in which data is stored only at the leaves and the rest of the tree holds search key values and, of course, pointers. Since this nonhomogenous type of B-tree is the only one we consider, we retain Knuth's term B*-tree for B-trees with overflow facilities, whether they are homogenous or not. Of all the file structures described in this section, the B-tree and its variants are the only ones that have been used extensively, hence the title of Comer's survey: the ubiquitous B-tree.

Orenstein's [Orenstein and Merrett, 1982] class of multidimensional structures based on Z-ordering enable us to use any one-dimensional order-preserving access method to store and search multidimensional data. Most data structures of this sort are logarithmic, such as B-trees, but Orenstein has suggested that linear hashing can be converted to a dynamic, order-preserving access method (see virtual hashing in Section 1.2-3). Burkhard [1982] has suggested a very similar combination of Z-ordering and linear hashing. Z-ordering has the noteworthy advantage that it is a linear ordering, with the consequence that any multidimensional file has a unique *merge sequence,* and so operations such as set intersections and unions can easily be applied to two files if they have the same attributes.

1.4-5   Cost Analysis and Modeling

The topic of physical file design, which includes both algorithms and their assessment, has received much attention. Schkolnick [1978] gives a selected survey. The subject is part of the broader field of database design, which includes requirements analysis, logical database design and physical database design. Fry *et al* [1978] did an extensive survey of tools, both manual and automated, for the various aspects of database design and, more recently, Sevcik [1981] provides an index to the literature. A workshop on database design was held in New Orleans and summarized by Lum *et al.* [1979].

The objective of physical database design is to choose among the great variety of file structures and methods of linking files into a database, and to tune the parameters of the chosen method for optimum performance. Studies can be made by empirical investigation of running systems, by simulation and by analytical models, in order of increasing generality and decreasing detailed accuracy of assumptions. For instance, the study by Magalhaes [1981] of the usage at Ontario Hydro of five databases on System 2000, learned some specific things about that situation which may or may not be generally applicable. Thus the facts, that most transactions are small and simple, a few are very complicated and not many lie between these extremes, could be due to the query and programming facilities provided by System 2000 and to the needs of Ontario Hydro. So could the fact that simple retrievals were more frequent than updates. The facts, that values in the database are not distributed uniformly and that the most often used processing module was the one to do selections, may be of more universal validity. The study predicted improvement in performance if parameters governing data buffering were changed—this result is very local to the system and this particular usage, although the savings predicted are 37 percent of all disk accesses. Since we are interested in generality, we will consider analytical models, and, moreover, those which encompass many different file structures.

We start with the one-dimensional model of Hsiao and Harary [1970], which considered the multilist file at one extreme and the inverted key file at the other. A multilist file has a starting address containing a record with a pointer to its successor, which points to its successor and so on. An inverted key file has a directory with a pointer to each record, which can thus be retrieved in one access.

A general inverted file occupies some point between these extremes, which can be described by the value of a single parameter. Severance [1975] added a second dimension to distinguish between physical adjoining of records in a sequence, as opposed to their being linked by pointers. Yao [1977a] increased the amount of detail that could be handled by observing, like Held [1975], that direct files and logarithmic files form a spectrum governed by the number, ℓ, of levels in the access structure: ℓ is 1 for direct files and O(log n) for logarithmic. His model required many more parameters, $4\ \ell$ to be exact, which demand knowledge of the fanouts, overflows, load factors and overflow thresholds at each level. His model was implemented by Teory and Das [1976].

As opposed to automated methods incorporating refinements of detail, Merrett [1977a] argued that costs in practical installations are dominated by salaries, software and overhead and that simple manual procedures to analyze performance costs are of sufficient value. He therefore returned to the direct access/sequential access dichotomy of Hsiao and Harary, pointing out that all files could be placed into this one-dimensional spectrum, and outlining analyses that could be performed, either simply or more elaborately, in terms of these two extreme categories. If it turns out that, for instance, the fine-tuning recommendations of Magalhaes [1981] really do achieve a 37 percent performance improvement[2], it is clear that very detailed study at a level well below that of general analytical file models is significant for performance. However, the system must be designed and implemented before such studies can be made, and simple, general techniques may still be the best for this. Severance and Carlis [1977] also adopt this approach from the practical point of view by classifying file organization in three dimensions: response speed (interactive *vs* deferred processing required), volatility and activity.

The discussion so far is limited to simple files and has not covered the logical or physical links between files that make a set of files into a database. These were addressed by Batory [1981]. From our point of view, a good file organization precludes the necessity of physical links between files because it gives direct access to any specified value of any attribute (which is the best a pointer can do), because pointers tend to freeze the addresses of records and lock the file against reorganization, and because using pointers permits us to forget that data must be clustered for efficient access and allows performance to degenerate to one access per record instead of one access per block. Logical links between files bring us to the relational algebra, discussed in Part 2.

All the general file models built apply only to files with single-attribute keys, or rather with a single set of attributes as search keys. Access on more than one search key has to be done indirectly via secondary indexes which are themselves one-dimensional files. The procedure for choosing which attributes of a file should be provided with secondary indexes has been considerably researched: Schkol-

---

[2] Apparently Magalhaes's study ignored some practically important considerations, such as the fact that Ontario Hydro charges by the amount of data transferred not by number of disk accesses. Thus implementing his suggestions is not straightforward. [Walker 1982].

nick [1978] has some references. The worst case complexity of the problem is exponential in m, the number of attributes, because there are 2^m possible sets of attributes which could be indexed [Comer, 1978]. Even restricting attention to single attributes, the problem of choosing which of m indexes to build and maintain requires knowing the probabilities that given attributes and given values are requested, probabilities which are not usually known and are certainly not uniformly distributed. Analytically, we can use usage distributions, although we have found the resulting expressions intractable except when very special distributions are assumed (Sections 1.3-3, 1.3-5: incidentally Fung [1978] showed that the 80-20 family is unable to fit the distribution of some quite simple data). This gets us into detailed studies of how users use databases.

Multidimensional storage structures such as multipaging largely avoid the problem of secondary index selection, although multipaging raises the issue of which attributes to use as axes, and we have designed multipaging so that indexes can be built as auxiliary access structures. The selection of axes is hard to treat as a cost problem, because adding axes does not increase the cost of multipaging the file or the size of the storage space. If there are more axes, there are fewer segments on each axis and the selective power of the axial directory is less. Choosing attribute sets for auxiliary indexing in multipaging is mostly a matter of finding keys, since multipaging is weakest in searching for keys if they form a proper subset of the attributes used as axes.

Another issue that is bypassed by dynamic multidimensional storage structures is the problem of reorganization. Schkolnick [1978] mentions two reasons for reorganizing: the transaction mix changes and the database access structure is no longer optimal; and performance degrades because of overflows caused by volatility. The first does not affect multipaging or similar structures because they are not built to optimize a particular transaction mix but to be flexible. The second does not apply to dynamic file organizations, which do not degrade by definition.

In summary, the evolution of file structures up to dynamic multipaging has reduced the importance of detailed analysis of competing structures in specific environments, given that we are satisfied with an adequate but not necessarily optimal physical structure. If we want to squeeze the last ounces of performance out of our computer system, these analyses are necessary. The advantage of picking a single file structure for all applications is the uniformity of implementation and reduction of software development.

2

OPERATIONS ON RELATIONS

BASICS: Relational Algebra

The use we advocate for relations in information systems is as the primitive units of data, just as integers and reals are the primitive units of data in a numerical computation. It is not adequate simply to have a way of describing data: we also need a way to manipulate it. The relational approach is the best of the major data models for our purpose because it gives us not only the relational form for data but also the *relational algebra* to process data with.

The essence of an *algebraic* approach to manipulating relations is that relations are considered as atomic objects by the operations. Thus access to tuples within a relation is precluded. This greatly simplifies the notation and manipulations that must be done. It may also seem unduly restrictive: this book aims to demonstrate, however, that an appropriate selection of algebraic operations is remarkably flexible in an area of applications such as Information Systems.

We will establish a notation for relational operations which, while not formal, aims to be as simple as possible. We start with assignments.

2.1-1 Assignments

The assignment operation assigns a value to a relation, or, in the terms of Part 1, establishes an instance of the relation. It acts in the same way that assignment of values to variables acts in programming languages such as COBOL, FORTRAN or Pascal. Because relations are more complex, it is useful to consider a few variations.

Exhibit 2.1-1. Four Types of Assignment

	By Name	By Position
Replacement	$T \leftarrow R$	$T[B,C \leftarrow D,E]S$
Incremental	$T \leftarrow\!\!+ R$	$T[B,C,A \leftarrow\!\!+ A,D,E]S$

Using relations R(A,B,C), S(A,D,E) and T(B,C,A) we illustrate the notation for the four different types of assignment in Exhibit 2.1-1. Assuming R and S to be initialized with one tuple each, we show the effect of these assignments in sequence below.

INITIAL VALUES	R(A B C)	S(A D E)
	a b c	w d e

ASSIGNMENT	RESULT T(B , C , A)
T ← R	b c a
T[B,C ← D,E]S	d e w
T ↩ R	d e w
	b c a
T[B,C,A ↩+ A,D,E]S	d e w
	b c a
	w d e

These examples make some obvious assumptions about the *compatibility* of attributes A with E, B with D and A, and C with D and E, namely that all are associated with the same domain {a, b, c, d, e, w, . . .}. Most of the assignments needed in this book will be by Name, either Replacement or Incremental.

Note that to update a relation in general, even to the extent of changing only one tuple, requires a replacement assignment such as T′ ← T. This is necessitated by the algebraic approach, but does not preclude a computer implementation from finding an efficient way of making the change, without copying unchanged tuples.

2.1-2   Taking Relations Apart— Unary Operations

In Section 1.1-1 we split the relation ORDERBOOK (Exhibit 1.1-1) into two relations, ORDERS and ORDLINE (Exhibit 1.1-2). This split can be accomplished by the *projection* operations

ORDERS ← ORD#, CUSTOMER, SALES in ORDERBOOK
ORDLINE ← ORD#, ASSEMBLY, QTY in ORDERBOOK.

Projection specifies a subset of the attributes of a relation and the resulting relation is defined on those attributes. Note that the result is a relation and so must contain no duplicate tuples. Thus the relation ORDERS has only eight tuples instead of the fifteen that were in ORDERBOOK.

Exercise 2.1-1:   ORDLINE has exactly as many tuples as ORDERBOOK. Why?

A second way of taking a relation apart is by *selection*. Here is the result of selection ORD# = 4 from ORDERBOOK.

ORDER4 ← **where** ORD# = 4 **in** ORDERBOOK

ORDER4 (ORD#	CUSTOMER	SALESMAN	ASSEMBLY	QTY)
4	Pennsylvania Railroad	Hannah Trainman	Car	37
4	Pennsylvania Railroad	Hannah Trainman	Toy Train	11

The clause between **where** and **in** in the notation may be any logical expression that can be evaluated to **true** or **false** on any one tuple of the relation. Thus

'P' ≤ CUSTOMER **and** CUSTOMER < 'Q'
even (ORD#) **and** (ASSEMBLY = 'Car' **or** ASSEMBLY = 'Toy Train')
    and SALESMAN ≥ 'H'

are valid selection clauses (which happen to give the same answer as ORDER4).

•   •   •

The notation used here is unorthodox but has the advantage of enabling projection and selection to be combined into the *T-selector,* as illustrated:

ORDLINE4 ← ORD#, ASSEMBLY, QTY **where** ORD# = 4 **in** ORDERBOOK

ORDLINE4 (ORD#	ASSEMBLY	QTY)
4	Car	37
4	Toy Train	11

This notation is more readable than the usual, and extends easily to the QT-selector, which we discuss in Part 4. The significance of T in "T-selector" is that each *T*uple of the source relation contains all the information necessary to determine whether it will contribute to the result relation.

It is, of course, permitted to nest T-selectors, provided always that the expression following "**in**" is a relation. Thus

where ORD# = 4 **in** (ORD#, ASSEMBLY, QTY **in** ORDERBOOK)

or

ORD#, ASSEMBLY, QTY **in** (**where** ORD# = 4 **in** ORDERBOOK)

are legal, if cumbersome, equivalents to ORDLINE4.

The Relational Editor

A unary operation that is a little different from projection and selection is *edit*. This has both an algebraic and an interactive component. Its function is to alter any relation (or the value of any expression on relations) in a way to be determined by an interactive user. Algebraically it is very simple, having a form such as

ORDERS ← **edit** ORDERS

or

$$\text{NEWORDERS} \leftarrow \textbf{edit ORDERS}$$

or even

$$\text{ORDERS} \leftarrow \textbf{edit.}$$

In these statements, ORDERS is respectively changed, replaced or created. In the second case, ORDERS is unchanged and available to subsequent expressions, while NEWORDERS is the edited version. The notation above looks like a simple form of projection. As far as the programmer writing at the level of the relational algebra is concerned, **edit** does something instantaneous but unspecified to its operand. He is unaware of the other side of **edit,** which presents a command language, possibly elaborate, to an interactive user, who may sit all day at his keyboard making changes.

This somewhat strange two-faced operator allows the applications programmer to view a relation algebraically, as a set of tuples, and the applications user to view it a tuple-at-a-time. We have argued already for the appropriateness and power of the algebraic approach for the programmer. But it is evident that the end user needs to work with individual tuples of his data. Some discussion is, of course, needed between the programmer and the end user to ensure the smooth working of the edit operation for the end user in the context of a program, but then such discussion is always necessary.

We do not here elaborate on the command language that could be provided by **edit,** except to say that it should provide for adding, changing and deleting tuples and that it should allow scanning the relation in various orders including the order in which the tuples were inserted during the current session, as well as a direct access to any tuple specified by key. Some kind of *validation* of data as it is entered is also important: checking that domain values have the right form and are not out of range, that keys and functional dependences are not violated, that integrity constraints on the relation or on its effect on other relations are intact.

2.1-3   Putting Relations Together— Binary Operations

Natural Join

In Section 1.1-1 we mentioned the possibility of reconstructing ORDERBOOK from its projections ORDERS and ORDLINE. The *natural join* is the appropriate means:

$$\text{ORDERBOOK} \leftarrow \text{ORDERS } \textbf{ijoin } \text{ORDLINE.}$$

We will see shortly why **"ijoin"** is used to specify the natural join. First we discuss this important operation and give more examples to show why it deserves the attribute "natural."

The above expression specifies that a tuple of ORDERBOOK is to be formed for every tuple from ORDERS and every tuple from ORDLINE which have the same value of the common attribute, ORD#. Alternatively, ORD# can be specified explicitly:

$$\text{ORDERBOOK} \leftarrow \text{ORDERS [ORD\# \textbf{ijoin} ORD\#] ORDLINE}.$$

Formally for binary relations R(X,Y) and S(Y,Z), we can define

Definition   2.1-1:   The *natural join*

$$R \textbf{ ijoin } S \overset{\Delta}{=} \{(x,y,z) \,|\, (x,y)\epsilon R \text{ and } (y,z)\epsilon S\}$$

or

$$R[Y \textbf{ ijoin } Y]S \overset{\Delta}{=} \{(x,y,y,z) \,|\, (x,y)\epsilon R \text{ and } (y,z)\epsilon S\}$$

Since X,Y and Z can be not just single attributes but *sets* of attributes, any relation can be considered a binary relation and this definition is quite general. Notationally, we require the second form if the join is done on distinct attributes from the two relations or if there is ambiguity. Thus we would write

$$R[X \textbf{ ijoin } Y]S = \{(x,y_1,y_2,z) \,|\, (x,y_1)\epsilon R \text{ and } (y_2,z)\epsilon S \text{ and } x=y_2\}.$$

Note also that the second form of notation may require renaming one of the attributes: T in

$$T \leftarrow R[X \textbf{ ijoin } Y]S$$

is a relation on the attributes (X,Y,Y,Z) with different values appearing in general in a tuple under the two attributes named Y. The domain algebra discussed in Part 3 deals gracefully with this.

Exercise   2.1-2:   ORDERBOOK has exactly as many tuples as ORDLINE. Why?

In the example, each ORD# is associated with exactly one {CUSTOMER, SALESMAN} pair and with a set of ASSEMBLYs. The natural join associates each {CUSTOMER,SALESMAN} pair, via ORD#, with the set of ASSEMBLYs. Now consider a case in which the join attribute is associated with a set of items in each of the relations to be joined:

WAREHOUSEMEN (FLOOR	STOCKMAN)	INVENTORY (FLOOR	ITEM)
1	Joe	1	Tractor
1	Moe	1	Snowmobile
2	Jan	2	Computer
2	Dan	2	Video Disk
2	Nan		

RESPONSIBILITY ← WAREHOUSEMEN **ijoin** INVENTORY

RESPONSIBILITY (STOCKMAN	FLOOR	ITEM)
Joe	1	Tractor
Joe	1	Snowmobile
Moe	1	Tractor
Moe	1	Snowmobile
Jan	2	Computer
Dan	2	Computer
Nan	2	Computer
Jan	2	Video Disk
Dan	2	Video Disk
Nan	2	Video Disk

Exercise   2.1-3:   How many tuples are in RESPONSIBILITY? Why?

It is instructive to look at the graph and matrix versions of this last example. Exhibit 2.1-2 shows the typical dragonfly-wing pattern of the graph associated with a natural join. The natural join connects everything on one side of the join attribute with everything on the other side. (Compare, however, Exhibit 1.1-4b, in which ORDERS is the natural join of OC with OS.) Exhibit 2.1-3 shows the typical rectangles in the planes of the join attribute in the matrix form of the natural join—which must necessarily be three-dimensional. The values of the attributes may be arranged so that the rectangles are less evident, and the rectangles may be "degenerate" with a width or breadth of only 1.

Exercise   2.1-4:   What is the smallest (largest) possible number of tuples in R **ijoin** S?

Note that if we were to add a tuple (Moe, 1, Lawnmower) to RESPONSI-BILITY, or delete, say, (Dan, 2, Computer), RESPONSIBILITY would no longer be the natural join of WAREHOUSEMEN and INVENTORY. In the latter case, WAREHOUSEMEN and INVENTORY would both still be projections of RE-SPONSIBILITY, but if we stored only the projections and not RESPONSIBIL-ITY we would have lost some information, namely the fact that (Dan, 2, Computer) is not a tuple of RESPONSIBILITY. Splitting a relation into two projections which can be combined again by natural join to give the original relation is called *decomposition*. Decomposition is possible when the rectangular patterns in the matrix representation, or their equivalent, are present. A relation with this form is said to contain a *multivalued dependence,* although the term is misleading and the relation is better/described as being *natural-join-decomposable.*   *why the term?*

Exercise   2.1-5:   If a functional dependence X → Y holds in a relation R(X,Y,Z), show that R = (X,Y **in** R) **ijoin** (X,Z **in** R).

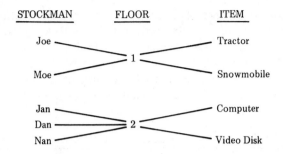

Exhibit 2.1-2. Graph form of RESPONSIBILITY.

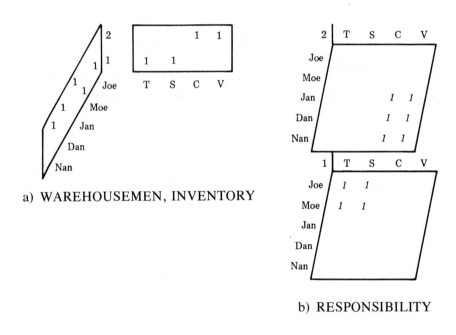

a) WAREHOUSEMEN, INVENTORY

b) RESPONSIBILITY

Exhibit 2.1-3. Matrix form of RESPONSIBILITY

The natural join, we have seen, has the effect of making all possible connections between the two sets of items that are mutually connected to some other item. If one or more of these possible connections is not made by a relation, that relation is not the natural join of any two relations: it is not natural-join-decomposable. It is in this sense that the natural join is "natural." It makes the connections that are plausible in the absence of information to the contrary.

Exercise 2.1-6:   Show that R   (X,Y in R) **ijoin** (X,Z in R) for any relation R(X,Y,Z).

Now consider the effect of natural join on a binary relation with both attributes from the same domain. Exhibit 2.1-4 shows R(X,Y), S(Y,Z) a renamed copy of R, and T(X,Y,Z), R joined with *itself*. Exhibit 2.1-5 shows the graph forms of R and X,Z in T. It is apparent that this projection of T is just the graph of *paths of length 2* in R. The further join of R with T (projected and renamed U) is also shown in Exhibits 2.1-4 and 2.1-5 and evidently gives the paths of length 3 in R.

Exhibit   2.1-4.   Natural Join of R with Itself.

R(X,Y)	S(Y,Z)	T(X,Y,Z)	U(Y,Z)	V(X,Y,Z)
Q A	B E	K B E	K E	K B A
K B	B Q	K B Q	K Q	K B R
L B	K B	L B E	L E	L B A
B E	L B	L B Q	L Q	L B R
L P	L P	B Q A	B A	
B Q	Q A	B Q R	B R	
Q R	Q R			

Connect with Y

Note: S[Y,Z ← X,Y]R; T← R **ijoin** S; U[Y ← X] (X,Z in T); V ← R **ijoin** U

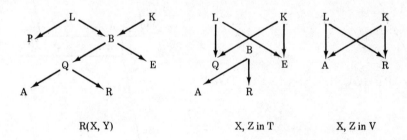

R(X, Y)   X, Z in T   X, Z in V

Exhibit   2.1-5.   Graph Forms of R and R Joined with Itself.

This projection of the result of a natural join on the attributes other than the join attribute is called the *natural composition* of the operand relations. Using the relations of Definition 2.1-1 we have

Definition   2.1-2: △   R **icomp** S = R[Y **icomp** Y]S $\overset{\Delta}{=}$ {(x,z)|(x,y)∈R and (y,z)∈S}

The advantage of defining the natural composition in its own right is that we avoid the problem of renaming attributes, which arises when we use join and projection to find the natural composition of a relation with itself. We can even write

$$R^2 \overset{\Delta}{=} R[Y \text{ **icomp** } X]R$$

$$R^3 \overset{\Delta}{=} R^2[Y \text{ **icomp** } X]R = R[Y \text{ **icomp** } X]R^2$$

etc.

where R^1 is the graph (relation) of paths of length ℓ in R.

Exercise   2.1-7:   How many tuples are there in R^4, R^5, . . . , for R in Exhibit 2.1-4?

It is instructive to look at the effect of natural composition on the matrix form of R. Exhibit 2.1-6 shows R and R^2 in matrix form. It is apparent that the matrix representing R^2 is just the square of the matrix for R, and so on. This is generally true of the matrix form of the natural composition

$$(R \textbf{ icomp } S)_{ij} = \sum_k R_{ik} \times S_{kj}$$

where we must use the following modified multiplication and addition operations

$\times$	0	x		$+$	0	x
0	0	0		0	0	1
x	0	1		x	1	1

for any $x \neq 0$. (These are just the operations of Boolean algebra.)

Generalized Joins

The natural join is reminiscent of the *intersection* operation on sets. Indeed, for relations R(X,Y) and S(X,Y), the natural join R **ijoin** S is exactly the intersection of the set of tuples in R with the set of tuples in S. In this section we consider extensions of the other set operations (union, symmetric difference, etc.) which adapt them to relations in the same way that natural join extends set intersection.

Rather than discuss set terminology, we will use examples to give practical motivation to the more important new relational operators. First, the *union join*. Consider two relations, GAIN (ACCT, TOTIN) and LOSS (ACCT, TOTOUT),

	A	B	E	K	L	P	Q	R
A								
B			1				1	
E								
K		1						
L		1			1			
P								
Q	1						1	
R								

	A	B	E	K	L	P	Q	R
A								
B	1						1	
E								
K				1			1	
L				1			1	
P								
Q								
R								

Exhibit   2.1-6.   Matrix Forms of R, R^2

derived from a financial accounting system. Exhibit 2.1-7 shows instances of these two relations and their union join, GAIN **ujoin** LOSS. The object of the computation is to subtract TOTOUT from TOTIN for each account in order to find the net change in the account. We will not deal with the subtraction here but merely observe that to do it we need to match the tuple in GAIN with the tuple in LOSS for each account. The natural join might do this for us, but the tuple for account F is missing from GAIN: evidently this account suffered only a loss and nothing was put into it for the period. The natural join would fail us here, because it would exclude account F altogether from the result, and we would not even know about the $.22 (or $.22 thousand or whatever the amount signifies) that was taken from the account. Instead we use the union join.

Exhibit   2.1-7.   Union Join of GAIN and LOSS.

GAIN		LOSS		GAIN **ujoin** LOSS		
(ACCT	, TOTIN)	(ACCT	, TOTOUT)	(ACCT	, TOTIN	, TOTOUT)
A	2.73	A	2.33	A	2.73	2.33
C	3.99	C	9.57	C	3.99	9.57
G	2.33	F	.22	F	*DC*	.22
M	1.01	G	3.19	G	2.33	3.19
R	5.40	M	1.30	M	1.01	1.30
P	7.70	R	3.99	R	5.40	3.99
T	1.87	P	3.12	P	7.70	3.12
E	3.28	T	.95	T	1.87	.95
		E	3.64	E	3.28	3.64

Notice that a new symbol, *DC*, appears in the TOTIN column of the tuple for account F. This is one of the two *null values* we must introduce and which are discussed in Section 2.1-4. We only note here that $DC - .22$ is equivalent to $0 - .22$, so that the subtraction when we come to it will be correctly performed.

In general, the union join consists of three disjoint sets of tuples, the *center,* the *left wing* and the *right wing.* For given operand relations, $R(X,Y)$, $S(Y,Z)$, these three sets of tuples are each defined on the attributes (or attribute groups) X, Y, Z.

Definition   2.1-3: R **ujoin** $S \overset{\Delta}{=}$ *left wing* $\cup$ *center* $\cup$ *right wing*

$center \overset{\Delta}{=} R$ **ijoin** S

$left\ wing \overset{\Delta}{=} \{(x,y,DC)\,|\,(x,y)\epsilon R\ \textbf{and}\ \forall\ z((y,z)\notin S)\}$

$right\ wing \overset{\Delta}{=} \{(DC,y,z)\,|\,(y,z)\epsilon S\ \textbf{and}\ \forall\ x((x,y)\notin R)\}.$

The *left wing* consists of all tuples from R which match no tuple from S, augmented by the *DC* null value, and the *right wing,* conversely, consists of all tuples from

S which match no tuple from R, augmented by DC. In the GAIN/LOSS example, the right wing is the tuple $(F, DC, .22)$. A similar definition may be given for union joins on attributes not common to the two operand relations, but we do not go into it.

Exercise   2.1-8:   a) If null values are present, is the relationship $R \subseteq (X, Y$ **in** $R)$ **ijoin** $(X, Z$ **in** $R)$ valid?

b) Show that $R \subseteq (X, Y$ **in** $R)$ **ujoin** $(X, Z$ **in** $R)$ for any $R(X, Y, Z)$.

The three components of the union join can also be combined in different ways to give other joins which we now define.

Definition   2.1-4:   a) *left join* R **ljoin** $S \overset{\Delta}{=} left\ wing \cup center$

b) *right join* R **rjoin** $S \overset{\Delta}{=} center \cup right\ wing$

c) *symmetric difference
  join* R **sjoin** $S \overset{\Delta}{=} left\ wing \cup right\ wing$

In the example, since the left wing is empty, GAIN **ujoin** LOSS = GAIN **rjoin** LOSS. The symmetric difference join is very useful for exception reporting. Thus GAIN **sjoin** LOSS, consisting of the tuple $(F, DC, .22)$, answers the query "find all accounts with either no gains or no losses." This could be used to detect omissions in preparing data for the relations GAIN and LOSS.

The *difference joins* are defined a little differently to avoid attribute columns containing nothing but the DC null value.

Definition   2.1-5   a) *left difference* R **dljoin** $S \overset{\Delta}{=} X, Y$ **in** *left wing*

b) *right difference* R **drjoin** $S \overset{\Delta}{=} Y, Z$ **in** *right wing*

We can limit these to just the left difference join, called the *difference join,* R **djoin** $S \overset{\Delta}{=} R$ **dljoin** S. This is useful for finding items which do *not* satisfy some criterion. Thus accounts which have had no gains might be given by (ACCT **in** (GAIN **ujoin** LOSS)) **djoin** (ACCT **in** GAIN).

Finally, we have the *intersection join*

$$R \text{ \textbf{ijoin} } S = center$$

which is just the natural join.

The family of joins defined here is collectively called the "μ-joins."

Set Selectors

The T-selector accepts a tuple if it satisfies a given logical condition. The set selector, which we are about to discuss, accepts a value (of an attribute or attribute set) if the *set of tuples* associated with it satisfies a specified condition. If we allowed the condition to be completely arbitrary, the set selector would be a unary operation, involving only one relation, like the T-selector. In that case we would have to define a rather complicated notation to describe all possible set conditions. Instead we restrict ourselves to set comparisons and use a second relation as operand, making set selection a binary operation.

The matrix form is the most revealing in this context. Consider the relations R(W,X) and S(X) shown in Exhibit 2.1-8. In R, each value w of W is associated with a set, R_w, of values of X. S is a set of values of X. We can make set comparisons between R_w and S, such as $R_w \subseteq S$, $R_w = S$, $R_w \supset S$ etc. There are four basic set comparisons from which all the others can be derived:

$R_w \supseteq S$	R_w includes S
$R_w \subseteq S$	R_w is included in S
$R_w \ominus S$	R_w and S do not intersect, $R_w \cap S = \phi$
$R_w \cup S$	R_w and S together span the universe, U, of all possible values of X; $R_w \cup S = U$ or $(U - R_w) \subseteq S$.

We mention the last for completeness but will not pursue it further since it requires

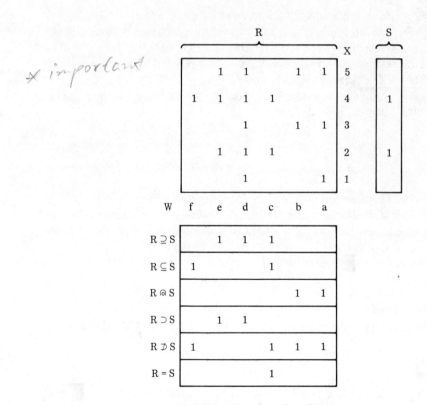

Exhibit 2.1-8. Set Selectors

knowing the "universe" of all possible values, which is not always possible.

Exercise   2.1-9:   Show that the four set comparison operators, $\supseteq$, $\subseteq$, $\cap\!\!\!\!\supset$, $\cup\!\!\!\!\supset$, can be used to give all possible comparisons on two sets in a given universe.

This notation can be extended directly to give set selectors.

Definition   2.1-6: $R \supseteq S \overset{\Delta}{=} \{(w) \mid R_w \supseteq S\}$

$R \subseteq S \overset{\Delta}{=} \{(w) \mid R_w \subseteq S\}$

$R \cap\!\!\!\!\supset S \overset{\Delta}{=} \{(w) \mid R_w \cap\!\!\!\!\supset S\}$

Exhibit 2.1-8 shows the values that result for the fundamental set selectors, $R \supseteq S = \{c,d,e\}$, $R \subseteq S = \{c,f\}$, $R \cap\!\!\!\!\supset S = \{a,b\}$. It also shows values for some of the set selectors that can be derived from the basic ones:

Definition   2.1-7: $R = S \overset{\Delta}{=} (R \supseteq S)$ **ijoin** $(R \subseteq S)$

$R \supset S \overset{\Delta}{=} (R \supseteq S)$ **djoin** $(R = S)$

$R \subset S \overset{\Delta}{=} (R \subseteq S)$ **djoin** $(R = S)$

$R \not\supset S \overset{\Delta}{=} (W$ **in** $R)$ **djoin** $(R \supset S)$

etc.

$(R \not\supset S$ could be written R **not** $\supset$ S.)

The extension to the notation is similar to what we have already seen if the set selection is to be done on attributes not common to both relations. Thus if S were defined on attribute Y, not X, with Y associated with the same domain as X, we would write $\underline{R[X \supseteq Y]S}$, etc. In the examples, $R[X \supseteq X]S$ would be an exactly equivalent alternative to the notation $R \supseteq S$, etc.: the number of attributes in the result does not change with the notation as it does for the μ-joins. Note again that the set selection attribute B in the definitions could be a *set* of attributes, so that Definitions 2.1-6 and 2.1-7 have general validity.

For readers familiar with the literature on relational databases, set selectors are an extension of relational *division* (Codd [1971b]) which is the same as the inclusion selector, $\underline{R \div S \equiv R \supseteq S}$.

Exercise   2.1-10:   What is an appropriate extension of these operations to $R[X \ \sigma \ Y]S$ where σ is one of $\supseteq$, $\subseteq$, $\cap\!\!\!\!\supset$, $\supset$, $\subset$, $=$, etc. and where we have operand relations $R(W,X)$ and $S(Y,Z)$?

Exercise   2.1-11:   Which of the operations in Exercise 2.1-11 is identical to natural composition?

The family of operations defined in Exercise 2.1-11 is collectively called the "σ-joins." We also use the notation **sup** or **div** for $\supseteq$, **sub** for $\subseteq$, **sep** or **icomp** for ⋈ and **span** for ∪.

Range Joins

The *Cartesian product* R × S of two relations R and S is the set of tuples made up by concatenating every tuple of S to every tuple of R. It is not useful in practice but gives a helpful perspective on the next operation we want to consider. There are various ways we can select tuples from the Cartesian product to give the effect of different joins of the two relations. For instance with relations R(W,X) and S(Y,Z), the T-selector

where X = Y **in** R × S

is equivalent to the natural join

R[X **ijoin** Y]S,

which is called the *equi-join* in this context.

Other selections from the Cartesian product give the "less-than" join and the "greater-than" join. Exhibit 2.1-9 shows two relations and, symbolically in matrix form, their less-than join (<), equi-join (=) and greater-than join (>). The Cartesian product is, of course, the union of these three joins.

Exhibit 2.1-9. The Joins **where** SALARY θ FLOOR **in** SALS × TAXES, $\theta \in \{<,=,>\}$.

SALS		TAXES						
(EMP	SALARY)	(FLOOR	TAX%)	<	<	<	500	35
TC	390	350	20	<	<	←	450	30
PF	400	400	25	≤	=	>	400	25
AP	425	450	30	→	>	>	350	20
		500	35	390	400	425		
				TC	PF	AP		
(a)		(b)		(c)				

The two *range joins* which we now introduce cannot be defined solely in terms of selection from the Cartesian product but require comparisons between tuples of the Cartesian product. They are formed of tuples from the "less-than-or-equal" join on one hand and the "greater-than-or-equal" join on the other.

The *low range join*, SALS[SALARY **lojoin** FLOOR]TAXES, consists of the tuples

EMP	SALARY	FLOOR	TAX%
TC	390	350	20
PF	400	400	25
AP	425	400	25

namely the tuple with the symbol '>' or '=' and the highest value of FLOOR in each column of the Cartesian product (Exhibit 2.1-9c). This is plainly useful in an application such as illustrated by the example. The relation TAXES can be taken to mean "if your income is between \$400 and \$450 then you must pay 25% tax," etc. The low range join informs us that TC must pay 20% tax (\$350 ≤ \$390 < \$400) while PF pays 25% (\$400 ≤ \$400 < \$450) as does AP (\$400 ≤ \$425 < \$450). (In Section 6.1-3, the TAXES relation is elaborated a little and treated more realistically.)

The *high range join,* SALS[SALARY **hijoin** FLOOR] TAXES, consists of the tuples

EMP	SALARY	FLOOR	TAX%
TC	390	400	25
PF	400	400	25
AP	425	450	30

namely the tuple with the symbol '<' or '=' and the lowest value of FLOOR in each column of the Cartesian product (Exhibit 2.1-9c). A high range join would not be used in a taxtable application, but the example illustrates the operation.

If the second relation does not contain a tuple with a value corresponding to one or more of the tuples in the first relation, those tuples are concatenated with the null value DC. Thus in the example for **lojoin,** if the tuple (350, 20) were absent from TAXES, the first tuple in the result would be (TC, 390, DC, DC).

Exercise 2.1-12:   (For mathematically inclined readers.) Construct formal definitions of **lojoin** and **hijoin.**

The family of joins introduced here (equi-join, less-than join, etc, but not the range joins) is collectively called the "θ-joins."

2.1-4   Null Values

The generalized joins required the introduction of the DC null value. This has the significance "don't care." A second type of null value, DK, means "don't know." The first describes irrelevant information, the second missing data. In this section we specify the properties of these two types of null value.

The "don't care" null value is taken to behave as a special value, with properties similar to those of non-null values. We assume that every domain is a set containing at least DC. In particular the test $DC = x$ is **true** or **false** depending on whether x is DC or non-null. Thus the μ-joins can be performed in the usual way even if the join attribute contains DC values. Other comparisons with DC we take to be DC so that Boolean operations ignore any comparison expression involving a DC[1] ($x < DC$, $DC \subseteq x$) except where $DC = DC$ makes the comparison **true** ($DC \geq DC$) or **false** ($DC > DC$). Thus the range joins and θ-joins ($\theta \in \{<, \leq, =, \geq, >, \neq\}$) are well defined if DC appears in the join attribute. Similarly a set containing DC cannot be a subset of a set not containing DC, DC can be the intersection of two sets and so on, leading to well-defined set selectors (σ-joins).

In Part 3 we will need to know the properties of null values in arithmetic. The DC null value behaves as the identity value of *both* $+$ and $\times$. That is, $DC + x = x$, $x \times DC = x$, $x - DC = x$, $DC - x = -x$, $x \div DC = x$, $DC \div x = 1/x$. Similarly DC **max** $x = x$ and DC **min** $x = x$. Logical operators are treated in the same way: DC **and** $x = x$, DC **or** $x = x$. Unary operations on DC are ignored: $-DC = DC$, **not** $DC = DC$. The consequence of these rules is that, by and large, DC is ignored, as it should be.

The "don't know" null value, DK, is less straightforward. It is not a special value but is best thought of as a *variable* with a range of all the non-null values of the domain. (This range may be restricted by partial knowledge—"his age is between 25 and 40"—but we do not investigate this possibility.) The basic way to evaluate expressions involving DK is to substitute for DK all the non-null values in its known range. If the result is always the same, this is the value of the expression, otherwise the expression has value DK. Thus, if a has the value DK, $(a > b)$ is DK and $((a < b)$ **or** $(a \geq b))$ is **true**. Ways of dealing with this are discussed in Lipski [1979] and Vassiliou [1979].

The above interpretation of DK can be approximated using "three-valued logic." Since the result of any simple comparison, such as $DK = x$, $DK < x$, is DK, we can think of DK as being a third value, in addition to **true** and **false**, attainable by a logical expression. The consistent rules for **and, or** and **not** are $(DK$ **and** $x)$ is DK (unless x is **false** when the result is **false** too), $(DK$ **or** $x)$ is DK (unless x is **true** when the result is **true** too) and (**not** DK) is DK. This approach does not achieve the full subtlety of the substitution approach, since it would cause $((a < b)$ **or** $(a \geq b))$ above to be DK, but it is simpler.

The result of joins and set selectors containing DK in the join attribute needs to be respecified. If we select tuples for the result on the basis of the comparison being **true** we exclude all tuples with DK in the join attribute. A weaker join, called the *maybe join* [Codd 1975], selects tuples if the comparison is not **false,** and so does not exclude DK tuples. This extension applies to σ-joins as well as to μ-joins and θ-joins. For instance, $(\{DK,b\} \supseteq \{DK\})$ is DK, so the value associated with $\{DK,b\}$ would be included in a *maybe* division but excluded from strict division.

Clearly the result of any arithmetical operation on DK is DK.

---

[1] In general, wherever the type of the result differs from the type of the operands, a DC operand gives a DC result.

Note that *DK* is considered to be one value for the purpose of checking a relation for duplicate tuples: e.g. {a,*DK*,*DK*} is not a set because of the duplication of *DK*.

• • •

Using the multivalued logic approximation, the above rules for *DC* and *DK* are illustrated and partially summarized in Exhibit 2.1-10. In this table, x stands for any non-null value and a stands for some particular non-null value. T and F mean **true** and **false** respectively. Finally, we specify the existence of a logical valued function, dontknow(x), which is **true** if x is *DK* and false otherwise. (A function dontcare(x) could also be specified, but is equivalent to x = *DC*.)

and	F	T	DC	DK
F	F	F	F	F
T	F	T	(T)	DK
DC	F	T	DC	DK
DK	F	DK	DK	DK

or	F	T	DC	DK
F	F	T	(F)	DK
T	T	T	T	T
DC	F	T	DC	DK
DK	DK	T	DK	DK

=	x	DC	DK
x		F	DK
DC	F	T	(F)
DK	DK	F	DK

<	x	DC	DK
x		(F)	DK
DC	F	F	F
DK	DK	F	DK

≤	x	DC	DK
x		F	DK
DC	F	T	F
DK	DK	F	DK

⊂	{a}	{a,DC}	{a, DK}
{a}	F	T	T
{a,DC}	F	F	F
{a,DK}	F	F	F

⊆	{a}	{a,DC}	{a, DK}
{a}	T	T	T
{a,DC}	F	T	F
{a, DK}	F	F	DK

+	x	DC	DK
x		x	DK
DC	x	DC	DK
DK	DK	DK	DK

−	x	DC	DK
x		x	DK
DC	−x	DC	DK
DK	DK	DK	DK

Exhibit 2.1-10. Some Rules for Operating on Nulls.

2.1-5   Simplicity, Normalization and Hierarchies

In Section 1.1-1 we included simplicity of values as an element of the definition of a relational instance. Now that we have discussed operations on relations we can say more clearly what is meant by "simple." In this context, *simple* is usually taken to mean *atomic* or *having no components*. This would exclude sets, tuples, relations, etc. as legitimate values. But it would also exclude integers, reals, etc. because on a computer these are made up of bits. (A set often requires fewer bits than an integer.) The reason integers, for instance, are usually considered simple is that all the operations we ever want to do on integers do not require dividing the integer into simpler units. That is, integers are treated *algebraically*. But so can sets or even relations be treated algebraically. Thus we allow objects such as sets or relations to be valid values of attributes within a tuple of a relation *provided that* they are not subdivided by any operation.

This stipulation is a little subtle and we give some examples. First, some relations and operations that are allowed

R (	A	B	C	)	S (	D	E	)
	1	−2	{a, b, c}	"andy"		1	"and"	a
	2	−1	{a, c}	"dandy"		2	"candy"	d
	3	121	{b, c}	"handy"				

where A < 0 **in** R   (tuples 1,2 of R selected)

where A **mod** 2 = 0 **in** R   (tuple 1 of R selected)

(Note that only one bit of the usual representation of integers needs to be tested in these selectors, but the operations are nevertheless viewed as operations on the whole integer.)

where b ε B **in** R   (tuples 1,3 of R selected)

(Again, this is an operation on the whole set, even though it is a membership operation.)

where C is a substring of D **in** R × S   (tuple 1 of R is combined with tuple 2 of S)

where E ε B **in** R × S   (tuples 1,2 of R are each combined with tuple 1 of S)

The last two operations could be called "substring join" and "membership join" if we were inclined to specify new join operations. In the substring join it is assumed that "is a substring of" is a recognizable operation; it would probably be indicated by a more concise notation if implemented and used frequently. Similarly, an unusual operation on integers might be implemented, making the following a valid selection.

where the second digit of A = 2 **in** R   (tuple 3 of R selected)

It is a quibble whether or not this is really an operation on a whole integer. The point is that if an application requires it, the operation "second digit of" or "nth digit of" can be defined and considered to be an operation on integers.

Now consider some less abstract data and operations that are not allowed. The following relations are valid, but will turn out to be inappropriate for the operations we want to perform on them.

FAMILY	(PARENTS	WEDDING	CHILDBIRTH	)
	{Roy, Joy}	74/8/29	{76/4/25, 78/5/10}	
	{Gus, Lee}	74/9/13	{77/9/14, 80/7/17}	

PICTURE (COORDINATES COMPONENT)   SQUARE (BOTLEFT TOPRIGHT)

(−5, −5)	SQUARE		(−1, −1)	(1, 1)
(0, 0)	TRIANGLE			
(5, 5)	SQUARE	TRIANGLE (FIRST	SECOND	THIRD)
		$(-1, -\sqrt{3}/2)$	$(1, -\sqrt{3}/2)$	$(0, \sqrt{3}/2)$

Here we have sets, dates, vectors and relations as values. All of these are valid provided they are used algebraically. For instance the following selectors are valid, assuming the various operations are well defined.

PARENTS **where** cardinality (CHILDBIRTH) > 1 **in** FAMILY

gives the relation {{Roy, Joy}, {Gus, Lee}}, assuming the cardinality operation gives the number of elements in the set.

where COORDINATES = (0, 0) **or** empty (COMPONENT) **in** PICTURE

gives the middle tuple of PICTURE, assuming the empty test is defined for relations (neither SQUARE nor TRIANGLE in this instance is empty).

Strictly speaking, the following operations on components are *not* allowed, although it is usual to make some notational provision to permit them.

WEDDING.YEAR **where** Roy ϵ PARENTS **in** FAMILY

finds the year Roy was married, assuming that a date is a tuple (YEAR, MONTH, DAY). We use the qualifier notation WEDDING.YEAR to extract the appropriate component.

COORDINATES · Y **in** PICTURE

gives the relation {−5, 0, 5} of y coordinates assuming (X,Y) is the form of COORDINATES. Whether or not we allow

CHILDBIRTH · YEAR **where** WEDDING > 74/0/0 **in** FAMILY

depends on whether or not it is worth our while to implement an operation that extracts components of all tuples in a set. The result of this selection would be the relation {{76, 78}, {77, 80}}. (We assume comparisons such as > are allowed for dates.)

We cannot at all, however, find out who had a shotgun wedding (WEDDING + 0/9/0 > "first element of CHILDBIRTH") or what the BOTLEFT coordinates of the squares in PICTURE are (COORDINATES + "BOTLEFT in COMPONENT"). The phrases in quotes are illegal because they attempt to change *levels,* from a value to a subdivision of a value. Operations which change levels could be devised, but they would be *ad hoc* and would greatly complicate the relational algebra. The restriction is made for simplicity.

There is a way to avoid operating on data at different levels, by *normalization.* This is a rearrangement of the relations so that the operations needed can always access data at one level. To normalize FAMILY for the shotgun wedding query we can do various things.

FAMILY1 (PARENT	WEDDING	CHILDBIRTH)
Roy	74/8/29	76/4/25
Roy	74/8/29	78/5/10
Joy	74/8/29	76/4/25
Joy	74/8/29	78/5/10
Gus	74/9/13	77/9/14
•	•	•
•	•	•

where WEDDING + 0/9/0 > CHILDBIRTH **in** FAMILY1

or

FAMILY2 (MOTHER	FATHER	WEDDING	CHILDBIRTH)
Joy	Roy	74/8/29	76/4/25
Joy	Roy	74/8/29	78/5/10
Lee	Gus	74/9/13	77/9/14
Lee	Gus	74/9/13	80/7/17

where WEDDING + 0/9/0 > CHILDBIRTH **in** FAMILY2

or

FAMILY3A (MOTHER	FATHER	WEDDING	SURNAME)
Joy	Roy	74/8/29	Smith
Lee	Gus	74/9/13	Jones

and

FAMILY3B (SURNAME	CHILDBIRTH)
Smith	76/4/25
Smith	78/5/10
Jones	77/9/14
Jones	80/7/17

where WEDDING + 0/9/0 > CHILDBIRTH **in** (FAMILY3A **ijoin** FAMILY3B)

(In terms of conciseness of representation and closeness to the original meaning of FAMILY, each of these alternatives is an improvement over its predecessor. Notice the importance of being able to define new attributes; this makes the process of normalization described here more flexible than what is usually called normalization.

Exercise   2.1-13:   Find the decomposition (multivalued dependence shown by FAMILY1. Why did we not use it?)

The problem of calculating coordinates in PICTURE requires more extensive normalization and is even more interesting. We replace the relations SQUARE and TRIANGLE by SUBPICTURE

SUBPICTURE (COMPONENT	CORNERS)
SQUARE	$(-1, -1)$
SQUARE	$(1, -1)$
SQUARE	$(1, 1)$
SQUARE	$(-1, 1)$
TRIANGLE	$(-1, -\sqrt{3}/2)$
TRIANGLE	$(1, -\sqrt{3}/2)$
TRIANGLE	$(0, \sqrt{3}/2)$

and, if we stretch our selector notation a little to include arithmetic (see Chapter 3 for a full discussion), we can write

COORDINATES + CORNERS **in** (PICTURE **ijoin** SUBPICTURE)

assuming that vector addition has been implemented. This gives the relation $\{(-6, -6), (-4, -6), (-4, -4), (-6, 4), (-1, -\sqrt{3}/2), (1, -\sqrt{3}/2), (0, \sqrt{3}/2), (4, 4), (6, 4), (6, 6), (4, 6)\}$ of all points in the picture.

This normalization accommodates the possibility of pictures having subpictures, but does not allow for a more extensive hierarchy of sub-subpictures and so on. When we encounter the Bill of Materials hierarchy in Part 5 we will need to handle such a situation, so we investigate PICTURE a little further here.

PICTURE1	(FIGURE	COMPONENTS	COORDINATES)
	ZIG	SQUARE	$(-5, -5)$
	ZIG	TRIANGLE	$(0, 0)$
	ZIG	SQUARE	$(5, 5)$
	ZAG	TRIANGLE	$(-5, 5)$
	ZAG	SQUARE	$(0, 0)$
	ZAG	TRIANGLE	$(5, -5)$
	ZIGZAG	ZIG	$(-7, 0)$
	ZIGZAG	ZAG	$(7, 0)$
	ZZZ	ZIGZAG	$(0, 0)$

ZZZ	ZIGZAG	(21, 0)
ZZZ	ZIGZAG	(42, 0)
SQUARE	POINT	(−1, −1)
SQUARE	POINT	(1, −1)
•	•	•
•	•	•

PICTURE1 defines a hierarchy in which a ZZZ consists of three ZIGZAGs, which each consists of a ZIG and a ZAG. A ZIG is our original picture and a ZAG similarly contains SQUAREs and TRIANGLEs. We specify that the components of SQUAREs and TRIANGLEs are primitive POINTs, eliminating SUBPIC-TURE altogether. The result is simpler and much more general than the original set of relations.

Of course, the coordinate calculation problem remains to be solved. To find the first point of the first square we must add coordinates all the way up the hierarchy: $(−1, −1) + (−5, −5) + (−7, 0) + (0, 0) = (−13, −6)$. Arithmetic is discussed in the next chapter. But processing a hierarchy, now that we have eliminated all the differences of level, is not straightforward. If we had retained the different levels and were able to consider each component in the hierarchy as *contained in* its parent component then we could use *recursion,* one of the most powerful programming techniques discovered by computer science. A recursive routine to draw a FIGURE might have the form

```
DRAW (FIGURE, ACCUM)
    for each COMPONENT of FIGURE
        if COMPONENT = 'POINT' then PLOT (ACCUM + COORDINATES)
            else DRAW (COMPONENT,
                                ACCUM + COORDINATES)
```

where ACCUM is initially set to be the (vector) position of the FIGURE to be drawn and is shifted by the coordinates of each parent component until a POINT is reached, which is drawn by PLOT. Implementation of such a routine on a relation would require a mechanism to find individual tuples, which is non-algebraic. Implementation of the routine for data on secondary storage would require repeated accesses, which is inefficient. There is a close connection between algebraic processes and efficient processing on secondary storage and so we regretfully disallow the kind of operations which permit recursive programming.

This restriction affects none of the processing discussed in this book, and most applications of relational information systems do not need recursive routines or even tuple-at-a-time access. The nearest approach to this kind of need is made by Bill of Materials processing and the related Project Evaluation and Review Technique. Algebraic operations for this category of application are discussed in Part 5.

In summary, we take the concept of simplicity and the process of normalization to be relative to the operations to be performed on the data. Or, to put it another way, these are both highly *semantic* notions.

Review Questions and Exercises, Chapter 2.1

2.1-14 Characterize assignment by Name and by Position; Replacement and Incremental assignment.

2.1-15 What is a T-selector?

2.1-16 What are the matrix forms of the relations in Exercise 1.1-13. Are they decomposable? Why?

2.1-17 What is a connection between a multivalued dependence in a relation and the natural-join-decomposability of the relation?

2.1-18 Given a relation PARENT (SENIOR, JUNIOR), how would you derive from it the relation GRANDPARENT?

2.1-19 Given relations MIDTERM (STUDENT ID, MTMARK) and FINAL (STUDENT ID, FIMARK), how would you combine them into a single relation giving both the mid-term mark, MTMARK, and the final mark, FIMARK?

2.1-20 Given a relation PC (PART, COLOR) in which the same part may have different colors, how would you find a) the parts that come in all primary colors, b) all colors except those used on parts P1 or P2, c) all colors except those used on parts P1 and P2?

2.1-21 Given the relations WAREHOUSEMAN and INVENTORY as in Section 2.1-3,
   a) find all items looked after by Joe, and their floor;
   b) find all personnel who are responsible for both Tractors and Computers.

2.1-22 Given the relation FINAL in Exercise 2.1-19, above, and a relation MG(MARK, GRADE), specifying the lowest mark (in percentage) required to get each letter grade, A, B, . . . , find the letter grades for all students.

2.1-23 Explain the difference between *DC* and *DK* null values.

2.1-24 What is x + *DC*? *DK* − x ?

2.1-25 Explain "simplicity" of attribute values in the context of the relational algebra.

2.1-26   a. Given the relations SUPPLY(SUPPLIER, PART, PROJECT) ("SUPPLIER supplies PROJECT with PART"), COULD(SUPPLIER, PART) ("SUPPLIER is able to supply PART") and NEEDS(PROJECT, PART) ("PROJECT needs PART"), write two expressions using the relational algebra which express the constraints that parts actually supplied are those that can be supplied and that all needed parts are supplied.
       b. Given that no superfluous parts are supplied to any project in Exercise 2.1-26a, what is the relationship between SUPPLY and COULD **ijoin** NEEDS?

2.1-27 How many meanings can you attach to the relation on the intersection of the attributes of R1(BANK, CUSTOMER, ACCOUNT NO) and R2(BANK, CUSTOMER, LOAN NO) where ACCOUNT NO and LOAN

NO identify accounts and loans respectively (the amounts are not given)? Give relational algebra expressions on R1 and R2 for each meaning.

2.1-28 Given the relation RESULTS, shown, what is the most appropriate way to break it down into two separate relations? Show the relations using the given data. What operation of the relational algebra is needed to reconstruct RESULTS?

RESULTS(STUDENT	COURSE	MARK	GRADE)
a	1	80	A
a	2	79	B
b	1	65	B
b	3	64	C
c	2	55	C
c	3	54	F

2.1-29   a. Given the relations MAKES(PART, DIVISION) and USES(PART, DIVISION) which express, respectively, that a DIVISION makes a PART and a DIVISION used a PART, explain the meaning of MAKES[PART **icomp** PART]USES and give correct algebraic expressions which eliminate duplicate attribute names. Do the same for USES[DIVISION **icomp** DIVISION] MAKES.

b. How many different queries can in principle be formulated on MAKES and USES in which a DIVISION is given and one or more DIVISIONs are sought as the answer? Give some of the simpler ones, using the relational algebra.

2.1-30   a. Given the relations RESPONSIBILITY and LOCATION, with extents as shown below, show the results of joining them on their common attribute using each of the μ-joins and each of the σ-joins.

RESPONSIBILITY			LOCATION	
(AGENT	ITEMS	)	(ITEMS	FLOOR)
Raman	Micros		Micros	1
Raman	Terminals		Terminals	1
Smith	V.C.R.s		Terminals	2
Hung	Micros		Videodisks	2

b. For each of the relations resulting from the joins in (a), give the predicate which is true tor all tuples in the result. Assume the following predicates hold for RESPONSIBILITY and LOCATION.

RESPONSIBILITY	AGENT is responsible for ITEMS
	e.g., Raman is responsible for Micros
LOCATIONS	ITEMS are located on floor FLOOR
	e.g., Micros are located on floor 1

IMPLEMENTATION

2.2-1   Sort-Merge Techniques

It is appropriate to start with the simplest implementation of the relational algebra. In this way learning how to construct the operations of the algebra will increase our understanding of them with minimum distraction from technical details. The simplest implementation is to store relations as unstructured sequential files ("flat" files), to sort them appropriately when an operation is to be performed and, for binary operations, to use merge techniques on the sorted files. Most of the operations of the relational algebra are high-activity processes, since every tuple of the participating relations is involved. Thus it will turn out that sequential files, which we have seen are unexcelled for high-activity processing, are not only very simple but also a surprisingly good way to implement the relational algebra.

We will now discuss projection, μ-joins, σ-joins and range joins in terms of sort-merge techniques. Selection, which is most commonly used in low-activity situations, is left out.

Projection

The only problem that arises in projection is eliminating the duplicate tuples. Otherwise, each tuple would simply be truncated by removing the unwanted attributes and we would have the result. This result, however, will contain duplicates (unless the projected attributes include a key) even though the relation being projected is free of duplicate tuples. To eliminate duplicates requires comparing every projected tuple with every other, or, more simply, sorting and comparing adjacent tuples.

If the projection attributes include a key of the relation, we know there will be no duplicates and so the sort need not be done.

Exercise   2.2-1:   Write a subroutine implementing the above method for projection. The sort used must be external since the projected relation is likely to be too large to fit into RAM.

Exercise 2.2-2: Extend your projection subroutine to a high-activity implementation of T-selectors.

μ-Join

The whole family of μ-joins can be included in a single sort-merge implementation. The two operand relations are sorted on the join attributes, then merged together on these attributes. The particular type of μ-join dictates what action to take when tuples of the two relations match or not.

To investigate this more closely, let us join $R(W, X)$ and $S(Y, Z)$ as follows

$$R[X \text{ join } Y]S$$

where *join* represents any one of {**ijoin, ujoin, sjoin, rjoin, ljoin, dljoin, drjoin**}. This is a completely general case, since W, X, Y and Z can be groups of an arbitrary number of attributes. Once R is sorted on W and S is sorted on Y, they are merged according to the algorithm displayed as a flowchart in Exhibit 2.2-1.

This flowchart shows the classical logic for a two-way merge. "X low" means that $(X \text{ in } R) < (Y \text{ in } S)$ for the tuples being considered, while "Y low" means the converse. When X is low, since the relations have been sorted, there is a tuple for R with no matching tuple in S. Thus this tuple will be included in the result, suitably padded with null values, if *join* is **ujoin, sjoin, ljoin** or **dljoin**. The case Y low is treated similarly. When the tuples of R and S match on X and Y respectively, we must output to the result *all* tuples of R with the matching value of X, each combined with *all* tuples of S with the matching value of Y. This is not shown explicitly in the flowchart, and requires a divergence from the traditional merge process which usually assumes that the merge is being done on keys. In most cases values of the join attributes are duplicated over relatively few tuples, and it is usually safe to suppose that one of the relations, say S, has no more tuples for any one value of Y than can fit into RAM. An implementation can cope with the rare violations of this assumption by resorting to multiple passes of the offending part of S. For the majority of cases, then, the merge logic is simply augmented by instructions to load all tuples of S with duplicated values of Y into RAM and to combine each one in turn with any matching tuple of R.

Exhibit 2.2-1 does not specify how to terminate the merge, which we must do when all tuples of both R and S have been read. This is most gracefully done by putting an impossibly high value in the attributes of X or Y when R or S is exhausted. Then the other will always be low until it is finished. A test for this high value must be made at the "match" outcome of the comparison, and the merge terminated when it is found.

Exercise 2.2-3: Write a subroutine to implement μ-join.

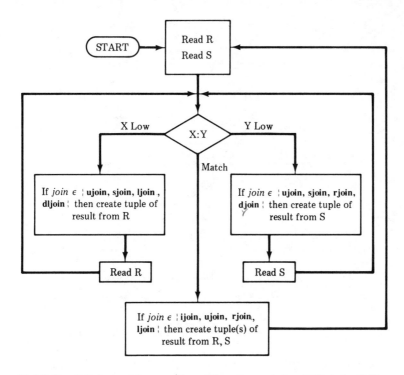

Exhibit 2.2-1   Merge Algorithm for μ-join: R[X *join* Y]S

Exercise   2.2-4:   How can *ijoin* be used to implement an important subcase of selection?

σ-Join

The family of σ-joins can also be handled in a single implementation. Without loss of generality, we consider right away the case of R(W, X) and S(Y, Z) joined to give

$$R[X\ join\ Y]S$$

where *join* is one of $\{\subseteq, \cap, \supseteq, \supset, =, \subset\}$ or one of the complementary symbols, $\{\textbf{not} \subseteq, \textbf{not}\ \cap, \textbf{not} \supseteq, \textbf{not} \supset, \textbf{not} =, not \subset\}$.

We sort R on X within W and S on Y within Z. Then, for each value w in W **in** R) and each z in (Z **in** S) we do the merge of R_w with S_z shown in Exhibit 2.2-2. All this merge does is set one of three logical variables to **false** for each possible outcome of the comparison. At the end of the merge, a tuple of the result, with value x, is output if the following correspondence holds between *join* and the three logical variables of "test."

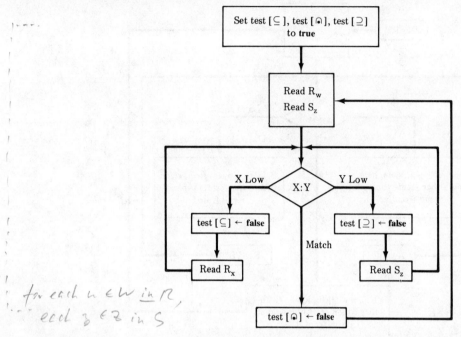

for each $w \in W$ in R,
each $z \in Z$ in S

Exhibit   2.2-2   Merge Algorithm σ-Join: $R\lceil X join Y \rceil S$. This must be placed within loops for each value **w** and each value **z**.

join	condition	*join*	condition
$\subseteq$	test $[\subseteq]$	**not** $\subseteq$	**not** test $[\subseteq]$
$\circleftharpoondown$	test $[\circleftharpoondown]$	**not** $\circleftharpoondown$	**not** test $[\circleftharpoondown]$
$\supseteq$	test $[\supseteq]$	**not** $\supseteq$	**not** test $[\supseteq]$
$\supset$	test $[\not\subseteq]$ **and** test $[\supseteq]$	**not** $\supset$	**not** (test $[\not\subseteq]$ **and** test $[\supseteq]$)
$=$	test $[\subseteq]$ **and** test $[\supseteq]$	**not** $=$	**not** (test $[\subseteq]$ **and** test $[\supseteq]$)
$\subset$	test $[\subseteq]$ **and** test $[\not\supseteq]$	**not** $\subset$	**not** (test $[\subseteq]$ **and** test $[\supseteq]$)

Thus if X goes low at any point of the merge it is impossible for $R_w \subseteq S_z$, since R_w contains a value of X not found in (Y **in** S). For this reason, test $[\subseteq]$ is set to **false** for this value, (w, z), and (w, z) cannot be included in $R[X \subseteq Y]S$. A similar argument applies to each of the other cases.

We are not entitled to assume that S_z can fit entirely in RAM, although this is a likely case. When it does, we can get away with reading S only once, rather than once for each value of (W **in** R).

Exercise   2.2-5:   Write a subroutine to implement σ-join.

An implementation of σ-join is possible which avoids repeated scans of the relation S, and whose basis is just the natural join. It requires that we be able to count the number of different values of X for each value of W in $R(W, X)$ and in $R[X \textbf{ ijoin } Y]S$, and depends on the following facts.

$$R_w \supseteq S_z \text{ is equivalent to } |R_w \cap S_z| = |S_z|$$
$$R_w \subseteq S_z \text{ is equivalent to } |R_w \cap S_z| = |R_w|$$
$$R_w \text{ ⊚ } S_z \text{ is equivalent to } |R_w \cap S_z| = 0 \tag{2.2-1}$$

and obvious extensions for $R_w \supset S_z$, $R_w \not\supset S_z$, $R_w = S_z$, etc.

An algorithm is

1) Count the number of values of X for each value of W in R (this involves sorting R on W, unless R is multipaged—see Section 3.2-2).

2) Find $R[X \textbf{ ijoin } Y]S$ (this involves resorting R on X as well as S on Y).

3) Count the number of values of X for each value of W in $R[X \textbf{ ijoin } Y]S$ (again, a sort on W).

4) Merge the results of (1) and (3), selecting values of (W, Z) which satisfy the appropriate condition in Expression 2.2-1 above.

For example, using R and S from Exhibit 2.1-8, ($|S| = 2$),

R:W	# of X	R ijoin S : W	X	R ijoin S : W	# of X
a	3	c	2	c	2
b	2	d	2	d	2
c	2	e	2	e	2
d	5	c	4	f	1
e	3	d	4		
f	1	e	4		
		f	4		

Thus $R \supseteq S = \{c, d, e\}$, $R \subseteq S = \{c, f\}$, $R \text{ ⊚ } S = \{a, b\}$, $R \supset S = \{d, e\}$, $R \not\supset S = \{a, b, c, f\}$, $R = S = \{c\}$, etc. as before.

Under certain circumstances, this approach might be preferable to the merge logic of Exhibit 2.2-2.

Range Joins

To implement the two range joins using sort-merge techniques, we can use the one flowchart shown in Exhibit 2.2-3 provided that we previously sort the operand relations in ascending order (the usual) if *join* is **lojoin** or in descending order if *join* is **hijoin**. The merging process is terminated as soon as the left-hand operand (R in Exhibit 2.2-3) is exhausted. Exactly one tuple of the result is produced for each tuple in R.

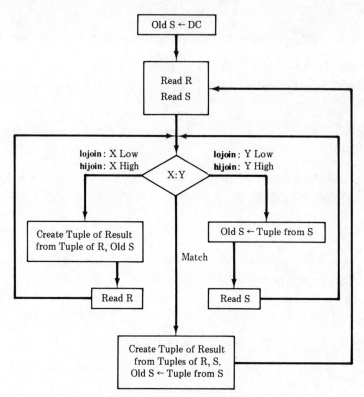

Exhibit   2.2-3   Merge Algorithm for Range Join: R[X *join* Y]S. NB, relations sorted in descending order for **hijoin.**

Exercise   2.2-6:   Write a subroutine to implement the range joins.

2.2-2   Multipaging Techniques

As a data storage structure, multipaging is at the other extreme of sophistication from sequential flat files. It is interesting to see what it can do for us in implementing the relational algebra. We start by using some one-, two- and three-dimensional diagrams to review the possibilities. We will assume that the relevant set of attributes—i.e., the projected attributes or the join attributes—are represented by one of the axes. This situation is trivially generalizable to any case in which the relevant attributes are associated with axes of the multipage space. Cases in which some of the relevant do not contribute to the basis of the space are hybrid cases: some advantage may be taken of the multipaging, but not full advantage.

In each of the operations depicted in Exhibit 2.2-4, multipaging breaks the implementation problem into subproblems of the sizes of the segments or even the blocks. In projection, each segment of axis X is projected in turn. In the μ-join, each block of R is matched with each block of S in the same segment of the join attribute Z. (The Exhibit shows absent values of Z **in** R and Z **in** S in an exaggerated way, spanning a whole segment, in order to indicate the effect of the μ-join.) In the σ-join, each X-segment of R is processed against each Y-segment of S.

The diagrams are oversimplified, in that the segment boundaries shown match each other exactly across different relations. This conflicts with the fact that the multipaging algorithms generate boundaries tailored to the distribution of each individual relation. Thus we cannot expect the operand relations in μ-join and σ-join to segment the join axis, Z, the same way. Nor can we expect that the partitions of axes X or Y of the various operand relations will give efficiently placed boundaries for the result relations.

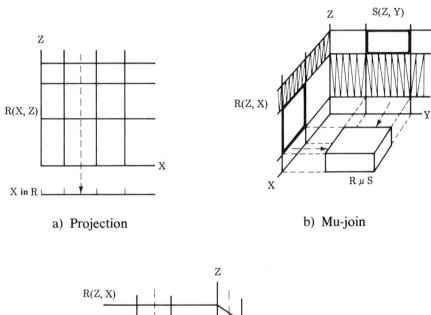

a) Projection

b) Mu-join

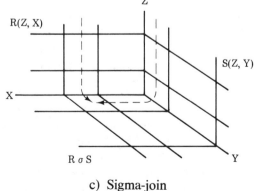

c) Sigma-join

Exhibit 2.2-4 Multipaging Implementation for the Regional Algebra

In fact, it does not seem possible to make multipaging participate in the algebraic nature of the operations. Ideally we should have algorithms which take multipaged operands and, in the most effective way, generate a multipaged result. The result can in fact be multipaged only by post-processing, such as adding a streamlined dynamic multipaging procedure. (It can be streamlined because the result tuples can be generated systematically with respect to the values of the result attributes.) If we accept this limitation, we do not need to worry about the mismatch between operand and result multipaging. Only the discontinuity of boundaries between join operands now concerns us. In the case of σ-join, mismatched Z-segments do not have a serious effect because the obvious implementation is to merge each X-segment with each Y-segment: merging can cope easily with mismatches. Mismatched Z-segments do not greatly aggravate the μ-join either, except that the problem aggravated is already serious enough that multipaging gives only small benefits, as we shall see.

We shall now elaborate multipaging techniques for select, project, σ-join and μ-join.

Select

We have not discussed selection so far because sequential search is unlikely to give an acceptable implementation—although it does give the most versatile implementation, in that any T-selector can be satisfied by scanning every tuple of the relation. Multipaging reduces significantly the search space required by any T-selector while preserving most of the flexibility of the exhaustive scan.

The multipage data structure is so simple that the implementation algorithms are trivial and we will be content to illustrate the retrieval of various subclasses of T-selector by example. The examples will be drawn from TOYMAKERS as multipaged in Exhibit 1.2-19.

The *exact match* query is satisfied by a single tuple and ideally costs one access. With multipaging it costs about $\pi \simeq 1$ accesses on the average. For instance, to find the tuple for Tricycles made by Mettal Toys, we look up Mettal Toys in the MAKER index and Tricycle in the TOY index (this costs no accesses since the indexes are assumed to be in RAM) and the correct block is immediately indicated to us.

The *partial match* query specifies k of the d attributes forming the multipage axes, k < d, and requires access to all blocks in the k-dimensional subspace. Multipaging identifies this subspace exactly and retrieves only those blocks in it. For example, find all makers of Locomotives. (If the k attributes contain a key, one tuple will satisfy the request and only one block needs to be accessed. By itself, multipaging will search too many blocks—but not the whole file. It is easy to add an index to the multipage data structure to reduce this search to the one relevant block: these techniques are detailed when we discuss low activity.)

The *range query* specifies a range of values to be sought on one or more attributes. For example, find toys made by Canloco, Dink or Extrafun. Because multipaging preserves the order of the attribute values, this is no more difficult than the match queries, and is answered in the ideal minimum number of accesses.

The *restriction* seeks tuples satisfying an ordering comparison on two attributes, e.g., MAKER < TOY. (This sort of query is more suitable for attributes drawn from the same domain.) If the attributes are both multipage axes, this T-selector identifies triangular or diagonal regions of the multipage space. The blocks in these regions should be accessed and are easily determined in a multipage data structure.

Conjunctions, disjunctions or *negations* of any of the above classes of query are easily handled using multipaging. Special cases: an exact match is a conjunction of partial matches; a range query is a disjunction of partial or exact matches.

Exercise   2.2-7:   Specify a general algorithm to implement T-selectors assuming all attributes specified by the selector have corresponding multipage axes.

Project

It is plausible to assume that the computer has enough RAM to allocate one bit for each possible value of any one segment of a multipage axis. When this assumption holds, the projection operation need only apply the following steps to each segment of the axis whose attribute is being projected. Set all bits to zero, then scan each block, setting bits to one if the corresponding value of the attribute is found on the block. The values finally in the projection are just those that have been found in the segments.

This procedure can be extended to implement projections on many attributes if all attributes have associated axes in the multipage space. RAM will be more crowded.

If RAM is overcrowded, this method will not work, and we must resort to sort-merge techniques. Multipaging benefits us a little even here, since we only need to sort one segment at a time. If there are f segments of n/f blocks each, the cost of sorting all f individually is $f(n/f) \log (n/f) = n(\log n - \log f)$, a small reduction from the $n \log n$ required to sort all n blocks at once.

Exercise   2.2-8:   Give the algorithm to implement Project with multipaging.

Sigma Join

The σ-join of Exhibit 2.2-4 requires comparing the set of Z-values for each X-value with that for each Y-value. This is best implemented by a merge on Z-values of each X-segment with Z-values of each Y-segment. If we have enough

RAM to allocate two bits for each pair (x, y) of possible X and Y values, we can keep track of the three basic results, test [⊆], test [⋒] and test [⊇] (see Exhibit 2.2-2), as we do the merge block by block. In this case, σ-join can be implemented without sorting.

For σ-joins with many attributes other than the join attributes, or when RAM is overcrowded, the above remarks for projection apply.

Exercise   2.2-9:   Specify the details of the σ-join algorithm for multipaged relations.

Mu Join

Multipaging offers two different ways of implementing the μ-join. One is to sort each segment of the join axis (Z in Exhibit 2.2-4b) and merge in the usual way. This has the advantage of reducing the sort cost by n log f accesses, as for project, where there are f segments of the Z axis. The second way is to avoid sorting but to compare every X block from R with every Y block from S in the Z segment. This method is much more likely to exceed RAM capacity than the first, and so to require repeated accesses to the same block. This is because the assumption, in the sort-merge method, that all tuples of the smaller relation for a given value of Z can fit into RAM is much weaker than the corresponding assumption required for the method without sorting, namely that all tuples of the smaller relation for a given *set* of values of Z—corresponding to the Z segment—can fit into RAM. The second method is further undermined when the Z segments for R do not coincide with the Z segments for S, a situation which does not affect the sort-merge method at all.

The best bet is probably to take advantage of the pre-sort offered by multipaging to speed up the sort-merge method.

2.2-3   Techniques for Low Activity

It is likely that multipaging methods cannot be improved on for implementing individual full projections, σ-joins and μ-joins. For selection we have already indicated that secondary indexes can significantly improve those types of search that result in only a few tuples. We called these searches *low-activity* processes in Chapter 1.2. We now discuss briefly some methods for some of the relational algebra operations that are faster than sort-merge or multipaging techniques under special circumstances.

These special circumstances usually require that a key of the relation be involved. For instance, projection on a key, whether low-activity or not, does not require a check for duplicates and so does not require sorting. Selection on a key is, of course, a low-activity process, and is best implemented by a secondary index unless the attributes in the key coincide exactly with the attributes defining the multipage space. The μ-join, $R \mu S$, of $R(X, Y)$ with $S(Y, Z)$, where $X \rightarrow Y$ and $X \rightarrow Z$ and where a selection has already been performed on X, is a frequent special case that needs the paraphernalia of neither sort-merge nor multipaging. The σ-join, $R \sigma S$, of $R(X, Y)$ and $S(Y, Z)$ with $X \rightarrow Y$, is trivial in that it boils down either to a natural composition or to natural composition followed by projection.

In Chapter 1.2 we have discussed secondary indexes in detail. Here we show how they can be used for low-activity μ-joins. Consider the two relations shown in Exhibit 2.2-5 and their indexes. A natural join after selecting Andrea Porter would use the index on PERSONNEL to look up tuple 4 and find the Gluing DEPT. Looking up Gluing in the CORPORATE index gives tuple 1 and the Manufacturing DIVISION. Thus the select and join give the single tuple (Andrea Porter, Gluing, Manufacturing).

Another natural join involving selection, but not necessarily keys, benefits from secondary indexes which are combined to form a *mutual index*. Here the selection is done on the join attributes. Suppose we selected ORD# = 4 in the relations ORDERS (ORD#, CUSTOMER, SALESMAN) and ORDLINE

Exhibit   2.2-5.   Two Relations and Their Indexes

PERSONNEL

	EMP	DEPT	
(			)
0	Eric Brakeman	British	
1	Toby Conductor	Assembling	
2	Natacha Engineer	American	
3	Patrick Fireman	Assembling	
4	Andrea Porter	Gluing	
5	Hannah Trainman	American	

a) Personnel file

CORPORATE

	DEPT	DIVISION	
(			)
0	Assembling	Manufacturing	
1	Gluing	Manufacturing	
2	American	Sales	
3	British	Sales	

b) Corporate structure

EMP

Eric Brakeman	0
Toby Conductor	1
Natacha Engineer	2
Patrick Fireman	3
Andrea Porter	4
Hannah Trainman	5

c) PERSONNEL Index on EMP

DEPT

American	2
Assembling	0
British	3
Gluing	1

d) CORPORATE Index on DEPT.

(ORD#, ASSEMBLY, QTY) (see Exhibit 1.1-2). Then with a suitable index on ORD# for each relation we could find quickly the one relevant tuple from ORDERs and the two from ORDLINE, giving the following result for the select and join:

ORD #	CUSTOMER	SALESMAN	ASSEMBLY	QTY
4	Pennsylvania Railroad	Hannah Trainman	Car	37
4	Pennsylvania Railroad	Hannah Trainman	Toy Train	11

If we assume tuple numbers from 0 to 7 for ORDERS and tuples 0 to 14 for ORDLINE in the order shown in Exhibit 1.1-2, the *mutual index* on ORD# for the two relations would be that shown in Exhibit 2.2-6. Since ORD# is not a key of ORDLINE, there is more than one entry in most of the →ORDLINE column. If there are too many entries, the activity ceases to be low and it becomes preferable to multipage the relation, select and then use sort-merge to implement the join.

Exhibit 2.2-6. Mutual Index on ORD# for ORDERS, ORDLINE.

→ORDERS	ORD#	→ORDLINE
6	1	8, 13
2	2	2
1	3	1, 4, 12
0	4	0, 11
4	5	5, 9
7	6	10
3	7	3, 6, 14
5	8	7

Exercise   2.2-10:   State the necessary conditions for a natural join to be a low-activity process.

2.2-4   Techniques for Algebraic Expressions

When we combine individual operations into an expression of the relational algebra, the opportunities for streamlining the implementation increase. The complications also increase, and, in view of the fact that practical expressions rarely involve more than a select, a project and one dyadic operation (see Chapters 5.1, 6.1), it may not be worthwhile to invest too much effort in studying these opportunities. In this section we content ourselves with noticing one or two aspects and we do not attempt to investigate general rules.

● ● ●

The first thing we can notice is that different algebraic expressions may be equivalent. This leads to opportunities to *optimize* an expression by transforming it into a cheaper equivalent—for instance by rearranging the order of the operations. As an example of this, consider the expression

ROUTING **ijoin** TEAMS **ijoin** SALARY .

Since intersection join is associative, we do not need to use any brackets and either ROUTING **ijoin** TEAMS or TEAMS **ijoin** SALARY can be done first. The relations are ROUTING (TEAM:2, ASSEMBLY:10, EQUIP:14, HOURS:1), TEAMS (TEAM:2, EMP:15) and SALARY (EMP:15, WAGE:2) where the keys are underlined and the notation :b gives the size of each attribute in bytes. Let us investigate the differences in cost for sample data.

ROUTING	(TEAM	ASSEMBLY	EQUIP	HOURS)
	A	Car	Gluset	24
	A	Caboose	Gluset	8
	PT	Base	Wheel Jig	16
	T	Toy Train	String Stapler	24
	AP	Body	Gluset	8
	P	Locomotive	Wheel Jig	16

SALARY (	EMP	WAGE)	TEAMS	(TEAM	EMP	)
	Andrea Porter	8.00		AP	Andrea Porter	
	Toby Conductor	7.50		AP	Patrick Fireman	
	Patrick Fireman	6.00		PT	Patrick Fireman	
				PT	Toby Conductor	
				A	Andrea Porter	
				P	Patrick Fireman	
				T	Toby Conductor	

The sizes of the two alternative intermediate results are

ROUTING **ijoin** TEAMS	8 tuples × 42 bytes
TEAMS **ijoin** SALARY	7 tuples × 19 bytes

From this, it is clearly preferable to compute TEAMS **ijoin** SALARY as a first step: one of the two equivalent expressions is significantly cheaper in computation and intermediate storage requirements.

To perform the above kind of optimization requires a method for estimating the number of tuples in the result of an algebraic operation. Such a method is described in Section 2.3-2. In the above example, of course, we obtained the sizes by computing the two joins, a method which hardly helps us to minimize the cost.

Some general remarks can be made about optimization through expression rearrangement. Since the objective is to minimize the size of intermediate results, it is clear that selection operations should be performed at the earliest possible moment, since selection eliminates tuples—often *most* tuples—from its operand. Projection is not so clear, since it may involve a sort to eliminate duplicates. In unsophisticated implementations, projections should be postponed until the final operation. It may be possible to *trim* a relation, however, to eliminate unnecessary attributes without checking for duplicates. Trimming is projection retaining duplicate tuples: the result is not in general a relation.

As an example of trimming, suppose we wanted the following projection of our earlier example:

ASSEMBLY, WAGE, HOURS **in** (ROUTING **ijoin** TEAMS **ijoin** SALARY).

We can trim EMP from TEAMS **ijoin** SALARY to reduce the size after the join to 7 tuples × 4 bytes. Note that this is not a projection since two employees may have the same wage: for some final computation not indicated here (see Exercise 5.1-4) we may need to distinguish the wages of these two employees. We can trim EQUIP from ROUTING and this *is* a projection because EQUIP is not in the key of ROUTING. The size of ROUTING drops from 6 tuples × 27 bytes to 6 tuples × 13 bytes.

We can eliminate intermediate results by *combining* operations. All successive selections on the same relation can be combined, as can all successive projections on a single relation. Indeed, the definition of the T-selector suggests that selections and projections should be combined: this should be tempered by the considerations about project we have just mentioned.

Here is an example of how joins can be combined. In

PRICE **ijoin** PARTPROFIT **ijoin** ORDLINE

the relations are PRICE (ASSEMBLY:10, FGPRICE:2), PARTPROFIT (ASSEMBLY:10, PPROFIT:2) and ORDLINE (ORD#:1, ASSEMBLY:10, QTY:1). The two joins are on the universally common attribute, ASSEMBLY, and can be done all together, after sorting, using a three-way merge. This eliminates calculating any of PRICE **ijoin** PARTPROFIT (4 tuples × 14 bytes), PRICE **ijoin** ORDLINE (15 tuples × 14 bytes) or PARTPROFIT **ijoin** ORDLINE (15 tuples × 14 bytes) as intermediate products. (The numbers of tuples in the sizes are derived from the sample data in Section 5.1-4.)

Exercise   2.2-11:   Determine all properties of the relational operators of Chapter 2.1 relevant to determining equivalence of arbitrary expressions—such as commutativity, associativity, distributivity.

Exercise   2.2-12:   Devise an algorithm which finds the cheapest among any set of equivalent expressions given an estimate of the sizes of the intermediate results.

• • •

A second thing we can notice about algebraic expressions is that we do not necessarily have to complete one operation before starting the next. Instead, tuples can be *pipelined* from one operation to the next as they are created by the first operation. Where pipelining is possible, it saves the work of creating and then reading the intermediate result, and it saves the storage space for the intermediate result. A pipeline can connect several operations but must stop at an operation which needs to sort or process the data into a different sequence.

Of the two categories of implementation techniques for the relational algebra, sort-merge and multipaging, multipaging is more suited for pipelining because it requires less sorting and so the pipelines can be longer. However, pipelining can work just as well for sort-merge implementations if the relations can be sorted in advance. We now give a fairly elaborate example of pipelining in either of these implementations involving two projections, σ-joins and an intersection join.

The example is summarized in Exhibit 2.2-7, which we now explain. The circled letters $T, \ldots, Y$ are the attributes and there is an additional attribute Z which has the values 0 or 1. The relations on these attributes correspond to the cubical volumes or square faces (which could represent the multipage spaces) as follows (keys underlined):

A (Z, Y, <u>X, W</u>)
B (Z, <u>X, W</u>)   B ← Z, X, W **in** A
C (<u>X, V</u>)
D (<u>Z, W, V</u>)   D ← C **div** B   (i.e. C $\supseteq$ B)
E (<u>W</u>, U)
F (<u>Z, V</u>, U)   F ← E **icomp** D   (i.e. E $\not\supseteq$ D)
G (U,<u>T</u>)
H (<u>Z, V, T</u>, U)   H ← G **ijoin** F
I (<u>V, T</u>, U)   I ← V, T, U **where** (select values of V, T, U with
                                          2 different values of Z) **in** H

The result, I, is thus the value of a complicated expression involving A, C, E and G. You should identify the plane or volume corresponding to each of the above relations. Tuples are indicated either by an asterisk or by a 0 or 1 in the corresponding location.

We can use Exhibit 2.2-7 to follow the pipelining. We must do the projection B ← Z, X, W **in** A in the order X within W. (This can be either the order on which A has been sorted or else it can be the order of scanning the multipage space. If we were sorting, we would probably use Y within X within W within Z. With multipaging, to keep the number of passes of A down to 1, the different values of Z would be processed within X within W.) With this processing order, an X-column of B can be compared with each X-column of C as soon as it is built up, giving a V-row of D ← C **div** B. At this point, the pipeline must stop, because to calculate F ← E **icomp** D, we will need the order W within V and not V within W, which has just been produced. So we must build up an intermediate result, either in multipage form or to be sorted. We must stop again at F, because calculating

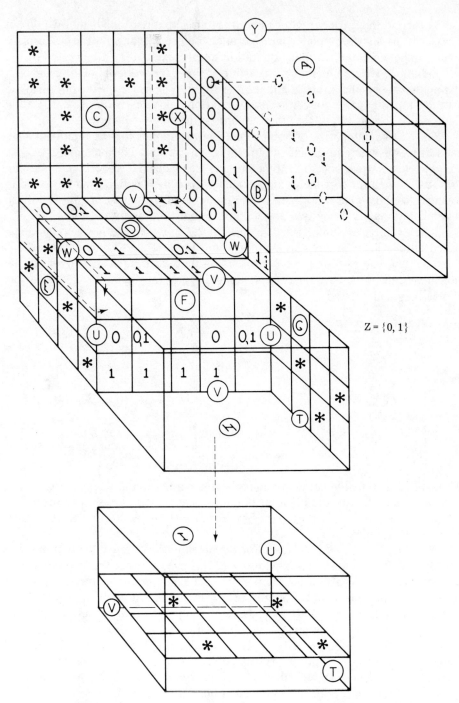

Exhibit 2.2-7 Pipelining a Relational Algebra Expression

H ← G **ijoin** F requires sorting. No sort is needed for the final projection, since it includes a key and duplicates are not possible. A sort may be needed, however, for the operation of selecting values of V, T, U with both values of Z: not for multipaging, if done as suggested above, but certainly for sort-merge.

Thus the six operations shown are performed using only three or four pipelines.

Exercise   2.2-13:   How would the number of pipelines change if the key were U instead of T in G?

Exercise   2.2-14:   Can you rearrange the sequence of operations to reduce the cost of evaluating I from A, C, E and G?

Exercise   2.2-15:   What can you say about the keys and functional dependences generated by arbitrary sequences of relational algebra operations such as in the example?

Review Questions and Exercises, Chapter 2.2

2.2-16 How many good ways can you think of to eliminate duplicate tuples from a relation?

2.2-17 Is there a better way to implement the natural join than the one described in the text?

2.2-18 Express the merge logic of Exhibit 2.2-2 in algorithmic form.

2.2-19 Give three methods of implementing the σ-join. Which is fastest?

2.2-20 A file of n = 100,000 blocks is multipaged 400×250. How many passes of the file are saved when sorting it on the first attribute using the multipaged version as opposed to a conventional sort of the whole file? Assume a 20-way merge.

2.2-21 A file of n = 100,000 blocks is multipaged 400×250. Assuming $V/f =$ constant, how many different values along each axis would be the maximum permitting a 1-pass projection using 1000 bytes of RAM?

COST ANALYSIS

This section has two parts. In the first we argue that no-one can do better than sort-merge to implement the natural join. In the second, we give a methodology to estimate the sizes of the relations resulting from most of the operations introduced in Sections 2.1-2 and 2.1-3.

2.3-1   Sort-Merge is Best for Natural Join

The sort-merge implementations are very simple. Now we will see how good they are, particularly in the case of the natural join. The cheapest possible way of computing the natural join will, in any case, require us to write each tuple of the result. The sort-merge implementation adds two more costs: sorting each operand relation and, in the merge, reading each tuple of each operand relation. The dominant cost is sorting and we must ask whether sorting can profitably be avoided. We must also ask if we need to read each operand in its entirety.

It is easy to imagine examples in which the natural join can be calculated at far less cost than by sorting and merging. For instance if we were computing R **ijoin** S for $R(X, Y)$ and $S(Y, Z)$ and Y **in** R = {a, c, e, g} while Y **in** S = {b, d, f} and *if we knew* that the intersection of these two sets was empty, we would have the result, ϕ, at no cost whatsoever. The important caveat, however, is "if we knew." We must ask how much it will *cost* us to know. In this case, if we are not told by some previously given integrity constraint, the cost of knowing is the cost of sorting each relation and merging. The basis of our argument in this section will be that, apart from prior knowledge given to us by integrity constraints, the cost of knowing that a method cheaper than sort-merge is applicable generally exceeds the cost of sorting and merging.

We start by investigating the optimal join of two relations with arbitrarily ordered tuples. This will lead us to introduce *mutual clustering* as a necessary condition for a join to have minimum cost. Sorting is the only known way to achieve mutual clustering, and has the advantage that each relation can be sorted on the join attributes independently of the other. To save ourselves the expense of sorting, we need a method of detecting mutual clustering that is cheaper than sorting and also a join algorithm that takes advantage of the mutual clustering. Merging is the only known way to make use of mutual clustering and merging works only for the special form of mutual clustering produced by sorting.

To aid our thought, we present the join of two relations as a matrix. This is best described by a trivial example which the reader can extend in his imagination. Suppose the relations WAREHOUSEMEN and INVENTORY of Section 2.1-3 were not conveniently presented in order of FLOOR but were arranged some other way. Exhibit 2.3-1 displays the two relations, in another order, as a matrix with the tuples of INVENTORY, down the side, heading rows and the tuples of WAREHOUSEMEN, along the top, heading columns. (Thus INVENTORY is shown in the traditional table form while WAREHOUSEMEN appears as a *horizontal* table with STOCKMAN being the upper row and FLOOR the lower row.) The entries in the matrix are 1 if the two relations have matching values of FLOOR. The matrix thus represents the natural join.

Exhibit 2.3-1. Natural Join of INVENTORY with WAREHOUSEMAN

		Dan	Jan	Joe	Moe	Nan
		2	2	1	1	2
Computer	2	1	1			1
Snowmobile	1			1	1	
Tractor	1			1	1	
Video Disk	2	1	1			1

Since relations are assumed to be too big for RAM and to require secondary storage, the connections between tuples interest us less than the connections between the *blocks* on which the tuples are stored. The dashed lines in Exhibit 2.3-1 show how WAREHOUSEMEN and INVENTORY might be divided up on two blocks each and how these divisions affect the connections required to form the natural join. The connections between the pairs of blocks of INVENTORY and WAREHOUSEMEN are shown in the *pair-page* graph of Exhibit 2.3-2. The blocks of INVENTORY are denoted r_1, r_2 and those of WAREHOUSEMEN are s_1, s_2. A node of the graph corresponds to a connected pair, (r_i, s_j), of blocks. Clearly, in this example, every block of INVENTORY must be compared with every block of WAREHOUSEMEN in order to effect the join.

The edges of the graph in Exhibit 2.3-2 give one of the optimal paths required to form the join. The graph is interpreted as follows. First the pair of blocks r_1 and s_1 is read (diagonal edge from corner). Then block s_1 is swapped for block s_2 (horizontal edge). Next, block r_1 is swapped for r_2 (vertical edge). Finally block s_2

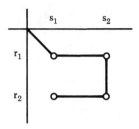

Exhibit   2.3-2.   Page-Pair Graph for Join of Exhibit 2.3-1.

is swapped for s_1. Thus every block of INVENTORY is compared with every block of WAREHOUSEMEN. The cost, in terms of page accesses, is s = 2 (for r_1, s_1) plus 1 (for s_2) plus 1 (for r_2) plus 1 (for s_1). A horizontal or vertical edge costs 1 access while a diagonal edge costs 2. The optimal path is clearly one which minimizes the number of diagonal edges.

Exercise   2.3-1:   Show that the problem of finding the optimal page-pair graph for an arbitrary join is NP-complete.

It turns out to be very difficult to find the optimal path (Exercise 2.3-1), but this does not concern us so much here. We look instead at the situation when the relations are sorted on the join attribute, FLOOR. Exhibits 2.3-3 and 2.3-4 show respectively the matrix and the page-pair graph for the join. The blocking has been arranged to give the best possible page-pair graph, diagonal in form. From this example it is easy to see, qualitatively speaking, that if the relations are sorted on the join attribute, the nodes are inclined to lie on or close to the diagonal of the page-pair graph. Otherwise they will be scattered all over the graph and there will be many more nodes. More quantitatively, if there are n blocks in each relation, there will be on the order of n nodes in the page-pair graph for sorted relations, and on the order of n^2 nodes in the graph for unsorted relations. (This last statement must be hedged with significant reservations; it is quite possible for the graph for

Exhibit   2.3-3.   Natural Join of Sorted INVENTORY, WAREHOUSEMEN

| | | Joe | Moe | Dan | Jan | Nan |
		1	1	2	2	2
Snowmobile	1	1	1			
Tractor	1	1	1			
Computer	2			1	1	1
Video Disk	2			1	1	1

sorted relations to have n^2 nodes. For instance, the join attribute could be constant in both relations. However the graph for sorted relations will never have more nodes than the graph for unsorted relations and will usually have far fewer nodes.)

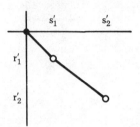

Exhibit   2.3-4.   Page-pair graph for Join of Exhibit 2.3-3

Exercise   2.3-2:   The above discussion assumes that only two buffers are available in RAM, one for each relation participating in the join. Discuss the situation if more than two buffers are provided.

The number of nodes in the page-pair graph depends on the arrangement of data on the blocks. The fact that sorted data gives the fewest nodes motivates a definition of *mutual clustering* as an indication that a minimum-cost join may be possible. Two relations are said to be mutually clustered if their page-pair graph has no more nodes than the page-pair graph of the same two relations when sorted. Mutual clustering is a necessary condition for a minimally cheap join.

We now have two questions to answer. Is there a cheaper way of mutually clustering two relations than by sorting them on the join attributes? Is there a cheap way of detecting that two relations are already mutually clustered? The answer to the first question is that no way cheaper than sorting is known. The answer to the second question is yes—if we know in advance that the relations are sorted. If, however, somebody else sorted them, we can still detect this in one pass of the data by verifying the non-descending (or non-ascending) order of the tuples.

Exercise   2.3-3:   If somebody else sorted the data, can we find out in less than one pass?

Another answer to the second question applies if simple *clustering* of the relations on their join attributes is sufficient to give mutual clustering. Clustering means that common values of the join attributes are grouped together on common blocks for each relation. Any attribute which is a key is clustered by definition; but two relations need not be mutually clustered with respect to their keys. The data may still be arranged so that there are n^2 nodes in the page-pair graph. Only if the number of tuples per value of the join attributes is at least as large as the blocksize does clustering imply mutual clustering. Clustering can be detected in $O(n \log n)$ accesses by building a tree—say a B-tree—and checking that each leaf is never revisited after another leaf has started being filled. This cost is, of course, comparable to sorting.

Detecting mutual clustering in general is as much an open problem as creating two mutually clustered files by means other than sorting. It is likely to be a problem of complexity comparable to the problem of finding optimal paths (Exercise 2.3-1) and is unlikely to be as cheap as sorting.

Exercise 2.3-4:   Suggest a sampling method of detecting mutual clustering in $O(1)$ time.

We conclude that we cannot now improve on sort-merge for calculating the natural join.

2.3-2   Tuple-Density Models of Relations

If we are given one or two relations and an algebraic operator involving them, we do not know how big the result will be. It is important to be able to estimate the size of the result since costs depend on the amounts of data. For instance we considered in Section 2.2-4 the problem of optimizing ROUTING **ijoin** TEAMS **ijoin** SALARY and discovered, by actually evaluating the alternatives, that TEAMS **ijoin** SALARY was smaller than ROUTING **ijoin** TEAMS, so that using ROUTING **ijoin** (TEAMS **ijoin** SALARY) was cheaper than using (ROUTING **ijoin** TEAMS) **ijoin** SALARY.

How can we estimate sizes before evaluating? This section describes a way to model the data stored on secondary memory by data stored entirely in RAM. To make this model useful, we describe the operations on it which correspond to the various algebraic operations on relations.

The Tuple-Density Model

Our model, like multipaging, derives from a view of an m-ary relation as an arrangement of points (tuples) in an m-dimensional space. The idea is simply to build an m-dimensional histogram whose cells are integers which give the number of points in the corresponding region of the space. Unlike multipaging, which seeks to equalize the number of points in each cell, the cells of the tuple-density histogram all have the same sizes, measured in terms of the numbers of different values of each attribute. That is, a relation $R(X, Y, Z)$ with 50 different X-values, 100 different Y-values and 20 different Z-values could be modelled by a $5 \times 10 \times 5$

histogram, in which case each cell would span 10 different X-values, 10 different Y-values and 4 different Z-values.[1]

The histogram therefore tells us the density of the tuples in the m-dimensional space. We use it to calculate the histogram of the relation which results from an algebraic operation. To do this we make two assumptions about how the tuples are distributed within each cell. First we suppose that tuples are distributed uniformly. Thus in a $10 \times 10 \times 4$ cell containing 27 tuples, the probability that there is a tuple at any of the $10 \times 10 \times 4 = 400$ possible sites is considered to be $27/400$. Second, whenever two cells (perhaps from different relations) are used together in a computation—for instance, to estimate the size of a join—the distributions of tuples in the cells are assumed to be independent. These assumptions are simplifications, of course, but with enough cells they will probably not cause significant errors. The consequence of this approach is, however, that the tuple-density histogram calculated for the result of an operation consists of *expected values* in each cell. Where possible, we also indicate how to calculate *variances* so that the precision of the result can be accessed.

Now we introduce, by examples, some notation for the tuple-density histograms. The relations $R(X, Y, Z)$ will have a set of cells $\{(x, y, z)\}$. The value of the count in cell (x, y, z) will be denoted $c_{xyz}^{XYZ}(R)$, or, if the context is clear, variously as $c_{xyz}(R)$, c_{xyz}^{XYZ} or c_{xyz}. The whole histogram is an array, written $c^{XYZ}(R)$ and abbreviated similarly where unambiguous. We are sometimes interested in *reduced* histograms, involving sums over values of one or more attributes. For example, $c_{xy}^{XY}(R) \overset{\Delta}{=} \sum_{z} c_{xyz}^{XYZ}(R)$. The ultimate reduced histogram consists of one cell which simply counts the number of tuples in the relation, $|R| \overset{\Delta}{=} c(R) = \sum_{x, y, x} c_{xyz}(R)$.

We will now restrict our attention to binary relations, without loss of generality, since any relation of more than one attribute may be considered as a binary relation on two attribute-groups. The relational algebra always operates on binary relations, in this sense, although some operations (project) result in unary relations and some (μ-join) result in ternary relations. We work with three example relations, shown together with typical tuple-density histograms in Exhibit 2.3-5 (R), (S) and (T). The matrix forms of the relations are shown partitioned into cells, for which the counts are given in the histograms. The interior cells have the following

---

[1] What if the number of values is not a multiple of the histogram size? For instance, suppose there were 47 X-values instead of 50 and we still wanted to use a $5 \times 10 \times 5$ histogram. Then there would be a set of cells on one face of the histogram with only 7 different X-values each. Thus we must devise a model in which cells can have varying numbers of different values of each attribute. In the model discussed in this section, only cells on a face of the histogram will differ in size from the majority of (interior) cells. But this raises the possibility that we could build a histogram model with different numbers of values in each cell, i.e., a model that (like multipaging) tries to equalize the number of *tuples* in each cell.

sizes: 3 Z-values, 2 Y-values, 2 X-values and 2 W-values. Thus the cell of $R(Z, Y)$ has $3 \times 2 = 6$ sites, each of which may or may not be occupied by a point (tuple).

It is clear that, given any relation, a tuple-density histogram which fits into RAM can be formed in a single pass of the relation. It may be useful to know the number of different values for each attribute; these can be found directly if the

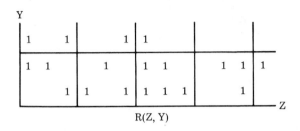

R(Z, Y)

$c^{ZY}(R)$

Exhibit 2.3-5(R).   Example relation $R(Z, Y)$ and tuple-density histogram $c^{ZY}(R)$.

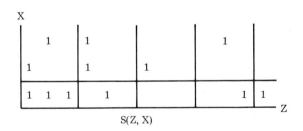

S(Z, X)

$c^{ZX}(S)$

Exhibit 2.3-5(S).   Example relation $S(Z, X)$ and tuple-density histogram $c^{ZX}(S)$.

Exhibit 2.3-5(T). Example relation T(Y, W) and tuple-density histogram $c^{YW}(T)$.

relation is multipaged, or else they can be found by sorting or constructing index trees.

Exercise 2.3-5:   Suppose R bits of RAM are available to hold a tuple-density histogram for a file of N tuples. If the tuple density is perfectly uniform, how many cells, C, should the histogram have and how many bits, b, should there be per cell? In an m-dimensional space, how many values will there be along each axis of each cell?

Exercise 2.3-6:   If RAM holds C cells, what value, C_i, would we use for the number of *segments* into which the histogram divides the ith axis, i = 1, . . . ,m a) to have the same average number of tuples per segment, N/C_i ? b) to give each axis the same segment width, V_i/C_i values, where V_i is the number of different values of the ith attribute?

Projection

The expected value for cell z of the tuple-density histogram of R projected on Z is

$$c_z^Z (Z \text{ in } R) = \ell \left[1 - \binom{k\ell - k}{c_z} \middle/ \binom{k\ell}{c_z} \right] \xrightarrow[k \to \infty]{} \ell [1 - ((\ell - 1)/\ell) \uparrow c_z]$$

$$(2.3\text{-}1)$$

where $c_z = c_z^Z(R) = \sum_y c_{zy}^{ZY}(R)$. The number of different values of attribute Z in cell z is ℓ and k is the number of different values of Y in R: the limit $k \to \infty$ corresponds to selection with replacement in the derivation of the expected value; it gives an adequate approximation except when m is very small. Compare Equation 2.3-1 with Equation 1.3-22.

Exercise 2.3-7:   Derive Equation 2.3-1.

As an example, we do the projection Z **in** R. Exhibit 2.3-6 shows the actual projection (a), the derived expected value ((b), using m = 3, n = 3 for the first four segments and n = 1 for the last segment) and the approximation of selection with replacement (c). It is evident that the estimates in c should be lower than those in (b), as they are.

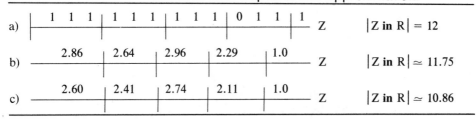

Exhibit 2.3-6. a) Z **in** R   b) c_z^Z(Z **in** R)   c) c_z^Z(Z **in** R) Using Selection with Replacement Approximation.

| | | | | | | | | | | | | | | | | | | |
| a) | 1 | 1 | 1 | 1 | 1 | 1 | 1 | 1 | 1 | 0 | 1 | 1 | 1 | Z | $|Z$ **in** $R| = 12$ |

| | | | | | | | |
| b) | 2.86 | 2.64 | 2.96 | 2.29 | 1.0 | Z | $|Z$ **in** $R| \simeq 11.75$ |

| | | | | | | | |
| c) | 2.60 | 2.41 | 2.74 | 2.11 | 1.0 | Z | $|Z$ **in** $R| \simeq 10.86$ |

In Exhibit 2.3-6 the estimates are sometimes low and sometimes high. It is useful to know how good they are, so we calculate the variance

$$\text{var }(c_z) = \ell \left[1 - \left(\frac{k\ell - k}{c_z} \right) \Big/ \left(\frac{k\ell}{c_z} \right) \right] \quad \left(\frac{k\ell - k}{c_z} \right) \Big/ \left(\frac{k\ell}{c_z} \right) \qquad (2.3\text{-}2)$$

For the example, the standard deviations are shown in Exhibit 2.3-7. We see that the errors are running at around 20%—not bad for such a tiny example. (If we had estimated the size of the projection using a single cell of 3 × 13 values containing 19 tuples, we would have found 11.78 ± 1.19 (10.16 ± 1.49 using selection with replacement) an error of 10%.)

Exhibit 2.3-7. Standard deviations

selection without replacement

| | | | | | | |
| b) | 0.37 | 0.56 | 0.19 | 0.74 | 0 | total = 1.86 |

selection with replacement

| | | | | | | |
| c) | 0.59 | 0.69 | 0.49 | 0.79 | 0 | total = 2.56 |

If we study the ratio of the standard deviation to the mean, we see that it can become very large, but only when the tuple density is very low and the mean is thus small. Thus, almost empty cells can give large errors. These cells do not, however, contribute much to the overall size of the projection. As a function of ℓ, the ration is $O(1/\sqrt{\ell}$: however, it is small for large ℓ. The answer to Exercise 2.3-5 gives some typical values for ℓ, the number of values per axis of each cell.

Exercise   2.3-8:   Derive Equation 2.3-2.

Natural Join

The expected values for cell (z, y, x) of the tuple-density histogram of R **ijoin** S is

$$c_{zyx}^{ZYX} (R \textbf{ ijoin } S) = c_{zy}^{ZY}(R) \times c_{zx}^{ZX}(S)/\ell \qquad (2.3\text{-}3)$$

where ℓ is the number of values in each segment of the common attribute Z. This result assumes that both R and S are segmented in the same way on Z. If instead R and S have overlapping but not identical segments z_1 and z_2 respectively, with ℓ_1 values in z_1, ℓ_2 values in z_2 and ℓ values in $z_1 \cap z_2$, we have

$$c_{z_1\ z_2 yx}^{Z\ YX} (R \textbf{ ijoin } S)= \frac{\ell}{\ell_1 \ell_2} c_{z_1 y}^{ZY}(R) \times c_{z_2 x}^{ZX} (S) \qquad (2.3\text{-}4)$$

Exercise   2.3-9:   Derive Equation 2.3-3.

The variance is given by the rather unwieldy expression

$$\text{var}(c_{zyx}) = \ell \frac{c_{zy}}{\ell_1} \left[\frac{(c_{zy} - 1)(k_1 - 1)}{k_1 \ell_1 - 1} + 1 \right] \frac{c_{zx}}{\ell_2} \left[\frac{(c_{pg} - 1)(k_2 - 1)}{k_2 \ell_2 - 1} + 1 \right]$$

$$- \ell \left(\frac{c_{zy}}{\ell_1} \frac{c_{zx}}{\ell_2} \right)^2 \qquad (2.3\text{-}5)$$

where k_1 and k_2 are respectively the number of Y values in cell (z, y) of R and the number of X values in cell (z, x) of S. Analysis of a simple case ($\ell_1 = \ell_2 = \ell$; $k_1, k_2 \to \infty$) shows that the ratio of standard deviation to mean behaves similarly to that for projection. For large ℓ, this ratio is $\sqrt{(1 + a + b)/\ell\, a\, b}$ where $a = c_{zy}/\ell$ and $b = c_{yx}/\ell$.

Exhibit 2.3-8 shows the natural join R **ijoin** S and the expected histogram c^{ZYX} (R **ijoin** S). There are 18 tuples in the join, while the total, c (R **ijoin** S)

$$\overset{\Delta}{=} \sum_{x,y,x} c_{zyx}^{ZYX} = 17.3,$$ an error of 7%. Equation 2.3-5 gives a total variance of 13.5,

so the result is 17.3 ± 3.7. (If we had used a single 3×13 cell of 19 tuples for R and a single 3×13 cell of 12 tuples for S, we would have 17.5 ± 5.5.)

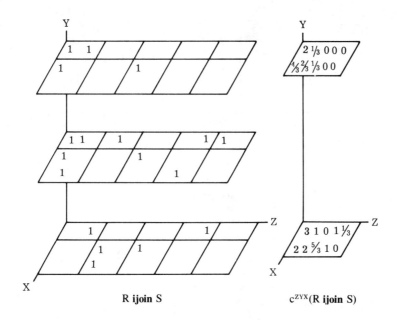

R ijoin S c^{ZYX}(R ijoin S)

Exhibit   2.3-8   The Natural Join of R and S, and the Expected Distribution c^{XYZ}.

Exercise   2.3-10:   Which order of evaluation of R **ijoin** S **ijoin** T is best?

To illustrate Equation 2.3-4 suppose that $R(Z, Y)$ were partitioned 1×3 (i.e., three cells of size 3×5, 3×5, 3×3) and $S(Z, X)$ were partitioned 1×5 (i.e., five cells of size $3 \times 3, 3 \times 3, 3 \times 3, 3 \times 3, 3 \times 1$). Exhibit 2.3-9 shows the relations partitioned this way, the tuple density histograms, the expected tuple density and its variance for the join.

The following extensions of Equation 2.3-4 are useful when multiple joins are to be analyzed. For $j-1$ joins all on the same attribute Z (written $\overset{j}{\bowtie} R_i$ for relations $R_i(Z, Y_i)$ $i = 1, \ldots, j$) the expected tuple density is

$$c_{\underset{i=1}{\overset{j}{\cap} z_i\, y_1\, \ldots\, y_j}}^{Z\ Y_1\, ..\, Y_j}(\overset{j}{\bowtie} R_i) = \frac{\ell}{\ell_1 \ldots \ell_j} \prod^{j} c_{z_i\ y_i}^{Z\ Y_i}(R_i) \qquad (2.3\text{-}6)$$

where ℓ_i is the number of different Z-values in the cell of relation R_i and ℓ is the number of different Z-values in the intersection of cells of each of the j relations. It is nice that the extension turns out to be so simple.

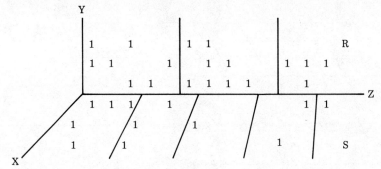

a) Relations R and S. R is partitioned 1×3, S is partitioned 1×5.

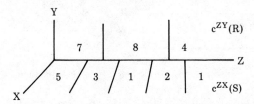

b) Tuple-density histograms for R and S.

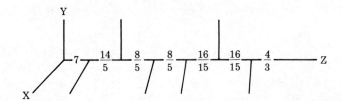

c) Expected histograms for **R ijoin** S. Total = 20.7 ± 4.6

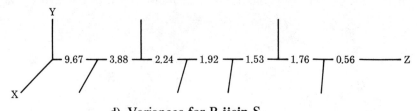

d) Variances for **R ijoin** S.

Exhibit 2.3-9. R **ijoin** S using nonidentical partitions.

If we examine two joins on different attributes, such as (R **ijoin** S) **ijoin** T above, we have

$$c \begin{matrix} Z & Y & X & W \\ z_1 \cap z_2 & y_1 \cap y_2 & x & w \end{matrix} ((R \text{ ijoin } S) \text{ ijoin } T)$$

$$= \frac{k_{13}}{k_1 k_3} \frac{\ell_{12}}{\ell_1 \ell_2} c \begin{matrix} Z & Y \\ z_1 y_1 \end{matrix} (R) \; c \begin{matrix} Z & X \\ z_2 x \end{matrix} (S) \; c \begin{matrix} Y & W \\ y_3 w \end{matrix} (T) \qquad (2.3\text{-}7)$$

where ℓ_{12} is the number of different Z-values in the intersection of Z-partitions for R and S and k_{13} is the number of different Y-values in the intersection of Y-partitions for R and T.

Exercise 2.3-11: Show that Equations 2.3-6 and 2.3-7 result from simply applying Equation 2.3-4 successively to the subexpressions.

μ-Join

The μ-join, as defined in Section 2.1-3, involves a *center*, which is just the natural join, a *left wing* and a *right wing*. These are all present in the union join, so we consider that

$$c \begin{matrix} Z & Y & X \\ z_1 \cap z_2 & y & x \end{matrix} (R \text{ ujoin } S) = \frac{\ell}{\ell_1 \ell_2} c \begin{matrix} Z & Y \\ z_1 y \end{matrix} (R) \; c \begin{matrix} Z & X \\ z_2 x \end{matrix} (S)$$

$$+ \delta_{x, DC} \frac{\ell}{\ell_1} c \begin{matrix} Z & Y \\ z_1 y \end{matrix} (R) \left(\frac{k_2 \ell_2 - k_2}{c_{z_2}^Z (S)} \right) \bigg/ \left(\frac{k_2 \ell_2}{c_{z_2}^Z (S)} \right) \qquad (2.3\text{-}8)$$

$$+ \delta_{y, DC} \frac{\ell}{\ell_2} c \begin{matrix} Z & X \\ z_2 x \end{matrix} (S) \left(\frac{k_1 \ell_1 - k_1}{c_{z_1}^Z (R)} \right) \bigg/ \left(\frac{k_1 \ell_1}{c_{zx_1}^Z (R)} \right)$$

In Equation 2.3-8 the symbol $\delta_{a, DC}$ has the value 1 when a is *DC* ("don't care": see Section 2.1-4) and 0 otherwise. We illustrate Equation 2.3-8 by the example R **ujoin** S before we go further. The center term is just the result we have already shown for the natural join and presents no further problem. The two wing terms can be visualized in the matrix framework of Exhibit 2.3-8 if we add two new planes, X = *DC* (left wing) and Y = *DC* (right wing). Exhibit 2.3-10 shows these planes for R **ujoin** S and the expected numbers of tuples in each cell from Equation (2.3-8). The total in the left wing is 6.44 tuples (the union join actually has 5 tuples in the left wing) and the right wing adds up to 1.08 tuples (actually, none).

Exercise 2.3-12: Derive the right wing term in Equation 2.3-8 in the case where $\ell_1 = \ell_2 = \ell$, $z_1 = z_2 = z$.

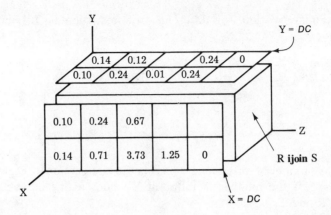

Exhibit   2.3-10.   Left wing ($X = DC$) and right wing ($Y = DC$) planes added R **ijoin** S to give R **ujoin** S. Numbers are expected numbers of tuples.

As the answer to Exercise 2.3-12 shows, Equation 2.3-8 can be approximated by taking the limits as k_1, $k_2 \to \infty$ (selection with replacement). For the example of Exhibit 2.3-10 in these limits, we expect 7.18 tuples in the left wing and 1.84 in the right.

σ-Join

The expected value for cell (x, w) of the tuple-density histogram of R **sup** T is

$$c_{xw}^{XW}(R \text{ sup } T) = mp \prod_{y=1}^{|Y|/n} \left[\sum_k \binom{mn-k}{c_{xy}-k} \binom{n}{k} \binom{np-n}{c_{yw}-k} \right] / \binom{mn}{c_{xy}} \binom{np}{c_{yw}} \tag{2.3-9}$$

where cell (x, w) of R **sup** T has m x-values and p w-values, cell (x, y) of R has m x-values and n y-values and cell (y, w) of T has n y-values and p w-values. (Equation 2.3-9 assumes that $|Y|/n$, the number of segments of Y in the histogram, is an integer: small modifications must be made if it is not, since n will have different values in some cells.)

Exercise   2.3-13:   Derive Equation 2.3-9.

Equation 2.3-9 is unwieldy, so we will consider special cases which give tuple-density histograms for R **sup** V and R **sub** V where V (Y) is a relation on attribute Y only. For instance, c_x (R **sup** V) can be found by changing T to V, c_{yw} (T) to c_y (V) and setting p = 1 in Equation 2.3-9:

$$c_x^X (R \text{ sup } V) = m \prod_y \binom{mn - c_y}{c_{xy} - c_y} / \binom{mn}{c_{xy}}$$

$$= m \prod_{y} \begin{cases} 1 & \text{if } c_y = 0 \\ \prod_{j=0}^{c_y-1} \dfrac{c_{xy} - j}{mn - j} \end{cases}$$

$$\xrightarrow[\substack{m \to \infty \\ c_{xy}/mn \,=\, \text{const.}}]{} \quad m \prod_{y} (c_{xy}/mn)^{c_y} \tag{2.3-10}$$

where the last is the approximation in the limit of selection with replacement.

Similarly C_w (V **sup** R) can be found (by setting n = 1 in Equation 2.3-9) and then turned around to give

$$c_X^X (\text{R sub V}) = m \prod_{y} \binom{mn - n + c_y}{c_{xy}} / \binom{mn}{c_{xy}}$$

$$= m \prod_{y} \begin{cases} 1 & \text{if } c_y = n \\ \prod_{j=0}^{n-c_y-1} (1 - \dfrac{c_{xy}}{mn - j}) \end{cases} \tag{2.3-11}$$

Derivations similar to Equation 2.3-9 followed by specializations to V give us tuple-density histograms for R **sep** V and R **span** V once we see that, for sets A and B, A **sep** B = A $\subseteq$ B' = B $\subseteq$ Y' and A **span** B = B' $\subseteq$ A = A' $\subseteq$ B where the prime means set complementation.

$$c_X^X (\text{R sep V}) = m \prod_{y} \binom{mn - c_y}{c_{xy}} / \binom{mn}{c_{xy}}$$

$$= m \prod_{y} \begin{cases} 1 & \text{if } c_y = 0 \\ \prod_{j=0}^{c_y-1} (1 - \dfrac{c_{xy}}{mn - j}) \end{cases} \tag{2.3-12}$$

$$c_X^X (\text{R span V}) = m \prod_{y} \binom{mn - n + c_y}{c_{xy} - n + c_y} / \binom{mn}{c_{xy}}$$

$$= m \prod_{y} \begin{cases} 1 & \text{if } c_y = n \\ \prod_{j=0}^{n-c_y-1} \dfrac{c_{xy} - 1}{mn - 1} \end{cases} \tag{2.3-13}$$

For the R used already as an example and $V = \{0, 1, 1\}$, we have the following total numbers of tuples, actual and estimated.

	R sup V	R sup V	R sep V	R span V
Actual	2	8	5	7
Estimated	2.33	7.5	5.83	6

Exercise 2.3-14: Derive tuple-density expected values for the σ-joins $R = V$, $R \neq V$, $R \supset V$, $R \subset V$.

2.3-3   Costs of Multipaging

In Section 2.2-2 we discuss various types of query implemented using multipaging. Here we examine *partial matches,* one of the varieties of query permitted by the Select operation. If a relation is multipaged on m attributes with f_i segments of n/f_i blocks on the ith axis, $i = 1, \ldots, m$, and if k of these attributes, $i_1, \ldots, i_k$ are specified in a query, then the number of blocks accessed is

$$n/(f_{i_1} \times \ldots \times f_{i_k}) \qquad (2.3\text{-}14)$$

As a simplification we will suppose that $f_1 = \ldots = f_m = f = \sqrt[m]{n}$: this is what we would expect to put if we did not know the values of f_i, $i = 1, \ldots, m$. Then the number of blocks accessed for a partial match query on k of the m attributes is

$$\frac{n}{f^k} = n \uparrow (1 - \frac{k}{m}) \qquad (2.3\text{-}15)$$

This is just the answer to Exercise 1.2-14. Now we discuss this quantity a little.

First, it is significantly smaller than n: multipaging answers partial match queries in sublinear time. Geometrically it is a subspace of a hypercube, with negligible volume in comparison with the hypercube, as illustrated for the case $k = 2$, $m = 3$ in Exhibit 2.3-11. In practice the geometry is discrete, not continuous, so Equation 2.3-14 is not just a plane or a line but has some volume.

Second, the quantity $n \uparrow (1 - \frac{k}{m})$ has been conjectured (Rivest [1971]) to be the least number of block accesses needed in a partial match query.

Third, in some circumstances, however, this cost is much too high. Suppose that attributes 0 and 1 in Exhibit 2.3-11 form a key. Then, once a query specifies values for these attributes, there is only one tuple satisfying it and only one block access should be needed instead of $n \uparrow (1 - \frac{k}{m})$. In this situation, we are well advised to construct a secondary index for key attributes, as discussed in Section 2.2-3.

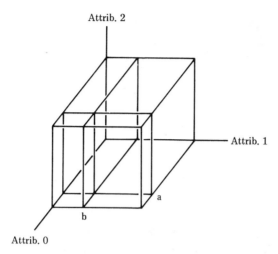

Exhibit 2.3-11. The Partial Match Query (Attrib. 0 = **a and** Attrib. 1 = b) in a Cubical Space.

When k = m in Expressions (2.3-14) and (2.3-15), we have the case of an *exact match* query, costing 1 access (n = $f_1 \times .. \times f_m$). We can use geometrical arguments to get estimates for *range queries* and *restrictions*. Exhibit 2.3-12 shows a range query on two attributes out of three and shows that the number of blocks accessed is just the *volume* of the range query. Exhibit 2.3-13 shows a restriction identifying

two out of three attributes, and shows that $n \uparrow (1 - \frac{1}{m})$ estimates the number of

blocks accessed for this kind of restriction. Inequality restrictions must access half ($<, \leq, \geq, >$) or almost all ($\neq$) the blocks in the space.

In all of these searches, the costs given above must be multiplied by π, the probe factor determined when the space is constructed, to give the actual number of accesses.

We can make other applications of quantities like Expression 2.3-14 and 2.3-15. For instance, the size of the indexes or directories that must be stored in RAM for a multipaged file is

$$m \sqrt[m]{n} \qquad (2.3\text{-}16)$$

under the same assumption of ignorance of f_i, i = 1, . . . , m, or

$$\sum_{i=1}^{m} f_i . \qquad (2.3\text{-}17)$$

This is just the total linear dimensions of the data space, and is likewise negligible (in principle) compared with n, the volume.

In dynamic multipaging, (Algorithm MSI, Section 1.2-3) we must split whole segments each time the file grows. The size of a segment of the ith axis is

$$\frac{n}{f_i} \tag{2.3-18}$$

or, assuming $f_i = f$, $i = 1, \ldots, m$,

$$n \uparrow (1 - \frac{1}{m}) \tag{2.3-19}$$

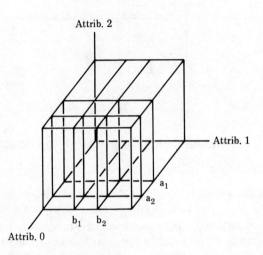

Exhibit 2.3-12.   The Range Query ($a_1 \le$ Attrib. $0 \le a_2$ **and** $b_1 \le$ Attrib. $1 \le$ b_2) in a Cubical Space

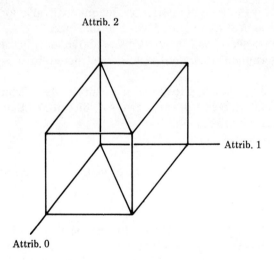

Exhibit 2.3-13.   The Restriction (Attrib. $0 =$ Attrib. 1) in a Cubical Space.

This is just the area of one of the faces of the data space. When we search for the best axis to shift, we may need to examine

$$\sum_{i=1}^{m} \frac{n}{f_i} \tag{2.3-20}$$

or

$$m \times n \uparrow (1 - \frac{1}{m}) \tag{2.3-21}$$

blocks: this is half the total surface area of the data space.

Exercise   2.3-15:   Show that the cost of building a dynamic multipage space of n blocks is linear, i.e., is proportional to n, assuming no shifting is done.

2.3-4   Summary of Costs

Exhibit 2.3-14 gives a summary of the cost of performing the various algebraic operations introduced in this chapter. The symbols n and N give the number of blocks and tuples in the operands, respectively, and for binary operators, they give the maximum for the two operands. The starred versions, n* and N*, give the sizes of the result—used in the case of μ-join where the result can be the Cartesian product. In keeping with our emphasis on practical cost analysis, the estimates

Exhibit 2.3-14. Estimates of Performance Costs for Relational Algebra.

Operation	Sort-Merge	TECHNIQUE Multipaged	Indexed
Project	n log n	n	N
Select	n	$n \uparrow (1 - \frac{k}{m})$ [1]	1 [2]
Edit	n log n	n	N
μ-Join [3]	max (n log n, n*)	max (n log n, n*)	N*
σ-Join [4]	max (n log n, nf)	nf	Nf
Range Join	n log n	n	N

Notes

1 Exact match, partial match, restriction: k is determined by number of attributes involved.
2 Exact match (including "partial match" on a key).
3 N* can be as bad as N^2, n* as n^2, in Cartesian products.
4 f is number of segments of non-join attributes in one of the operands: a function of n.

given are not asymptotic results describing worst cases but give reasonable expectations of the cost. Thus, the asymptotic cost of exact match in Select using a logarithmic index is O (log n) and using a hash or a tidy index is O (n): we give 1 as the estimate, since this is what we expect from a hash or a tidy index, the best possible case. In the Sort-Merge column, the estimates given happen all to be the worst-case costs. The use of N instead of n in the Indexed column emphasizes the likely case that the data values as stored are in no particular order with respect to the ordering (if any) determined by the index: Exercise 1.2-44 shows that almost every tuple sought will require accessing a fresh block. Indexing is best used in connection with multipaging for low activity queries.

Not all of the estimated presented have been derived in the text, but they should follow from a perusal of Chapter 2.3 and a little thought. To understand the assumptions and approximations involved requires a study of the rest of the chapter.

ADVANCED TOPICS

2.4-1   Operations on Relations

Unlike other data models, such as DBTG [CODASYL, 1971], the relational model was conceived from the outset with algebraic operators [Codd, 1970], which were elaborated by Codd [1971b]. Relations were proposed so that operations could be defined which manipulated the whole relation rather than require the user to consider individual tuples, and especially so that "navigation" from one tuple to another by the programmer is not needed. This difference between the relational and DBTG models is elaborated in a famous debate [Rustin, 1974] and can be taken as a characterization of the relational approach as opposed to most other data models. It can be summarized by saying that the relational algebra is less *procedural* than approaches that require the manipulating of individual records inside explicitly-written program loops. In the relational algebra, the loops are hidden in the general operators.

Codd proposed [1971b] and elaborated less formally [1971c] a "relational calculus" to extend this process of removing procedurality by using the descriptive formalism of the first-order predicate calculus (see e.g. Suppes [1957]). Since predicate calculus was devised as a vehicle for quantified logic by mathematicians before computers were invented, it does not specify how statements are to be verified or any other procedure. Procedurality had to be re-introduced into the relational calculus to some extent, however, with notions such as the workspace and verbs such as Get, Put and Update. And, unfortunately, the program loops were implicitly resurrected in the guise of ranges and tuple variables. Still, the calculus is less procedural than the algebra. We leave the discussion of other, less procedural formalisms (needless to say, there is no such thing as a "non-procedural" computer language) to Part 4 on Queries. Here we only note that a programmer user should have a rather more procedural formalism than an end-user, and we have chosen the relational algebra as a suitable level for programmers.

The notion of variables as used in the predicate calculus is painful to many people including Tarski who introduced the notion of a *cylindric algebra* [Henkin and Tarski, 1961] as a way to algebraize the first-order predicate calculus. A cylindric algebra is, roughly, a Boolean algebra with a set of additional unary operations, called *cylindrifications,* each corresponding to existential quantification on a domain of discourse. This operation can be illustrated graphically using the matrix representation of relations. In Exhibit 2.4-1 suppose the relation R (X, Y) consists of the set of points contained in the area enclosed by the solid curve. This can be interpreted as the set of points for which the proposition P = "the relation R holds between X and Y" is true. Then the proposition (∃Y) P = "for some Y, the relation R holds between X and that Y" is true in the cylinder bounded by dashed lines containing the area for P.

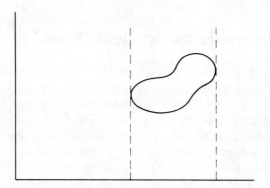

Exhibit   2.4-1.   The Cylinder (Y)^P for Proposition P

Tarski's algebraization of the predicate calculus was used by Imielinski and Lipski [1981a] to embed the relational algebra in a cylindric algebra and to show, among other things, that the general problem of establishing the equivalence of two different expressions of the relational algebra is undecidable. The embedding of a relation consists of extending each tuple in all possible ways to the whole set of attributes. Thus, if (x, y) is a tuple of R (X, Y) and {W, X, Y, Z} is the full set of attributes under consideration, (x, y) is extended to {(w_1, x, y, z_1), (w_1, x, y, z_2) · · · (w_2, x, y, z_1), (w_2, x, y, z_2), · · ·} where w_1, w_2, · · · covers the full set of W values and z_1, z_2, · · · covers the full set of Z values. Then the operations selection, union and difference extend to their obvious counterparts, natural join becomes the usual set-theoretical intersection and projection becomes cylindrification. Note that the extension of (x, y) could be written (*, x, y, *) where * is a new kind of null value representing "all possible values". This embedding by Imielinski and Lipski of the relational algebra in a cylindrical algebra may not lead to a practical implementation but to some extent rationalizes that part of the relational algebra they consider and is theoretically highly suggestive.

The relational algebra outlined in Chapter 2.1 owes its origin to Codd [1970, 1971b] but is somewhat generalized. In extending the relational algebra we have been motivated by the practical consideration of making the algebra more widely useful, but we have tried to avoid *ad hoc*ery by defining only operations that are applicable to *all* possible relations and by concentrating on generalizing the earlier operations. Thus the μ-join generalizes the natural join and the σ-join generalizes division and natural composition. The union join, which is the senior member of the μ-join family, was independently proposed by Heath in 1971 (see [Codd 1979]) by Hall, Hitchcock and Todd [1975], by Zaniolo [1976] and by LaCroix and Pirotte [1976b]. The μ-join was introduced by Merrett [1976].

Relational division has always been a little difficult to understand. Codd [1971b] saw it as a counterpart for the universal quantifier and Adiba and Delobel [1976, §4.2.4] took this a little further by viewing division as an extension of "anti-projection", a unary operator which outputs values for the projected attribute(s) only if they are related to *every* value of the other attribute(s). (Projection can be described similarly, with *some* replacing *every*.) However, the motivation for the σ-join is quite different and due to some notions in the algebra of quotient relations [Furtado and Kerschberg, 1977]. This novel variant of the relational algebra introduces a set-processing capability by operating on partitioned relations, where the partitions are equivalence classes defined by equal values of a given attribute. Since division can be seen as a comparison of sets of tuples in a relation with a set of values, limited to the comparison of set inclusion, the σ-join generalization achieves most of the goals of the quotient algebra. The σ-join is implicit in Merrett and Otoo [1979], where the tuple-density model of Section 2.3-2 was used to analyze relational operations. It is described in Chiu [1982] and a restricted version appears in Merrett and Zaidi [1981].

2.4-2   Decomposition

The converse of the natural join, decomposition of a relation into two or more relations which could join together to reconstruct the original, was explored by Delobel [1972] in connection with functional dependence and the hierarchical representation of data. The "first-order hierarchical decomposition" (FOHD) of Delobel and Leonard [1974] is a multi-way decomposition exemplified by

$$R = (W, X \text{ in } R) \text{ ijoin } (W, Y \text{ in } R) \text{ ijoin } (W, Z \text{ in } R) \qquad (2.4-1)$$

where R is a relation on the disjoint sets W, X, Y, Z of attributes. W is called the *root* of the decomposition and X, Y, Z the *branches*. Equation 2.4-1 can be abbreviated $W \twoheadrightarrow X \,|\, Y \,|\, Z$.

A special case of the FOHD became known as the "multivalued dependency" (MVD), introduced independently by Zaniolo [1976] and Fagin [1977]. This is an FOHD with only two branches, e.g., $W \twoheadrightarrow X \,|\, Y$, which is usually written W $\twoheadrightarrow$ X to indicate the relationship with functional dependence: if W $\rightarrow$ X then W $\twoheadrightarrow$ X for a relation R (W, X, Y) with W, X, Y disjoint (Exercise 2.1-5). The context-sensitivity and the symmetry of the MVD makes it quite different from a functional dependence: W $\twoheadrightarrow$ X implies W $\twoheadrightarrow$ Y in R (W, X, Y). It is preferable to think of MVDs as decompositions, or, as in Section 2.1-3, *natural join decompositions*.

Armstrong and Delobel [1977] use the notation (X, Y) for a decomposition of a relation R on a set of attributes U = X $\cup$ Y. The attribute sets are not necessarily disjoint and the root of the decomposition is X $\cap$ Y. Thus (X, Y) means R = (X **in** R) **ijoin** (Y **in** R) where the join is on X $\cap$ Y. If X $\cap$ Y = ϕ, the empty set, **ijoin** is the Cartesian product. They establish four axioms

E	Empty Decomposition	(ϕ, U)
S	Symmetry	if (X, Y) then (Y, X)
RE	Root Enlargement	if (X, Y) and Z $\subseteq$ U then (X $\cup$ Z, Y $\cup$ Z)
BI	Branch Intersection	if (X, Y) and (Z, W) and Z $\cap$ W = Y
		then (X $\cap$ Z, W)

Exercise   2.4-1:   Prove axioms E, S, RE, BI.

The rest of Armstrong and Delobel's [1977] paper uses saturated sets and *antiroots,* the corresponding "dual" for decompositions, to explore the relationships between functional dependences and decompositions and to uncover other useful properties. The antiroot is a somewhat more complicated notion than the saturated set, and the theorems of this paper have to contend with more special conditions than those in [Armstrong, 1974]. It may still be necessary to improve on the approach of Armstrong and Delobel, but it seems more satisfactory than other axiomatizing work. For instance, Beeri, Fagin and Howard [1977] formulate axioms for MVDs reminiscent of the FD axioms—e.g., reflexivity, augmentation, transitivity. They add mixed axioms for MVDs and FDs and show completeness of the collection.

From about this point, research into dependency theory begins to get highly involved. For instance, because of their context-dependence, MVDs can exist in a projection of a relation but not in the original relation. These are called *embedded* MVDs or EMVDs. Parker and Parsaye-Ghomi [1980] show that an infinite number of axioms are necessary for EMVDs. Over a dozen new dependences have been invented—a review is given by Kambayashi, Tanaka and Yajima [1981]. The practical interest of these studies is in database design: decomposition rules allow us to break big relations down into smaller ones with consequent elimination of redundancy and avoidance of the processing anomalies encouraged by redundancy. Starting with one big relation involves a controversial assumption, the universal relation assumption—see Kent [1981], Ullman [1982]. But the whole area of research is hard to apply in its current state.

2.4-3   Null Values

The use of two null values, representing "don't know" and "don't care" has its origin in the early development of the Information Algebra [Bosak *et al.*, 1962], in which all data was held in (from the relational point of view) one big relation and the "don't care" value, ω, was needed to indicate irrelevant attributes for any given tuple. The "don't know" value, θ, of the Information Algebra was later called @ by Codd [1975], who elaborated a three-valued logic for it. The four-valued logic of Section 2.1-4 uses a truth-function approach which is overly simplistic, as was pointed out by Lipski [1979] and Vassiliou [1979]. Vassiliou uses denotational semantics (see Section 1.4-3) which also results in two null values, enabling him to display truth tables for **and** and **or** which are identical to those of Section 2.1-4 for T, F, *DK* but have only *DC* entries in the *DC* rows and columns. That these truth tables are peripheral to his approach, however, is shown by the fact that no "truth table" is possible for $<$ since the result for $DK > x$ depends on comparing *all* values in the first set with x. This is clearly more realistic than our assumption, $DK > x = DK$.

Lipski [1979] proposes upper and lower *ranges* of values for unknown information, and distinguishes the internal from the external interpretation of a query, Q, involving incompletely represented data. The external interpretation is for the user who is not aware of the incompleteness of the information or who does not want to make sophisticated use of this incompleteness. The obvious thing for the system to do is to return lower and upper bounds to the query: $||Q||^*$ is the set of objects (from the real world and modelled incompletely by the system) which certainly satisfy the query Q; $||Q||_*$ is the set of objects which certainly do not fail to satisfy Q (i.e. which may satisfy Q). The internal interpretation, $||Q||$, derives directly from the data stored in the system, and obeys the usual rules, such as $||Q_1 \text{ or } Q_2|| = ||Q_1|| \cup ||Q_2||$. Lipski gives an example: a, b, c, d are possibly white objects; c, d, e, f are possibly black objects; b, c, f, g are possibly red objects. Then

$$||\text{white or black}||_* = \{a, d, e\}$$
$$||\text{white or black}||^* = \{a, b, c, d, e, f\}$$
$$||\text{white or black}|| = ||\text{white}|| \cup ||\text{black}|| = \{a\} \cup \{e\} = \{a, e\}$$
$$||\text{not white}||_* = \{e, f, g\}$$
$$||\text{not black}|| = [b, c, d, e, f, g\}$$

Multiple null values are all right until we come to operate on them—an extreme case of nulls without operations being taken into account is the 14 different null values proposed by the ANSI/X3/SPARC Study Group on DBMSs [ANSI, 1975, p. IV-28]. It is important to understand the effects of relational operators and expressions of relational operations. A study was made by Imielinski and Lipski [1981b] of the completeness of two systems of null values under the operators project, select, union and join. A null system is complete if all valid conclusions expressible by relational expressions using the operators are in fact derivable in the system. Imielinski and Lipski found that Codd's @-null system supports project-select, but (in [Imielinski and Lipski, 1982]) they showed that it does not support either project-select-union or project-join. The trouble with join seems to be that two different occurrences of @ (''don't know'' or DK) can represent the same value. The way out is to use a set of *variables* to represent ''don't know'' such that the recurrence of the same variable means a recurrence of the value. This system supports project—positive select—union—join, where *positive select* is select with no negations in the selection condition. In evaluating operations, the variables are treated exactly as if they were values. Variable nulls, however, do not support project—select, which Codd's null does. A system which supports project—select—union—join involves a less practical system of incomplete values, in which arbitrary conditions (from a limited class) are appended to each tuple. This work is related to the lower bound, $||\cdot||_*$, of Lipski [1979] in that the criterion throughout is that no incorrect conclusion be derivable using the relational operators on the incomplete data.

The effect of null values on integrity constraints is also important. Functional dependences are discussed by Vassiliou [1979] and by Imielinski and Lipski [1981b]. An integrity system that supports two-valued nulls is described by Ho [1982].

2.4-4   Implementing Operations and Expressions

Whitney [1974] discusses three early systems which use sort-merge techniques to implement set operations, join and composition. He points out that sequential processing is good for operations that deal with all the tuples of a relation. Todd [1974] discusses qualitatively three implementations of the natural join/Cartesian product operator used in PRTV [Todd 1976]: a nested-loop method which does a complete scan of one relation for each block of the other; a sort-merge method; and a method which joins indexes and then realizes the full result using the index pointers. The first is clearly good for Cartesian products or joins that almost give the Cartesian product. The third corresponds with methods proposed by Palermo [1972]: the realization phase requires two sorts and is itself a double join.

Gotlieb [1975] considers three algorithms to implement the θ-join (Codd [1971b]: the equi-join, less-than join and greater-than join discussed in Section 2.1-3 are members of this family of joins). He compares the costs using a simple analytic model with parameters such as N (number of tuples in relation), w (size of each tuple), K (block size), v (size of join attributes). The first method uses nested loops for the general θ-join and the other two use indexes for equijoins on non-key and key attributes respectively. The I/O times are order N^2, N and N respectively, with RAM requirements that are independent of N. The linear costs of the second and third methods are due to the fact that indexes are assumed already built and to the use of hashing. Chapter 5.3 shows that hashing is more expensive than sorting in practice, despite the O (N log N) complexity of sorting, because of the blocking of data on secondary storage. Using indexes is similarly expensive.

Blasgen and Eswaran [1977] did a similar analysis, including sort-merge, and obtained results which immediately support the sort-merge technique. They observed the importance of physical clustering of tuples according to the values of the join attributes. The only case in which sort-merge did not give the best, or nearly the best, performance was the one in which both relations were clustered on the join attributes. In Section 2.3-1 we have already raised the problem of the cost of detecting this condition. Blasgen and Eswaran's analysis applies not to isolated joins but to a query that involves restricting both operands before, and projecting the result after, the join. Evidently the join cost dominates, however.

Smith and Chang [1975] describe 21 different implementations of the 8 operations project, select, join, union, intersection, difference, Cartesian product and divide, with up to 4 methods for any one operator. These are used by a procedure to rearrange expressions in the relational algebra to improve their performance. No cost analysis is done in the paper and only qualitative indication is given for which method to use. Some of their general conclusions are expressed in Section 2.2-4. Pecherer [1975] also discusses transformation of expressions to equivalent but cheaper expressions, based on simple cost analyses of restriction, Cartesian product, θ-join, project and divide. With suitable ordering of intermediate results, he claims linear times for project and divide, which means that these operations can be included in a pipeline. The class of algebraic expressions to which this applies is generated by Codd's [1971b] algorithm to convert relational calculus to relational algebra expressions.

In their work on PRTV [Todd, 1976], Hall and Todd [1974] and Hall [1974] addressed important specific issues in improving the execution of relational expressions. Factorizing algebraic expressions [Hall and Todd, 1974] is useful in dealing with Boolean selection conditions applied to a join. For instance, "find employees who either were born before 1930 and today earn less than £4000, or were born after 1950 and last year earned between £1000 and £2000" applied to EMPLOYEE (MAN#, NAME, BIRTHDATE) and SALARY HISTORY (MAN#, JOBDATE, SALARYDATE, SALARY) gives the condition

(b1 and d1 and s1) or (b2 and d2 and s2 and s3)

where b1 = (BIRTHDATE < 1930), b2 = (BIRTHDATE > 1950), d1 = (SALARYDATE = 1974), d2 = (SALARYDATE = 1973), s1 = (SALARY < 4000), s2 = (SALARY > 1000), s3 = (SALARY < 2000). It would be preferable to use the equivalent condition

$$(b1 \text{ or } b2) \text{ and } \{[b1 \text{ or } (d2 \text{ and } s2 \text{ and } s3)] \text{ and } [(d1 \text{ and } s1) \text{ or } b2]$$
$$\text{and } [(d1 \text{ and } s1) \text{ or } (d2 \text{ and } s2 \text{ and } s3)]\}$$

which has the form (b1 **or** b2) **and** {residue}. This has the advantage of being a selection condition with a factor involving birthdate references only, which can be applied to EMPLOYEE and reduce its size before joining. The residue is more complicated than the original expression, but this does not matter since it still can be applied as a whole to each tuple resulting from the join.

Hall's [1974] work on identifying common subexpressions helps us to avoid evaluating the same subexpression more than once.

In view of the results of Imielinski and Lipski [1981a], mentioned in Section 2.4-1, there are limits to the process of optimizing relational expressions, since the equivalence of some relational expressions is undecidable.

2.4-5   Systems and Languages

Kim [1979] "lists . . . every database system which has been designed or implemented to support the n-ary relational model of data". His list is expanded by Fernandez [1980]. An exhaustive coverage of relational database systems is even more difficult since 1980 when systems, especially for microcomputers, began to proliferate. We will here limit discussion to early developments.

Activity at M.I.T.'s Project MAC [Goldstein and Strnad, 1970] was already in progress but clearly influenced [Strnad, 1971] by publication of Codd's [1970] paper as well as by an M.Sc. thesis in Electrical Engineering at M.I.T. [Kraning and Fillat, 1970]. The original version of the MacAIMS Data Management System (MADAM: Goldstein and Strnad [1970]) provided union, intersection, difference and project. Join, composition and Cartesian product were added [Strnad, 1971]. MADAM represents attribute values in a standard, encoded and hence (for strings at least) compressed form. Processing modules are provided to encode and decode values. The advantages are that the same item will be represented in the same way and thus recognized internally (e.g., the equality of 6, Jan. 1962 and January 6, 1962 or of MacAIMS and MACAIMS is ensured) and that internal operations such as joins are on smaller data elements and so faster. The "reference numbers" encoding data preserve collating order where possible, so that comparisons and ranking can be done without decoding. A parallel feature of MADAM is the provision for as many physical representations of relations as the implementor cares to write code for, enabling him to use the best data structures for an application. To keep the amount of code down in the case of binary operations on relations represented differently, each relational processing module must be able to handle a "canonical form"—a sequence of tuples implemented as a linked list—as well as its own special physical representation. (This multiplicity of representations is valuable, although the need is diminished by the advent of flexible data structures like multipaging.)

BASICS: Domain Algebra

We encountered in Part 2 the need for arithmetic and related operations on the data in relations. If we were content to process relations a tuple-at-a-time (TATI), such operations could be left to the programmer to incorporate in his TATI loops. With atomic relations, these operations could be implemented by predefined procedures or functions such as SUBTRACT (e.g., SUBTRACT (TOTIN, TOTOUT, DIFF) to create DIFF, the difference of TOTIN minus TOT-OUT in each tuple of Exhibit 2.1-7) or TOTAL (e.g., TOTAL (DIFF) to give the sum of all the differences calculated by SUBTRACT, above.) This is somewhat inflexible.

However, the form of SUBTRACT, above, is very suggestive. In subtracting TOTOUT from TOTIN for each tuple, we have had to create a new attribute, DIFF, to hold the result. Here is a direct interaction among attributes, DIFF = TOTIN − TOTOUT, suggesting that an *algebra of attributes* might be possible. In SUBTRACT, we did not even mention the relation on which the operation was to be applied. We might have, of course, but clearly we will be more free if we can avoid it. One way to set up such an operation independently of the relations to which it is to be applied is to recognize that DIFF = TOTIN − TOTOUT is itself a relation, a ternary relation of infinite cardinality. We could then use the natural join on (TOTIN, TOTOUT) to append DIFF to the relation on which the computation is to be performed. It is not obvious how this approach will handle TOTAL, above, however. So we adopt a viewpoint that simplifies the problem of applying the computation while allowing considerable variety in the types of computation available.

The relation DIFF = TOTIN − TOTOUT cannot, of course, be stored explicitly. It must be a *virtual relation*, the tuples of which are *actualized* when needed. In getting away from the problem of combining different types of virtual relation with explicit relations, we apply the notion of virtuality to attributes instead of relations. DIFF is a *virtual attribute*, which can be *actualized* on any relation containing the attributes TOTIN and TOTOUT. The usual way we actualize an attribute is by naming it in a projection. Thus

$$\text{CHANGE} \leftarrow \text{ACCT, DIFF in (GAIN ujoin LOSS)} \qquad (3.1\text{-}1)$$

includes a projection that actualizes DIFF. Note that the operand attributes, TOTIN and TOTOUT, are not necessarily retained in the result.

We define a virtual attribute by a statement such as

$$\text{let DIFF be TOTIN} - \text{TOTOUT}$$

or

$$\text{let SUM be red} + \text{of DIFF.}$$

(The significance of this latter syntax will appear in Section 3.1-2.) These statements are operations of the algebra of attributes, which we call the *domain algebra* for euphony.

3.1-1   Scalar Operations

The simplest operations of the domain algebra generate the value in a tuple for the virtual attribute in terms only of the values in the same tuple of the operand attributes. These operations work along a tuple and are sometimes referred to as *horizontal operations* for this reason. We call them *scalar operations* because the values they operate on are the simplest (in the sense of Section 2.1-5) values considered in the application, i.e., scalars.

The subtraction already discussed is a scalar operation,

$$\text{let DIFF be TOTIN} - \text{TOTOUT.}$$

We do not limit the variety of scalar operations except by the constraint that each expression must be able to be evaluated completely on any single tuple of the relation. Here are some examples.

```
let QTY1 be 1      <<defines a constant attribute>>
let FGPRICE be (1.0 + PR%/100.0) × FGCOST
let SUAMT be abs (FF)      <<abs is a function giving absolute value>>
let PL be if FF≥0 then 'Profit' else 'Loss'      <<conditional expression>>
let PLDESCR be 'Net '||PL||' after tax'      <<concatenation>>
let FF be if ACTYPE = 'Asset' then TOTIN − TOTOUT
                                else TOTOUT − TOTIN
let ACCT be ACCTCR      <<renaming an attribute>>
```

It is also implicit in the above examples that virtual attributes can be defined in terms of each other, e.g., PLDESCR depends on PL which is in turn defined in terms of FF (the sequence of the above examples does not reflect their order of appearance in an application).

3.1-2   Reduction

Now we come to domain algebra operations which combine values from more than one tuple—the "vertical" operations. We discuss *reduction* in this section and *functional mapping* in the next.

Simple reduction (or just *reduction*) produces a single result from the values from all tuples of a single attribute in the relation. Summation is an example:

let SUM be red + of DIFF

where **red** indicates a reduction operation and the operator + is one of many operations that can be specified. For instance

let PRODUCT be red × of DIFF

and so on.

Before specifying the effects of reduction and characterizing the operators permitted, we note that the result is a virtual attribute and is treated in just the same way as the virtual attribute resulting from a scalar operation. That is, it might be actualized by

TOTAL ← SUM **in** CHANGE

on CHANGE (Equation 3.1-1). Note that TOTAL consists of one number, namely the sum of all the DIFF values in CHANGE (27.30—see Exhibit 2.1-7 or Exhibit 6.1-5). Nevertheless, for consistency it is a relation and an expression such as 2.0 × TOTAL would be illegal due to the incompatibility of levels of the scalar 2.0 and the relation TOTAL. The application might require a different, if improbable, actualization, such as

TOTAL 1 ← ACCT, SUM **in** CHANGE.

Then SUM would be a constant attribute and every tuple would have the same value, 27.30, for SUM. Such an actualization would be redundant, and rare in practice, but is consistent with the whole approach of the domain algebra. It also makes it very easy to use the result of a reduction in scalar operations of the domain algebra. For instance, we can find the average difference very easily:

let AVG be (red + of DIFF)/(red + of 1)

divides SUM (i.e., **red + of** DIFF) by the number of tuples (i.e., **red + of** 1). This statement can be conceived as creating temporary attributes for the sum and for the number of tuples, which are then combined by the scalar operation of division. How much work is actually done in an implementation depends, of course, on how the result is actualized.

Not every operator is allowed to replace <op> in **red** <op> **of**. In fact, legal reduction operators must be *commutative,* a <op> b = b <op> a, and *associative,* a <op> (b <op> c) = (a <op> b) <op> c. For instance, +, ×, **max, min, and, or,** =, ≠ are allowed, but −, /, ↑ (exponentiation), **mod,** < are not. This is because reduction operates between tuples but no order is specified for the tuples in a relation. If we allowed a noncommutative operator such as − or a nonassociative operator such as **mod,** the result would depend on the order the tuples happen to be in and so might not be the same for different implementations of the same relation. (Is 8 **mod** 5 **mod** 2   0 or 1?)

Given that the reduction operator is such that the result does not depend on the order of the tuples, we can define reduction algorithmically. Let there be an accumulator, ACCUM, which is set equal to the value of the specified attribute, A, in the first tuple (in any ordering of the tuples). The value of **red** <op> of A is the final value, after all tuples have been processed, in ACCUM, which is changed as follows by each tuple:

$$ACCUM \leftarrow ACCUM <op> A \qquad\qquad (3.1\text{-}2)$$

Exercise   3.1-1:   What is the expression which gives total quantity of assemblies ordered in ODERBOOK (Exhibit 1.1-1)?

Exercise   3.1-2:   What is the expression which gives total quantity of Cars ordered in ODERBOOK (Exhibit 1.1-1)?

• • •

Equivalence reduction is like simple reduction but produces a different result for different sets of tuples in the relation. Each set is characterized by all tuples having the same value for some specified attribute—an "equivalence class" in mathematical terminology. Subtotalling is an example, and GAIN and LOSS (Exhibit 2.1-7) might each be derived from a relation TRANSACTIONS (ACCTCR, ACCTDB, AMOUNT) (compare Exhibit 6.1-5):

> **let** TOTIN **be equiv** + **of** AMOUNT **by** ACCTDB
> **let** ACCT **be** ACCTDB
> GAIN ← ACCT, TOTIN **in** TRANSACTIONS

> **let** TOTOUT **be equiv** + **of** AMOUNT **by** ACCTCR
> **let** ACCT **be** ACCTCR
> LOSS ← ACCT, TOTOUT **in** TRANSACTIONS

Here **equiv** indicates equivalence reduction and the attribute after **by** is used to group the tuples into equivalence classes. The calculation of GAIN sums the amounts debited from each account, ACCTDB, and that of LOSS sums the amounts credited to each account, ACCTCR. (The accountant reader is asked to defer his criticisms of the examples until Part 6.)

Exercise   3.1-3:   Using Exhibit 6.1-5, apart from the column Δ^+ and the row Δ^-, as TRANSACTIONS, verify that the above calculations give GAIN and LOSS in Exhibit 2.1-7.

The same process of actualizing the virtual attribute and the same restriction on the legal operators apply to equivalence reduction as to simple reduction. The algorithmic definition, above, of simple reduction defines equivalence reduction for any equivalence class. It must be applied to each equivalence class in turn.

Exercise 3.1-4:   For each different type of ASSEMBLY (Car, Locomotive, etc.) in ORDERBOOK (Exhibit 1.1-1), express the query, "how many are ordered?"

Exercise 3.1-5:   For each different ORD# in ORDERBOOK (Exhibit 1.1-1), express the query, "how many assemblies are ordered?"

3.1-3   Functional Mapping

We will discuss the second type of "vertical" domain algebra operation only briefly here, as it does not enter much into the commercial applications we consider later in the book. It is, however, useful for simulations, operations research, and engineering calculations. Functional mapping, like equivalence reduction, involves an operand attribute and a controlling attribute. In this case, the controlling attribute serves to specify an *order* of processing the tuples. The two kinds of functional mapping are best presented through examples.

Simple functional mapping (or just *functional mapping*) is illustrated by the cumulative total

let CUM **be fcn** + **of** AMOUNT **order** YEAR

as applied to

SALES (PRESIDENT	YEAR	AMOUNT)	CUM
Smith	1979	150	150
Smith	1980	175	325
Smith	1981	200	525
Brown	1981	200	525
Brown	1982	210	735
Brown	1983	225	960

The column to the right of the relation SALES shows how the virtual attribute CUM would appear if actualized. It gives the cumulative sum of AMOUNT over the years starting in 1979.

For a functional mapping to be properly defined, the operand attribute (e.g., AMOUNT) must be functionally dependent on the controlling attribute (e.g., YEAR). The resulting virtual attribute is also functionally dependent on the controlling attribute. This is shown in the example by the fact that CUM has the same value in the two tuples for 1981, as does AMOUNT. The otherwise irrelevant attribute PRESIDENT is included solely to make this point: we can suppose that the presidency changed in 1981, although the total sales for the year is accounted for only once.

(The mathematically inclined reader will reorganize the concept of a *functional* embodied in this property of the functional mapping. A functional is a mapping which transforms one function to another. For instance integration, $\int_0^y f(x)\,dx = g(y)$, maps the function f to the function g. In the domain algebra, functional mapping gives, among other uses, a facility for numerical integration, which is useful for simulation, data smoothing, and other purposes in operations research and related applications. The notion of functional used in the domain algebra is somewhat less general than the mathematical concept.)

As the example suggests, functional mapping is not restricted to sums, and the operator + can be replaced by other operators just as with reduction. In this case, since an order is imposed on the tuples, we need not be so restrictive. Thus non-commutative and non-associative operations such as −, ÷ are permitted. We define functional mapping so that − gives an alternating sum, ÷ an alternating product, and so on. This can be done algorithmically, as we did for reduction. In particular, we keep an accumulator which is altered the same way as Equation 3.1-2. The successive values of this accumulator are the values of the virtual attribute for successive tuples. (In reduction, the virtual attribute had only one value for all tuples, the final value in the accumulator.)

That is, the value of the virtual attribute in the tuple, r_i, for the ith distinct value of the controlling attribute (in ascending order) is

$$\triangle \quad r_i\,[\textbf{fcn}\ \beta\ \textbf{of}\ y\ \textbf{order}\ x] = r_i\,[y]\ \beta\ (.\,.\beta\,(r_3\,[y]\ \beta\ (r_2\,[y]\ \beta\,r_1\,[y]))\,.\,.) \qquad (3.1\text{-}3)$$

where β is the operator, y the operand attribute, x the controlling attribute and **fcn** β **of** y **order** x is the virtual attribute resulting from the functional mapping.

● ● ●

Partial functional mapping is the obvious extension of functional mapping in the same way that equivalence reduction extends reduction. For example,

let DCUM be par + of AMOUNT order YEAR by DIV

might be applied to

DIVSALES (DIV	YEAR	AMOUNT)	DCUM
A	1982	80	80
B	1982	60	60
C	1982	90	90
A	1983	110	190
B	1983	75	135
C	1983	110	200

giving, if DCUM were actualized, the right-hand column. This operation performs simple functional mapping within each equivalence class of tuples having the same value for the classifying attribute (e.g., DIV).

(Partial functional mapping is closely related to partial integration. The result and the operand attribute (e.g., AMOUNT) are functions of the controlling and classifying attributes (e.g., YEAR, DIV respectively).)

Exercise 3.1-6: Write domain algebra expressions to find the number of different values of YEAR in SALES and the number of different values of YEAR within each DIVision in DIVSALES.

● ● ●

A useful process which falls under the general category of functional mapping is the *successor* function, illustrated by

let NEXT be succ AMOUNT order YEAR

SALES (PRESIDENT	YEAR	AMOUNT)	NEXT
Smith	1979	150	135
Smith	1980	175	200
Smith	1981	200	210
Brown	1981	200	210
Brown	1982	210	225
Brown	1983	225	150

Note the functional dependence YEAR → AMOUNT and the consequent dependence YEAR → NEXT. Note also the convention that the successor is cyclic: if we do not want a cycle, it is easy to get rid of the last tuple after computing successors. The successor function is useful for subsequent scalar operations. For instance, we could go on to compute the increase, NEXT − AMOUNT, in SALES, or the percentage growth.

There is an easy analogue to partial functional mapping, as in

let SUBSEQ be succ AMOUNT order YEAR by DIV

DIVSALES (DIV	YEAR	AMOUNT)	SUBSEQ
A	1982	80	110
B	1982	60	75
C	1982	90	110
A	1983	110	80
B	1983	75	60
C	1983	110	90

Note that there are three cycles here, one for each division, so the successor tuple for (A, 1983, 110) is (A, 1982, 80) and so on.

It is convenient, but not necessary, to define a *predecessor* function, **pred**, working in a similar way.

Review Questions and Exercises, Chapter 3.1

3.1-7   In Review Question 2.1-19, Chapter 2.1, suppose the marks MTMARK and FIMARK are both given as percentages. What is the domain algebra expression required to combine them into TOTMARK with respective weights of .2 and .8?

3.1-8   In the relation SHIPPED (DEPT, ITEM, QTY, UNIT VALUE) find the total value of items shipped by department.

3.1-9   Find the average marks by course and by student in STUDRECORD (STUDENT, COURSE, MARK).

3.1-10 Find the students with the highest marks in each course in STUDRECORD (STUDENT, COURSE, MARK).

3.1-11 In the relation STUDRECORD (STUDENT, COURSE, MARK) find the number of courses taken by each student.

3.1-12 Use the renaming capability of the domain algebra and the natural join to answer Review Question 2.1-18, Chapter 2.1.

3.1-13 Suppose relations A (VALUEA, I, J) and B (VALUEB, J, K) represent two matrices A and B. Use the natural join and equivalence reduction to obtain AB (VALUE, I, K), which represents the matrix product A × B.

IMPLEMENTATION: Actualization

The domain algebra must be implemented in two phases. First is the construction of an expression which corresponds to the **let** statement and which defines a virtual attribute. Second is the actualization. The first involves techniques for processing in RAM and we do not discuss it. The second requires that some stipulation be made about when a virtual attribute is to be actualized. This can raise considerations of how to design a programming language which we prefer to avoid in the context of this book. We will suppose that a simple linguistic facility is provided for actualization, such as an extended projection.

Another linguistic matter that we leave unspecified is whether the arithmetic and other operators in the domain algebra are restricted to a set of predetermined operations (such as $+$, $\times$, **max,** etc.) or whether they can include user-defined operations.

This chapter will discuss techniques for actualizing individual domain algebra operations and then considers briefly the implementation of expressions.

3.2-1 Sequential Techniques

The simplest implementation of the part of the domain algebra which actualizes expressions uses files which are accessed sequentially and which may or may not be sorted. Scalar operations apply to every tuple of the relation and so can be actualized as efficiently on a sequential file as on any other organization. Reductions also must access all tuples, and are defined in such a way that the order of the tuples does not matter. Equivalence reductions require grouping by like values of the control attributes, which can be achieved by sorting. Functional mapping specifies an order of processing the tuples. Partial functional mapping needs both a grouping and an ordering within the groups. We will discuss the examples from Chapter 3.1 for equivalence reduction and partial functional mapping rather than give the very simple implementation algorithms.

Exercise   3.2-1:   Give an algorithm to actualize the scalar operation **let Z be X** <op> Y in the projection X, Y, Z **in** R.

Exercise   3.2-2:   Give an algorithm to actualize the reduction **let Y be red** <op> **of** X in the projection Y **in** R.

The equivalence reductions (from Section 3.1-2) **let TOTIN be equiv + of** AMOUNT **by** ACCTDB and **let TOTOUT be equiv + of** AMOUNT **by** ACCTCR on TRANSACTIONS (ACCTCR, ACCTDB, AMOUNT) are shown in Exhibit 3.2-1. Both Exhibits 3.2-1 and 3.2-1b show the same relation, TRANSACTIONS, but sorted on ACCTDB and ACCTCR respectively. The virtual attributes TOTIN and TOTOUT are shown as the sums of AMOUNT within the appropriate groups. Actualizing them is straightforward once the relation has been sorted.

Exhibit 3.1-1. TRANSACTIONS Sorted to Actualize Equivalence Reductions.

TRANSACTIONS				TRANSACTIONS			
(ACCTDB	ACCTCR	AMT)	TOTIN	(ACCTDB	ACCTCR	AMT)	TOTOUT
A	M	1.30		G	A	2.33	2.33
A	E	1.43	2.73	P	C	7.70	
C	R	3.99	3.99	T	C	1.87	9.57
E	F	0.22		A	E	1.43	
E	P	2.11		R	E	2.21	3.64
E	T	0.95	3.28	E	F	0.22	0.22
G	A	2.33	2.33	R	G	3.19	3.19
M	P	1.01	1.01	A	M	1.30	1.30
P	C	7.70	7.70	M	P	1.01	
R	G	3.19		E	P	2.11	3.12
R	E	2.21	5.40	C	R	3.99	3.99
T	C	1.87	1.87	E	T	0.95	0.95
	a) Sorted by ACCTDB				b) Sorted by ACCTCR		

Exercise   3.2-3:   Give an algorithm to actualize the equivalence reduction **let Z be equiv** <op> **of** Y **by** X in the projection X, Z **in** R.

Exercise   3.2-4:   Give an algorithm to actualize the functional mapping **let Z be fcn** <op> **of** Y **order** X in the projection X, Y, Z **in** R. (See e.g., SALES in Section 3.1-3.)

The partial functional mapping (from Section 3.1-3) **let DCUM be par + of** AMOUNT **order** YEAR **by** DIV on DIVSALES (DIV, YEAR, AMOUNT) is shown in Exhibit 3.2-2. DIVSALES is sorted on YEAR within DIV, and the calculation accumulates AMOUNT within each group with a fixed value of DIV. The virtual attribute DCUM is shown as the cumulative sum.

Exhibit 3.2-2. DIVSALES Sorted to Actualize Partial Functional Mapping.

DIVSALES	(DIV	YEAR	AMOUNT)	DCUM
	A	1982	80	80
	A	1983	110	190
	B	1982	60	60
	B	1983	75	135
	C	1982	90	90
	C	1983	110	200

Exercise 3.2-5:   Give an algorithm to actualize the partial functional mapping **let** Z **be par** <op> **of** Y **order** X **by** W in the projection W, X, Y, Z, **in** R.

3.2-2   Multipaging Techniques

For equivalence reduction, functional mapping, and partial functional mapping, we turn to multipaging to eliminate the need to sort, or at least to reduce the cost of sorting.

As with projection and σ-join (see Section 2.2-2), multipaging reduces the problem on the whole set of blocks in the file to a problem on the blocks in only one segment of the controlling attribute. More to the point, multipaging reduces the problem on the full set of values of the controlling attribute to a problem on the set of values in one segment. The number of different values in a segment is not a function of the size of the file, and so it is permissible to suppose that the RAM capacity of some computer might be capable of storing an accumulator for each different value. This is a bigger demand than the projection requirement of one bit per value or the σ-join requirement of two bits per value. As in the relational algebra implementation, the demand may exceed the capacity of the computer to be used, in which case the file must be sorted after all or some compromise adopted. We now look at equivalence reduction and the two forms of functional mapping.

If the attribute X is segmented by multipaging in the equivalence reduction **let** Z **be equiv** <op> **of** Y **by** X, and if RAM can hold an accumulator for each different value of X in a segment, then the sort to find groups of X can be omitted. An example of this is discussed for the equivalence reductions of TRANSACTIONS in Section 6.3-1. If RAM can hold only accumulators for half the different values of X in some segments, we may decide to do two passes on those segments rather than resort to sorting. Or we may be able to avoid sorting some segments even if others must be sorted. Thus there is a spectrum of compromises ranging from taking full advantage of the multipaging to sorting the file. Finally, sorting itself is cheaper, as described in Section 2.2-2, if the file is multipaged.

Functional mapping is helped by multipaging only by the reduction in the cost of sorting. The sorting must be done in any case. If there is an axis for X, the mapping **let** Z **be fcn** $<$op$>$ **of** Y **order** X will be speeded up by this consideration. If there are axes for both W and X in the mapping **let** Z **be par** $<$op$>$ **of** Y **order** X **by** W, the sort may be for only one block at a time and so can be done in RAM. In any case, the sort will be cheaper by log f_W + log f_X passes, where there are f_W segments of the W-axis and f_X segments of the X-axis. This is illustrated in Exhibit 3.2-3. The dashed line shows the order of processing for one of the values of W. Each of the twelve blocks shown can be sorted independently of the others.

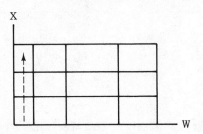

Exhibit   3.2-3.   Multipaging and **let** Z **be par** $<$op$>$ **of** Y **order** X **by** W.

3.2-3   Pipelining

In the domain algebra, methods for combining operations efficiently into expressions are more important than in the relational algebra. A virtual attribute may have a quite complicated definition and, at a cost of at least one pass per operation, creating each intermediate result separately is unacceptable. Of the two techniques discussed in Section 2.2-4 for algebraic expressions, rearrangement into equivalent expressions and pipelining, we will discuss pipelining briefly.

It is clear from the last section that functional mapping and partial functional mapping must terminate any pipeline since they require a sort. Equivalence reduction may participate in a pipeline if the data is multipaged and the conditions of the last section are met. Reduction and scalar operations are easy to evaluate in a pipeline without needing to stop and build up an intermediate relation. Since the applications of Parts 5 and 6 use only scalar, reduction, and equivalence reduction operations, we can use some of them as examples.

The first example is

let OPS% **be** 100 × (**equiv** + **of** PPROFIT × QTY **by** ORD#)
/(**equiv** + **of** FGPRICE × QTY **by** ORD#),

to be actualized on a single relation which is a join of PRICE (<u>ASSEMBLY</u>, FGPRICE), PARTPROFIT (*ASSEMBLY,* PPROFIT) and ORDLINE (<u>ORD #</u>, <u>ASSEMBLY</u>, QTY) (keys <u>underlined</u>). First we consider the scalar operations PPROFIT × QTY and FGPRICE × QTY. These can be performed on each individual tuple and the results pipelined along to the appropriate equivalence reduction. (If it happens that QTY and PPROFIT or FGPRICE have axes in the multipage space, the effect of the scalar operations can be seen as a reduction of the dimensionality of the space and represented schematically as in Exhibit 3.2-4a.

The space that results from the join of the three relations is essentially two-dimensional, since ORD# and ASSEMBLY together form the key of the result. If the join, on which OPS% is being actualized, were multipaged in this space and if the range of different ORD# in each segment were small enough to permit accumulators in RAM, then both equivalence reductions can be done simultaneously and have the effect of collapsing the ORD#—ASSEMBLY plane into an ORD# line, as shown in Exhibit 3.2-4b. (Notice how the behavior of equivalence reduction depends on the keys and, in general, on the functional dependences.) Even if the join were not multipaged, a single sort on ORD# would be the only sort necessary in evaluating the equivalence reductions and OPS%.

The division of the two equivalence reductions, and the scalar multiplication by 100, can be commenced as soon as values of **equiv + of** PPROFIT × QTY **by** ORD# and **equiv + of** FGPRICE × QTY **by** ORD# have been found for a given

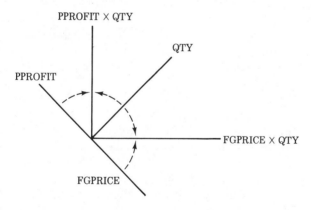

a) Scalar operations reduce dimensionality

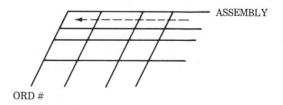

b) Equivalence reductions do too.

Exhibit   3.2-4.   100 × (**equiv + of** PPROFIT × QTY **by** ORD#)
/(**equiv + of** FGPRICE × QTY **by** ORD#)

value of ORD#. Whether the join is multipaged or simply sorted on ORD#, this can be done in the pipeline with the earlier operations.

The second example is more complicated because it involves more dimensions and because the domain algebra operations intersect with the relational algebra operations. It could be written

> let EQUIP$ be equiv + of ((EQCOST − SALVAGE/(LIFE) × HOURS/
> (equiv + of HOURS by EQUIP) by ASSEMBLY,

actualized on a join of FIXED ASSETS (EQUIP, EQCOST, SALVAGE, LIFE) and ROUTING (TEAM, ASSEMBLY, EQUIP, HOURS). However, it is more comprehensible and correct as

> let PROPOR be HOURS/(equiv + of HOURS by EQUIP)
> let DEPR be (EQCOST − SALVAGE)/LIFE
> let EQUIP$ be equiv + of DEPR × PROPOR by ASSEMBLY,

actualized on (EQUIP, DEPR in FIXED ASSETS) ijoin (EQUIP, ASSEMBLY, TEAM, PROPOR in ROUTING).

We now look at the actualization of EQUIP$ as an alternation of domain algebra actualizations with a natural join. It is still not straightforward. The innermost equivalence reduction is a reduction of the three-dimensional space of TEAM, ASSEMBLY and EQUIP to the linear axis EQUIP, as indicated by the diagonal dotted arrow in Exhibit 3.2-5a. However, in order to divide HOURS by the result, we need to keep the full space, not just the EQUIP axis, since HOURS depends on the full space.

The key of the result, after calculating DEPR and doing the natural join, is still{TEAM, ASSEMBLY, EQUIP}, so we do not alter the space of Exhibit 3.2-5a. (This is not to say that additional attributes could not be included as multipage axes, but that only the key attributes determine the essential dimensionality of the relation.) The final equivalence reduction reduces the three-dimensional space to the ASSEMBLY axis, as shown by the diagonal dotted arrow in Exhibit 3.2-5b.

All the steps in actualizing EQUIP$ can be included in two pipelines, if the space for ROUTING is multipaged at least on EQUIP and ASSEMBLY with few enough different values of each of these per segment for the equivalence reductions to be done by accumulators in RAM. First, the equivalence reduction by EQUIP is performed for a given segment of EQUIP values. Since EQUIP is a key of FIXED ASSETS, the value of DEPR can be found immediately for each value of EQUIP in this segment and divided by the result of the equivalence reduction: thus the natural join goes into the pipeline. The value of this division is stored for each value of EQUIP and the other segments of EQUIP are then processed similarly. This terminates one pipeline. The second pipeline is required because the equivalence reduction, on ASSEMBLY, is in a different direction. We process this time on segments of ASSEMBLY, doing multiple passes of the file holding the quotients for each EQUIP value, multiplying these quotients by HOURS and summing.

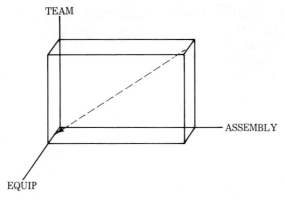

a) **equiv + of** HOURS **by** EQUIP

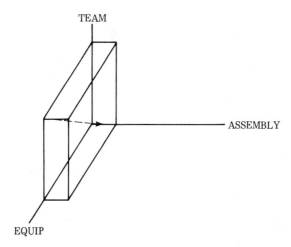

b) **equiv + of** DEPR × PROPOR **by** ASSEMBLY

Exhibit   3.2-5.   Examples of dimension reduction.

If ROUTING were not multipaged, it would have to be sorted, first on EQUIP, then on ASSEMBLY. The quotients that were stored separately in the multipaged version would be passed, repeating the same quotient for each tuple with the same EQUIP value, to the second sort.

These two examples suggest a few generalities, such as that scalar operations pose no problems, the effect of equivalence reductions is dictated by functional dependences, and equivalence reductions by different attributes impose breaks in the pipeline. They also suggest that a general pipelining procedure would be complicated and would have to include a pipelining procedure for the relational algebra. Since domain algebra expressions seem to be broken up naturally by the relational algebra operations needed to assemble the result relations on which the virtual attributes are actualized, a sustained effort to find an optimizing implementation of the domain algebra should at least be preceded by discovering the same for the relational algebra.

ADVANCED TOPICS

3.4-1   The Domain Algebra

The need for arithmetic and similar processing of the values of attributes in individual tuples is apparent and has been incorporated in one way or another in all serious database languages. Long before the relational model was elaborated, the Information Algebra [Bosak *et al.*, 1962] contained scalar operations, "functions-of-areas" for reduction and "functions-of-glumps" for equivalence reduction. SEQUEL (Chamberlin and Boyce [1974], now called SQL) in System R and QUEL [Zook *et al.*, 1976] in INGRES both support at least scalar arithmetic and the aggregation functions of count, sum, average, minimum and maximum. The fact that most developers of query languages have found it valuable to embed their language into a programming language such as C, COBOL or PL/I, and the tuple-at-a-time facilities of all the specially designed programming languages (except Aldat) discussed in Section 2.4-5, attest to the need for this kind of data processing.

The Domain Algebra was proposed [Merrett, 1976] entirely to avoid tuple-at-a-time operations for processing attributes in individual tuples. It makes this processing algebraic and integrates it into the data manipulation formalism (in this case the relational algebra) in an unprecedented way. The tuple-at-a-time extensions of ISBL [Todd, 1976] in PRTV are perhaps more elegant, but are limited to scalar operations applied repetitively to all tuples in a relation.

In Aldat [Kamel, 1980], expressions of the domain algebra are separated from statements of the relational algebra, which is an unfortunate divorce. In Chapters 5.1 and 6.1 of this book, we follow the practice of writing small chunks of code, with domain algebra statements first, followed by relational algebra statements. A programming language could mingle the two further, to the extent of using expressions of the domain algebra in selection conditions, and so on. This raises points of programming language design which are beyond the scope of this book but excellent topics for further research.

4

QUERIES AND QUANTIFIERS

BASICS: QT-Expressions

A major activity in database research and development, particularly since the introduction of relations in 1970, has been the formulation of query languages. The facilities offered by query languages usually include the ability for a user, who is not particularly trained in the use of computers or the implementation of data-bases, to interact with his data by sitting down at a suitable terminal and using it himself. The interest in query languages has been twofold:

a)   how great a variety of queries can a database cope with?

b)   how close can we make the query facilities to what the user is accustomed to so as to minimize the period of special training he must endure?

These are separate issues and are to some extent antithetical to each other. We focus, with limitations, on the first, since this book is intended for readers acquainted with computers. For the second, we only note here that, given the relational algebra and the extensions discussed in this chapter, a programmer has the facility to build a query interface for a user's particular application, and this is probably going to be the best way to cope with "naive" users' needs for the next few decades.

The query facilities we shall discuss are limited in two important ways. First, they are confined to interactions with the data stored explicitly in the databases. Thus we exclude systems which make deductions from the explicit data—or rather we consider these to be artificial intelligence applications which can be built upon the explicit query formalisms such as the one to be described. (One application for such a system would be to provide information about the integrity constraints which apply to the explicitly stored relations. To a certain extent, however, such information can be provided by formulating the constraints as relations, as mentioned in Section 1.1-1, and using the explicit query mechanism to access them.)

Second, they are confined to queries on single relations. This may not at first sight seem a limitation, since several relations can be combined into one by the relational algebra. It may be a limitation, however, if we include updating in our query capability. Consider a relation, T, which is the natural join of relations R and S:

R	(X	Y)		S	(X	Z)
	a	1			a	3
	a	2			a	4

Deleting the tuple (a, 1, 4) from T (X, Y, Z) cannot be expressed as a change to either R or S because the new T will no longer be the natural join of any two relations. Similar problems occur with changing tuple (a, 1, 4) to (b, 1, 4) since changing a tuple is tantamount to deleting then adding a tuple. This example shows one of the problems that can arise when updating a *view,* which is a relation not explicitly held in the database, but is an algebraic combination of relations which are. Our approach to this issue is to say that if a relation is defined only in terms of algebraic components, then this is a meaningful property of the relation, and it *should not* be updated in any way that is incompatible with this definition. Thus, for the example, the decomposability of T into R **ijoin** S is an *integrity constraint* on T which should not be violated by updates.

4.1-1   QT-Selectors

We can start our single-relation query system with the T-selectors discussed in Section 2.1-2. In this section we extend them to include *quantifiers*.

Our approach to quantification is to provide a facility, and a notation, to count the *number of different values* of an attribute in a given relation or in a given subset of tuples of a relation. Exercise 3.1-2 approaches this problem from the point of view of the domain algebra. We now deal with it more directly. Let us start with some sample data (See Exhibit 4.1-1).

Exhibit 4.1-1.   Relations to Illustrate QT-Selectors

LOC (DEPT	FLOOR)	SUPPLY (COMP	DEPT	ITEM	VOL)
Rug	1	Domtex	Rug	Yarn	10
Rug	2	Playsew	Rug	Yarn	17
Shoe	2	Playsew	Toy	Yarn	20
Toy	1	Oddball	Toy	Yarn	13
		Domtex	Rug	String	5
		Domtex	Toy	String	2
CLASS (ITEM	TYPE)	Playsew	Toy	String	10
Yarn	A	Playsew	Shoe	String	5
String	A	Shoeco	Shoe	String	15
Ball	B	Playsew	Toy	Ball	2
Sandal	C	Oddball	Toy	Ball	2

We start with a quantified query

find items supplied to more than two departments

and express it as a QT-**selector** as follows.

ITEM **where** (# > 2) DEPT **in** SUPPLY   *[:)—(ITEM, more then two DEPT]*

The phrase (# > 2) is a quantifier, prescribing "there must be more than two different values of. . . ." So that (# > 2) DEPT states "there must be more than two different values of DEPT." To see how it is used in the QT-selector, we show SUPPLY projected on ITEM and DEPT. The column to the right of the relation gives the value of a virtual attribute, (#) DEPT, which counts the number of different departments associated with each item.

ITEM, DEPT **in** SUPPLY (ITEM   DEPT)   (#) DEPT *> 2 ? ITEM*

ITEM	DEPT	
Yarn	Rug	2
Yarn	Toy	
String	Rug	3
String	Toy	
String	Shoe	1
Ball	Toy	

To calculate the final value of the QT-selector, we just select on (#) DEPT > 2 and project on ITEM to get {STRING} as the sole ITEM for which the condition is true.

The effect of the QT-selector is thus to project SUPPLY on the named attributes (ITEM, DEPT), to count the number of different values of DEPT for each value of ITEM and to select values of ITEM for which the count satisfies the condition described in the quantifier. This could all be expressed as a series of statements in the relational and domain algebras, but it is sufficiently interesting to deserve its own notation. This notation extends easily to much more general specifications, all of which are straightforward to implement in not more than one pass of the relation (after sorting, if necessary).

The reason for writing the quantifier as we do is so that we can stipulate any condition we like on the quantity. For instance "between 3 and 7 of" is (3 ≤ # **and** # ≤ 7), "an odd number of" could be (**mod** (#, 2) = 1), and so on.

Here is an example which shows that conditions are evaluated from right to left if there are more than one:

find all items except those supplied in volumes of less than 10

ITEM **where** (# = 0) VOL, VOL < 10 **in** SUPPLY

This also shows how to negate a condition (e.g., VOL < 10) by selecting values (e.g., of ITEM) to which it does not apply (# = 0). To see the result of this selector, we show the selection operations, from left to right, in the columns to the right of SUPPLY projected on ITEM and VOL. The only ITEM satisfying the combined conditions is Yarn.

ITEM, VOL **in** SUPPLY

(ITEM	VOL)	VOL < 10	# VOL PER ITEM	= 0 ?
Yarn	10	f		
Yarn	13	f		
Yarn	17	f	0	t
Yarn	20	f		
String	2	t		
String	5	t		
String	5	t	2	f
String	10	f		
String	15	f		
Ball	2	t	1	f
Ball	2	t		

We can similarly try two quantifiers and note that <u>interchanging them gives</u> a different result.

find items supplied by at least two companies to more than one department

can be two companies
two dept

ITEM **where** (# ≥ 2) COMP, (# > 1) DEPT **in** SUPPLY

ITEM, COMP, DEPT **in** SUPPLY

(ITEM	COMP	DEPT)	#DEPT per (ITEM, COMP) >1?	#COMP per ITEM ≥2?	
Yarn	Domtex	Rug	1		
Yarn	Playsew	Rug	2	t	1
Yarn	Playsew	Toy			
Yarn	Oddball	Toy	1		
String	Domtex	Rug	2	t	
String	Domtex	Toy			2	t
String	Playsew	Toy	2	t	
String	Playsew	Shoe			
String	Shoeco	Shoe	1		
Ball	Playsew	Toy	1		
Ball	Oddball	Toy	1		

Note that the count (#COMP per ITEM) is made only on tuples selected by (#DEPT per (ITEM, COMP) > 1). Here, String is the only ITEM accepted. The formulation

must be ≥ 1 companies
to the same dept.

ITEM **where** (# > 1) DEPT, (# ≥ 2) COMP **in** SUPPLY

produces {Yarn, String} as a result. (This difference is an appearance in QT-selectors of the usual non-exchangeability in predicate calculus of the classical quantifiers, e.g.,

$$\forall x\ \exists y\ y > x \neq \exists y\ \forall x\ y > x \ .)$$

Classical logic supports two quantifiers, ∃ ("for some") and ∀ ("for all"). The first is easy to express in our notation: (# ≥ 1). The second suggests that we introduce a second quantifier symbol, say **.** , representing "proportion of." Then "for all" would be (**.** = 1) or "the whole of," and we also get (**.** > .5) for "most of," (**.** = 3/4) for "three-quarters of" and so on. This second quantifier symbol is a little less trustworthy than the first, because the "proportion of" must be taken with respect to some total quantity. This total could be taken to be the total number of different values in the domain corresponding to the attribute, or it could be the number of different values of the attribute in the relation (or relational expression) specified after **in** in the QT-selector. We choose the latter because the former could presumably be supplied by a built-in function and used with the "number of" quantifier symbol, #. But this means that, say,

$$\text{where (. = 1) B, A = B in (R × S)} \qquad (4.1\text{-}1)$$

is not necessarily the same as

$$\text{where (. = 1) B in (R [A ijoin B] S)}$$

despite the fact that R [A **ijoin** B] S ≡ **where** A = B **in** (R × S). This is because there may be fewer different values of B in R [A **ijoin** B] S than in R × S. Caution must be observed in using the "proportion of" quantifier symbol.

(Another useful interpretation of the total quantity in the "proportion of" quantifier is the total number of different values of the quantified attribute within the *groups* specified by the attributes on its left in the QT-selector. Thus

$$\text{ITEM where (. = 1) COMP, DEPT = 'Toy' in SUPPLY}$$

would be interpreted "find items" such that all companies *supplying the item* supply it to the Toy department. Answer: 'Ball'.)

● ● ●

The QT-selectors described above have relations as values and so are a part of the relational algebra. *QT-predicates* and *QT-counters* can be defined which have scalar values.

The *QT-predicate*

$$\text{(. = 1) COMP, VOL > 10 in SUPPLY}$$

expresses the false statement

$$\text{all companies supply volumes in excess of 10 .}$$

(Domtex and Oddball are companies with no tuples in SUPPLY with volumes greater than 10.)

The *QT-counters*

$$\text{# ITEM where (# ≥ 2) COMP, (# > 1) DEPT in SUPPLY}$$

and

. ITEM **where** (# ≥ 2) COMP, (# > 1) DEPT **in** SUPPLY

have the values 1 and 1/3 respectively.

Exercise   4.1-1:   Using projection and equivalence reduction, give a definition
of the QT-selector

A **where** (Q_1) B_1, · ·, (Q_k) B_k, T **in** R

for R (A, B_1, . . , B_k, C) .

4.1-2   Updates

Adding and deleting tuples of a relation is relatively straightforward using the
relational algebra, but changing values of tuples is a little more awkward to express. This section outlines a notation for updates which does not extend the
combined capabilities of the relational and domain algebras, but is easier to use
and understand.

Consider first two relations on the same attributes, R (A, B) and S (A, B). We
set up some simple equivalences for addition and deletion. In Exhibit 4.1-2, S may
be replaced by any relational expression involving the attributes A and B.

Exhibit 4.1-2. Simple Additions and Deletions

update R **add** S	≡	R ←+ S
update R **delete** S	≡	R ← R **djoin** S

Changes involve modifying values of specified attributes in certain tuples.
We select the tuples by a relational expression which is combined with the relation
to be modified by one of the operations of the relational algebra, such as **ijoin,**
djoin or one of the σ-joins. We specify explicitly the attributes to be modified. We
illustrate the procedure with relations CLASS (ITEM, TYPE) (see Exhibit 4.1-1)
and RECLASS (ITEM, TYPE).

RECLASS	(ITEM	TYPE)
	Yarn	A
	String	B
	Top	A

1.   **update** CLASS **change** TYPE ← 'B' **using ijoin on** RECLASS   (4.1-2)

We find CLASS **ijoin** RECLASS, which is the single tuple (Yarn, A). The change
instruction, TYPE ← 'B' alters this to (Yarn, B). This altered version of CLASS
ijoin RECLASS then replaces the tuples of CLASS which contributed to CLASS
ijoin RECLASS, giving the new CLASS

CLASS (ITEM   TYPE)
　　　　　Yarn   B
　　　　　String   A
　　　　　Ball   B
　　　　　Sandal   C

Since **ijoin** is the most commonly used operation in updates, we will assume it as a default and write the following equivalent to Equation 4.1-2.

$$\text{\underline{\textbf{update} CLASS \textbf{change} TYPE} \leftarrow \text{`B' \textbf{using} RECLASS}} \qquad (4.1\text{-}2a)$$

We could also use

update CLASS **change** TYPE ← 'B' **using where** ITEM = 'Yarn' **in** CLASS
(4.1-2b)

to get the same result.

2. **update** CLASS **change** TYPE ← 'B' **using** ITEM **in** RECLASS   (4.1-3)

Here we have projected RECLASS. Finding CLASS **ijoin** (ITEM **in** RECLASS) gives two tuples, (Yarn, A) and (String, A). (NB. In this and subsequent examples we work with the original CLASS from Exhibit 4.1-1, not the changed values from preceding examples.) Altering these to (Yarn, B) and (String, B) and replacing gives

CLASS (ITEM   TYPE)
　　　　　Yarn   B
　　　　　String   B
　　　　　Ball   B
　　　　　Sandal   C

3. **let** NEWTYPE **be** TYPE
    update CLASS **change** TYPE ← NEWTYPE **using** ITEM, NEWTYPE **in**
    RECLASS   (4.1-4)

This is a more flexible update. CLASS **ijoin** (ITEM, NEWTYPE **in** RECLASS) gives two tuples, (Yarn, A, A), (String, A, B), similar to case 2 above only these are on ITEM, TYPE and NEWTYPE. The change and replacement leaves

CLASS (ITEM   TYPE)
　　　　　Yarn   A
　　　　　String   B
　　　　　Ball   B
　　　　　Sandal   C

4. The update to CLASS that seems most appropriate, given RECLASS, is

> **let** NEWTYPE **be** TYPE
> **update** CLASS **change** TYPE ← NEWTYPE **using ujoin on** ITEM, NEW-
> TYPE **in** RECLASS   (4.1-5)

The intermediate union join gives the unnamed relation shown on the left and CLASS becomes the relation on the right, below.

ITEM	TYPE	NEWTYPE		CLASS	(ITEM	TYPE)
Yarn	A	A			Yarn	A
String	A	B			String	B
Ball	B	*DC*			Ball	B
Sandal	C	*DC*			Sandal	C
Top	*DC*	A			Top	A

Note that *DC*, the "don't care" null value, does not replace a known value in the change operation.

5. We may want to update every tuple but some specified ones.

> **update** CLASS **change** TYPE ← 'B' **using djoin on** RECLASS   (4.1-6)

The intermediate difference join is shown to the left and the new value of CLASS to the right, below. Here, (Yarn, A) is the tuple common to CLASS and RE-CLASS, which is not updated.

CLASS **djoin** RECLASS	(ITEM	TYPE)		CLASS	(ITEM	TYPE)
	String	A			Yarn	A
	Ball	B			String	B
	Sandal	C			Ball	B
					Sandal	B

6. Some degenerate forms of update are

> **update** CLASS **change** TYPE ← 'B'   (4.1-7)

and

> **update** CLASS **using** RECLASS

The second has no effect on CLASS and is not particularly interesting. The first replaces all values of TYPE in CLASS with 'B'. This has useful variations such as

> **let** NEWTYPE **be if** TYPE = 'C' **then** 'B' **else** TYPE
> **update** CLASS **change** TYPE ← NEWTYPE   (4.1-7a)

which will change type C to type B and leave other types unchanged. Or

> **let** NEWTYPE **be if** ITEM = 'Yarn' **then** 'B' **else** TYPE
> **update** CLASS **change** TYPE ← NEWTYPE   (4.1-7b)

which has the same effect as (4.1-2b).

7. This approach allows some quite elaborate forms of update, such as

> **update** CLASS **change** TYPE ← 'A' **using**
> **where** COMP = 'Playsew' **in** SUPPLY   (4.1-8a)

which changes the TYPE of Yarn, String and Ball to 'A' (only Ball was not already type A).

> **update** CLASS **change** TYPE ← 'A' **using** SUPPLY **ijoin**
> **where** FLOOR = 1 **in** LOC   (4.1-8b)

makes the same change—for a different reason, of course.

> **update** CLASS **change** TYPE ← 'B' **using** ITEM
> **where** (# ≥ 2) COMP, (# > 1) DEPT **in** SUPPLY   (4.1-8c)

changes the type of String to B.

● ● ●

The notations for add, delete and change can be extended in an obvious way to handle relations on different attributes. Thus, with a relation T (C, D), we might have

> **update** R [A, B **add** C, D] T   ≡   R [A, B ←+ C, D] T
> **update** R [A, B **delete** C, D] T ≡   R ← R [A, B **djoin** C, D] T
> **update** R **change** A ← 2 **using** [A, B **ijoin** C, D] **on** T.   (4.1-9)

4.1-3   Integrity, Concurrency, Reliability

Updates give rise to three considerations which are primarily implementation problems but which may be mentioned briefly here. First, *consistency constraints* must be enforced. If {COMP, DEPT, ITEM} → VOL is a functional dependence imposed on SUPPLY (Section 4.1-1, we may not

update SUPPLY **add** NEWTUP

where NEWTUP is the singleton relation {(Domtex, Rug, Yarn, 17)}. Nor may we

> **let** NEWCOMP **be if** COMP = 'Playsew' **then** 'Domtex' **else** COMP
> **update** SUPPLY **change** COMP ← NEWCOMP

for the same reason. Three ways of checking this are: post-processing, query modification, and special checking. Other ways are discussed in Section 4.4-3.

With *post-processing,* the update is performed and then the whole relation checked to see if the integrity constraint (e.g., the functional dependence) is still satisfied. This is the slowest but most thorough and also, because any integrity constraint can be expressed as a query in a sufficiently powerful query formalism, the most easily implemented method in general. *Query modification* combines the update command with the formulation of the integrity constraint. This can be easily applied to a constraint like "VOL must not exceed 20": the first update is modified to

update SUPPLY **add where** VOL $\leq$ 20 **in** NEWTUP

It is harder to apply to a constraint like functional dependence which involves combinations of tuples of the relation. *Special checking* is still more geared to the type of consistency constraint but can be more efficient and may even be carried out on the syntactic form of the update before it is run. In the case of functional dependence A $\rightarrow$ B, the check might be that a new value of (A, B) requires a new value of A. This would stop both versions of the above update.

We consider that both integrity constraints and the update operations allowed reflect the semantics of the application, and should be expressed at a higher level than that of the data manipulation formalism. The relational algebra with the query and update facilities described in this chapter is intended for *any* data, apart from its use or semantic interpretation. The designer of a particular application is in the best position to specify the constraints on his data, and an important way for him to do this is to write a carefully worked out set of update operations using the facilities described in this book.

$$\bullet \quad \bullet \quad \bullet$$

The second implementation problem we touch on arises from *concurrent updates*. Two users may safely read the same tuple simultaneously but they cannot both change it at the same time without risk. The danger arises because updates are usually processed in several separate transactions, and the transactions of two "simultaneous" updates will be intermingled in an unpredictable—and unreconstructible—fashion. For instance, the following two updates, if run simultaneously,

> **let** NEWTYPE **be if** TYPE = 'A' **then** 'B' **else** TYPE
> **update** CLASS **change** TYPE $\leftarrow$ NEWTYPE

and

> **let** NEWTYPE **be if** TYPE = 'A' **then** 'C' **else** TYPE
> **update** CLASS **change** TYPE $\leftarrow$ NEWTYPE

could change the type of Yarn to B but the type of String to C, or any of three other possible changes, and it would be impossible to roll back and reestablish the original data in order to run the two updates again independently. Or we could imagine a scenario in which the manager of the Rug department became dissatisfied with the quality of goods supplied by Domtex and ordered

> **let** NEWVOL **be if** DEPT = 'Rug' **and** COMP = 'Domtex'
> **then** 0.8 $\times$ VOL **else** VOL
> **update** SUPPLY **change** VOL $\leftarrow$ NEWVOL

while the store general manager received too many complaints about the unwillingness of Playsew to refund for deficient items and specified

> **let** NEWCOMP **be if** COMP = 'Playsew' **then** 'Domtex' **else** COMP
> **update** SUPPLY **change** COMP $\leftarrow$ NEWCOMP

If these updates were run simultaneously, we would not know whether the tuple (Playsew, Rug, Yarn, 17) was changed to (Domtex, Rug, Yarn, 17) or to (Domtex, Rug, Yarn, 13).

One solution to this problem is to force an update to be a single transaction by *locking* other updates out of the relation until the first update has completely finished. It may be, however, that each user has specified two updates in his request. Suppose the Rug department manager wants to change SUPPLY, then type A in CLASS to type B, while the general manager wants to change type A in CLASS to type C, as above, then change SUPPLY. This will lead to SUPPLY being locked by the Rug manager and CLASS by the general manager, and since each must change both relations before completing his update and releasing his locks, each will wait for the other indefinitely in a state appropriately called *deadlock*. Deadlocks can be avoided by requiring processes to lock all resources at once, by allowing a process to pre-empt another or by ranking resources in a non-circular hierarchy and requiring processes to lock resources only in the order dictated by the hierarchy. Their probability of occurrence can be reduced, at the cost of reduced concurrency, by increasing the "granularity" of the locking: if an update locked the whole database instead of just a relation, deadlock would be impossible, to give the extreme case.

Section 4.4-4 looks in more detail at research into concurrency control.

● ● ●

The third implementation problem arises when there is a *failure of hardware or software* during an update. Suppose we are doing

let NEWTYPE **be if** TYPE = 'B' **then** 'C' **else if** TYPE = 'A' **then** 'B'
update CLASS **change** TYPE ← NEWTYPE

and there is a power cut just before the third tuple of CLASS, (Ball, B), is written back to secondary storage. Then CLASS has not been completely updated, yet if we run the update a second time it will be over-updated because Yarn and String will have type C instead of B. We can cope with this problem by keeping a copy of an earlier state of the database and logging all transactions as they are processed. When a failure occurs, the database can be restored by repeating the updates on the log since the last saved "snapshot" of the database. A differential file does this without actually applying the transactions to the database; the earlier state is just the main file, which is periodically reorganized to bring it up to date. The approach of keeping a correct early version, then substituting a correct up-to-date version for it, can also be used at the level of individual relations or even individual blocks of data, at the expense of an index informing us which is the current version of each relation or block.

Review Questions and Exercises, Chapter 4.1

4.1-2 Use the relational and domain algebras only to express the queries of Section 4.1-1.

4.1-3 Show that Expression 4.1-1 is equivalent to R [A $\supseteq$ B] S.

4.1-4 Express the following queries on SUPPLY using QT-expressions.

   a) Find items which are not supplied to all departments.
   b) Find items supplied by most companies.
   c) Find items supplied by at least two companies to most departments.
   d) Find items supplied by at least two but less than 3/4 of the companies.

4.1-5 Express the following queries on SUPPLY, LOC and CLASS, together with EMP (NAME, SAL, MGR, DEPT) and SALES (DEPT, ITEM), using the relational and domain algebras and QT-expressions.

   a) Find companies, each of which supply every item of type A to some department on the second floor.
   b) Find companies which do not supply balls.
   c) Find departments which sell no items of type B.
   d) Find departments which sell all items supplied to the departments on the same floor.

4.1-6 Given the relations SUPPLIER (SNO, SNAME, SLOC, SBUDGET)
             PART(PNO, PNAME, DIM, PRICE, COLOR)
             PROJECT(JNO, JNAME, JBUDGET, JLOC)
             SHIPMENT(SNO, PNO, JNO, QTY)
   formulate the following queries:
   a) Find supplier numbers of suppliers which supply parts whose unit price is higher than 25.
   b) Find the names of suppliers which supply all red parts that are priced higher than 25.

4.1-7 For the same database as (Exercise 4.1-6), formulate:

   a) Find the highest part number of parts whose unit price is greater than 25.
   b) Find supplier numbers of suppliers which supply parts whose part numbers are the highest of those parts used by each of the projects located in New York.

4.1-8 Given the database

        R1(STUDENT, ADVISOR)   ADVISOR supervises STUDENT
        R2(STUDENT, HOBBY)   STUDENT has HOBBY
        R3(ADVISOR, HOBBY)   ADVISOR has HOBBY
   formulate the following queries.

a) Find advisors and students who share some hobbies.

b) Find advisors and their students if they share some hobbies.

4.1-9 Given the database

DIV(DIVISION, MANAGER, BUDGET)
DEPT(DEPARTMENT, DIVISION, MANAGER, BUDGET)
EMP(EMPLOYEE, SALARY, DEPARTMENT, SENIORITY, RECRUITER)

formulate the following queries

a) For each department in the marketing division, list the department name and a count of its employees.

b) Sum employee salaries over departments, and then average these sums over divisions. Give division names and the averages.

4.1-10 The following sixty-six queries are from Lacroix and Pirotte [1976]. Use QT-expressions to express them, devising suitable relations where necessary.

(1) Find the names of employees in the toy department.

(2) Find the items sold by no department on the second floor.

(3) Find the items sold by departments on the second floor.

(4) Find the items sold by all departments on the second floor.

(5) Find the items sold by at least two departments on the second floor.

(6) Find the salary of Anderson's manager.

(7) Find the names of the employees who make more than their manager.

(8) Find the departments where all the employees make less than their manager.

(9) Find the names of the employees whose salary equals the salary of their manager.

(10) Find the names of the employees who are in the same departments as their manager (as an employee).

(11) List the departments having an average salary greater than 25000.

(12) List the departments where the average salary of the employees of each manager is greater than 25000.

(13) List the name and salary of the managers who manage more than 10 employees.

(14) List the name and manager of the employees of the shoe department who have a salary greater than 25000.

(15) List the name of the employees who make more than any employee in the shoe department.

(16) Among all departments with total salary greater than 100000, find the departments which sell dresses.

(17) List the items supplied by all companies that supply all items of type A.

(18) Find the companies that supply pens.

(19) Find the companies that do not supply pens.

(20) Find the companies that supply an item other than pens.

(21) List the departments that do not sell all the items of type A.

  (a) departments that sell some but not all of the items of type A.

  (b) all departments except those that sell all items of type A (includes all the departments that sell no item at all);

  (c) departments that sell something excluding those that sell all items of type A.

(22) List the departments that sell all the items that they are supplied.

(23) List the supplier-department pairs where the department sells all items it is supplied by the supplier.

(24) List the items supplied to all departments by all suppliers.

(25) List the items sold only by departments which sell all the items that they are supplied.

(26) What are the companies that supply all the items.

(27) List the suppliers who supply all and only the items sold by the toy department.

(28) List the suppliers who supply only items sold by the toy department.

(29) List the companies that supply every item of type A to one same department on the second floor. [Logical order of quantifiers: ($\exists$ department) ($\forall$ item)]

(30) List the companies that supply every item of type A (to departments) on the second floor. [Logical order of quantifiers: ($\forall$ item) ($\exists$ department)]

(31) List the companies that supply at least two items of type A to one same department on the second floor. [Logical order of quantifiers: ($\exists$ department) ($\exists2$ Item)]

(32) List the companies which supply all the items of type A to departments on the second floor which sell all the items of type B. [Logical order of quantifiers: ($\forall$ item of type A) ($\exists$ department) ($\forall$ item of type B)]

(33) List the companies which supply all the items of type A to one same department on the second floor which sells all the items of type B. [Logical order of quantifiers: ($\exists$ department) ($\forall$ item of type B) ($\forall$ item of type A)]

(34) List the items supplied by exactly one supplier. [= List the items always supplied by the same supplier]

(35) List the companies that are the only supplier of some item.

(36) List the companies that are the only supplier of at least 10 items.

(37) For each item, give its type, the departments which sell the item and the floor of these departments.

(38) Find the companies and their location for those companies that supply all departments.

(39) Find the companies and their location for those companies that supply all departments supplied by company PHILIPS.

(40) List the departments for which each item supplied to the department is supplied to some other department as well.

(41) List each item supplied to at least two departments by each company that supplies it.

(42) List the items which are only supplied by companies which supply something to all the departments. [= items such that every company that supplies it supplies something to all the departments].

(43) List the items supplied by Levi and sold in the men's department.

(44) List the items supplied by Levi or sold in the men's department.

(45) List the departments selling items of type A which are supplied by Levi and/or which are sold by the men's department.

(46) Find the average salary of the employees in the SHOE department.

(47) Give, for each department, the average salary of the employees.

(48) Give, for each department on the second floor, the average salary of the employees.

(49) Give, for each department which sells items of type A, the average salary of the employees.

(50) Give, for each department, its floor and the average salary in the department.

(51) What is the number of different items supplied by each company which supplies all the departments.

(52) What is, for each company that supplies all the departments, the number of different items supplied to each department.

(53) Find the total volume of items of type A sold by departments on the second floor.

(54) Give, for each item, the total volume sold by departments on the second floor.

(55) List companies that supply a total volume of items of type A and B which is altogether greater than 1000.

(56) List the employees in the shoe department and the difference of their salary with the average salary of the department.

(57) List the employees in the shoe department and the difference of their salary with the average salary computed on all departments.

(58) List each employee and the difference of his salary with the average salary of the department where he works.

(59) What is, for each supplier, the average number of items per department that the supplier supplies.

(60) For each department, find the average salary of the employees who make more than the average salary of the department.

(61) Give the overall average of the average salary per department.

(62) List, for each employee, his salary, the average salary of the department where he works and the difference of his salary with the average salary of the department where he works.

(63) What is the average volume of items of type A supplied per company that supplies them.

(64) What is the average volume of items of type A supplied per company and per department. [such that the company supplies the items of type A to the department].

(65) What is the number of pairs company-department such that the company supplies at least one item of type A to the department.

(66) Is it true that all the departments that sell items of type A are located on the third floor.

IMPLEMENTATION

The major advantage of QT-expressions is the ease of implementing them. In this chapter we describe the QT-expression in terms of projection and equivalence reduction, then we streamline this description into a one-pass implementation. Combined with multipaging and the selective effect of the tuple part, T, of the QT-expression, this gives us an implementation that is optimal in many cases, and usually sub-linear. It also leads easily to an implementation of updates, which, however, we do not elaborate on.

4.2-1 Using Projection and Equivalence Reduction

We said in Section 4.1-1 that QT-expressions essentially represent special sets of statements in the relational and domain algebras. According to Exercise 4.1-1, the QT-selector A **where** QT **in** R on R $(A, B_1, \ldots, B_k, C)$ can be defined by projections and equivalence reductions:

$$A \text{ where } (Q_1) B_1, \ldots, (Q_k) B_k, T \text{ in } R \stackrel{\Delta}{=} A \text{ where } Q_1 \text{ in } R_1$$

where we specify

> **let** Q_{k+1} **be** T $(A, B_1, \ldots, B_k, C)$
> $R_{k+1} \leftarrow A, B_1, \ldots, B_k, Q_{k+1}$ **in** R
> **let** S_k **be equiv** + **of** (**if** T **then** 1 **else** 0) **by** $(A, B_1, \ldots, B_{k-1})$
> **let** Q_k **be** Q_k $(S_k, S_k / \#_k)$ $A, B_1, \ldots, B_{k-1})$
> $R_k \leftarrow A, B_1, \ldots, B_{k-1}, Q_k$ **in** R_{k+1}
> $\vdots$
> **let** S_j **be equiv** + **of** (**if** Q_{j+1} **then** 1 **else** 0) **by** $(A, B_1, \ldots, B_{j-1})$
> **let** Q_j **be** Q_j $(S_j, S_j / \#_j)$
> $R_j \leftarrow A, B_1, \ldots, B_{j-1}, Q_j$ **in** R_{j+1}.

Here T is the Boolean-valued function on some of the attributes $A, B_1, \ldots, B_k,$ C defined for each tuple by the query. Q_j is the Boolean-valued function on one or both of $\#, \cdot$ defined by the query. The symbol $\#$ in the quantifier-predicate Q_j is replaced by S_j when evaluating, and the symbol $\cdot$ is replaced by $S_j/\#_j$, where $\#_j$ is the cardinality of B_j in R and by convention $Q_j(S_j, S_j/\#_j)$ is **true** if $\#_j = 0$. (This definition is limited, in that Q_j can depend only on the values of attributes $A, B_1, \ldots, B_{j-1}$. This is usually sufficient, but if there is a functional dependence of A or any $B_i, i = 1., , ,.j - 1,$ on C or any $B_i, i = j, \ldots, k,$ it might be acceptable for Q_j to use the value of C or B_i for some $i = j, \ldots, k.$)

Implementation of the QT-selector is straightforward given this definition: we just make a loop forming $R_{k+1}, \ldots, R_1$. Here is an illustration using

$$\text{ITEM \textbf{where} } (\# \geq 2) \text{ COMP}, (\# > 1) \text{ DEPT \textbf{in} SUPPLY}$$

from Section 4.1-1. Exhibit 4.2-1 shows R_3, R_2 and R_1 defined as follows

> **let** T **be true**
> $R_3 \leftarrow$ ITEM, COMP, DEPT, T **in** SUPPLY
> **let** S_2 **be equiv** + **of** (**if** T **then** 1 **else** 0) **by** ITEM, COMP
> **let** Q_2 **be** $S_2 > 1$ $<<$ # is replaced by S_2 $>>$
> $R_2 \leftarrow$ ITEM, COMP, Q_2 **in** R_3
> **let** S_1 **be equiv** + **of** (**if** 1_2 **then** 1 **else** 0) **by** ITEM
> **let** Q_1 **be** $S_1 \geq 2$
> $R_1 \leftarrow$ ITEM, Q_1 **in** R_2

Exhibit 4.2-1 also shows the virtual attributes S_2 and S_1, and the final result.

QT-predicates and QT-counters can similarly be defined and implemented. The QT-predicate $(Q_0) A, (Q_1) B_1, \ldots, (Q_k) B_k$ **in** R, is Q_0 **in** R_1 where Q_j and R_j are defined as before with suitable modification to introduce S_0 and Q_0. The QT-counter, $\# A$ **where** $(Q_1) B_1, \ldots, (Q_k) B_k$ **in** R, uses $R(A, B_1, \ldots, B_k, C)$ and is defined to be S_0 **where** Q_1 **in** R with **let** S_0 **be red** + **of** 1.

4.2-2   Using a Single Pass

Inspecting the definition of the last section more closely reveals that we can pipeline the whole set of expressions into one pass of the relation R. The projections only serve the purpose of reducing the number of tuples in each intermediate relation R_{j+1} so that S_j really is a count of the number of different values of $A,$ $B_1, \ldots, B_{j-1}$ such that Q_{j+1} is **true**; without the projections, we might have duplicate **true** values of Q_{j+1} and the count would be too high. This is because the equivalence reduction counts *tuples* rather than different values of $A, B_1, \ldots,$ B_{j-1}. If we can count different values instead of tuples, we can avoid the projections. We notice, in any case, that the attributes in each projection are very simply related to the attributes of the preceeding projection, in such a way that only one sort would be needed for all projections (if R were represented by a sequential file

Exhibit   4.2-1.   Stages in Evaluating ITEM **where** (# $\geq$ 2) COMP, (# > 1) DEPT **in** SUPPLY

R_3 (ITEM	COMP	DEPT	T)	S_2		R_2 (ITEM	COMP	Q_2)	S_1
Yarn	Domtex	Rug	t	1		Yarn	Domtex	f	1
Yarn	Playsew	Rug	t	2		Yarn	Playsew	t	1
Yarn	Playsew	Toy	t	2		Yarn	Oddball	f	1
Yarn	Oddball	Toy	t	1		String	Domtex	t	2
String	Domtex	Rug	t	2		String	Playsew	t	2
String	Domtex	Toy	t	2		Ball	Playsew	f	0
String	Playsew	Toy	t	2		Ball	Oddball	f	0
String	Playsew	Shoe	t	2					
Ball	Playsew	Toy	t	1					
Ball	Oddball	Toy	t	1					

R_1 (ITEM	Q_1)		ITEM if Q_1 in R (ITEM)
Yarn	f		
String	t		String
Ball	f		

and any sort were needed at all). The same simple relationship holds between the control attribute sets of successive equivalence reductions.

Algorithm QT gives a one-pass implementation of A **where** $(Q_1) B_1, \ldots, (Q_k) B_k$, T **in** R on R $(A, B_1, \ldots, B_k, C)$, which is assumed to be a sequential file sorted in lexicographical order on $A, B_1, \ldots, B_k$. The "control break" is j, the position of the first attribute B_j at which the current tuple differs from the preceeding tuple. The counters, S_j, j = control break, $\ldots$, $k-1$, are incremented simultaneously, instead of in successive passes, as would be done by the iterated implementation of the last section. Algorithm QT also implements for the QT-predicate (Q_0) A, $(Q_1) B_1, \ldots, (Q_k) B_k$, T **in** R and the QT-counter # A **where** $(Q_1) B_1, \ldots, (Q_k) B_k$, T **in** R.

Algorithm QT: One-pass QT-expression evaluation.
Comment   A is at position 0. The first tuple is assumed identical with its "predecessor" and the "last tuple" is an imaginary successor to the actual final tuple, giving a control break of -1.
for each tuple
    if control break $\geq$ k
    then $Q_{k+1} \leftarrow (Q_{k+1}$ **or** T $(A, B_1, \ldots, B_k, C))$ << evaluate T>>
    else $S_k \leftarrow (S_k +$ **if** Q_{k+1} **then** 1 **else** 0)
        if control break = k
        then $Q_{k+1} \leftarrow$ T $(A, B_1, \ldots, B_k, C)$ << evaluate T >>
        else for each B_j, j $\leftarrow$ k-1 **by** -1 **to** max (0, control break)
            $Q_{j+1} \leftarrow Q_{j+1} (S_{j+1}, S_{j+1}/\#_{j+1})$ << evaluate Q_{j+1} >>
            $S_j \leftarrow S_j +$ **if** Q_{j+1} **then** 1 **else** 0
        if control break $\leq$ 0 **then**
            if not last tuple **and** QT-selector **then** add tuple to result

              else if last tuple **and** QT-predicate **then** value is Q_0
              else if last tuple **and** QT-counter **then** value is S_0
          if not last tuple **then**
              $Q_{k+1} \leftarrow T(A, B_1, \ldots, B_k, C)$ $<<$ evaluate T$>>$
              for $j \leftarrow$ max (0, control break) + 1 **to** k **do** $S_j \leftarrow 0$
end for each tuple

As a consequence of getting rid of the projections and using only one pass, Algorithm QT extends the definition of the QT-expression a little to allow the QT-predicate Q_j to use values of $B_j, \ldots, B_k, C$. This extension is of limited use, but it is nice to improve efficiency by a factor of k + 1 and also get a more powerful operator.

If $R(A, B_1, \ldots, B_k, C)$ were multipaged on A, $B_1, \ldots, B_k$, we could do the same pipelining without having to sort beforehand. We would just process the attributes in the order B_k within ... within B_1 within A. The control breaks would correspond to changing loops in

        for each A
          for each B_1
            ●
                ●
                   ●
                  for each B_k

Exercise 1.2-24 gives an implementation for k + 1 nested loops of this sort, where k is variable.

In general, a QT-expression requires access to each tuple, so that the multipaged one-pass implementation is optimal. Some special cases require less processing. A QT-predicate with an existential quantifier such as $(Q_0) = (\# > 3)$ may be satisfied before the whole relation has been inspected, and we can stop processing. $(Q_0) = (\# = 1)$ is not, however, such a predicate. An important special case is the T-selector, major categories of which have been discussed in Section 2.2-2.

General QT-expressions may be significantly speeded up if the T-predicate is very selective and if the data structure can take advantage of this. Thus a multipaged relation with secondary indices can be substantially reduced by the T-predicate before the pass to evaluate $(Q_1) B_1, \ldots, (Q_k) B_k$ begins.

The one-pass algorithm is also valuable if the result of a QT-selector is to be used in updating a relation, since it effectively flags the tuple selected, i.e., to be changed or deleted.

ADVANCED TOPICS: Queries and Updates

4.4-1   Query Languages

As with relational database systems, an exhaustive list of relational query languages would be prohibitively long. We shall select query languages for discussion with an emphasis on novelty of form and features. The important aspects of query languages that have been promoted and developed by research are the generality and flexibility of facilities and the degree of "non-procedurality", i.e. the capacity of a language to express what should be done without being concerned about how it is to be done. Query languages usually have the capacity to update the database as well as just find out what is stored on it. Finally, especially for a query language intended for end-users (as opposed to programmer users), human factors analysis is necessary to ensure that it can be used effectively.

The first relational languages were the relational algebra [Codd, 1970; Kraning and Fillat, 1970] and the relational calculus [Codd, 1971c], of which the calculus, being less procedural, is more suitable as a query language. Codd [1971b] showed that the algebra has at least the selective power of the calculus by giving an algorithm to translate all calculus expressions into algebraic equivalents. This discussion is the basis of the notion of "relational completeness" of data languages, which has been used subsequently as an assessment of query languages —unfortunately, because a relationally "complete" language may omit all sorts of processing power, such as the capabilities of the domain algebra, or the ability to compute fixed-point operations like the transitive closure (see Chapter 5.2).

The Structured English QUEry Language SEQUEL (Chamberlin and Boyce [1974]: part of System R and now called SQL) is an extended and syntactically smoother elaboration of SQUARE (Specifying QUeries As Relational Expressions), which avoids the variables and quantifiers of the relational calculus by being based on "mappings". A mapping is a unary operation on relations, a T-selector, in fact, which generates a set of tuples on specified attributes from a relation selected according to some condition. It is a mapping from a set (the original relation) to a set (the result relation) and so avoids tuple-at-a-time notions or the use of variables, which somewhat conceals these notions in the calculus. The trick which enables SEQUEL to use this unary algebraic operation to express a join (or other binary operation) is that the selection condition can depend on the result of a previous mapping. Consider the query "find items sold by departments on the second floor" which, applied to the relations LOC (DEPT, FLOOR) and SALES (DEPT, ITEM), is written in the algebra

$$\text{ITEM in (SALES ijoin DEPT where FLOOR} = 2 \text{ in LOC).} \quad (4.4\text{-}1)$$

If we allowed selection conditions to include sets produced from another T-selector, we could write this as the following nested T-selector

$$\text{ITEM where DEPT} \in \{\text{DEPT where FLOOR} = 2 \text{ in LOC}\} \text{ in SALES}$$

and, turning this around so that clauses at the same level are not so widely separated, we have almost exactly the format of the SEQUEL expression for this join:

$$\text{ITEM in SALES where DEPT} \in \{\text{DEPT in LOC where FLOOR} = 2\}.$$

This kind of notation got into difficulty in SEQUEL, because it appears to dictate an unsymmetrical nested-loop implementation of the join and because attribute names appearing twice in a join (for instance as a result of joining a relation with itself: try the query "find employees who earn more than their managers" in EMP (NAME, MGR, SAL)) must be distinguished by a difficult mechanism of labelling the levels of the query. So the next version of SEQUEL [Astrahan *et al.*, 1976] made the join more symmetrical but was forced to introduce the relation names as qualifiers to distinguish the sources of ambiguous attributes. Thus, continuing to use fancied extensions to T-selector notation, we would write the query above as

$$\text{ITEM in SALES, LOC where SALES. DEPT} = \text{LOC. DEPT and}$$
$$\text{LOC. FLOOR} = 2.$$

This was in turn criticized by Lochovsky [1978], who recommended replacing this calculus-like predicate with an explicit join specification, giving, say,

$$\text{ITEM in SALES, LOC joined by DEPT where FLOOR} = 2.$$

The human factors study by Welty and Stemple [1981] supported this change, as part of a more general finding that procedural languages are easier to formulate queries in than non-procedural languages when the queries are complicated. Reisner [1981] cautions us that this study does not isolate non-procedurality as the source of the difficulty. (Incidentally, Welty and Stemple characterize "procedurality" of a query formulation by three measures including the number of intermediate results assigned to variables. Gray and Bell [1979] find that having intermediate results from the relational algebra helps thinking about a query and have built a simulator which enables a user to see these results on a sample of data before running an expensive query on a large database.) It is noteworthy that this evolution in SEQUEL away from the join then back again was anticipated by COLARD [Bracchi, Fedeli and Paolini, 1972], which uses relational calculus constructs to query single relations and the relational algebra to combine relations.

The QUEry Language QUEL [Held, Stonebraker and Wong, 1975] is based on the relational calculus, but uses set functions instead of quantifiers. Thus, the query "find items sold by all departments on the second floor", which we would phrase using the σ-join

$$\text{SALES } \textbf{sup (where } \text{FLOOR} = 2 \textbf{ in } \text{LOC)} \qquad (4.4-2)$$

(**sup** is equivalent to **divide** or $\supseteq$) could be expressed in QUEL [Lacroix and Pirotte, 1976]

> **range** s ϵ SALES, ℓ ϵ LOC;
> **get** s. ITEM **where set** (s. DEPT **by** s. ITEM)
> $\supseteq$ **set** (ℓ. DEPT **where** ℓ. FLOOR = 2).

The relations are, as before, SALES (DEPT, ITEM) and LOC (DEPT, FLOOR). The **by** clause in the query causes a set of departments to be formed for each item, and just makes explicit the grouping implicit in the division operator, **sup**.

QUEL uses the **set** function, in conjunction with the five predefined aggregation operators COUNT, SUM, AVG, MAX and MIN, to obtain the major reduction operations of the domain algebra. AVG (SET $(\cdot\ \cdot)$) is abbreviated AVG $(\cdot\ \cdot)$. The **by** clause, with these aggregates, gives *equivalence reductions*. An interesting aspect of QUEL is its recursive definition in terms of aggregates, allowing any degree of nesting of aggregation operations. Thus the query on SUPPLY (S#, P#, PRICE), "find suppliers whose price for every part that he supplies is greater than the average price for the part", expressed algebraically as

let AVPRICE **be (equiv** + **of** PRICE **by** P#)/(**equiv** + **of** 1 **by** P#)
S# **where** (**.** = 1) P#, PRICE > AVPRICE **in** (S#, P#, PRICE, AVPRICE **in**
SUPPLY), (4.4-3)

is in QUEL

> RANGE OF S IS SUPPLY
> RETRIEVE INTO W (S, S#)
> WHERE COUNT (S. P# BY S. S# WHERE S. PRICE >
> AVG' (S. PRICE BY S. P#))
> = COUNT (S. P# BY S. S#).

Note the use of COUNT, which is cheaper than using SET to express the universal quantification "every part"—see the counting implementation of σ-join suggested in Section 2.2-1. The prime in AVG' means that duplicates are not to be eliminated in SET (S. PRICE BY S. P#) before the average is taken: the equivalence reduction always works this way. The domain algebra operators are also intended for arbitrary nesting, and recursive implementation is essential.

Query by Example [Zloof, 1975] is a query language intended for ease of use rather than to add facilities beyond those already available. Its major contributions are to provide for the user templates of the relations he must work with and to allow him to specify *examples* of the sort of answer he wants. This saves him from the need to remember syntax or abstract notions. For instance, a simple query on a single relation, EMP (NAME, SAL, MGR, DEPT), such as would be expressed by a T-selector, is "list the names, salaries and managers of employees in the toy department". The first line in Exhibit 4.4-1 is the template provided by the system, and the second line is the on-line response of the questioner. TOY is a *constant*, the underlined values represent *variables*—the values may or may not turn out to be in the answer—and the operator P. instructs the system to *print* the answer. Exhibit 4.4-1 shows the answer given by Zloof [1975] to this query, according to his example database.

Exhibit   4.4-1. Query by Example—simple case.

EMP	NAME	SAL	MGR	DEPT
	P. Jones	P. 10K	P. Smith	Toy

a) The Query

NAME	SAL	MGR
Anderson	6K	Murphy
Nelson	6K	Murphy
Hung	9K	Smith

b) The Answer

Things get more complicated, however, with more difficult queries. A natural join of two relations is specified by entering the *same* variable (i.e. the same value, underlined) in the join attributes of the two relations, or, in some cases, by explicitly invoking a JOIN: operator—as when a view is to be formed. Exhibit 4.4-2 shows this in the classic case of "find the names of employees who earn more than their managers"—a join of EMP with itself. Queries requiring the Boolean operations **and** and **or** need two rows in their template, as in Exhibit 4.4-3. So far, human factors studies [Thomas and Gould, 1975] do not reveal any difficulties. When it comes to quantification, however, misconceptions appear to arise. Query by Example handles quantification by a hidden notion of set comparison generating a set with the keyword ALL and using notations such as

$$\text{ALL } \underline{\text{Pen}}, \qquad \begin{bmatrix} \text{ALL } \underline{\text{Pen}} \\ \bullet \end{bmatrix} \qquad \text{and} \qquad \begin{bmatrix} \text{ALL } \underline{\text{Pen}} \\ \underline{\text{Pencil}} \\ \bullet \end{bmatrix}$$

in the attribute columns. Here, the relationships

$$\text{ALL } \underline{\text{Pen}} \subseteq \left[\begin{array}{c} \text{ALL } \underline{\text{Pen}} \\ \bullet \end{array} \right] \quad \text{and} \quad \text{ALL } \underline{\text{Pen}} \subseteq \left[\begin{array}{c} \text{ALL } \underline{\text{Pen}} \\ \underline{\text{Pencil}} \\ \bullet \end{array} \right]$$

hold by convention. Perhaps set notions cannot be simplified and hiding them generates rather than clears up confusion.

A comparative study [Greenblatt and Waxman, 1978] shows, not surprisingly but not very diagnostically, that Query by Example is easier for novices to learn and use than SEQUEL or a limited algebraic language.

Exhibit 4.4-2. Join of EMP with Itself

EMP	NAME	SAL	MGR	DEPT
	P. <u>Jones</u> Peter	> <u>10K</u> 10K	Peter	

Exhibit 4.4-3. Conjunctive and Disjunctive Queries

SALES	DEPT	ITEM
	P. <u>Toy</u> Toy	Pen Pencil

SALES	DEPT	ITEM
	P. <u>Toy</u> P. <u>Shoe</u>	Pen Pencil

a) Departments selling <u>Pens</u> *and* Pencils

b) Departments selling <u>Pens</u> *or* Pencils

Zloof [1978] indicates three potential types of user of a query facility: casual, professionals who are not programmers, and applications programmers. Query by Example is intended for the second category, and Zloof supposes that the casual user is best served by a natural language interface such as RENDEZVOUS [Codd 1978]. A full natural language recognition system is still very expensive, and languages such as SYNGLISH [Kerschberg, Ozkarahan and Pacheco, 1976] and ILL [Lacroix and Pirotte, 1977] have been proposed which are based on English grammar but still formal. The danger with this approach (see Thomas and Gould [1975]) is that *interference* develops between daily language usage and the query language, leading to errors when the user does not use just the right construct or term. (Incidentally, English keywords were found to be the best delimiters in QUEL—see Held, Stonebraker and Wong [1975]. They are probably easier to remember.)

QT-expressions [Merrett, 1978b] were not formulated for the casual or for the non-programmer user but because they provide an easily implementable, powerful query facility within the framework of the relational algebra. It happens that simpler queries formulated as QT-Expressions have very straightforward translations into English, but this is a benefit of the notation rather than a design motive. This direct correspondence is probably a result of the *domain orientation* as opposed to the *tuple orientation* of QT-expressions, a distinction made by Pirotte [1977]. In his Domain Relational Calculus, the query "find items sold by departments on the second floor" on SALES (DEPT, ITEM) and LOC (DEPT, FLOOR) is:

$$\{i \mid \exists d \text{ SALES (DEPT:d, ITEM:i) \textbf{and} LOC (DEPT:d, FLOOR:'2')}\}$$

while in the Tuple Relational Calculus (Codd's [1971b] relational calculus) it is

$$\{s. \text{ITEM} \mid \text{SALES(s) \textbf{and} } \exists \ell \in \text{LOC} (\ell . \text{DEPT} = s. \text{DEPT \textbf{and} } \ell . \text{FLOOR} = 2)\}.$$

Expressing these in words, the first becomes "find the ITEM, i, which is associated in SALES with some DEPT, d, which LOC gives on the second FLOOR". This is more straightforward than the translation of the tuple formulation: "find the ITEM part of tuple s, which is a tuple of SALES and whose DEPT part matches the DEPT part of some tuple, ℓ, in LOC, with FLOOR part equal to 2". The QT-expression (ℓ) for this query uses **ijoin** to connect SALES and LOC, but avoids variables. Nevertheless, the domain orientation of QT-expressions is clear. Query by Example is also domain-oriented. For more complex queries, introspection found [Merrett, 1978b] that thinking procedurally was the best way to disambiguate the English and to formulate the query. Although the subject is a programmer and more objective studies must be done, this finding is supported by Welty and Stemple [1981].

Reisner [1981] conjectures that *inconsistency* of strategies indicated to the user by a query language causes confusion and hypothesizes this as the source of difficulty with the GROUP BY function in SEQUEL, which conflicts with the mapping conception. I would like to speculate, continuing that conjecture, that there is a requirement for *deep friendliness* in query languages or other interfaces between man and machine. This is as opposed to, say, *syntactic friendliness*: Reisner, Boyce and Chamberlin [1975] found little difference in the performances of programmers using SQUARE, which has a mathematical notation, and SE-QUEL, which uses English keywords. The main difference is in the improved syntactic friendliness of SEQUEL. (Non-programmers, on the other hand, found SEQUEL much preferable.) Deep friendliness, which I shall not define, depends on the simplicity and fewness of the underlying concepts. The relational algebra, as elaborated in Chapters 2.1, 3.1 and 4.1 of this book, is not intended for untrained users but has the following valuable characteristic. It makes clear distinctions among the three areas that have different conceptual bases, so that the student can learn them separately and only later try putting them together into complex formulations. The first is the simple query on a single relation, formalized by T-selectors and QT-selectors, and easily translatable to and from natural language. The second is the collection of binary algebraic operators for putting relations together: to a naive user, the very fact that the data has been separated into different relations appears arbitrary (it is done for deep technical reasons that theoretical research is far from unveiling), and so it is appropriate that the mechanisms for putting them back together should require more sophistication to master. The third is calculations, aggregations and grouping on attributes, which the domain algebra divorces clearly from the operations on relations. If several conceptual bases are involved in manipulating data, it follows from Reisner's conjecture that they should be kept well apart in the formalisms.

4.4-2   Updating Views

We have not discussed the update formalisms of the query languages described in the last section, because minimal extensions to the syntax are required, as in Section 4.1-2, and because updating raises a number of problems which we would like to review separately. This section addresses the problem of updating views, while the following three sections discuss integrity enforcement, concurrency and reliability.

A *view* of a database is a relation derived from the given relations of the database by some expression, say using the relational operators, domain operators and QT-expressions of Chapters 2.1, 3.1 and 4.1. An important reason for having a view is the difficulty users have with combining relations: the joins and other binary operations can be done in advance and the end-user presented with a single relation containing everything that concerns him. It follows that, if he needs to change the database, he should be allowed to do so through his view. A second reason is that there may be certain aspects of the database we do not want a particular end-user to see or change. These can be removed from his view through projection, selection or aggregation.

The Natural Forms Query Language NFQL [Embley, 1982] is an example of a query language which presents the user with attributes independently of the relations they are associated with in the database. A *form* in NFQL is a view consisting of the natural join of the underlying relations, selected according to the user-supplied values of certain attributes and projected on the requested attributes. (It is, moreover, hierarchically displayed so that common values of some attributes are not repeated: in other words the view becomes an *unnormalized* relation. A form of this sort is a useful view for the end-user because it resembles documents which many potential users are already familiar with.)

(For queries only, in the context of projection and natural join operators, the Access Path Producing LanguagE APPLE [Carlson and Kaplan, 1976] and the query language of Maier *et al.* [1982] use semantic information to allow the enquirer to specify only attribute names, not relation names. The semantic information for APPLE is given with the database, in the form of functional dependences and join paths interestingly expressed as set relationships between join attributes, such as *same as, contained in,* etc. Osborn [1979] gives algorithms and a theoretical basis for automatic generation of answers to queries expressed in terms of attributes alone. She uses second-order relations in the form of two acyclic graphs whose vertices are the relations of the database and whose edges reflect the containment of the key of one relation in the attribute of the other. The graphs can be generated automatically during the database design by using algorithms [Osborn, 1978] to construct third-normal-form relations which include all functional dependences and from which the universal relation can be reconstructed by natural joins.)

We thus have the need to be able to update views. On the other hand, we saw at the beginning of Chapter 4.1 that some views—e.g., natural join—cannot be updated and still remain consistent with their definition. Let us investigate which views can be updated. Furtado, Sevcik and dos Santos [1979] discuss updatable views on the Quotient Algebra [Furtado and Kerschberg, 1977], which we can easily relate to the relational algebra: Exhibit 4.4-4. We limit attention to additions, deletions and changes to tuples in views defined by projection, selection and union (simple union, not the general union-join). Deletions and changes can be applied directly to the underlying relation. Additions require more thought. Adding a tuple to a view that is a projection requires us to add a don't care null value to each attribute in the base relation that is not in the projection. Adding a tuple to a selection is straightforward, with the reasonable requirement that the added tuple be a legal member of the selection. Thus, if the view is defined as "**where** TYPE > 'A' **in** CLASS" from Exhibit 4.1-1, it would be forbidden to add the tuple (ITEM, TYPE) = (Top, A) to the view. Adding a tuple to a union produces ambiguous effects on the underlying relations: we do not know whether to add it to one or the other relation, or both. Note that those difficulties in *adding* tuples do not carry over to *changing* values, so that a change is not equivalent to a combination of add and delete for the purpose of updating views.

When we combine operations into a relational expression, however, updates to the resulting view may be less restricted than to views defined by the individual operators. Furtado, Sevcik and dos Santos suggest that, for instance, a projection of a selection can avoid the null value problem, as in the following case. Update "ITEM **where** TYPE = 'A' **in** CLASS" from Exhibit 4.1-1 by adding "Top": this clearly adds (Top, A) to CLASS, not (Top, DC). Thus we cannot know everything about updating views simply by knowing how to update the results of individual operations.

	ADD	DELETE	CHANGE
PROJECT V = X **in** R	(x, DC)	OK	OK
SELECT V = **where** cond **in** R	OK	OK	OK
UNION V = R **ujoin** S	?	OK	OK

Exhibit 4.4-4. Updating Simple Views, V, of Base Relations R (X, Y) and S (X, Y)

Dayal and Bernstein [1978] seek rules for translating view updates to updates on the base relations according to the *extent* of the relations. Rules such as those of Exhibit 4.4-4 are too simple and, where they disallow updates as in natural joins, are too restrictive, and so it is necessary to look at the actual data present in the view and relations. In the case of joins we find that some joins can be updated. For instance, we can delete (Natacha, Deli, 3) from STORE, the natural join of LOC and STAFF in Exhibit 4.4-5, because removing (Natacha, Deli) from STAFF accomplishes this without *side effects* (i.e., changing other tuples in the view). If, however, we delete (Andrea, Rug, 1), we would also lose (Andrea, Rug, 2) from STORE (by removing (Andrea, Rug) from STAFF) or we would lose (Patrick, Rug, 1) from STORE (by removing (Rug, 1) from LOC). To delete a tuple from a view, in general, Dayal and Bernstein require that there be a tuple in a base relation that can be removed with the effect *only, of deleting the required tuple from the view*—i.e., no side effects. Furthermore, they require that there be a *unique* base relation with such a tuple, otherwise we must arbitrarily decide which base relation to update. They give similar rules for additions and changes, and include the further criteria that the update be minimal, in the sense that it does not change the hidden part of the database unnecessarily, and that it should not violate any other integrity constraints.

These rules of Dayal and Bernstein appear to require inspection of the tuples of the database—at run time—and so would be, at least, expensive to implement. Accordingly they make an interpretation of the rules in terms of functional dependences. The result is more restrictive than the rules on relational extents ("semantic" rules) but has the advantage of being checkable at compile time ("syntactic" rules). Thus we would allow deletions from STORE, by removing tuples from STAFF, if there were a functional dependence DEPT → FLOOR in LOC. This is in fact why we allowed deletion of (Natacha, Deli, 3). In LOC, apart from the Rug department, we do have DEPT → FLOOR. This observation can be used to give a weaker requirement than that of Dayal and Bernstein. Armstrong and Delobel [1977] show (in section 10) that both deletions and additions can be made to a view which has a *degenerate decomposition*. That is, the view is a natural join, giving it a decomposition (X, Y) and the decomposition is moreover such that the view

Exhibit 4.4-5. Partially Updatable View, STORE = STAFF **ijoin** LOC with EMP → DEPT

STAFF (EMP	DEPT)	LOC (DEPT	FLOOR)		STORE (EMP	DEPT	FLOOR)
Andrea	Rug	Rug	1		Andrea	Rug	1
Eric	Toy	Rug	2		Andrea	Rug	2
Hannah	Deli	Deli	3		Patrick	Rug	1
Natacha	Deli	Shirt	3		Patrick	Rug	2
Patrick	Rug			updat-	Toby	Shirt	3
Toby	Shirt			able	Hannah	Deli	3
				part	Natacha	Deli	3

is the union of two disjoint relations, in one of which $X \cap Y \to X$ and in the other $X \cap Y \to Y$. This does not apply to STORE, so that deletions can only be made to *part* of STORE, but STORE has a decomposition, ({EMP, DEPT}, {DEPT, FLOOR}) and in the updatable part of STORE it is true that {EMP, DEPT} {DEPT, FLOOR} $\to$ FLOOR i.e., DEPT $\to$ FLOOR.

Todd [1977a] proposes weakening the update if it is *overspecified* (there are no changes that can be made to the base relations which satisfy all constraints and update the view without side effects) as in the case of join, or strengthening it if it is *underspecified* (the minimal update is not unique) as in the case of union. He is able to do this because he views an update as specified by constraints. Thus, if we wanted to insert the tuple (Toby, Rug, 2) into STORE—which would put (Toby, Rug) into STAFF and generate the side effect tuple (Toby, Rug, 1) in STORE—we could allow side effects by specifying the update as

$$\text{STORE}' \supseteq \text{STORE} \cup (\text{Toby, Rug, 2})$$

which is weaker than the usual

$$\text{STORE}' = \text{STORE} \cup (\text{Toby, Rug, 2}).$$

Or, to add (Toy, 1) to the union of LOC with some other relation, say R (DEPT, FLOOR),

$$\text{VIEW} = \text{LOC } \textbf{ujoin } \textbf{R},$$

we could resolve where to place the new tuple by specifying

$$\text{VIEW}' = \text{VIEW} \cup (\text{Toy, 1}) \textbf{ and } \text{R}' = \text{R}$$

which is stronger than

$$\text{VIEW}' = \text{VIEW} \cup (\text{Toy, 1}).$$

(Here, STORE', VIEW' and R' are the results of the updates to STORE, VIEW and R respectively.)

Both Todd [1977a] and Dayal and Bernstein [1978] require uniqueness of minimal update to the base relations before allowing an update to the view. Such uniqueness is unlikely, as the case of union shows. Bancilhon and Spyratos [1981] define the notion of the *complement* of a view, namely another view which can be used together with the original view to reconstruct the database. They show that minimal complements are unique only for trivial views but that, for a given view, complement, and set of updates (which contains the composition of every pair of updates in the set and the rollback of every update in the set), there is a unique translation of the updates to the base relations which does not affect the complement. This gives the database administrator, or whoever defines user views, the responsibility of selecting the appropriate complement as well—not to mention devising algorithms to implement the abstract results of this paper.

Exercise   4.4-1:   Characterize the updatability of views defined by μ-joins, σ-joins or domain algebra.

If the end-user is presented his view by a programming language such as RIGEL or ASTRAL (Section 2.4-5) using a data abstraction mechanism, all this discussion may be circumvented by allowing the programmer to define the updates in advance, specifying the base relations to be changed for each update.

4.4-3   Enforcing Integrity Constraints

In Section 4.1-3, post-processing, query modification and special checking are suggested as methods to verify that integrity constraints are not violated by updates. Loosely, to give a framework for a more extensive discussion in this section, these can be classified as post-processing, run-time processing and compile-time processing techniques. Post-processing uses brute force, but is not unreasonable for specialized checking such as validating large amounts of data being used to create a database. Integrity constraints involving aggregates—such as sums, averages and functional dependences—often require scanning many tuples or even all of a relation, so that post-processing is not necessarily ineffi-cient. MRDS uses post-processing to validate new data and to check keys and functional dependences [Ho, 1982].

Besides the usually unnecessary exhaustive scan of post-processing meth-ods, there is the problem of rolling back the update when an error is detected. There are two directions in which we can improve on post-processing. One is to *reduce* the proportion of the database that needs to be checked and the other is to *anticipate* errors before doing the update so that rollback is not needed. If possi-ble, we should like to do all or part of the checking at *compile time,* when the constraint is defined. At *run time,* when we are processing the update, we can if necessary do the rest of the checking. Both special checking, by means of data abstraction, and query modification, which we discuss next, have compile time and run time components. In special checking by data abstraction, the constraints are embedded in the procedural code for the update and compiled with it, although parameter values must be checked at run time.

Query modification [Stonebraker, 1975] classifies constraints and updates and provides general mechanisms for modifying the update at run time. If we limit our attention to constraints which do not contain aggregates, Stonebraker de-scribes three categories of increasing complexity. Constraints that can be evalu-ated on single tuples of a single relation are enforced by a direct conjunction (**and**) of the update qualification and the constraint, as in the update to SUPPLY such that VOL $\leq$ 20 in Section 4.1-3. Constraints which can be evaluated on single tuples of the relation to be updated, together with information from other relations, require that the new values be checked against those other relations before accepting the update. Since QUEL uses tuple variables ranging over the Cartesian product of the participating relations, it is forced to implement this check along the lines of the following example. We wich to add the tuples in STAFF' to the relation STAFF, subject to the "weak knees" constraint that nobody can work in a department whose floor (in relation LOC) is higher than he can climb: "if DEPT in STAFF = DEPT in LOC then CLIMB in STAFF ≥ FLOOR in LOC". To test this, QUEL takes the Cartesian product of STAFF' with LOC and, for each tuple from STAFF', compares the number of tuples from LOC in the Cartesian product with the number of tuples from LOC that satisfy the constraint "if DEPT in STAFF' = DEPT in LOC then CLIMB in STAFF' ≥ FLOOR in LOC". An example is given in Exhibit 4.4-6, showing that one of the two tuples in STAFF' is rejected. The third category of constraint involves multiple-tuple comparison within the relation to be updated and requires comparisons of the new tuples among themselves and against the updated relation in 2^k-1 ways, where k is the number of tuples that must be compared within the relation to evaluate the constraint. Constraints with aggregates are also not practical to enforce using query modification.

A general analysis of the conditions of query modification was made by Blaustein [1981]. Constraints were expressed in *prenex* form in first-order predicate calculus: any predicate may be put into prenex form, which is a sequence of quantified variables (the *prefix*) followed by a Boolean expression (the *matrix*) with free variables but no quantifiers. The quantifiers are the classical ones— universal (∀, "for all") and existential (∃, "for some"). The constraint can include references to any number of relations, but updates are limited to single-tuple additions and deletions to a single relation. Blaustein first shows that a deletion can always be made from a relation which is associated only with a universal quantifier, that an addition can always be made to a relation associated only with an existential quantifier, and that these are the only "trivial" updates—in the sense that the update can always safely be performed without checking. Since Stonebraker's [1975] discussion is implicitly limited to universal quantifiers, this result justifies his dismissial of deletions in all categories as not needing consideration. But the result that no other combination of assertion and update is trivial disappoints any (unlikely) hope we may have had that we need only do compile-time checking.

The rest of Blaustein's work has the dual objective of reducing the amount of work we need to do at run-time by various compile-time substitution rules that *restrict* the processing to critical parts of the database, and of transforming the formulation of the constraint from one that is valid *after* the update has been done to one that is valid *before*. The following three substitution rules restrict the parts of the database that must be checked (they are paraphrased from Blaustein's formal notation). First, if the constraint prefix has the form ∃ ∃ . . ∃ ∀ and we are adding a tuple to the relation associated with the ∀, then we need only check

Exhibit 4.4-6. Testing S. DEPT = L. DEPT => CLIMB ≥ FLOOR by Counting Tuples in the Cartesian Product, STAFF' × LOC.

LOC (DEPT FLOOR)

DEPT	FLOOR
Rug	1
Rug	2
Deli	3
Shirt	3

STAFF (EMP DEPT CLIMB)

EMP	DEPT	CLIMB
Andrea	Rug	6
Natacha	Deli	14
Patrick	Rug	4
Eric	Toy	15

STAFF' (EMP DEPT CLIMB)

EMP	DEPT	CLIMB
Toby	Shirt	5
Hannah	Deli	2

STAFF' × LOC

EMP	S. DEPT	CLIMB	L. DEPT	FLOOR	
Toby	Shirt	5	Rug	1	⎫
Toby	Shirt	5	Rug	2	⎬ 4
Toby	Shirt	5	Deli	3	
Toby	Shirt	5	Shirt	3	⎭
Hannah	Deli	2	Rug	1	⎫
Hannah	Deli	2	Rug	2	⎬ ~~4~~
Hannah	Deli	2	Deli	3	3
Hannah	Deli	2	Shirt	3	⎭

269

what we call the "satiator" from each ∃-relation against the tuple to be added to the ∀-relation. The satiator of a relation R is the set of tuples of R for which the constraint holds. For example "not every item in the catalog is sold" is a constraint with the form we are discussing—(∃ cat ∈ CAT) (∀ sells ∈ SELLS) (cat. ITEM ≠ sells. ITEM)[1]—and the satiator of CAT is just those tuples of CAT for which (∀ sells ∈ SELLS) (cat. ITEM ≠ sells. ITEM). Clearly no other tuples in CAT can cause trouble if we add a tuple to SELLS, but the new item we have decided to sell might just be the only one in the catalog hitherto not sold (i.e., in the satiator of CAT) and therefore upholding the constraint. The satiator can be computed for each relation at run time, but this is not efficient and Blaustein suggests it be stored redundantly. If there are no existential quantifiers before the ∀, we need only check the incoming tuple, which gives us Stonebraker's first category of constraint.

The second and third substitution rules concern deletions from existentially quantified relations, respectively governed by and governing a universal quantifier. These rules are less effective in reducing the number of tuples in the database to be considered, although they can be applied iteratively with benefit (the first rule cannot). The second rule controls deletions from relation R_j if the constraint prefix has the form ∃ . . ∃ ∀$_i$ . . ∃$_j$. We can restrict our attention to those tuples of R_i which match the tuples to be deleted from R_j in the database after deletion. Thus, a deletion of a whistle from BUYS in a database subject to "every item in the catalog is bought and sold"—(∀ cat ∈ CAT) (∃ buys ∈ BUYS) (∃ sells ∈ SELLS) (cat. ITEM = buys. ITEM **and** buys. ITEM = sells. ITEM)—requires checking only the whistles in CAT and SELLS against the remaining tuples in BUYS.

The third rule controls deletions from relation R_j if the constraint prefix has the form . . ∃$_j$ . . ∀$_i$. We must look at those tuples remaining in R_j after deletion to see if they still satisfy the constraint. Thus, deleting an item from the catalog when "not every item in the catalog is sold"—(see example for first rule)—requires us to look at the remaining items in CAT to see that there is still one not in SELLS.

If we hope we can do better than this, particularly for deletions, we are disappointed by Blaustein's result that the substitution rules are *complete,* in the sense that no smaller set of tuples is adequate for checking constraints. This does not prevent us entirely from improving performance—for instance in the situation considered by the third rule we could check the satiator of CAT (items in CAT not sold) to see if it is emptied by the update. Blaustein applies her results to the problem of maintaining such redundant information, "concrete views", in her Chapter 7.

---

[1] Literally "there is a tuple in CAT (catalog) such that, for all tuples in SELLS, ITEM in the CAT tuple ≠ ITEM in the SELLS tuple (the ITEM in the catalog is not sold)".

The substitution rules reduce the checking needed, but this checking must be done on the updated database. It would be better if we could do the check before the update, to save having to undo the update, and we can. The only problematical update is deleting from an existentially quantified relation, and that can be handled by replacing the matrix, M, of the constraint assertion by M **and** "the tuple does not equal the tuple to be deleted".

Aggregates, such as MAX, MIN and COUNT, can be useful in enforcing constraints, since they are single values and cheaply stored. Blaustein discusses the circumstances under which MAX can replace the combination $\forall$, $<$, or $\exists$, $>$, and similarly MIN can replace $\forall$, $>$ or $\exists$, $<$. For instance "no volume supplied is greater than 20"—$(\forall s \in$ SUPPLY) (s. VOL $\leq$ 20)—is equivalent to MAX (VOL) $\leq$ 20. Also, COUNT can replace $\forall$, $=$, and we have seen in Section 2.2-1 how COUNT can implement set comparisons. If a constraint involves MAX, MIN, SUM or COUNT, adding or deleting a tuple is easy if the aggregate is separately stored and maintained. Thus if the constraint involves SUM, we just add the value in the tuple to the stored sum and check the constraint. This takes care of reduction aggregates. Equivalence reductions can be handled similarly, at the expense of more storage. Further details on using MAX, MIN and COUNT aggregates, separately stored as concrete views, to enforce constraints are in Bernstein, Blaustein and Clarke [1980].

Deletions and additions can be combined to give any update, so the above considerations are necessary. But they are not sufficient. As we saw with view updates, a replacement can be legal even though the component deletion or addition is not. Individual additions and deletions may violate an integrity constraint, yet be combined into a single *transaction* which does not: the violations are transient, and, if we take the transaction to be the atomic unit of updating, need not be considered. Gardarin and Melkanoff [1979] use the same proof techniques (see [Hoare, 1969]) as Blaustein [1981] to consider transactions: general rules are, of course, more difficult to specify.

We have seen the value of concrete views—redundantly stored data—for integrity enforcement. Defined views—just the expressions specifying the views —are also useful. An integrity constraint is just an assertion, and an assertion can be represented by the set of tuples for which it is true or by the complement, the set of tuples for which it is false. If we consider this complementary set to be a view, it should be empty, and we can enforce the constraint by requiring that updates do not add tuples to this view. Buneman and Clemons [1979] investigate the effect of additions, deletions and changes of single tuples in the base relations to views defined on them using the relational algebra. For instance, additions and deletions to operands of union, intersection, join, projection, and to the left operands of difference and division, may cause additions and deletions, respectively, to the result. On the other hand, an addition to the right operand of difference or division may cause a deletion in the result and vice versa. Thus, if we want to avoid additions to the view, we must avoid additions to the base relations if the view is a union or deletions from the right operand if it is a division. Buneman and Clemons give recursive algorithms to propagate the effect of their rules through the entire tree representing the algebraic expression defining a view. They start at the top with a constraint to the view, such as "no additions", and do a breadth-first scan of the tree, using the rules to compute the "relevance" to this constraint of additions, deletions and changes to each attribute in the operands. All this can be done at compile time and defines the trivial updates for the given constraint — the updates that do not need to be checked further. For other updates, the relevance of each node in the tree can be used to limit the run-time checking: when a relation is irrelevant, it does not need to be checked, nor do any of its components if it is itself a view. (This method can be used to check not only integrity constraints but any condition: Buneman and Clemons call such a checking routine an *alerter*. System R [Astrahan *et al.* 1976] uses the term *trigger* to include an alerter and the specification of action to be taken if the condition arises, such as changing the count of employees — a redundantly stored aggregate — if the Employee relation is updated.)

Hammer and Sarin [1978] call the complementary view, to which additions may not be made, the *error set*, and discuss ways of reducing the computation required to check nontrivial updates. For instance, changing the subject of a course in COURSE (COURSE#, SUBJECT) under the constraint "every trainee employee must be enrolled in at least two salesmanship courses" requires a check at run time only if the update changes a salesmanship course to something else. Then, assuming the relations EMP(EMP#, JOB-CLASS) and ENROL (COURSE #, EMP#), the error set is those employees with JOB-CLASS = 'trainee' and the following COUNT greater than two:

> **let** COUNT **be red** + **of** 1
> EMP, COUNT **where** SUBJECT = 'salesmanship' **in**
>   (EMP **ijoin** ENROL **ijoin** COURSE)

A subgoal on the way to determining that the error set remains empty is to assure that COUNT does not decrease: Hammer and Sarin propose that the tree of the expression defining the error set be analyzed in terms of subgoals from the bottom up.

We should note, however, that the error set method is not general. The constraint that an error set should be empty is equivalent only to a constraint involving a universal quantifier on the relation associated with the error set. Universal quantification can be treated this way because of the equivalence in predicate logic of $\forall x\, p\,(x)$ and **not** $(\exists x\, \textbf{not}\, p\,(x))$: the error set for $\forall x\, p\,(x)$ is thus $\{x \mid \textbf{not}\, p\,(x)\}$. For the existential quantifier we can define a corresponding set or view, but the constraint now is that it should contain at least one tuple: $\exists x\, p\,(x)$ becomes $|\{x \mid p\,(x)\}| \geq 1$. For the exact quantifiers of QT-expressions, we could have other numerical requirements on the size of the corresponding view. Buneman and Clemons avoid this limitation by not using the term "error set" or requiring emptiness of the derived view as a criterion.

Buneman and Clemons raise the possibility that run-time checking could use a *filter,* like the Bloom filter discussed in Section 1.2-6. If the filter shows that the update has not altered the view, we need check no further. If not, we may still be safe but must check more thoroughly. Such a filter could be used to check only the tuples added to R if the constraint required R **ijoin** S not to exceed a certain size. If the added tuples, say R', produce no extra tuples in the view, $|$ R' **ijoin** S $| = 0$, then we are safe. If not, it may or may not be true that $(R \cup R')$ **ijoin** S exceeds the size specified in the constraint.

Relational database systems that have been implemented with integrity enforcement have tended to classify constraints into run-time and post-processing categories and deal with updates accordingly. The work of Buneman and Clemons [1979] was motivated by needs in DAISY, a decision aiding system. INGRES [Stonebraker *et al.* 1976] handles only the simplest category by query modification. System R [Astrahan *et al.* 1976] uses post-processing and transaction rollback. CASSM, a database system using associative hardware, also validates the transaction after the update is finished, and rolls back if necessary [Hong and Su, 1981]. Rolling back is a recovery mechanism and usually requires two copies of the updated data. System R allocates a new copy of the whole page to be updated, and simply sets the pointers back to the original location in case of rollback. CASSM takes advantage of its rotating associative memory to copy only the changed part of the tuple, and writes the new value to the original location on validation.

How to store the predicates expressing integrity constraints is a problem that has been approached in different ways. CASSM generates the code for doing the checking and stores that. INGRES and System R store a parse tree for the QUEL or SEQUEL statement giving the constraint. MRDS [Ho, 1982] does the same, using relations for storage so that the constraint can be interrogated like any other entry in the database. Wong and Edelberg [1977] describe a hierarchical structure for holding a restricted class of predicates, conjunctions of ranges, which can be represented as strings of "intervals".

Exercise 4.4-2:   What are the trivial updates for integrity constraints expressed using the generalized quantifiers of QT-predicates?

Exercise 4.4-3:   Devise a one-pass (at most) integrity enforcement scheme using QT-predicates to express the constraints.

4.4-4   Concurrency

The problem facing a concurrency control subsystem, like that of the integrity enforcer, is consistency of the database. Only the concurrency control must cope with the conflicts of separate transactions being processed at the same time. The problem is illustrated in Section 4.1-3 and arises in multi-user databases when relatively complicated transactions which include updates must be processed with short response time—such as booking flights in an airlines reservation system.

As with integrity enforcement, techniques for concurrency control can be classified as post-processing, run-time and compile-time, and, again, compile-time control is clearly preferable but not adequate for all situations. An obvious, but unworkable, post-processing approach is to let the transactions run then check the database against the integrity constraints. This does not work because we do not necessarily have enough integrity constraints. For example, consider the two simultaneous updates to CLASS in Section 4.1-3 which mistakenly change the type of Yarn from A to B and the type of String from A to C. There need not be an integrity constraint to stop this. Indeed, it is hard to see how such an integrity constraint would be formulated, although the result is clearly undesirable and even inconsistent. So instead of the vaguer constraint of "consistency" we impose a more precise but stronger condition [Rosenkrantz, Stearns and Lewis, 1980], [Stearns and Rosenkrantz, 1981], [Lynch, 1982], [Fischer and Michael, 1982]. This is usually taken to be *serializability:* the transactions, running concurrently, should produce the same effect as some (any) serial ordering of the transactions such that each transaction is completely finished before another transaction starts. Serializability has the advantage that it allows us to restrict integrity enforcement to individual transactions running alone: if each transaction, running separately, preserves integrity, then so does a series of transactions and so, by definition, does a serializable concurrent running of the transactions.

This leads to a trivial concurrency control: run the transactions in a series, i.e. not concurrently at all. This is unsatisfactory because of the need stated above for short response time, and because, of course, there is no concurrency. To decrease response time over such batched transactions, we need to increase concurrency by interleaving the transactions together. This is possible because the "atomic unit" of the system — usually a read or a write to a tuple — is smaller than the "atomic unit" of the end-user, namely the transaction. But it must be subject to a non-trivial concurrency control. The objective of concurrency control is to maximize concurrency control. The objective of concurrency control is to maximize concurrency by maximizing the interleaving of the reads and writes of different transactions, while preserving serializability.

At compile time, we may be able to determine that two transactions do not *conflict* with each other: that one does not write to an object in the database used (either read or written) by the other. At run time we may be able to cause one transaction to wait for another through a mechanism called *locking*. Or, we may need a post-processing mechanism that *rolls back* and then *restarts* a partially completed transaction. We consider these in reverse order, first looking more closely at the nature of serializability.

Exhibit 4.4-7 illustrates the notion of the *progress space* [Kung and Papadimitriou, 1979] of two transactions. (We will limit discussion here to pairs of transactions: this does not always give general results, but it gives the ideas and the ideas are generalizable.) Transaction S progresses in time from the point marked "Start" to the point marked "Finish" on its axis. Similarly, transaction

T progresses from "Start" to "Finish" on *its* axis. At point s_1 in Exhibit 4.4-7a transaction S requests Object 1 in the database in such a way as possibly to put it into conflict with transaction T, which requests Object 1 at point t_1 on its axis: we call the potential conflict C_1. Transaction S no longer needs Object 1 after point s_1', and transaction T releases it at point t_1'. Similarly, C_2 is a potential conflict demanded at points s_2 and t_2 and released at points s_2' and t_2' by the respective transactions. Thus, both transactions start at the origin of the space, mutually labelled "Start", and jointly follow some path in the space to the diagonally opposite corner. Exhibit 4.4-7a shows three paths in the progress space which avoid these potential conflicts. For instance, if the two transactions progress simultaneously along path ST, transaction S demands and then releases Object 2, then Object 1, followed by transaction T, which uses Object 1 then Object 2. If C_1 and C_2 are the only potential conflicts then path ST is serializable and equivalent to transaction S followed by transaction T. Similarly, path TS is serializable and equivalent to the reverse sequence. The path labelled "?", however, is not serializable, as we can show. Suppose transaction S changes type from A to B in CLASS, as in Section 4.1-3, transaction T changes type from A to C, Object 1 is the tuple in CLASS for Yarn and Object 2 is the tuple in CLASS for String. Then the path in question causes the type of Yarn to change to B and the type of String to C (at about the same time: when the path passes through the box bounded by the lines from s_1 and s_1' and t_2 and t_2'). After this, nothing happens, because both Yarn and String have been changed from A and so do not satisfy the selection condition of the update. This argument can be made generally for two transactions, and it follows that any path is serializable which can be "moved" into one of the two serial paths (along the edges of the progress space) without passing through a potential conflict, and only such a path. (To interpret "moved", consider the path as a rubber band from (Start, Start) to (Finish, Finish), which can be deformed but not broken.)

Note that, in the ordinary course of events, a path is *monotonic:* neither coordinate is smaller at a later time than it was at an earlier time. Any decrease in a coordinate corresponds to a rollback of the corresponding transaction. The path is also a step function: its slope is either 0 or ∞ at any point because we suppose one transaction to be dormant at any time the other is processing.

Exhibit 4.4-7a makes it apparent how a serialization can be defined for a given set of transactions. Exhibit 4.4-7b shows six potential conflicts and the boundaries (dashed lines) for the serializable paths around them. In this sketch of the serialization procedure we note that in path p, transaction S crosses the first boundary (moving horizontally at point 1) and so is placed first in the serialization. In path q, transaction T is first across a boundary (moving vertically at point 3), and so the serialization is T then S. This can be generalized to any number of dimensions (transactions). The path is constrained from the point at which it touches the second boundary (p at point 2, q at point 4) until it crosses the last boundary. Exhibit 4.4-7b shows that the path may safely enter the rectangle enclosing all potential conflicts, but only if subject to further constraints. Of course, the convenient serialization of Exhibit 4.4-7b depends on knowing and analyzing in advance the transactions and their potential conflicts. If we do not have this advance knowledge or the time to analyze it, we must put up with the path running into the forbidden zone and encountering actual conflicts.

Exhibit 4.4-8a shows the possible responses to an actual conflict, which arises when the path hits the box containing the potential conflict, C. Here, transaction S causes the conflict, because T has already requested the object in contention. The three possibilities are shown by paths p, q and r: either S *waits* (p), or S pre-empts T causing T to restart (q), or S itself restarts (r). Note that we do not need to restart from the beginning of the transaction, although this is the usual procedure. Hadzilacos [1982] discusses the locating of *save points* to which a transaction can be rolled back. A fourth path, u, shows transaction T being rolled back only to the point where it requested the contended object. We now look at restarting, waiting and conflict detection in turn.

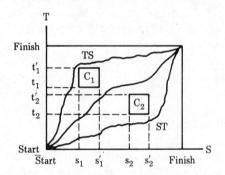

a) Serializable and Nonserializable Paths

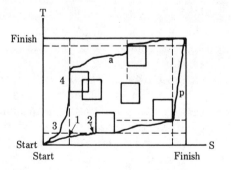

b) Serialization with Known Conflicts

Exhibit   4.4-7.   Progress Space for Transactions S and T with Potential Conflicts.

Exhibit 4.4-8a raises the question: if we can just wait, why should we go to the trouble of restarting a transaction? Exhibit 4.4-8b answers: if we just wait, we may produce a nonserializable path. For this reason restart procedures have been proposed for concurrency control. We must decide in advance on the serialization —which ordering of the transactions the path is to be equivalent to. This is usually taken to be a *timestamp* order: the chronological order in which the transactions reach some specified point in their activity, such as the start point. Exhibits 4.4-9a and b show two procedures proposed by Rosenkrantz, Stearns and Lewis [1978][2]. Their definition of a conflict is more strict than ours: a conflict, once raised, endures until one of the transactions either terminates or is restarted. Thus waits in Exhibit 4.4-9 extend right to the terminal boundaries of one or other transaction. In the Wait-Die system, the transaction causing the conflict waits if it is older, else it is restarted. The Wound-Wait system is pre-emptive: the transaction causing the conflict, if it is older, restarts the other, younger, transaction, else it waits. In the Wound-Wait system, the older transaction tends to finish first, as Exhibit 4.4-9b shows, and Rosenkrantz, Stearns and Lewis speculate that fewer restarts are necessary. Exhibit 4.4-9a is not typical of the Wait-Die system, which tends to favor younger transactions. Bernstein, Shipman and Rothnie [1980] and Kung and Robinson [1981] propose restart concurrency control, based not on the con-figurations of individual conflicts within transactions but on global conflicts be-tween transactions, determined by whether the "write set" of one—the set of database objects written to—overlaps with the write set or "read set" of the other.

The disadvantages of restart concurrency control are that rollback and re-starting are expensive and, overwhelmingly, that some "writes" may be perma-nent and impervious to rollback. Such a "write" might be a command by a database system to launch a nuclear attack, or, more locally, printing the accounts payable checks. (As Rosenkrantz, Stearns and Lewis ask, "how do you undrill a hole?")

This brings us to wait concurrency control, usually implemented by *locking*. A lock by one transaction of a database object causes another transaction request-ing the object to wait. To solve the problem of Exhibit 4.4-8b, Eswaran *et al.* [1976], proposed *two-phase locking*. A two-phase locking technique first goes through a phase of acquiring all the locks for a transaction, then a phase of releasing them: no lock may be acquired after any lock has been released. In our representation of conflicts in progress space, this requirement extends the conflict regions until they all overlap and no path can possibly pass among them. We see this in Exhibit 4.4-10a: each potential conflict is extended to overlap every other. Clearly, two-phase locking is an overly strong condition, since it is only necessary that a chain of overlaps exist, including all potential conflicts [Soisalon-Soininen

---

[2]From about 1978, an increasing proportion of concurrency work concerned *dis-tributed* systems. This section refers to some of this work, but limits discussion to *centralized* database systems.

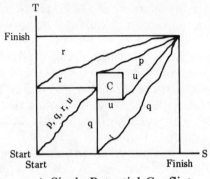

a) Single Potential Conflict

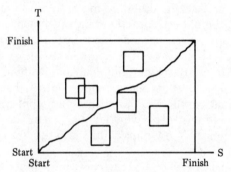

b) Waiting with Many Potential Conflicts

Exhibit 4.4-8. Restarting or Waiting.

and Wood, 1982]. The trouble with overlapping conflicts is that they cause *deadlock,* as described in Section 4.1-3 and shown in Exhibit 4.4-10b. The deadlock depicted in Exhibit 4.4-10b can be resolved only by restarting—either T, preemptively, or S. Other locking configurations which are deadlock-free, as described in Section 4.1-3, correspond to locking all objects at once (Exhibit 4.4-10c) and ranking objects hierarchically (Exhibit 4.4-10d) [Mohan, Fussell and Silberschatz, 1982].

The advantage and disadvantage of locking, even when free of deadlocks, is that each transaction sets its locks independently of all others. This is an advantage in simplicity and economy of implementation. It is a disadvantage in that locks may be set on objects for which there is no conflict with any currently running transaction. For instance, read operations may need to lock objects, if the transaction compares two values and does not want one changed while reading the other; but if the other transactions only read those objects, there is no conflict. Since most transactions could involve only reads, in many installations, locking can be wasteful.

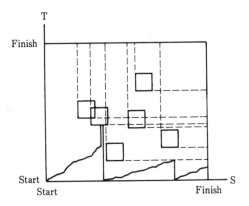

a) Wait-Die Concurrency Control

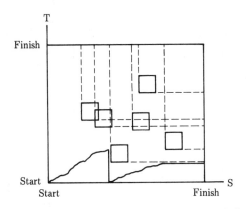

b) Wound-Wait Concurrency Control

Exhibit 4.4-9. Restart Concurrency Control Based on Timestamping, with S Older than T.

This brings us to conflict detection. Bernstein, Shipman and Rothnie [1980] make conflict detection a compile-time technique by pre-defining classes of transactions, according to their write-sets and read-sets. These classes can then be analyzed for conflict before running any transactions, and a graph constructed showing the read-write and write-write conflicts between classes. At run time, transactions are classified and if transactions from two classes that conflict are running concurrently, protocols are invoked to resolve the conflicts by restarting the reading transaction. Transactions can conflict with other transactions in the same class, and so are treated by serialization into timestamp order.

With the exception of SDD-1 [Bernstein, Shipman and Rothnie, 1980], concurrency control in implemented database systems uses locking. System R [Astrahan *et al.*, 1976, Chamberlin *et al.*, 1981] has user-defined transactions of variable size and system-controlled locking of objects of size varying from tuples

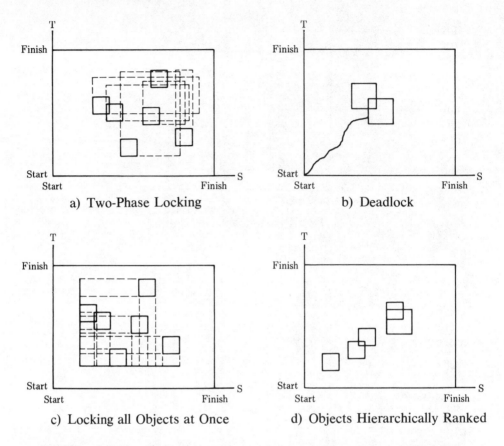

a) Two-Phase Locking

b) Deadlock

c) Locking all Objects at Once

d) Objects Hierarchically Ranked

Exhibit   4.4-10.   Wait Concurrency Control: Locking and Deadlock.

to several relations. (This issue of "granularity", mentioned in Section 4.1-3, was studied by Ries and Stonebraker [1977], who concluded from simulation studies that a small number of large granules was much cheaper and allowed plenty of concurrency. Intuitively, from the way that conflicts interact with each other in Exhibits 4.4-7—10, this result is not surprising. Different assumptions, however, lead to different results [Ries and Stonebrakcr, 1979].) The original intention was to use "predicate locks" [Eswaran *et al.,* 1976], which lock all tuples satisfying a given condition, such as VOL > 10 in SUPPLY in Section 4.1-1. These solve the problem of locking "phantom" tuples—tuples which are not present but may be added by concurrent transactions. If we had stored the fact that three companies supply some article in volumes > 10, and wanted to run a transaction verifying the consistency of this with SUPPLY, we would have to lock out transactions which add tuples with VOL > 10 to SUPPLY. Predicate locks proved too difficult to test for conflict—using syntactic information alone, the general problem is NP-complete [Hunt and Rosenkrantz, 1979], and semantic information, which is hard to process, can resolve apparent conflicts. "Precision locks" [Jordan, Banerjee and Batman, 1981] use predicates to read but specific tuples to write, avoiding the difficult testing for conflicting predicates.

INGRES [Stonebraker *et al.*, 1979] restricts a transaction to be one QUEL statement and locks attributes of relations. It locks all objects at once to avoid deadlock. SDD-1, despite its restart method of concurrency control, is subject to deadlock [McLean, 1981].

A survey, which classifies concurrency control methods into two-phase locking and timestamp ordering categories, is made by Bernstein and Goodman [1981]. They take advantage of this classification to generate several new permutations. Almost all methods fit into one of the two categories, which correspond to our "run-time" and "post-processing" categories respectively. Date [1979] gives a tutorial on the effects of locking on applications programmers.

Exercise   4.4-4:   Extend the serializability condition to an arbitrary number of dimensions (transactions).

Exercise   4.4-5:   (Refer to Exhibit 4.4-7b.) Characterize the serialization with maximum concurrency, in terms of areas or linear dimensions of the space a serializable path may traverse. Devise an algorithm that analyzes the sequence of requests in each transaction to constrain the path for a given serialization to its proper space. This algorithm could be used at run time on individual transactions or, if too slow, at compile time on classes of transactions.

Exercise   4.4-6:   Apply game theory to the problem of locking. [Devillers, 1977].

4.4-5   Reliability

Using Gray's [1981] distinction between reliability and availability (a system is unreliable if it does the wrong thing; it is unavailable if it does not do the right thing within a specified period of time) we see that a system can be made arbitrarily reliable in the absence of updates. We just need to ensure that our query algorithms give the right answers. (It can be made arbitrarily available, too, with sufficient redundancy in hardware and copies of the (static) database.)

Updates threaten reliability in two ways that we shall be concerned with. One way is through errors in the data being used to do the update. A transaction may consistently but wrongly update the database. The evident way to correct it is to run a *compensating transaction*. This does not necessarily simply undo the update. For instance, if it was intended to give an employee a $1000 raise and a

$1000 cut was applied by mistake, the compensating transaction would give a $2000 raise, cancelling the cut and effecting the originally intended raise. Compensating transactions are standard practice in book-keeping, where entries are never changed, but corrected by compensating entries. Compensation is made easy in traditional book-keeping, however, because arithmetical operations *commute,* in the sense that a $1000 cut followed by a $2000 raise gives the same result as a $2000 raise followed by a $1000 cut. The more general transactions on modern databases may not commute, in that errors, once made, may affect subsequent transactions, so that the compensation must not only correct the original error but also re-run the dependent transactions. Such re-runs, however, are only practical in the case that none of the re-run transactions had any permanent effects, such as raising the control rods of a nuclear reactor. These issues are raised by Gray [1981]. Since most information systems have strong external interactions, full compensation for errors is not practical and we must either avoid the error in the first place or learn to live with the consequences. Errors can be detected by thorough screening of input data by syntactical and integrity checks. The other aspects of this problem lie beyond the realm of database and information system techniques. However, we shall call such erroneous transactions *Dromio Updates* in light of Exercise 4.4-7.

Exercise 4.4-7:   Specify the compensating transaction(s) in the following scenario. Antipholus (*AS*), a merchant of Syracuse visiting Ephesus with his servant Dromio (*DS*), instructs him to deposit his recent profits safely. No sooner does Dromio (*DS*) leave on this mission than his long-lost identical twin Dromio (*DE*) of Ephesus arrives to summon Antipholus (*AS*) to supper at home, where the wife of *his* long-lost identical twin, and *DE*'s master, Antipholus (*AE*) of Ephesus awaits impatiently. Antipholus, astonished at Dromio's rapid return, beats him for losing the money. *DE* runs away, to be replaced by *DS,* returning after successful completion of his trust. *AS* beats *DS* for *DE*'s "jests". *AE*'s wife now comes in person to fetch *AS* home to dinner, chiding him, to his compounded confusion, for his attentions to other women. Meanwhile *DE* finds *AE,* complains about being beaten and proceeds home with him, only to be locked out by *AE*'s wife who is entertaining *AS* at dinner. *AE* goes off to a courtesan's house for supper, spitefully requesting his goldsmith to fetch the necklace he ordered for his wife so that he can now give it to the courtesan. Back home, *AS* falls in love with *AE*'s wife's sister and woos her. He is interrupted by the goldsmith, bringing the necklace, and, deciding it is time to embark, sends *DS* to prepare his ship. The goldsmith, returning to collect payment, finds *AE* in the town and has him arrested when he will not pay. *DS* appears and reports to *AE,* under arrest, that the ship is ready. *AE* sends *DS* home to get money for bail, which he does, and then gives it to *AS*. The courtesan meets *AS* on the way to his ship and demands the necklace, or at least to have back the ring which *AE* took. . . .

The second way in which updates threaten realiability is through failure. The kind of failure that concerns us here is the *soft crash*, but we digress first to discuss *hard crashes*. A hard crash destroys existing information, and is called by Scheuler [1977] an *Alexandria Update*, after the fire that destroyed the Library of Alexandria in 47 BC, even though it has nothing to do with updates. There may have been nobody writing in the library at the time of the fire. The Alexandria fire was just the first hard crash. Hard crashes can be avoided by using durable materials (e.g., not papyrus) and can be ameliorated by redundancy.

Soft crashes prevent a transaction from completing its updates, thereby leaving the database in an inconsistent state. This might be due to a power failure, a disk component going down or a condition unmanageable by the software. There is no choice, after a soft crash, but to rerun all transactions that may have done some but not all of their updates. Further, the rerun must not duplicate updates already made (such as giving a $1000 raise), nor must it be unsafe if further soft crashes occur during the rerun. The first clear rule for crashproof updates is that *updates must not be in place:* an update in place replaces the old value with the new. Both old and new values must be available for recovery. The second clear rule is that *a log must be kept*. A log is a record of transactions performed, so that they can be rerun. Possibly the first log was that used by Theseus (the credit is due to Adriane), who recorded his route through the Labyrinth by unravelling a ball of string, so that he could leave after slaying the Minotaur. (He could not, however, unslay the Minotaur, whose death must be regarded as a permanent write.) [Gray, 1981]. The third clear rule is that *reruns must be idempotent* in the sense that repeating a completed transaction must have no effect and repeating a partially completed transaction must have no effect on the updates that were successfully made. Theseus could have repeated his whole exploit, and, given that there were no more Minotaurs, would have changed nothing since slaying is idempotent.

Protection against soft crashes involves restoring the consistency that was lost because transactions stopped abnormally part-way through, and then resuming processing, possibly as of some time in the past, in order not to lose the transactions that were running at the time of the crash. Most techniques [Verhofstad, 1977] require rolling back the transactions in question, but if the *transactions* are idempotent (a stronger condition than the rule that reruns must be idempotent) rollback is not necessary. Rollback should be avoided because of the problems caused by permanent writes. Rolling back Theseus may have required unslaying the Minotaur. With idempotent transactions, resuming processing alone (as of a time preceding the crash) guarantees that consistency is restored, since the completed parts of the transaction are repeated without effect, and the rest is completed by the rerun. We now look at a way to ensure idempotency of transactions updating a database.

Each transaction must be uniquely identified and ordered (e.g., by a timestamp). Each update, whether it be a change or a delete, writes a new copy of the updated object to the database, flagged by the identifier of the transaction it comes from, and, presumably, by status information indicating change or deletion. This procedure automatically satisfies the first rule, that old and new copies must be kept: it keeps old and new copies for every active transaction in a straightforward way. Additions work the same way except, of course, there is no old copy. To detect a crash in the middle of writing the object, the transaction identifier should be recorded last. When a transaction is run, it is permitted to make changes only to versions of objects flagged with an identifier of a transaction that precedes it. The log is then simply a previously recorded list of the transactions and their identifiers. All updates are thus seen as additions, in the tradition of book-keeping. These additions can be permanently recorded, giving, for instance a *chronological relation* (see Chapter 6.2) which is also an archive of the history of the data, or they can be kept only for recent transactions. The evident mechanism, at least for the recent transactions, is the differential file. Timestamping techniques are discussed by Gray [1981].

Idempotency of transactions that include permanent writes requires special enforcement. For instance the permanent write "raise the control rods in the reactor by half a meter" can be inadvertently repeated with disastrous consequences.

No reliability mechanism is perfect, and crashes against which a reliability method is not proof are called *catastrophes*. Thus the Alexandria fire was a catastrophe: there was no backup. Catastrophes can be made arbitrarily unlikely by piling reliability measure on reliability measure, but cannot be eliminated.

Verhofstad [1978] reviews techniques that can be used to recover from failures.

Exercise   4.4-8:   Identify the following situations.

a) Aton, the sun god of Egypt, was fanatically worshipped by Amenophis IV, to the extent of requiring all his subjects to worship only Aton, and of changing his own name to Akhenaton. On Akhenaton's death in 1362 BC, every record pertaining to Aton was erased with hammer and chisel throughout the country.

b) Hansel and Gretel left a trail of crumbs behind them as they wandered in the woods in search of berries. Unfortunately the crumbs were eaten by birds.

c) MENE, MENE, TEKEL, UPHARSIN.

5

A MANUFACTURING PROFIT APPLICATION

BASICS: A Relational Model of a Manufacturing Firm

This section describes the manufacturing and product costing operations of a hypothetical firm that makes toy trains. We look first at the structure of the product (the bill-of-materials) and the operations used in making it (the routing). Then we show the contributions to the cost of finished goods, namely, the cost of raw materials, the cost of labor, and the cost of equipment. Finally, we discuss the information available about customer orders, which will eventually enable us to do profit analyses by part, customer, and salesman.

5.1-1   Bill of Materials and Routing

The components of the toy locomotive, railroad car, and caboose are shown in a typical "parts explosion" in Exhibit 5.1-1. The bill-of-materials is a hierarchical structure of assemblies and subassemblies corresponding to this. It is shown in graphic form in Exhibit 5.1-2.

Thus a locomotive, which is part of a toy train, consists of a body and wheels. The body is made of a cab, a burner, and a boiler. The wheels consist of two big wheel assemblies and a small wheel assembly. Each wheel assembly requires two wheels and an axle. In the bill-of-materials, the raw materials are at the bottom—cab, burner, big wheel, axle, etc. The intermediate assemblies appear in the middle—locomotive, body, wheels, etc. The final assembly is the toy train. (We shall also allow our firm to sell locomotives, cars, and cabooses that are not assembled into trains.) Note that the numbers in the bill-of-materials give the number of subassemblies, or raw materials parts, required for each assembly. A toy train consists of one locomotive, three cars, and one caboose. Note also that some subassemblies are common to more than one assembly. Locomotives, cars, and cabooses all have small wheel assemblies.

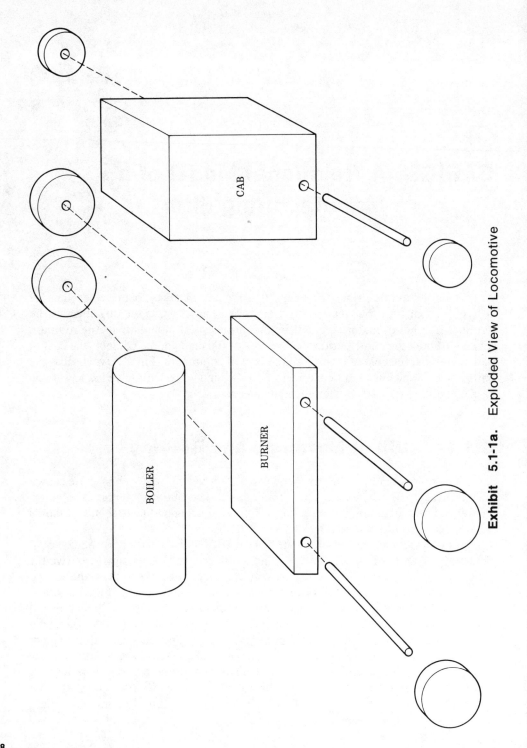

Exhibit 5.1-1a. Exploded View of Locomotive

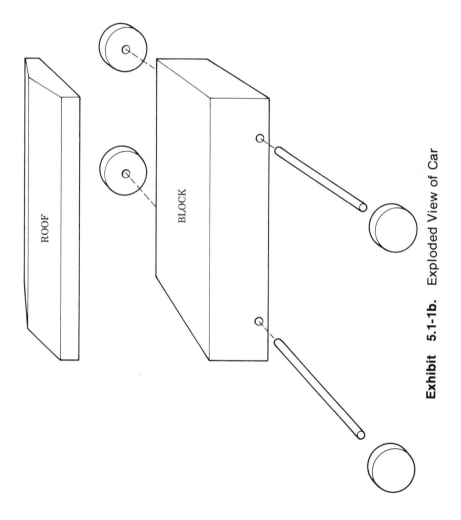

Exhibit 5.1-1b. Exploded View of Car

ROOF

BLOCK

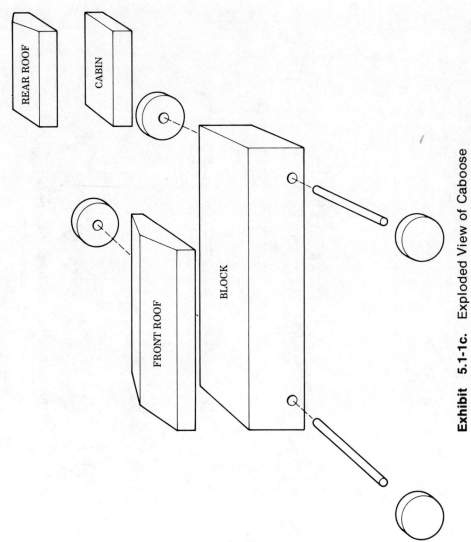

REAR ROOF

CABIN

FRONT ROOF

BLOCK

Exhibit 5.1-1c. Exploded View of Caboose

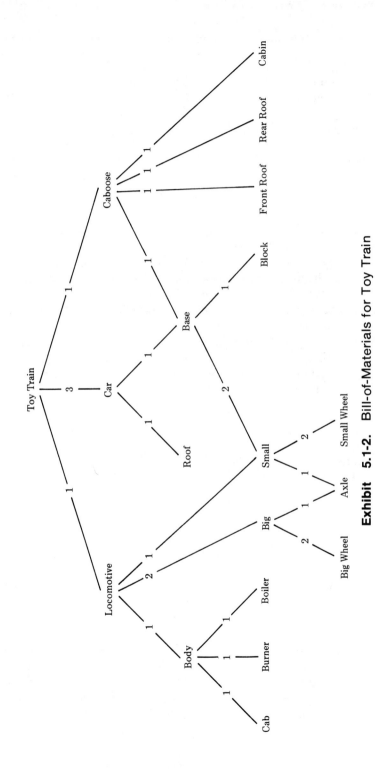

Exhibit 5.1-2. Bill-of-Materials for Toy Train

291

Exhibit 5.1-2 represents a ternary relation, which in tabular form would be

BOM (ASSEMBLY	SUBASSEMBLY	QTY)
Toy Train	Locomotive	1
Toy Train	Car	3
Toy Train	Caboose	1
Locomotive	Body	1
Locomotive	Big	2
Body	Cab	1
•	•	•
•	•	•

Exercise   5.1-1:   Write out fully the table form of the relation BOM.

A second way of looking at the components of a product emphasizes the process of putting them together. The diagram of Exhibit 5.1-3 shows the raw materials parts, the operations that are used, and the assemblies that result. Thus the cab, burner, and boiler are glued together to form the body of the locomotive. The wheels and axles are then assembled on the body.

If we now specify the equipment needed for each operation, we have a manufacturing routing. Our firm uses a "gluset" machine for gluing, a wheel jig for wheel assembly, and a string stapler to attach the cars to the locomotive and caboose. The following relation gives the manufacturing routing.

ROUTING (TEAM	ASSEMBLY	EQUIP	HOURS)
A	Car	Gluset	24
A	Caboose	Gluset	8
PT	Base	Wheel Jig	16
T	Toy Train	String Stapler	24
AP	Body	Gluset	8
P	Locomotive	Wheel Jig	16

Note that ROUTING does not contain any information about the relationship between subassemblies, since this is in BOM. Thus ROUTING does not indicate that the materials for making a Body are Cab, Burner, and Boiler. The team is the set of employees doing the assembly. The hours they spent on each assembly during the week is also given.

Exercise   5.1-2:   Considerable detail has been suppressed even for the very simple product described in this subsection. Specify full bill-of-materials and routing relations, supposing that axles are all made from wire of a common gauge, big wheels and boilers are cut from wood dowel, a funnel is added to the locomotive, the final products are painted, etc.

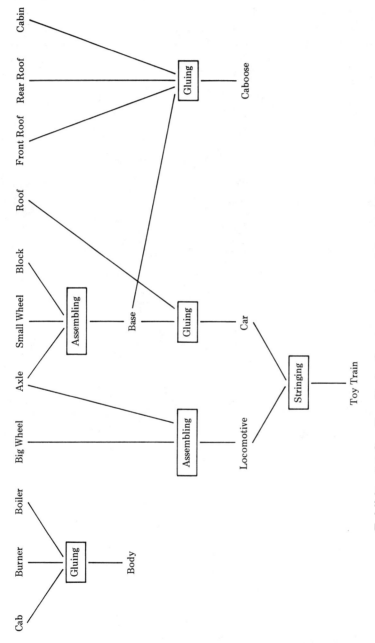

Exhibit 5.1-3. Toy Train Components and Assembly Operations

5.1-2   Production Costs

We will be concerned with three basic contributions to the cost of making toy trains: raw materials, labor, and equipment costs. We look at the basic data relations and from them find a summary of these three costs. In Section 5.2-1 we will show how the accumulated costs are calculated using the bill-of-materials.

The cost of raw materials is given by

RMCOST (PART	RMPRICE)
Cab	0.17
Burner	0.20
Boiler	0.25
Big Wheel	0.03
Axle	0.01
Small Wheel	0.02
Block	0.28
Roof	0.19
Front Roof	0.12
Rear Roof	0.07
Cabin	0.10

The cost of labor must be ascertained by combining data from the routing and the employee teams and salary records.

ROUTING (TEAM	ASSEMBLY	EQUIP	HOURS)
A	Car	Gluset	24
A	Caboose	Gluset	8
PT	Base	Wheel Jig	16
T	Toy Train	String Stapler	24
AP	Body	Gluset	8
P	Locomotive	Wheel Jig	16

SALARY (EMP	WAGE)	TEAMS (TEAM	EMP)
Andrea Porter	8.00	AP	Andrea Porter
Toby Conductor	7.50	AP	Patrick Fireman
Patrick Fireman	6.00	PT	Patrick Fireman
		PT	Toby Conductor
		A	Andrea Porter
		P	Patrick Fireman
		T	Toby Conductor

It is not hard to deduce from these three relations that the following shows the total labor costs for the week by each type of assembly

LABCOST (ASSEMBLY   LAB$)

ASSEMBLY	LAB$
Car	192.00
Caboose	64.00
Base	216.00
Body	112.00
Locomotive	96.00
Toy Train	180.00

For instance, bodies required 8 hours of Andrea Porter's time at $8 per hour plus 8 hours at $6 per hour for Patrick Fireman.

To find the cost per assembly, we require that the production department keep data on how many of each assembly were made that week:

PRODUCTION (ASSEMBLY   QTY)

ASSEMBLY	QTY
Car	60
Caboose	20
Base	160
Body	20
Locomotive	32
Toy Train	24

Now we can calculate that the cost was $3.20 per car, $1.35 per base, etc. Recall that these are *direct* labor costs and that although a base is a component of a car, the $1.35 is not included in the $3.20.

If the cost of equipment is due to depreciation, we must know the purchase value, salvage value, and effective life of each piece of equipment.

FIXED ASSETS (EQUIP   EQCOST   SALVAGE   LIFE)

EQUIP	EQCOST	SALVAGE	LIFE
Gluset	10,000	1000	300
Wheel Jig	20,000	2000	500
String Stapler	10,000	400	200

The depreciation in dollars per week is given by the straight-line method:

$$\text{DEPR} = (\text{EQCOST} - \text{SALVAGE})/\text{LIFE}$$

where LIFE is measured in weeks. Thus the gluset machine costs $30 per week, the wheel jig $36, and the string stapler $48.

We will assume that the depreciation figures are independent of usage and that they can be charged to each assembly in proportion to the amount of time the machine is used for the assembly. Thus the string stapler is dedicated to the toy train, which therefore has an equipment cost of $48 for the week, or $2 for each of the 24 toy trains. The gluset machine is used 24 hours out of 40 on cars and 8 hours out of 40 (with two operators) on locomotive bodies. The following gives the equipment cost for the week, computed from FIXED ASSETS and ROUTING.

EQUIPCOST (ASSEMBLY   EQUIP$)

	ASSEMBLY	EQUIP$
	Car	18.00
	Caboose	6.00
	Base	18.00
	Body	6.00
	Locomotive	18.00
	Toy Train	48.00

We can use PRODUCTION to give us the equipment cost per assembly.

Finally, we can put the raw materials cost, labor cost per assembly, and equipment cost per assembly together to give the basic production costs for all parts and assemblies in the process. RMPRICE gives the cost of raw materials in the following.

BASIC COSTS (PART   RMPRICE   LABPRICE   EQUIPPRICE)

PART	RMPRICE	LABPRICE	EQUIPPRICE
Cab	0.17		
Burner	0.20		
Boiler	0.25		
Big Wheel	0.03		
Axle	0.01		
Small Wheel	0.02		
Block	0.28		
Roof	0.19		
Front Roof	0.12		
Rear Roof	0.07		
Cabin	0.10		
Car		3.20	0.30
Caboose		3.20	0.30
Base		1.35	0.1125
Body		5.60	0.30
Locomotive		3.00	0.5625
Toy Train		7.50	2.00

Exercise 5.1-3:   The relation ROUTING is a summary of a week's work. Devise daily data for this application that can be summarized to give ROUTING.

Exercise 5.1-4:   Use the relational algebra to calculate LABCOST from ROUTING, TEAMS and SALARY and to calculate EQUIP-COST from ROUTING and FIXED ASSETS.

Exercise 5.1-5:   What operations of the relational algebra are needed to derive BASICCOSTS from LABCOST, EQUIPCOST, PRODUCTION and RMCOST?

5.1-3   Finished Goods Cost

This section shows how to calculate the costs of finished goods from the basic production costs using the bill-of-materials. It thus links the previous two sections. Section 5.1-2 gave the raw materials cost for each part not made by the firm, and the labor and equipment costs of assembling each part made by the firm from its immediate components. Section 5.1-1 gave the tree-like bill-of-materials describing the hierarchy of all assemblies and subassemblies. The task of this section is to propagate the costs up through the hierarchy so that the amount recorded for any assembly includes the costs of materials, equipment and labor for all, not just the immediate, component subassemblies.

This task can be split into two. First, we find the *closure* of the bill-of-materials. Then we apply BASIC COSTS of Section 5.1-2. Let us start by introducing informally the notion of closure. A more extensive discussion is given in Chapter 5.2.

To discuss closure, let us work with a very small subset of our bill-of-materials (Exhibit 5.1-2).

BOM (ASSEMBLY	SUBASSEMBLY	QTY)
Locomotive	Big	2
Locomotive	Small	1
Big	Axle	1
Big	Big Wheel	2
Small	Axle	1

The closure is a relation on the same attributes, giving *all* constituents of each assembly and the appropriate quantities.

CONSTITUENTS (ASSEMBLY	SUBASSEMBLY	QTY)
Locomotive	Big	2
Locomotive	Small	1
Locomotive	Axle	3
Locomotive	Big Wheel	4
Big	Axle	1
Big	Big Wheel	2
Small	Axle	1
•	•	•
•	•	•

Thus, a Locomotive has three Axles, one via each of two Big wheel assemblies and one via the Small wheel assembly. It has 2 × 2 Big Wheels because each Big Wheel assembly has two Big Wheels. This example should make the concept clear, although it does not illustrate all the possible things we could do with the non-key attribute, QTY. If we project both the original relation and the closure on the key, ASSEMBLY and SUBASSEMBLY, we have an acyclic graph and its *transitive closure,* which is the basis for our notion of relational closure. We will leave further elaboration to Chapter 5.2, and conclude this discussion with a possible notation,

CONSTITUENTS ← **closure** BOM (ASSEMBLY, SUBASSEMBLY,
× **of** QTY **meet** +)

This will remain partly mysterious until Chapter 5.2. It is introduced here to emphasize that CONSTITUENTS can be derived from BOM by an explicit procedure. Chapter 5.2 discusses two possible methods.

The second step in finding the finished goods cost is the combination of BASIC COSTS (Section 5.1-2) with CONSTITUENTS for the whole bill-of-materials. Here is an example using another subset of BOM. We show the constituents and relative costs of Car.

CONSTITUENTS

(ASSEMBLY	SUBASSEMBLY	QTY)
Car	Base	1
Car	Block	1
Car	Small	2
Car	Axle	2
Car	Small Wheel	4
Car	Roof	1
•	•	•
•	•	•

BASIC COSTS

(PART	RMPRICE	LABPRICE	EQUIPPRICE)
Car		3.20	0.30
Base		1.35	0.1125
Block	0.28		
Axle	0.01		
Small Wheel	0.02		
Roof	0.19		
•	•	•	•
•	•	•	•

A join of these two, multiplying QTY by RMPRICE + LABPRICE + EQUIPPRICE and summing over all tuples for Car, gives a final cost of $5.53. A similar exercise for each of the final assemblies sold by the firm gives the relation

FINAL COSTS (ASSEMBLY   FGCOST)

	ASSEMBLY	FGCOST
	Locomotive	10.27
	Car	5.53
	Caboose	5.63
	Toy Train	42.00

Exercise 5.1-6:   Confirm the values in FINAL COSTS using the values in BASIC COSTS and direct inspection of the graph of Exhibit 5.1-2.

Exercise 5.1-7:   Discover which join must be done on CONSTITUENTS and BASIC COSTS and verify that it gives the required final cost for the example.

Exercise 5.1-8:   Revise the derivation of Exercise 5.1-6 to give an extended relation FINAL COSTS which includes raw materials cost, labor cost, and equipment cost (RMCOST, LABCOST, EQCOST), the three components which sum to give FGCOST for each assembly.

5.1-4   Finished Goods Profit

We assume that the prices asked for finished goods by our company are fixed and given by the relation

PRICE (ASSEMBLY	FGPRICE)
Locomotive	11.99
Car	6.49
Caboose	6.75
Toy Train	46.95

Then it is easy to work out the profit per part

PARTPROFIT (ASSEMBLY	PPROFIT)
Locomotive	1.72
Car	.96
Caboose	1.12
Toy Train	4.95

This data is used in the rest of this section to find profit by customer and by salesman.

We will assess profit by orders, although this makes no provision for returned merchandise. The following two relations give the order book.

ORDLINE (ORD #	ASSEMBLY	QTY)
1	Toy Train	7
1	Locomotive	2
2	Locomotive	1
3	Car	23
3	Locomotive	5
3	Caboose	3
4	Toy Train	11
4	Car	37
5	Locomotive	13
5	Car	31
6	Car	17
7	Locomotive	47
7	Car	139
7	Caboose	43
8	Toy Train	37

ORDERS (ORD #	CUSTOMER	SALESMAN)
1	Great North of Scotland	Eric Brakeman
2	New York Central	Natacha Engineer
3	London & Southwestern	Eric Brakeman
4	Pennsylvania Railroad	Hannah Trainman
5	New York Central	Hannah Trainman
6	Baltimore & Ohio	Hannah Trainman
7	Grand Trunk Railway of Canada	Natacha Engineer
8	Great North of Scotland	Eric Brakeman

On the way to doing an analysis of profit by customer and by salesman, we find sales and profit by order. OPS% is 100% × OPROFIT/OSALES.

ORDERANAL (ORD #	OSALES	OPROFIT	OPS%)
1	352.63	38.07	11
2	11.99	1.72	14
3	229.47	33.96	15
4	756.58	89.85	12
5	357.06	52.01	15
6	110.33	16.28	15
7	1755.89	261.87	15
8	1737.15	183.06	11

The analysis by customer is

CUSTANAL (CUSTOMER	CSALES	CPROFIT	CPS%)
Grand Trunk Railway of Canada	1755.89	261.87	15
Great North of Scotland	2089.78	221.13	11
Pennsylvania Railroad	756.58	89.85	12
New York Central	369.05	53.73	15
London & Southwestern	229.47	33.96	15
Baltimore & Ohio	110.33	16.28	15

The analysis by salesman is

SALESANAL (SALESMAN	SSALES	SPROFIT	SPS%)
Natacha Engineer	1767.88	263.59	15
Eric Brakeman	2319.25	255.09	11
Hannah Trainman	1223.97	158.14	13

(This analysis shows, for instance, that the customer which accounts for the most sales, Great North of Scotland, also gives the lowest profit percentage. Our company might decide not to sell to this customer in the future, with unfortunate consequences for Eric Brakeman. Or we might decide to disallow sizeable orders for only Toy Trains, which are relatively unprofitable. Note that the sales volume for orders 7 and 8 are almost identical while the profit on order 7 is 42% greater than that on order 8.)

Exercise 5.1-9: Use the relational algebra to derive PARTPROFIT from FINALCOSTS (Section 5.1-3) and PRICE.

Exercise 5.1-10: Suppose our company had stipulated the percentage profit to be made on each finished item, in a relation PROFIT% (ASSEMBLY, PR%). How would we derive PRICE?

Exercise 5.1-11: What operations of the relational algebra are required to calculate ORDERANAL, CUSTANAL and SALESANAL from PRICE, PARTPROFIT, ORDLINE and ORDERS?

5.1-5 System Overview

The preceding examples and exercises give the whole cost and profit analysis system, apart from the closure operation, which remains to be discussed. Here we summarize the relational operations of the system in Exhibit 5.1-4.

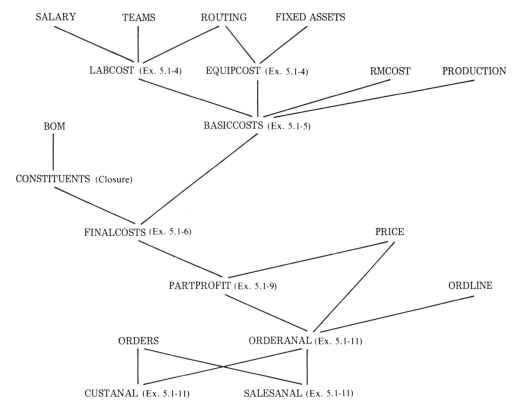

Exhibit 5.1-4. Relational Operations of the Manufacturing Cost and Profit Analysis System

Exercise 5.1-12:   How would we take into account cancellations and return of goods in doing profit analysis?

Exercise 5.1-13:   How many statements of the relational algebra and how many statements of the domain algebra are necessary to implement this system? Assuming it were written in a language which also required a declaration for each relation and each different attribute, how many printer pages would the program occupy?

Exercise 5.1-14:   Write out the whole system with the extensions that have been suggested in Exercises 5.1-3, 5.1-11 and any others that you feel are appropriate.

IMPLEMENTATION: Relational Closure

The operation of closure can be defined precisely (see e.g., Aho, Hopcroft & Ullman [1974] §§ 5.6, 5.7, 5.9), but to do so here would involve too much of a mathematical digression. Besides, we shall open the possibility not only of extending the concept but also of doing it some violence in certain cases. So we shall pursue it intuitively here, leaving formalization and generalization to the future.

We will consider relational closure in the context of networks. A *network* is a directed graph with one or more values associated with each edge. Thus it is represented by an m-ary relation, m > 2 with a binary key. Each tuple corresponds to an edge of the graph, and the values of the two key attributes give the start and finish points of the edge. The other m − 2 attributes give the values associated with the edge. We call the graph the *topological* component of the network and the other values the *quantitative* component.

The topological component of the relational closure is just the transitive closure of the graph.

The quantitative component of the relational closure tells us what to do with the non-key attributes, and depends on the application. Here it makes a practical difference if the graph contains cycles or not. If it does, each non-key attribute together with its operations must form a "closed semiring" (see Aho, Hopcroft & Ullman [1974] § 5.6: Boolean algebra is an example). We will consider only acyclic graphs, for which the quantitative component of the closure is quite unrestricted.

In Section 5.1-3, the non-key attribute of BOM is QTY, which has integer values, and the effect of closure on it is a combination of products and sums. If we compare CONSTITUENTS in Section 5.1-3 with Exhibit 5.1-2, we see that the value of QTY is multiplied with other values along a path of connected edges and that the values for paths that meet are added together. This was expressed in the closure notation introduced in Section 5.1-3,

$$\times \textbf{ of QTY meet } +.$$

Exercise 5.2-1:   A PERT network has an acyclic graph where each edge represents activities in some project (e.g., installing the windows in a construction project) and has an associated value, the duration of the activity. The nodes represent events, namely the start and finish of activities. A path is formed of edges representing activities that must follow each other, and so the duration of the path is the sum of the durations of the edges. Two parallel paths, with the same start and finish nodes, specify two sequences of parallel activities, and the total duration is the maximum of the two path durations. Show that + **of** DURATION **meet max** is the appropriate description of the quantitative component of the closure of PERT (SEVENT, FEVENT, DURATION).

BOM and PERT provide two practical examples of relational closure. We will next discuss implementing the closure of BOM using the relational algebra. Then we will examine the best direct implementation of relational closure. These discussions will be restricted to relations with acyclic topologies.

5.2-1   Closure Using Relational Algebra

We use the relational algebra to derive CONSTITUENTS, a closure of BOM. We first work an example with that part of BOM involving CAR.

BOM (ASSEMBLY	SUBASSEMBLY	QTY)
Car	Roof	1
Car	Base	1
Base	Small	2
Small	Axle	1
Small	Small Wheel	2
Base	Block	1
•	•	•
•	•	•

We do a natural join of BOM on SUBASSEMBLY with BOM on ASSEMBLY. We show the result with the necessary renaming of attributes.

(ASSEMBLY or SUBASSEMBLY	ASSEMBLYA	SUBASSEMBLYA	QTY	QTYA)
Car	Base	Small	1	2
Car	Base	Block	1	2
Base	Small	Axle	2	1
Base	Small	Small Wheel	2	2
•	•	•	•	•
•	•	•	•	•

We **let** QTYB **be** QTY × QTYA and project on ASSEMBLY, SUBASSEMBLYA and QTYB, renaming in an obvious way for convenience.

BOM2 (ASSEMBLY	SUBASSEMBLY	QTY)
Car	Small	2
Car	Block	1
Base	Axle	2
Base	Small Wheel	4
•	•	•
•	•	•

BOM2 contains all paths of length two in the part of the bill-of-materials graph (Exhibit 5.1-2) describing Car.

A second natural join, of BOM on SUBASSEMBLY with BOM2 on AS-SEMBLY, similarly projected, gives the paths of length three.

BOM3 (ASSEMBLY	SUBASSEMBLY	QTY)
Car	Axle	2
Car	Small Wheel	4
•	•	•
•	•	•

Further natural joins give empty results, so there are no paths of length four or more in the CAR subgraph of Exhibit 5.1-2.

The union of BOM, BOM2 and BOM3 is CONSTITUENTS, the closure of BOM. In the notation

CONSTITUENTS ← **closure** BOM (ASSEMBLY, SUBASSEMBLY,
× **of** QTY **meet** +),

the first two parameters are the attributes, drawn from the same domain, that specify the topology of the relation. The remaining parameter (there may be more than one) specifies additional attributes to be carried over to the closure and the reduction to be performed on them. This reduction is like that of the domain algebra except that it need not be associative or commutative since each path through the graph defines a unique ordering of its edges. In the example the reduction operator is multiplication. The second operator, +, is the *meet* operator and tells us what to do when alternative paths are found between subassemblies. This situation does not arise in the Car example. But a Locomotive uses three axles, two in the big wheel assembly and one in the small wheel assembly, and here the sum must be performed.

The closure of the above example can be specified using the relational algebra in a program loop.

```
BOMA[ASSEMBLYA,SUBASSEMBLYA,QTYA,
     ←ASSEMBLY,SUBASSEMBLY,QTY] BOM;
while not empty (BOMA) do
     CONSTITUENTS[ASSEMBLY,SUBASSEMBLY,QTY
          ←+ ASSEMBLYA,SUBASSEMBLYA,QTYA] BOMA;
```

> let QTYB be equiv + of QTY × QTYA by ASSEMBLY,SUBASSEMBLYA;
> BOMA[ASSEMBLYA,SUBASSEMBLYA,QTYA
>   ←ASSEMBLY,SUBASSEMBLYA,QTYB]
>   (BOM[SUBASSEMBLY ijoin ASSEMBLYA] BOMA)
> end   (5.2-1)

The successive projected natural joins are formed in BOMA using replacement assignment and accumulated in CONSTITUENTS using incremental assignment. The equivalence reduction uses the meet operator, +, and the product uses the reduction operator, ×.

Exercise 5.2-2:   Find the closure of the entire bill-of-materials shown in Exhibit 5.1-2 by working through the relational algebra above.

Exercise 5.2-3:   A PERT network is a set of activities of known duration, each activity specified by the two events which initiate and terminate it. The duration of a sequence of activities is the sum of the durations of the individual activities. The duration of alternative activities is the maximum of the duration of the activities. Find the expression which gives PATHS the duration of all sets of activities in

PERT (SEVENT	FEVENT	DURATION)
Start	Middle	2
Middle	End	2
Start	End	3

5.2-2   Topological Sorting of Large Files

This and the next section discuss a direct implementation of relational closure. The implementation has two stages, a topological sort, and a scan to find the closure. This is the best way to deal with large, acyclic relations.

To motivate the discussion, we begin with transitive closure of an acyclic graph. It is helpful to use the matrix form of the graph. Exhibit 5.2-1 shows the subset of BOM[ASSEMBLY, SUBASSEMBLY] involving Locomotive, from Section 5.1-3, with L for Locomotive, B for Big, S for Small, A for Axle and W for Big Wheel. (The 1's in the matrix indicate only the presence of tuples in the projection, not values of QTY.)

Warshall's [1962] algorithm to find the transitive closure applies to all graphs, whether cyclic or not:

```
for j ← 1 to n do
    for i ← 1 to n do
        if g(i,j) = 1 then for k ← 1 to n do g(i,k) ← (g(i,k) or g(j,k))
```

where g is the Boolean matrix representing the graph. Warren [1975] noted that the algorithm scans down columns but **or**s by rows: it would deal better with large matrices on secondary storage if it scanned *and* ored by rows. Warren found that this would work if the elements above the diagonal were scanned first, followed by a scan of the elements below the diagonal. If we now specialize to acyclic graphs, a topological sort puts *all* elements below the diagonal. This is our point of departure. We do not, however, consider a relation stored in matrix form, but adapt the procedure to a sequence of tuples.

Exercise 5.2-4:   Apply Warshall's algorithm to Exhibit 5.2-1.

Exercise 5.2-5:   Formulate Warren's algorithm and apply it to Exhibit 5.2-1.

Topological sorting (see e.g., Knuth [1968] § 2.2.3) arranges the nodes of an acyclic graph so that if the graph has an edge from node a to node b then node a precedes node b in the sorted arrangement. Alternatively, it lines the nodes up in such a way that all edges of the graph go from left to right. The arrangement is not necessarily unique. Here are some arrangements for the nodes A, B, L, S, W of the graph of Exhibit 5.2-1: L, B, S, W, A; L, B, W, S, A; L, S, B, A, W; etc.

Exercise 5.2-6:   Demonstrate for Exhibit 5.2-1 the claim of the text that a topological sort can put all elements below the diagonal. (Or it could put them all above.)

The algorithm discussed by Knuth [1968] § 2.2.3 assumes the tuples are presented to the algorithm as a sequence (in any order) of pairs of nodes. It uses a table of lists of direct successors, one list for each node. For a large relation, this is impractical, even using a hash table on direct access secondary storage, as we will show in Section 5.3-1. In its place, we use a method suggested by Norman Hardy (see Knuth [1973], ex. 5.1.1-24) for a graph which is just a path. This method turns out to be related to the algebraic method (Expression 5.2-1), but faster.

ASSEMBLY:	A	B	L	S	W
A		1		1	
B			1		
SUB-ASSEMBLY L					
S			1		
W		1			

Exhibit 5.2-1. A Subset of BOM.

We first discuss only the topological part of the operation. That is, we are dealing with a set of pairs, {(START, FINISH)}, representing each edge. If we make a copy of the set, sort the original on FINISH and the copy on START and merge, we will have a new set, {(START^2, FINISH^2)}, of all paths of length 2. Repeating the process inductively, we get {(START^4, FINISH^4)}, {(START^8, FINISH^8)}, etc. At the ith step we have all paths of length 2^i. After $\lfloor \log_2 (\text{max. path length}) \rfloor$ steps, we will get empty sets and can stop.

This process leads to a topological ordering of the nodes (or edges) of the graph if we add a mechanism for picking out first all nodes with no predecessors, then all nodes that are 1, 2, 4, . . . edges away from nodes that have already been picked out. That is, we generate a third set from the first step above, a set of nodes this time, namely those *START* nodes from the copied set of edges which match no *FINISH* node from the original set of edges. We label each of these nodes with a 0, to indicate that they have no predecessor. Each of their successors (*FINISH* nodes in the copied set of edges) is also added to the set of nodes and labelled 1. In the second step of the above paragraph, we merge the nodes labelled 0 and 1 with the paths of length 2. We add to the set the end-points of maths starting at nodes labelled 0 and label them 2. Similarly end-points of length-2 paths starting at nodes labelled 1 are added and labelled 3. The third step adds nodes that are 4, 5, 6 and 7 edges from a node with no predecessor, and so on.

Algorithm T: Here is the merge logic for the ith step of the algorithm, $i = 1, . . . ,$ $\lfloor \log_2 (\text{max. path length}) \rfloor - 1$, operating on P_i(START, FINISH), the set of all paths of length 2^i, and T_i(NODE, LABEL), the set of all nodes less than 2^i edges away from a node with no predecessors. At the beginning of the step, P_i^f is created by sorting P_i on FINISH, and P_i^s is created by sorting P_i on START.

1. read P_i^f, P_i^s, T_i
2. compare P_i^f[FINISH]: P_i^s[START]: T_i[NODE]
3. if P_i^f is low then {read P_i^f; goto 2}
4. if T_i is low then {read T_i; goto 2}
5. if $P_i^f = P_i^s$ and low then {P_{i+1} ↢ (P_i^f[START], P_i^s[FINISH]);
                     read P_i^f, P_i^s; goto 2}
6. if $P_i^s = T_i$ and low then {T_{i+1}^+ ↢ (P_i^s[FINISH], T_i[LABEL] $+2^i$);
                     read P_i^s, T_i; goto 2}

In this merge logic the input sets are not likely to be exhausted simultaneously. The merge attribute of any exhausted set is forced to an "infinitely" high value and the loop continues until all sets have this value: this is not shown. A second implicit convention is that duplicate values of P_i^f or P_i^s in step 5 enter P_{i+1} as a *Cartesian product*, just as in natural join. Thus if P_i^f has f tuples of one value of

FINISH and P_i^s has s tuples of the same value of START, P_{i+1} will increase by $f \times s$ tuples.

After the merge, T_{i+1}^+ must be sorted and merged with T_i to form T_{i+1}. In this sort and merge process, duplicate values of NODE are not allowed. Only the tuple with the highest value of LABEL is kept for any node. In this way, nodes at ends of paths of different length from some predecessorless node occupy the proper position in the topological ordering.

The 0th step is similar to the ith step, except that T_i is empty. A final step sorts T on LABEL to give the topologically ordered lists of nodes. If a list of edges is required, T is merged with P_0 before sorting on LABEL. Extending the method to include the values associated with the network edge (the "quantitative component") is just a matter of including these values in the final merge between T and P_0. They can be left out of the rest of the process.

Exercise 5.2-7:   Perform the topological sort on the set $\{(B, A, 1), (B, W, 2), (L, B, 2), (L, S, 1), (S, A, 1)\}$ (which is BOM (ASSEMBLY, SUBASSEMBLY, QTY) for locomotives, as shown in Exhibit 5.2-1, but with QTY added).

Exercise 5.2-8:   The merge logic, Algorithm T, does not include such cases as "P_i^s is low," or "$P_i^f = T_i$ and low." Why are these impossible?

Exercise 5.2-9:   Do the topological sort on the graph of Exhibit 5.1-2 and show the resulting graph in matrix form with rows and columns ordered according to the result of the Hardy topological sort.

5.2-3   Closure by Direct Methods

The Hardy topological sort of the last section partitions the nodes of the network into *layers*. The first layer, labelled 0, consists of all nodes with no predecessors. These are nodes that terminate no edges and can be called *root* nodes. The ith layer holds nodes terminating paths of length $\leq i$ from some root node. Thus a node belongs to layer 3 if there is at least one path of length 3 to it from some root, but no path longer than 3: there may also be paths of length 2 or 1 to it from a root. When we come to find the closure of the network, this ordering aids us because all paths go from some layer to a higher layer.

The graph of the network, in the matrix representation with rows and columns ordered according to the topological sort, is a subdiagonal triangle, with sets of consecutive rows forming each layer. Exhibit 5.2-2 shows this for the toy train bill-of-materials (the nodes are named by single letters for convenience: the correspondence with the subassemblies of Exhibit 5.1-2 does not matter here.) The closure algorithm described in this section is Warren's algorithm applied to layers instead of rows.

Exercise 5.2-10:   Write out the 1s in Exhibit 5.2-2 in graph form, with each layer occupying one horizontal line of nodes.

Applying layer 1 to layer 2 in Exhibit 5.2-2 tells us that B, C, F, J, M, O and P are descendents of S by paths of length 2 via K, L or N. The closure will thus contain additional tuples, shown as asterisks in layer 2. This extended layer 2 is

Layer		S	K	L	N	B	C	F	J	M	O	P	D	E	G	H	J	Q	A	R
0	S																			
	K	1																		
1	L	1																		
	N	1																		
	B	*	1	1																
	C	*			1															
	F	*			1															
2	J	*	1																	
	M	*	1																	
	O	*	1																	
	P	*		1																
	D	*			*	1														
	E	*	*	*		1														
	G	*			*		1													
3	H	*			*		1													
	J	*			*		1													
	Q	*	*	*	1	1														
	A	*	*	*	*	*	1											1		
4	R	*	*	*	*	*												1		

Exhibit 5.2-2. Topologically sorted graph, showing layers. Asterisks show extra tuples to complete closure.

applied to layer 3 in the same way and produces more tuples (asterisks in layer 3), and so on.

The process of "applying layer i to layer i + 1" is as follows. For each row, r, of layer i + 1, if there is an entry in column c, where row c is in layer i, copy row c to row r. (Note however that we may need to look back beyond layer i in order to generate all closure tuples for layer i + 1: in Exhibit 5.2-2, entries NQ and CA require this.) This process is just the natural composition of layer i on rows with layer i + 1 on columns, with the results then added to layer i + 1. This insight tells us how to specify the closure algorithm in terms of tuples as opposed to matrix entries.

Exercise 5.2-11:   Illustrate the point of the last paragraph by finding the natural composition of layer 2 in Exhibit 5.2-2 with layer 3.

The input to the closure algorithm is a set of tuples with the attributes START, FINISH, LFINISH and whatever quantitative (nonkey) attributes are in the original relation. (In BOM, START is ASSEMBLY, FINISH is SUB-ASSEMBLY, and the quantitative attribute is QTY.) We will include one such quantitative attribute, called Q, in the following discussion. LFINISH is the layer (called the *label* in Section 5.2-2) of the FINISH node. This input can be taken from the Hardy topological sort (e.g., Exercise 5.2-7).

If we call the input INP (START, FINISH, Q, LFINISH) and the output of the closure OUP (START, FINISH, Q), the closure algorithm effectively is

OUP ← START, FINISH, Q **in** INP
for each layer, ℓ, from $\ell = 2$
    OUP ↤ OUP [FINISH · START] (**where** LFINISH = ℓ **in** INP)

We describe it in finer detail, abbreviating (**where** LFINISH = ℓ **in** INP) as INP_ℓ. Our handling of the quantitative component, Q, corresponds to the reduction × **of** Q **meet** + .

Algorithm C:

1.   OUP ← INP_ℓ sorted on FINISH, START.
2.   Sort the rest of INP on LFINISH, START, FINISH.
3.   For ℓ ← 2, . . .
   3.1   Merge OUP on FINISH with INP_ℓ on START, creating TEM-PA (START, FINISH, Q) with START from OUP, FINISH from INP_ℓ and Q ← (Q from OUP) × (Q from INP_ℓ)
   3.2   TEMPB ← TEMPA sorted on FINISH, START, with dupli-

cates replaced by a single tuple whose Q value is the sum of the Qs from all tuples with this value of FINISH, START.

3.3   TEMPC ← INP_ℓ sorted on FINISH, START.

3.4   OUP ↔+ OUP ∪ TEMPB ∪ TEMPC with duplicates treated as in 3.2.

Exercise   5.2-12:   Apply algorithm C to the table form of Exhibit 5.1-2 and verify that the 1s and *s of Exhibit 5.2-2 result. If Q is QTY, what values of Q are output?

Exercise   5.2-13:   Write the network of Exhibit 5.1-2 as a matrix, with the values of QTY as the elements instead of 1. In working out the closure of BOM in this form, what is the operation that replaces natural composition in the discussion of transitive closure of the text? Verify that the resulting closure is the same as that of Exercise 5.2-12.

Exercise   5.2-14:   How would you change algorithm C to evaluate + of Q **meet max**?

We conclude our discussion of transitive closure by returning to the problem considered in Section 5.1-3. There we were interested in finding the constituents of certain final assemblies—Toy Train, Locomotive, Car and Caboose. These correspond to S, N, L and K, respectively, in Exhibit 5.2-2. Thus we only need to know columns S, K, L and N of Exhibit 5.2-2 in our final answer (along with the quantitative component), or tuples with START values of S, K, L or N in Exercise 5.2-12. Unfortunately, the other columns, or tuples, are important in deriving the needed results, as a review of Algorithm C will show. Since the graph has one root node, S, and its constituents are among those required, we must take the full closure in this case and then discard unwanted tuples.

In general, if we want only the constituents of some node n in layer ℓ, we can discard all lower layers before finding the closure. To discard nodes in higher layers, we must first ascertain that there is no connection from node n to the node to be discarded. This requires modifying the topological sort so that some kind of trace is transmitted from node n to all its descendents, and then discarding nodes that have not been marked by the trace. This may be worth doing, since inspection of Exhibit 5.2-2 shows that the number of tuples in the closure can be half the square of the number of tuples in the original relation.

Exercise   5.2-15:   Design a topological sort/closure algorithm which incorporates these features.

While Section 5.1-3 finds constituents of given final assemblies, it uses them only in *aggregate* to find the final costs. This can lead to further implementation savings, which we discuss in the next section.

5.2-4   Closure Joins

Computing the full closure of a relation sometimes gives more than we need. A case in point is the calculation of FINAL COSTS in Section 5.1-3 (see also Exhibit 5.1-4). The closure of BOM, which is joined with BASIC COSTS and aggregated by final assembly, contains many more tuples than the needed result and can be avoided.

We will discuss the alternative in this section, illustrating it first in a version suitable for data that can fit entirely in the primary memory of the computer. We abbreviate BASIC COSTS (Section 5.1-2) to

S 9.50	B 1.4625	M .12	E .28	Q 0
K 3.50	C 0	O .07	G .20	A .01
L 3.50	F 5.90	P .19	H .25	R .02
N 3.5625	J .10	D .03	I .17	

Here, single letters have replaced the part names (exact correspondence can be worked out but is not essential) and all prices for each part have been added together for simplicity. Thus Base, with a LABPRICE of $1.35 and an EQUIP-PRICE of $0.1125, becomes the entry (B, 1.4625). Note that the above list is in topological order, S, K, ... , R.

This list can be treated as a vector, T_c, of 19 entries, (9.50, 3.50, ... , .02), if the order of the values S, K, ... , R is given:

$$T_c \triangleq \text{RMPRICE} + \text{LABPRICE} + \text{EQUIPPRICE where PART} = c \text{ in}$$
$$\text{BASIC COSTS.}$$

BOM (ASSEMBLY, SUBASSEMBLY, QTY) becomes a matrix, R_{rc}, with the entry in the column corresponding to the ASSEMBLY and the row corresponding to the SUBASSEMBLY, giving the QTY (zero if no tuple corresponds to that row and column): $R_{rc} \triangleq \text{QTY where ASSEMBLY} = c \text{ and SUBASSEM-}$ BLY $= r$ in *BOM*. The following algorithm for computing the "× of QTY **meet** + closure join" of BOM and BASIC COSTS assumes that all BASIC COSTS can fit in main memory. The algorithm itself is intended to define the notion of a closure join, so a full example is also given.

Algorithm CJ:

For each row, r, from the last to the first
    For each c, $T_c \leftarrow T_c + T_r \times R_{rc}$

Note that the topological ordering of the rows of R is essential.

The result is a modified T giving the final costs for all parts and assemblies. It need only be restricted to the four final assemblies we are interested in to give FINAL COSTS.

The bill of materials of Exhibit 5.1-2 becomes the matrix

	S	K	L	N	B	C	F	J	M	O	P	D	E	G	H	I	Q	A	R
S																			
K	1																		
L	3																		
N	1																		
B		1	1																
C				2															
F					1														
J		1																	
M		1																	
O		1																	
P			1																
D						2													
E					1														
G							1												
H							1												
I							1												
Q				1	2														
A						1											1		
R																	2		

The successive values of the costs vector are (to 2 decimal places)

	start					finish
S	9.50	———————————————————	10.77	36.37	42.00	
K	3.50	—————————	3.57 3.69 3.79 ———	5.63 ———	5.63	
L	3.50	—————————	3.69 ———	5.53 ———	5.53	
N	3.56	——— 3.61 ———	10.13 10.27 ———	10.27		
B	1.46	——— 1.56 ——— 1.84 ———————————	1.84			
C	0	——— 0.01 ——— 0.07 ———————————	0.07			

F 5.90 ————————————6.07 6.32 6.52———————————————————— 6.52

J 0.10 ——— 0.10

M 0.12 ——— 0.12

O 0.07 ——— 0.07

P 0.19 ——— 0.19

D 0.03 ——— 0.03

E 0.28 ——— 0.28

G 0.20 ——— 0.20

H 0.25 ——— 0.25

   0.17 ——— 0.17

Q 0 ———0.04 0.05——————————————————————————————————— 0.05

A 0.01 ——— 0.01

R 0.02 ——— 0.02

This can he restricted to FINAL COSTS by extracting S, K, L and N: compare Section 5.1-3.

Exercise   5.2-16:   Suppose R represents a PERT network (see Exercises 5.2-1 and 5.2-3) and T initially gives the set of earliest times at which activities can commence, due to external constraints apart from the network. What modification of Algorithm CJ is needed to combine R and T to give the set of earliest times at which activities can commence, due to external and network constraints?

Algorithm CJ can be modified, if there is additional room in main memory, to process R by layers instead of by rows. Since nodes within layers are not connected by any paths, the order of processing rows within each layer does not matter.

If main memory cannot hold all of the BASIC COSTS vector, T, we must resort to a layer-by-layer sort and merge algorithm akin to the closure algorithm of the last section (but much faster in principle).

Exercise   5.2-17:   Devise a layer-by-layer sort-merge algorithm equivalent to Algorithm CJ.

Another way of looking at the closure join is graphically. Exhibit 5.2-3 shows a small part of the bill of materials graph (Exhibit 5.1-2: F is Body, I is Cab, H is Burner and G is Boiler) together with the amounts from BASIC COSTS corresponding to the nodes. The BOM edges are shown dashed. Superimposed on the graph are the computations required to work out the final cost of $6.52 for F (Body). Thus I (Cab) costs 17¢ and only one is in the Body, so 1 × .17 is added to the cost. The result, 6.52, is next used as a component in computing the final cost of N (Locomotive), and so on. The net effect is a piping of values up from the raw parts to the final assemblies.

This upwards piping of values is very systematic in the case of working out costs in the bill of materials. It is still systematic, but less simple, when we continue up to the orders (see ORDLINE in Section 5.1-4), which are made up of various final assemblies. Exhibit 5.2-4 shows how both FGPRICE (e.g., $11.99, $46.95) and FGCOST (e.g., $10.27, $42.00) are piped up from the final assemblies N (Locomotive) and S (Toy Train) to order number 1. This is the same process as computing final costs, above, but involves pairs of numbers. Further, subtractions must be performed to calculate profits at each level.

A more complicated process that can still be represented as an upwards piping of values occurs at the beginning of the whole costs computation. Exhibit 5.2-5 shows the derivation of the basic cost of $5.90 for F (Body). This combines the equipment costs of the Glueset machine, G, the labour costs of the Team AP, the 8 hours required per week to do the operation and the 20 units produced in the week. Each type of data needs a unique set of operations, so that a systematic description of the whole process is very difficult. Even to understand Exhibit 5.2-5 requires a careful review of Section 5.1-2. As an aid, the relevant attribute names are given and each different type of data at the nodes of the graph has a unique vertical position corresponding to the attribute name.

Since this graphical presentation may give the reader a clearer view of the example problem than the relations of Chapter 5.1, Exhibit 5.2-6 gives the whole graph for the example, using abbreviated node labels that are either self-evident or have been used earlier in Chapter 5.2. Only some of the values computed for each node are shown. Thus, only profits are shown at BOM nodes N, L, K and S and all nodes higher than these. While this graph may give a helpful perspective on the example of Chapter 5.1, it gives little indication of the *general* operations that we formulated in the relational algebra. A general method of proceeding from the relational algebra to such a piping graph and then of performing the calculations efficiently would be very desirable for some applications.

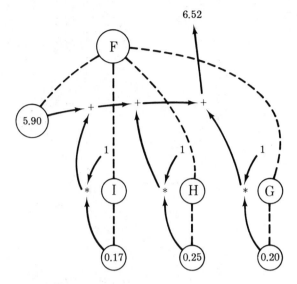

Exhibit 5.2-3. Value piping to give BOM final costs.

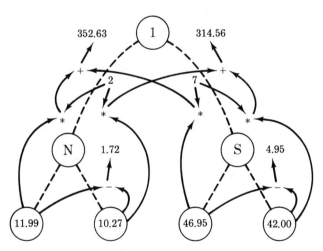

Exhibit 5.2-4. Value piping to give price and cost for Order #1.

ASSEMBLY

QTY

HOURS

TEAM

EMP

WAGE

EQUIP
LIFE

SALVAGE

EQCOST

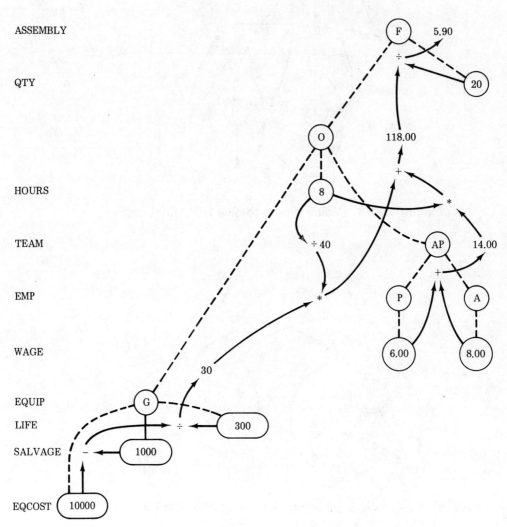

Exhibit   5.2-5.   Value piping to give basic cost for F (Body).

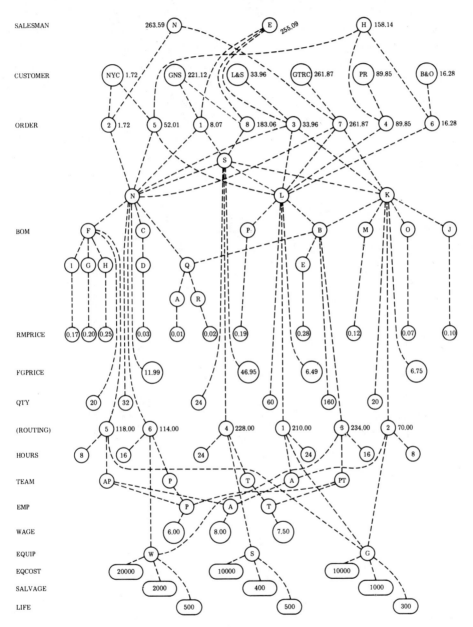

Exhibit 5.2-6. Graph of manufacturing profit example of Chapter 5.1.

COST ANALYSIS: Mainly Topological Sorting

Topological sorting using a truly random access memory is a linear process (see eg. Knuth [1968] § 2.2.3). The algorithm discussed in Section 5.2-2 for secondary memory was shown there to require $O((\log N)^2)$ passes of a file of N tuples. In this section we shall show that the linear method applied to secondary memory is more expensive than the Hardy topological sort for all practical cases, because of the relative inefficiency of accessing one record at a time from the blocks on secondary storage.

We will also look briefly at the cubic process of closure and the linear process of closure join, but will leave the reader to infer from the discussion of topological sorting that sort-merge methods are probably also best in these cases. It is also implied that a general implementation of the relational algebra would be a relatively good way of doing the manufacturing profit processing of Chapter 5.1.

5.3-1   The Cost of Hashing

The topological sort specified by Knuth's Algorithm T does the following:

1) Read the tuples, (START, FINISH, . . .), in any order.
2) For each node, build a list of its immediate successors every time it appears as a START node, and count the number of times it appears as a FINISH node. This step constructs a table of lists: each node heads a list of all nodes to which edges are directed from it. In addition, the number of edges that lead to that node is counted.

3) With the table built, output tuples as follows. Find each node whose count is zero and output it together with each of its successors. Diminish the count of each successor by one and repeat. This step outputs first all edges leading from root nodes, then edges leading from their immediate successors, and so on. The label or layer of Section 5.2-2 can also be generated at this step.

Exercise   5.3-1:   Show the table generated by Knuth's Algorithm T for the Toy Train example of Exhibit 5.1-2.

It is fairly straightforward to see, after working the example of Exercise 5.3-1, that the cost of Knuth's Algorithm T, using hashed secondary storage, is

Input	1 pass.
Build table	2p passes, where p is the effective number of passes to hash all nodes and where 2 is due to the need to add an entry to the list for START and a count to the list for FINISH.
Reduce counts	p passes, since we must change a count each time a node appears as a successor. (We assume with Knuth that a queue links all lists with zero counts at any time, so that search for zero counts is not needed.)
Output	1 pass.

In this analysis, we alter Knuth's approach by assuming that the table on secondary storage contains no links, so that all successors are obtained in a single access. It would be more realistic to suppose that the record size was large enough to hold more than one successor but not necessarily all of them, so that links would be required in a small number of cases. For instance, if each list contained the head node and two successors, the table in Exercise 5.3-1 would require four links, for the lists headed by F, K, N and S.

To make the analysis more precise, we must make such an assumption and commit ourselves to a record size. We suppose that each node requires 31 bytes and QTY requires 2 bytes, giving tuples of 64 bytes in the original file. Suppose the count requires 2 bytes and an overflow pointer (if used) needs 1 byte, and there are two successors per record (i.e., about 20% of records will overflow in this example). Then the record length in the hash table will be $2 + 3 \times 31 + 2 \times 2 + 1 = 100$ bytes.

From Exhibit 1.3-3, we have the optimum value of P for a hash table of 100-byte records: P is 142 effective passes. It is the size of this value that makes hashing so expensive. We must further multiply P by 100/64, the expansion factor of the hash record over the record of the original relation, since we would like to know the cost in terms of effective passes of the original file.

This gives a hashing cost of $2 + 3 \times 142 \times (100/64) = 668$ effective passes. This is the number the Hardy sort must beat.

5.3-2   Extrapolating Graphs

The cost of the hashing algorithm for topological sorting, given above, is essentially independent of the size of the bill of materials. To find the cost of the Hardy topological sort, we need to know quantities, such as the number of nodes in each layer of the bill of materials, which depend on the size. All we have to work with is an example of 19 nodes and 21 edges. To get an idea of costs in cases of realistic sizes we need a way of expanding the graph to 10^3, 10^6 and even 10^9 records (edges). The concern of this section is how to characterize the graph by means of parameters which we can control when we extrapolate from a simple example involving tens of edges to a realistic case involving thousands or millions of edges.

The discussion will be limited to graphs that are almost trees, in the sense of the Appendix, and even here we resort to handwaving. Trees have two characteristics which might be of interest in a given application: fanout, ϕ, and height, h. To keep things simple, we should try to fix one of these parameters so that only the other one changes. In the case of a tree representing a bill of materials, the full-scale case is likely to be both bushier (i.e. the fanout is larger) and higher than the example of Exhibit 5.1-2 ($\phi = 2.63$, h = 4). The relationship between ϕ, h and $|E|$ is, using ϕ in place of m in the m-ary tree formulas of the Appendix,

$$h = \lceil \log_\phi |L| \rceil \qquad (5.3\text{-}1)$$

where $|L|$, the number of leaf nodes, is $|E|(\phi - 1)/\phi - 1$ for a tree of $|E|$ edges. We can alternately fix $\phi = 2.6$ and then h = 4 to estimate the extreme cases of, respectively, a slender tree of variable length and a short tree of variable bushiness. In the latter case, we must find ϕ from Equation 5.3-1, which is difficult unless we allow h to take on non-integer values and use

$$h = \log_\phi(|E|(\phi - 1)/\phi - 1) \qquad (5.3\text{-}2)$$

(e.g. h = 3.62). Finding ϕ from Equation 5.3-2 given $|E|$ and h, requires writing a short program, say for a pocket calculator, to solve the implicit equation.

Exercise 5.3-2:   Confirm that $\phi = 2.63$ and therefore that h = 3.62 in the bill of materials example of Exhibit 5.1-2.

Exercise 5.3-3:   If we fix $\phi = 2.63$, what is h for $|E| = 10^3$, 10^6 and 10^9 edges?

Exercise 5.3-4:   If we fix h = 3.62, what values of ϕ satisfy Equation 5.3-2 for $|E| = 10^3$, 10^6 and 10^9 edges?

The analysis of topological sorting in the next section requires that we know two quantities for each level, ℓ, of an almost tree: p_ℓ, the number of paths of length ℓ; and v_ℓ, the number of nodes separated from the root by paths of length ℓ. If we model the almost tree by a ϕ-ary tree, clearly

$$
v_\ell = \begin{cases} \phi^\ell & \text{if} \quad \sum_{i=0}^{\ell} \phi^i \le |V|, \\[2em] |V| - \sum_{i=0}^{\ell-1} \phi^i & \text{otherwise.} \end{cases} \tag{5.3-3}
$$

We can also estimate p_1 using a ϕ-ary tree model. The number of edges starting at each internal node is ϕ, the fanout. The sum of this over all internal nodes is the number of paths of length 1, i.e., the number of edges: $p_1 = |E|$. The sum of ϕ over all internal nodes except the root gives $p_2 = |E| - \phi$. In general,

$$
p_\ell = |E| - \sum_{i=1}^{\ell-1} \phi^i = |E| - (\phi^\ell - 1)/(\phi - 1). \tag{5.3-4}
$$

Exercise 5.3-5:   What is p_ℓ for a forest of t ϕ-ary trees?

Exercise 5.3-6:   Compare p_ℓ given by Equation 5.3-4 with the true number of paths of length ℓ for Exhibit 5.1-2.

5.3-3   Cost of Hardy Topological Sort

The ith step of Algorithm 5.2-2T has four parts

    a)   3-way merge of P_i^f, P_i^s, T_i giving P_{i+1}, T_{i+1}^+
    b)   sort P_{i+1} twice, eliminating duplicates and giving P_{i+1}^f, P_{i+1}^s
    c)   sort T_{i+1}^+, eliminating duplicates
    d)   merge T_{i+1}^+, T_i giving T_{i+1}

We need to know the sizes of the various inputs and outputs for the parts of step i, in order to estimate the sort and merge costs. Let us use more specific notation for these inputs and outputs. The result of the merge of P_i^f and P_i^s is P_i^2: this is different from P_{i+1} in that duplicates have yet to be eliminated. We use R to indicate the set of root nodes and P^jR to indicate the set of nodes that are j edges away from a root node along some path. If the graph is a tree, P^jR and P^kR have no nodes in common ($j \ne k$), but in general a node may terminate one path of j edges from the root and another of k edges. Thus $|P^jR| + |P^kR| \ge |(P^j + P^k)R|$ with equality holding for trees but not in general, where $|S|$ denotes the number of elements in a set S and $(P^j + P^k)R$ is the set union of P^jR with P^kR.

The results T_{i+1}^{+} of part (a) above and T_{i+1} of part (d) can be expressed using P^j and R: T_1 is $(1 + P)R$, T_2 is $(1 + P + P^2 + P^3)R$, and generally, T_i is $(1 + \ldots + P^{2^i - 1})R$: i.e., T_1 contains roots and nodes one edge from a root, T_2, contains T_1 plus nodes two and three edges from a root, and so on. T_{i+1}^{+} has two versions: the result of part (a), containing duplicates, and the sorted version after part (c), with duplicates removed. These differ in size, so we will express only the *sizes* of T_{i+1}^{+}. T_1^{+} is T_1. The size of T_2^{+} is $|P^2R| + |P^3R|$ after (a) and $|(P^2 + P^3)R|$ or $|P^2(1 + P)R|$ after (c). In general, the size of T_i^{+} is $|P^{2^{i-1}}R| + \ldots + |P^{2^i - 1}R|$ after (a) and $|P^{2^{i-1}}(1 + \ldots + P^{2^{i-1}} - 1)R|$ after (c).

These formulas give us a feel for the sizes of the sets involved in Algorithm 5.2-2T, but they are unwieldy and we do not know how to calculate, in general, the individual quantities involved. What we shall do is approximate the graph with a ϕ-ary tree and use the quantities derived in Section 5.3-2. For a tree, $P_i^2 = P_{i+1}$ and the two versions of T_{i+1}^{+} have the same size since no two nodes have more than one path connecting them. This simplifies our cost formula for step i. It now contains three basic quantities instead of five:

$$X_i \overset{\Delta}{=} P_{i-1}^2 \quad \text{the number of paths of length } 2^i \text{ in P}$$

$$= P_i \quad \text{the number of pairs of nodes in P separated by paths of length } 2^i$$

$$Y_{i+1} \overset{\Delta}{=} |P^{2^i}R| + \ldots + |P^{2^{i+1}-1}R| = \sum_{j=2^i}^{2^{i+1}-1} \text{(number of nodes}$$

$$\text{separated from roots by paths of length j)}$$

$$= \text{size of } T_{i+1}^{+} \text{ after part (a)} = |P^{2^i}(1 + \ldots + P^{2^i-1})R|$$

$$= \text{size of } \sum_{j=2^i}^{2^{i+1}-1} \text{(nodes separated from roots by paths of}$$

$$\text{length j)} = \text{size of } T_{i+1}^{+} \text{ after part (c)}$$

$$Z_i \overset{\Delta}{=} |(1 + \ldots + P^{2^i-1})R| = \text{size of} \sum_{j=0}^{2^i-1} \text{(nodes separated from}$$

$$\text{roots by paths of length j)} = \text{size of } T_i$$

The cost of sorting a set S of tuples, $s(|S|)$ read requests to the secondary storage, is the quantity worked out in Section 1.3-5. The total cost of sorting S, including write requests, is $2s(|S|)$. The cost of merging S_1 with S_2 is $|S_1| + |S_2|$ reads and $|S_1 + S_2|$ writes, where $|S_1 + S_2|$ is the size of the result, which may not be a simple set union of S_1 with S_2.

For step i of Algorithm 5.2-2T, the costs are:

    a)   3-way merge: $2 X_i + Z_i$ reads and $X_{i+1} + Y_{i+1}$ writes

    b)   sort P_{i+1} twice: $2 s(X_{i+1})$ reads and $2 s(X_{i+1})$ writes

    c)   sort T_{i+1}^+: $s(Y_{i+1})$ reads and $s(Y_{i+1})$ writes

    d)   merge T, T^+: $Y_{i+1} + Z_i$ reads and Z_{i+1} writes

We are interested in knowing costs expressed as a number of *effective passes* of P_o, so we shall divide all results by $|P_o|$. If $i = 0$ then part (d) is omitted, $Z_i = 0$, and the step is preceeded by two sorts of P_o. The final step omits part (b) and modifies part (d) according to whether the edges are to be sorted or just the nodes.

The quantities X_i, Y_i and Z_i can be expressed in terms of the parameters of the ϕ-ary tree that we use to approximate the graph, X_i is just P_ℓ with $\ell = 2^i$.

Y_i is $\displaystyle\sum_{j=2^{i-1}}^{2^i - 1} v_j$ and Z_i is the sum of Y_j up through $j = i$.

If we consider the problem of extrapolating the bill of materials of Exhibit 5.1-2 to cases involving thousands and millions of records (edges), we can either fix ϕ or h, according to the discussion of Section 5.3-2. In addition we need to know $|V|$, the number of nodes, in order to find V_j. We will assume that $|V| / |E|$ is independent of $|E|$, the number of edges. Other assumptions could be made.

Exercise 5.3-7:   Fixing $\phi = 2.63$ for the ϕ-ary tree approximating the bill of materials of Exhibit 5.1-2, with $|E| = 10^3$, 10^6 and 10^9 records, derive the values of X_i, Y_i, Z_i from the root to the leaves. Assume $|V| = 19|E|/21$.

Exercise 5.3-8:   Fixing $h = 3.62$ for the same example, derive X_i, Y_i, Z_i.

What we must finally do is use the values for X_i, Y_i and Z_i to compute the total cost of the Hardy topological sort for various file sizes and various machines. In the analysis of sorting in Section 1.3-5, we characterized large, mini and micro computers in terms of buffer memory size: e.g., 15625, 1562 and 156 64-byte records respectively. We discovered good merge factors for sorting on each type of machine, and can use here the results of the sorting analysis. The computation of total cost requires a program, such as could be run on a pocket calculator. Using the results of Exercises 5.3-7 and 5.3-8 for X_i, Y_i and Z_i, we obtain Exhibit 5.3-1a for fixed ϕ and Exhibit 5.3-1b for fixed h.

In comparing Exhibit 5.3-1 with the cost required to do a topological sort using the linear algorithm with hashing of Section 5.3-1, we see that only files of greater than about 10^8 bytes, sorted on microcomputers, give worse results using the Hardy method. These cases are impractical: 668 passes of 10^8 bytes at a transfer time of 30 μsec/byte requires over three weeks. In all practical cases, Hardy sorting is better than hashing.

	MAIN	MINI	MICRO
$|E| = 10^3$			155.5
10^6	62.9	152.2	790.1
10^9	141.3	341.4	1684

(A) $\phi = 2.63$

	MAIN	MINI	MICRO
$|E| = 10^3$			128.6
10^6	47.3	114.0	591.1
10^9	88.8	214.3	1975

(B) $h = 3.62$

Exhibit 5.3-1. Costs of Hardy topological sort, in effective passes, for files of $|E|$ 64-byte records on various computers for a) fixed ϕ and b) fixed h.

Exercise 5.3-9:   Write a program and calculate Exhibit 5.3-1.

5.3-4   Closure and Closure Joins

The ϕ-ary tree model appears to work well for cost analysis of topological sort on graphs that have very few nodes with more than one incoming edge. Under this assumption, the results of the last section indicate that sort-merge methods are superior to direct access methods in practical cases. The reason for this is that hashing to individual records makes no use of the fact that many records are stored on a block of secondary storage, while sorting clusters associated records together on a block in the optimal way. Hashing requires one access per record, or many accesses to each block, while a sorted file can be processed with one access per block. Sorting itself requires several accesses per block, but, as the analysis of Section 1.3-5 shows, the number of accesses is relatively small.

The ϕ-ary tree model does not work well when we come to analyze closure, since the size of the closure of an (acyclic) graph that is not a tree depends very much not only on the number of nodes with two or more incoming edges but also on where in the graph they are. However, the general comparison, above, of sort-merge versus direct access methods with secondary storage, applies. Closure is a cubic process: Warshall's algorithm, say, requires time and operations proportional to the cube of the number of nodes. Topological sorting, by comparison, is linear. The sort-merge algorithms described in Chapter 5.2 for topological sorting and for closure are in principle worse than linear and cubic, respectively. But they both make use of the clustering of data possible on secondary storage and avoid the pitfalls of a naive adaptation of the classical linear and cubic algorithms. It is reasonable to suppose that where sort-merge is an improvement on direct access for the (linear) topological sort, it is at least as good an improvement for the (cubic) closure.

For our purposes, the closure join is more interesting than closure. As noted in Section 5.2-4, this is in principle a linear process. Sort-merge techniques increase the theoretical cost but again are likely to be better in cases that are not too large to be practical.

It must be borne in mind that the arguments leading to these conclusions, as well as being loose in places, are founded on assumptions that do not always apply. The main assumption in the topological sort analysis is that the graph can be successfully modelled for the purpose as a ϕ-ary tree. If the graph has many nodes with several incoming edges, the model may not work. The extension of the example graph to bills of materials of up to 10^9 edges makes assumptions about the ratio of edges to nodes, and other approximations are used. However, bills of materials are likely to conform to our assumptions and the methods described in Chapter 5.2 are probably the best methods possible for bill of materials processing.

It is of interest to see what advantage we gain in finding the transitive closure of an acyclic graph by first doing a topological sort. We can explore this by using the matrix representation of the graph and of its transitive closure. The matrix will be triangular, as a result of the sort. The cost of finding the transitive closure is proportional to at least the number of edges in the closure. In the diagrams, the transitive closure is shown and the edges of the original graph are circled. Graphs will have $n = |V|$ nodes.

If the original graph is a tree, the size of the transitive closure is at most $n(n-1)/2$ edges. This happens when the tree is a path (see Exhibit 5.3-2): the closure fills the triangle. The algorithm for finding the closure can simply scan once down the rows, copying each row, r, to the row with the 1 in column r, and so the worse cost is $O(n^2)$ for trees. This is better than cubic ($O(n^3)$), and so the topological sort is very useful if we are finding the closure of trees.

In general, however, we cannot do better than $O(n^3)$ because of *overlap*. If a row of the matrix has more than one 1, two or more other rows will be copied onto that row, and these rows will overlap wherever paths converging on one node have another common node. An example is given by a type of graph we shall call a *ϕ-ary braid*. Exhibit 5.3-3a shows a 3-ary braid, with three edges leading from each internal node. In the general case, ϕ edges start at each internal node and each level (apart from the root) has ϕ nodes. The ϕ-ary braid is an almost tree, under the definition of the Appendix, but it is a kind that does not much resemble a tree. It has a root, leaves, a fanout (ϕ) and a height ($h = (n-1)/\phi$) but the width (the number of root-to-leaf paths), $\phi^h = \phi(\sqrt[\phi]{\phi})^{n-1}$, is exponential in n. (A tree has a width of $< n$.)

In Exhibit 5.3-3b the unitalicized entries are not 1 but integers not less than 1. This is a convention we adopt to describe overlap: the entries are 3 in this case because each row with edges added in the transitive closure process has three *1*s and so each new edge is added three times. Thus the edge $5 \leftarrow 1$ is a consequence of $5 \leftarrow 2$ and $2 \leftarrow 1$, of $5 \leftarrow 3$ and $3 \leftarrow 1$ and of $5 \leftarrow 4$ and $4 \leftarrow 1$. So it is added 3 times, even though it appears only once in the final closure. Because of this overlap, we must refine what we said above about cost: the cost of finding the

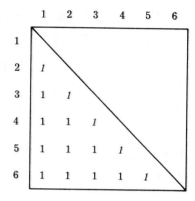

Exhibit 5.3-2. Closure of a path.

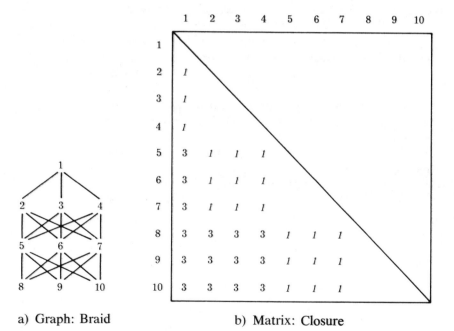

a) Graph: Braid   b) Matrix: Closure

Exhibit 5.3-3. Closure of a 3-ary Braid.

transitive closure is proportional to at least the number of edges in the closure plus the extra additions of edges due to overlap. For the ϕ-ary braid, each new edge is added ϕ times and $O(n^2)$ new edges are added. This last assertion is justified by inspection of Exhibit 5.3-3b: the ϕs ($\phi = 3$) form a rough triangle of sides $n - (\phi + 1)$ and $n - 2\phi$.

Exercise   5.3-10:   Show that the overlap generated in finding the closure of the ϕ-ary braid is $(\phi - 1)(n - \phi + 1)(n - 2\phi + 1)/2$.

If we have a class of ϕ-ary braids with ϕ proportional to n, say $\phi = .21n$, then the overlap and the cost of the closure process, is $0(n^3)$.

Exercise   5.3-11:   What ϕ gives the maximum overlap for the ϕ-ary braid for a given n?

Exercise   5.3-12:   Find other classes of graphs which require $O(n^3)$ operations to compute closure.

Graphs such as the ϕ-ary braid help to illustrate that there are some extremely poor ways of computing closure joins or piping values up a graph (as discussed in Section 5.2-4) and that unwariness can lead to disastrous costs. For instance, we could use a traversal algorithm which finds the contribution at a node by recursively examining each of its descendents. This is very suitable for processing trees, but becomes exponentially expensive even for other acyclic graphs. Thus, to find the total profit for Salesman S in Exhibit 5.2-6, we would find the profits for Orders 2 and 7. But each of these has descendents: to find the profit of Order 2 we must find that for BOM node N, and to find it for Order 7, we must examine BOM nodes N (again), L and K. From here, we are led to inspect *every* lower node in the graph, sometimes repeatedly as we process its various predecessors. To go from each root to all the data necessary to find its profit requires traversing all root-to-leaf paths in the graph.

For a ϕ-ary braid we have seen that the number of these paths, the *width* of the graph, is exponential in the number of nodes. For an arbitrary acyclic graph, we can calculate the width using the following definition. The *participation* of a node, n, in an acyclic graph, part (n), is defined

$$\text{part}(n) \stackrel{\Delta}{=} \begin{cases} 1 & \text{if n is a root} \\ \\ \displaystyle\sum_{n' \in \{\text{pred}(n)\}} \text{part}(n') & \text{otherwise} \end{cases}$$

where {pred (n)} is the set of immediate predecessors of n in the graph. It is easy to see by induction that part (n) is the number of paths to node n from some root. Thus the width of the graph is

$$w = \sum_{n = \text{leaf}} \text{part (n)}.$$

Exercise 5.3-13: Show that the width of the graph of Exhibit 5.2-6 is 1008.

Processing costs proportional to the width of the graph are incurred by traversal methods and by certain navigational approaches to database management. The width can easily become exponential in the number of nodes in the graph for classes of graph with nodes, that finish more than one edge, scattered from root to leaf.

6

A FINANCIAL ACCOUNTING SYSTEM

BASICS: An Information System Based on Funds Flow

Now we take a more global view of our hypothetical manufacturing firm and construct a general accounting/financial system. We will make some assumptions about the business strategies of the firm and will mention alternative strategies at the appropriate points of the text. We will adopt a particularly simple accounting technique, expressing the flow of funds by a spread sheet and reducing the number of separate accounts to manageable size. The funds flow approach to financial modelling will be extended to a general information model so that we can use operational data as a source for the financial entries of our accounting system.

6.1-1 Accounting and Information Systems

Accounting and information systems are closely linked. In its broadest sense, accounting is the measurement of the activities and performance of a firm. Only in the narrow sense does it have to do with records of money and production of statements required by law (e.g., balance sheet and statement of income). Information systems are thus a branch of accounting. Computers have made it possible to do accounting at much more elaborate and sophisticated levels, using not only money but many different measures.

We will distinguish two levels of accounting and information systems— *managerial* and *operational*. Managerial accounting provides summaries and overall performance measures as a basis for management decisions and control. A plan (or a budget) is made and the company activity monitored in comparison with that plan. Operational information systems, on the other hand, function at the lower, more detailed level of daily operations. They keep track of such transactions as invoicing and payments received, payments made, inventory, production in progress, etc.

The applications discussed in this book are reporting systems and thus mainly managerial in aim. It is operational data, however, that they summarize. Thus the manufacturing profit system of Part 5 used bill-of-materials and payroll data to produce an analysis of profit by part. The financial system of this chapter similarly will draw on basic operational data to produce the traditional financial statements.

To design a general financial system, we need a model of our company which can accommodate both the operational data and the established accounting conventions. We choose a model based on *funds flow*. Examining the funds flow of a firm gives an overview, in monetary terms, of all the operations of the firm. We shall see in the next section that it can be described by the accounting device of the spread sheet and that this can be used to generate the usual financial reports.

As Exhibit 6.1-1 shows, there is a basic cycle of funds flow, from liquidity to raw materials and labor to finished goods to sales and back to liquidity. The cycle is driven by a *source*, the profit, and it has *sinks* in the depreciation of fixed assets and in all the expenses that are necessary to run the firm but are hard to attribute directly to the components of the cycle.

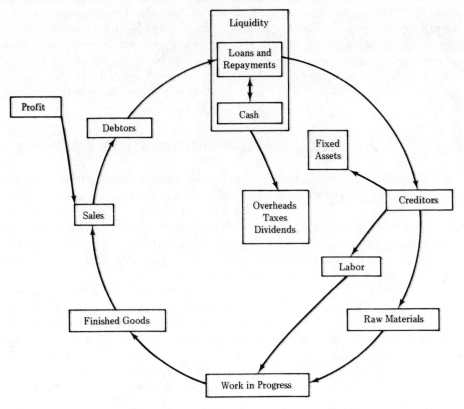

Exhibit   6.1-1.   The Funds Flow Cycle

Like the thermodynamic cycle of an engine, the funds flow cycle is the financial workhorse of the firm. The more funds that flow or the faster they flow, the faster the gain of the system. Thus a management which uses funds flow as an indicator of company performance is very interested in movements or turnover in basic items such as inventories, debtors, cash balances, overdrafts, and production. Improving funds flow is then, among other ways, a matter of speeding up processes such as production or debt collection, or minimizing the inverse of turnover such as average inventory or bank balances. Computerized information systems have the justification that they are supposed to be good at speeding up operational processes and at doing the involved calculations required for good minimization. On the other hand, computerized systems are not free. Making them significantly cheaper is the motivation of the techniques described in this book.

Funds flow gives a financial model of the firm. The operational model parallels it closely, as Exhibit 6.1-2 shows. Each of the boxes of this diagram names one of the information subsystems needed to run the manufacturing company. In this model, the data recorded and processed is not just financial but involves raw materials, labor and equipment hours, order forms, and many different sorts of documented information. The summary reports from the information systems list not only dollar aggregates for the accounting system but also non-monetary aggregates such as average lead times, total stockouts, various turnover rates, routing and location summaries, absenteeism and safety.

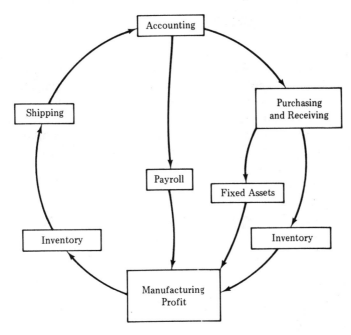

Exhibit 6.1-2. The Business Information Model

Exhibit 6.1-2 is a flow of events diagram which mimics the flow of funds cycle. After we purchase raw materials we receive them. They are stocked until assembled into finished goods. These are ordered by customers and then paid for.

It is worth noting the assumptions implicit in this particular model. First we have a *manufacturing* operation. If we were looking at, say, a *distributor,* there would be no assembly process and the "raw materials" and "finished goods" inventories would be one and the same. Or we might have two distinct inventories but of the same type of goods and in different locations; the assembly process would be replaced by a distribution activity. Another alternative would be a *point-of-sale* operation which would have no ordering process or any of the associated invoicing or accounts receivable activities. Goods are paid for immediately by the customer and any information is recorded at the cash register.

Within the order-based manufacturing framework there are some alternatives. A firm can *manufacture to order*. Each customer order initiates the process of raw materials purchase, assembly, etc. On the other hand, a mass-production setup *manufactures to stock,* with purchasing and assembly activities determined by desired changes in inventory levels. Apart from the problem of forecasting sales, manufacture to stock requires a simpler system and so will be emphasized here.

6.1-2   Spread Sheets and Financial Statements

The funds flow diagram of Exhibit 6.1-1 becomes a network of accounts and transactions in a straightforward way, as shown in Exhibit 6.1-4. The nodes of the network are accounts, summarized together with example beginning balances (in thousands of dollars) in Exhibit 6.1-3. Each account is either an Asset, Liability or Equity account by classification, indicated in the diagram by subscript A, L or E. The edges of the network are transactions from one account to another, with the arrow going from credit to debit. The accounting convention, for reasons that are explained a little further on, is to add debits to Asset accounts and subtract credits, and to do the opposite with Liability and Equity accounts. This conven-

Exhibit 6.1-3. Summary of Accounts, with Beginning Balances

	ASSETS (DB +)			LIABILITIES (CR +)	
A	Goods in Assembly	5.41	P	Accounts Payable	5.57
C	Cash	7.26	T	Taxes Payable	2.92
F	Fixed Assets	26.13			
G	Finished Goods	4.03			
M	Raw Materials	1.49		EQUITIES (CR +)	
R	Accounts Receivable	7.00	E	Stockholders' Account	42.83
		51.32			51.32

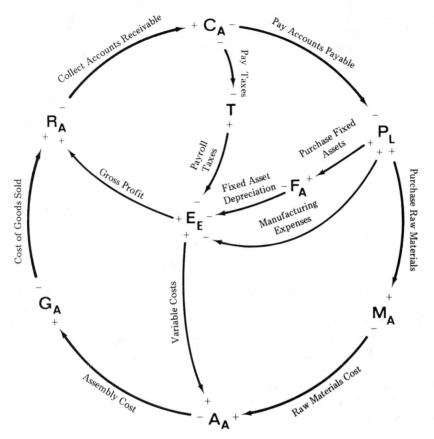

Exhibit 6.1-4. Transaction Network

tion is indicated by signs at the ends of each arrow in the network. An important improvement over the funds flow diagram is the introduction of the Equity account to tie up the loose ends of sources and sinks. We will see that a convenient simplification results from this.

The transactions represented by the arrows in the network could be the minute-by-minute financial transfers of the enterprise or they could be summaries, by day, month or year, of all the transactions between each pair of accounts. In the latter case, the transaction network is called a *spread sheet* and is conventionally written as a matrix (Exhibit 6.1-5). Note the summary row, Δ^-, and column, Δ^+: Δ^- gives the total outflows (in the sense of the arrows) for each account and Δ^+ gives the total inflows. The totals, in turn, of Δ^- and Δ^+, are both the same of course, and are entered as the amount 27.30 in the lower right corner. Ensuring that these last two totals are the same is called *balancing* in double-entry accounting. The spread sheet is a double-entry system because each amount appears both in a row (debit account) and in a column (credit account).

	CR→ DB↓	A	C	F	G	M	R	P	T	E	Δ⁺
		Assets						Liabilities		Equity	
A	A					1.30				1.43	2.73
	C						3.99				3.99
	F							0.00			0.00
	G	2.33									2.33
	M							1.01			1.01
	R			3.19						2.21	5.40
L	P		7.70								7.70
	T		1.87								1.87
E	E			0.22				2.11	0.95		3.28
	Δ⁻	2.33	9.57	0.22	3.19	1.30	3.99	3.12	0.95	3.64	27.30

Exhibit 6.1-5. Spread Sheet

To be a little more conventional about balancing the spread sheet, we total the *change in account balance,* $\Delta^+ - \Delta^-$, separately for Assets and for Liabilities and Equities. This gives the *flow of funds statement* (Exhibit 6.1-6). Note that the sign has been changed for Liabilities and Equities: the total now equals the total for Assets, which occupies the other half of the table. Otherwise the sum of $\Delta^+ - \Delta^-$ would be zero, of course, which is a perfectly reasonable way of checking the balance, but just does not happen to be traditional. To achieve this traditional balance, rather than zero sum, is the reason for treating Asset accounts differently from Liabilities and Equities

Exhibit 6.1-6. Flow of Funds Statement

Δ ASSETS		Δ LIABILITIES	
A	0.40	P	−4.58
C	−5.58	T	−0.92
F	−0.22		
G	−0.86		
M	−0.29	Δ EQUITY	
R	1.41	E	0.36
	−5.14		−5.14

Exhibit 6.1-7. Source and Use of Funds

SOURCE OF FUNDS		USE OF FUNDS	
C	5.58	A	0.40
E	0.36	P	4.58
F	0.22	R	1.41
G	0.86	T	0.92
M	0.29		
	7.31		7.31

Exhibit 6.1-7 shows the *source and use of funds statement,* which is related to the flow of funds; decreases in Assets (negative sign) and increases in Liabilities or Equity (positive sign) are sources of funds; while increases in Assets and decreases in Liabilities or Equity are uses. This is all fairly intuitive: selling equipment (an Asset) or borrowing (a Liability) gives you more money.

The sum of the flow of funds statement with the beginning balance sheet gives the *final balance sheet* (Exhibit 6.1-8).

Exhibit 6.1-8. Final Balance Sheet

ASSETS			LIABILITIES		
A	Goods in assembly	5.81	P	Accounts Payable	0.99
C	Cash	1.68	T	Taxes Payable	2.00
F	Fixed Assets	25.91			
G	Finished Goods	3.17			
M	Raw Materials	1.20		EQUITIES	
R	Accounts Receivable	8.41	E	Stockholders' Account	43.19
		46.18			46.18

Exhibit 6.1-9. Income Statement

EXPENSES			REVENUES		
DIRECT					
EP	Manufacturing expenses	2.11	RE	Gross profit	2.21
INDIRECT			AE	Variable Costs	1.43
EF	Depreciation of fixed assets	0.22			3.64
ET	Payroll taxes	0.95			
		3.28			
NET PROFIT					
	after taxes	0.36			
		3.64			

Going back to the spread sheet, we can derive the *income statement* for the period. We will do this in a slightly unorthodox way, to highlight the simplifying role of the Equity account. We introduce two new types of "accounts", which are really transaction summaries: *Revenue* accounts are entries in the Equity column, E, of the spread sheet and *Expense* accounts are entries in the Equity row, E, of the spread sheet. Our version of the income statement is just the summary of these two types of account (Exhibit 6.1-9).

The income statement becomes slightly more conventional if we add cost of goods sold (transaction R ← G) to both sides; on the Revenues side, this adds to gross profit (R ← E) to give Sales. Mentioning gross profit is considered to be unwise and possibly in poor taste.

Exercise 6.1-1:   The principle underlying the balances that we can make in all the above reports is that *money is conserved:* it does not appear from nowhere nor, normally, does it disappear. That is why accountants use the Equity accounts to make the transaction network free of sources or sinks. From a more subtle point of view, however, considering the effects of inflation on the *value* of money, money does disappear and is not conserved. How would you elaborate the above accounting procedures to accommodate a given rate of inflationary erosion? What if the rate depended on which account the money was in—e.g., inventories inflate less than bank accounts?

Now that we have reviewed the usual financial documents, we can describe them as relations and express their derivations in terms of relational operations. In this section we assume that we are given the spread sheet and initial balance for a specified period and are asked to produce the various statements. This given data could be a summary of the company Journal, the daily record of all financial transactions, or it could be derived directly from the operation data of the company. In the next section we discuss the latter derivation.

Exhibit 6.1-10. Relations for Financial Documents

Given	TYPE (<u>ACCT</u>, ACTYPE, ADESCR)
	TRANS (<u>ACCTCR, ACCTDB</u> TDESCR)
	BALANCE (<u>DATE, ACCT</u>, BAL)
	SPREAD (<u>PEREND, ACCTCR, ACCTDB</u>, AMOUNT)
Derived	FUNDFLOW (<u>ACCT</u>, ADESCR, ACTYPE, FF)
	SORUSE (<u>ACCT</u>, ADESCR, SUAMT, SU)
	REVENUE (<u>ACCTDB</u>, TDESCR, AMOUNT)
	EXPENSE (<u>ACCTCR</u>, TDESCR, AMOUNT)
	INCOME (<u>ACCT</u>, TDESCR, AMOUNT, RE)

Exhibits 6.1-10 and 6.1-11 show the relations we use and how they are derived from each other. The given relations are illustrated in Exhibit 6.1-12. Of these, two (TYPE and TRANS) are permanent and two (BALANCE and SPREAD) will be derived from more fundamental data in the next section. TYPE is a description of the company accounts and gives the classification of each account into Asset, Liability or Equity. A large company would have a hierarchical Chart of Accounts classifying them further into categories, subaccounts, etc. This adds an interesting dimension when summaries of subaccounts, accounts by category, etc. are required, but we bypass this topic here. TRANS is the specification and description of the allowed transactions. Both of these relations

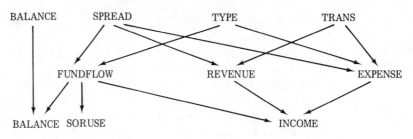

Exhibit 6.1-11. How the Relations are Derived

are relatively static and no provision for changing them is made in this discussion, although in a dynamic company they may well change frequently.

Exhibit 6.1-12. Relations Used to Derive Financial Statements

TYPE				TRANS			
(ACCT	ACTYPE	ADESCR	)	(ACCTCR	ACCTDB	TDESCR	)
A	Asset	Goods in assembly		A	G	Assembly cost	
C	Asset	Cash		C	P	Pay accounts payable	
E	Equity	Stockholders'		C	T	Pay taxes	
F	Asset	Fixed assets		F	E	Fixed asset depreciation	
G	Asset	Finished goods		G	R	Cost of goods sold	
M	Asset	Raw materials		M	A	Raw materials cost	
P	Liability	Accounts payable		R	C	Collect accounts receivable	
R	Asset	Accounts receivable		P	F	Purchase fixed assets	
T	Liability	Taxes payable		P	M	Purchase raw materials	
				P	E	Manufacturing expenses	
				T	E	Payroll taxes	
				E	A	Variable costs	
				E	R	Gross profit	

a) Type   b) Trans

SPREAD				BALANCE		
(PEREND	ACCTCR	ACCTDB	AMOUNT)	(DATE	ACCT	BAL)
●	●	●	●	●	●	●
●	●	●	●	●	●	●
1984/3/30	A	G	2.33	1984/2/29	A	5.41
1984/3/30	C	P	7.70	1984/2/29	C	7.26
1984/3/30	C	T	1.87	1984/2/29	E	42.83
1984/3/30	F	E	0.22	1984/2/29	F	26.13
1984/3/30	G	R	3.19	1984/2/29	G	4.03
1984/3/30	M	A	1.30	1984/2/29	M	1.49
1984/3/30	R	C	3.99	1984/2/29	P	5.57
1984/3/30	P	M	1.01	1984/2/29	R	7.00
1984/3/30	P	E	2.11	1984/2/29	T	2.92
1984/3/30	T	E	0.95			
1984/3/30	E	A	1.43			
1984/3/30	E	R	2.21			

c) Spread   d) Balance

BALANCE and SPREAD are the beginning/final balance and spread sheets respectively. New data is added to these relations at the end of each period and so the key of each must contain chronological information (DATE in BALANCE and PEREND, or period end, in SPREAD) to distinguish the entries from their predecessors. Chapter 6.2 discusses how to implement a relation containing an indefinite history, without occupying the entire storage area. An alternative would be to keep historical data at a more detailed level and simply re-derive SPREAD and BALANCE when needed. Which method to use depends on trade-offs. Here we arbitrarily choose the first.

On the other hand, the derived relations are not intended to be kept but to be printed as reports or displayed on request within the following time period. So they do not contain a chronological key. The meaning of the attributes listed in Exhibit 6.1-10 will appear as we discuss the derivation of each relation.

To compute FUNDFLOW, the flow of funds statement, we need to know the row and column totals (TOTIN and TOTOUT, respectively) of the spread sheet, which are not stored in the relation, SPREAD. For each account we find the difference,

$$FF \leftarrow \begin{cases} TOTIN - TOTOUT & \text{for Asset accounts} \\ TOTOUT - TOTIN & \text{for Liabilities or Equities.} \end{cases}$$

To find the type of account, ACTYPE, we must join in TYPE, and so we can also insert the account description, ADESCR. Here is the derivation.

let TOTIN **be equiv** + **of** AMOUNT **by** ACCTDB
let TOTOUT **be equiv** + **of** AMOUNT **by** ACCTCR
let FF **be if** ACTYPE = 'Asset' **then** TOTIN-TOTOUT **else** TOTOUT-TOTIN

FUNDFLOW ← ACCT, ADESCR, ACTYPE, FF **in**
   (TYPE [ACCT **ijoin** ACCTCR]
   ((ACCTDB, TOTIN **where** PEREND = 1984/3/30 **in** SPREAD)
   [ACCTDB **ujoin** ACCTCR] (ACCTCR, TOTOUT **where** PEREND
        = 1984/3/30 **in** SPREAD)))   (6.1-1)

Note the use of union join, **ujoin,** in combining the row and column totals: this handles the case where some account has no row or no column entries (e.g., F). Note also the selection of the most recent period.

Exercise 6.1-2:   Work out for the example data of this chapter the steps of the above computations.

Exercise 6.1-3:   Write the derivation of SORUSE, the sources and uses statement, from FUNDFLOW. SUAMT is the absolute value of FF and SU is either "Source" or "Use."

Exercise 6.1-4:   Use BALANCE and FUNDFLOW to calculate the balance sheet for the current period.

The INCOME statement derivation is more easily understood if split into a derivation of REVENUE and EXPENSE. To get REVENUE, we select the E column of the spread sheet and join in the E column of TRANS to get the description, TDESCR, of the transaction. To get EXPENSE we do the same thing with rows. The INCOME statement is the union of these, with the flag RE indicating "Revenue" or "Expense." We need to use FUNDFLOW to find the change in equity, which gives the net profit (loss) line on the statement.

Exercise 6.1-5: Derive REVENUE and EXPENSE from SPREAD and IN-COME from REVENUE, EXPENSE and FUNDFLOW.

The above calculations presuppose very simple requirements. Various extensions would be necessary in a practical environment. The most important extension is to include in the reports comparisons with previous time periods: last month, this time last year, and year-to-date. Another extension would be to include relative figures: expenses and revenues as percent of total revenues or balances as percent of total assets, for instance.

Exercise 6.1-6: Give the derivation of a modified relation FUNDFLOW which includes figures for last month, this time last year, and year-to-date, as well as those for the current month. Assume the current month is March 1984 and do not worry about the easy generalization to any month.

Exercise 6.1-7: Show how to calculate a modified BALANCE relation which also gives each entry as a percentage of total assets.

6.1-3   Operational Data and Spread Sheets

From the vantage of the accountant's overview we can work our way down to some of the operational details of the firm. This section outlines briefly the derivation of some of the entries in the spread sheet from parts of the operational systems shown in Exhibit 6.1-2. Note the limited role of the "Accounting" system in this operational context. The manufacturing profit system is discussed in detail in Part 5. Most of these systems are clearly discussed in Eliason & Kitts [1974].

Exhibit 6.1-14 shows the relations we will need from the operational systems and their connection to the spread sheet. (Spread sheet transactions that appear twice in the table are numbered in order of appearance). Exhibit 6.1-13 gives a diagrammatic form of Exhibit 6.1-14.

To show how to derive an entry of SPREAD, we start with one of the simplest edges, R → C. All we must do is add all amounts in CASHIN for the current period and create a tuple for SPREAD with the right date and account codes.

let TODAY **be** 1984/3/30
let ACCTC **be** 'R'

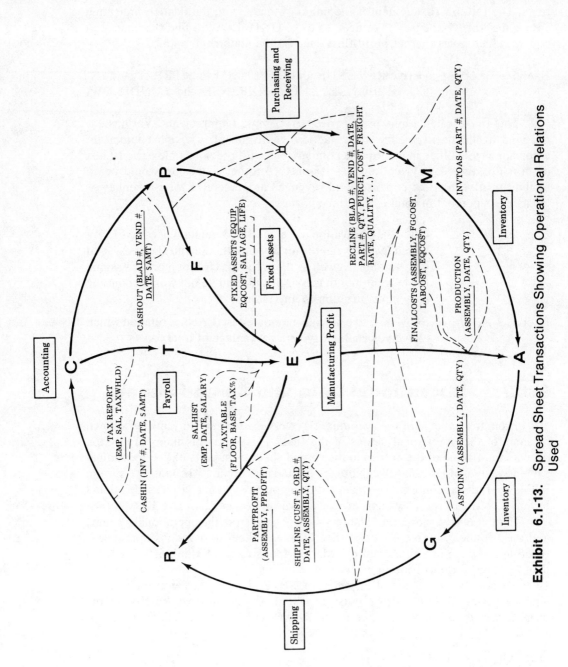

Exhibit 6.1-13. Spread Sheet Transactions Showing Operational Relations Used

Exhibit 6.1-14. Operational Relations Needed for Spread Sheet

SPREAD SHEET TRANSACTION	RELATIONS	OPERATIONAL SYSTEM (AND SUBSYSTEM)
C → P	CASHOUT (BLAD#, VEND#, DATE, $AMT)	ACCOUNTING (ACCOUNTS PAYABLE)
C → T	TAX REPORT (EMP, SAL, TAXWITHELD)	PAYROLL
T → E (1)	SALHIST (EMP, DATE, SALARY)	
T → E (2)	TAXTABLE (FLOOR, BASE, TAX%)	
P → F		PURCHASING AND RECEIVING
P → E	RECLINE (BLAD#, VEND#, DATE, PART#, QTY, PURCHASE COST, FREIGHT RATE)	
P → M		
M → A (1)		
F → E	FIXED ASSETS (EQUIP, EQCOST, SALVAGE, LIFE)	INVENTORY
M → A (2)	INVTOAS (PART#, DATE, QTY)	
A → G (1)	ASTOINV (ASSEMBLY, DATE, QTY)	
E → A (1)	PRODUCTION (ASSEMBLY, DATE, QTY)	
A → G (2)		
E → A (2)	FINAL COSTS (ASSEMBLY, FGCOST, LABCOST, EQCOST)	MANUFACTURING PROFIT
G → R (1)	PART PROFIT (ASSEMBLY, PPROFIT)	
E → R (1)		
E → R (2)	SHIPLINE (CUST#, ORD#, DATE, ASSEMBLY, QTY)	SHIPPING
G → R (2)		
R → C	CASHIN (INV#, DATE, $AMT)	ACCOUNTING (ACCOUNTS RECEIVABLE)

let ACCTD **be** 'C'
let SUM **be** red + **of** $AMT
SPREAD ↩+ TODAY, ACCTC, ACCTD, SUM **where** 1984/2/29 < DATE
    and DATE ≤ TODAY **in** CASHIN   (6.1-2)

A more complicated entry is T → E, which requires us to add up the taxes for each employee's salary. We assume that employees have only been paid once in the period and that the amount is the most recent SALARY in the salary history relation, SALHIST. We must find this latest figure and we must apply the TAX-TABLE to it to calculate the tax using the formula

$$\text{TAX} \leftarrow \text{BASE} + \text{TAX\%} \times (\text{SALARY}-\text{FLOOR})$$

where FLOOR is taken from the tuple of TAXTABLE such that FLOOR ≤ SALARY and no other tuple has a greater FLOOR which is also less than SALARY. This extraction requires a low-range join. Exhibit 6.1-5 shows sample data for TAXTABLE and SALHIST

Exhibit 6.1-15.   TAXTABLE and SALHIST

TAXTABLE			SALHIST		
(FLOOR	BASE	TAX%)	(EMP	DATE	SALARY)
350	50.00	20	Andrea Porter	1976/4	375
400	60.00	25	Toby Conductor	1977/9	390
450	72.50	30	Patrick Fireman	1978/5	400
500	87.50	35	Andrea Porter	1979/1	425

A few things can be said about the following code.

let SURFACE **be equiv max of** DATE **by** EMP
let SUM **be** red + **of** (BASE + TAX% × (SALARY-FLOOR))
let TODAY **be** 1984/3/30; ACCTC **be** 'T'; ACCTD **be** 'E'

SPREAD ↩+ TODAY, ACCTC, ACCTD, SUM **in** ((**where** DATE = SURFACE
    in SALHIST) [SALARY **lojoin** FLOOR] TAXTABLE)   (6.1-2)

First, the *surface* of a relation which contains historical information is the set of tuples containing the most recent information, and is extracted above using SUR-FACE. The most recent tuple for each employee is given by DATE = **equiv max of** DATE **by** EMP. Second, SALHIST and TAXTABLE are linked by low range join. This gives the following intermediate result, using the surface of SALHIST.

EMP	SALARY	FLOOR	BASE	TAX%	(TAX)	(SUM)
Toby Conductor	390	350	50.00	20	58.00	194.25
Patrick Fireman	400	400	60.00	25	60.00	194.25
Andrea Porter	425	400	60.00	25	66.25	194.25

Exercise   6.1-8:   Derive the spread sheet entry $F \rightarrow E$ from FIXED ASSETS.

Exercise   6.1-9:   Derive $E \rightarrow R$ from PART PROFIT and SHIPLINE.

Exercise   6.1-10:   Derive $E \rightarrow A$ from FINALCOSTS and PRODUCTION. (Note that FINALCOSTS is a projection of the version developed in Exercise 5.1-7 rather than that of the text of Section 5.1-3.)

IMPLEMENTATION: Chronological Relations

Financial data is particularly subject to fraud. The relations of this chapter deal with transfers of money or of goods from department to department and in and out of the company. This data is of central importance to the firm and must be easily accessible by qualified people. They must also be able to change it, in order to correct errors.

Keeping a history of all transactions, as we have proposed for relations such as CASHOUT, RECLINE, PRODUCTION, etc, is a good way to monitor for fraud and also to satisfy the auditors. We have not specifically provided a facility for making corrections in the discussion of the last section, but we must allow for it in the implementation to be described in this section.

The ability to update data without leaving any traces of the change is a temptation to fraud for employees in positions of trust. The technique discussed in this section is one of *updating by adding*. Old records are always kept but are superceded by more recent ones. The system mechanism for determining which information is currently in effect, is to maintain a *chronology* field, independently of keys and data, for each relation. The current data is just that with the highest value of the chronology field. This is the same notion of the *surface* of a relation that was computed for SALHIST in Section 6.1-3. Note, though, that DATE in that relation is an ordinary attribute and part of the key. The chronology attribute is a separate notion, a key itself. In fact the supposed key for the relation is perverted by this technique, because the method allows us to store several records with identical "keys" which are corrections of each other; the assigned key of the relation is now the key of the surface of the relation or of a given level of the relation (i.e., its surface at some point in the past) but not of the relation as a whole.

We will discuss the implementation of the spread sheet as such a chronological relation, using multipaging and differential files. The spread sheet is represented by the relation used in Section 6.1-2.

$$\text{SPREAD (\underline{PEREND, ACCTCR, ACCTDB}, AMOUNT)}$$

with the first three attributes as key. To the four attributes we must add a fifth, CHRONOL, to make SPREAD a chronological relation. This is a special attribute, which need not be visible to the user (or to the high-level programmer) except when he wants a full audit trail of activities involving the relation. It is, in fact, the only true key of the extended relation, as the following example of an update shows.

SPREAD (PEREND	ACCTCR	ACCTDB	AMOUNT)	CHRONOL
84.2.29	A	G	2.53	84.3.5.16.2.44.262
84.2.29	A	G	2.33	84.3.7.9.43.1.192
•	•	•	•	•
•	•	•	•	•

Here the incorrect entry of 2.53 from goods in assembly (A) to finished goods (G) for Feb. 1984 was made on the fifth of March (at two minutes 44.262 seconds after four p.m.) and corrected a day and a half later (probably as a result of a trial balance) to 2.33. This latter amount was used in computing the financial statements in Section 6.1-2, and, being part of the surface of the relation, is the only entry of interest to the auditors—until they have a fraud to investigate.

In this example, the two tuples have the same value for the assigned key, {PEREND, ACCTCR, ACCTDB}, and so only one of them can appear at any level of the relation, for which the three attributes are defined to be the key. (The surface is one such level.) The only key of the extended relation is CHRONOL. Note that CHRONOL can resolve to millisecond precision: this is probably extreme for this application and it is certainly inadequate for others, such as recording events in a bubble chamber.

6.2-1   Multipaging the Spread Sheet

The extended relation, SPREAD, has five attributes. We must select those that are valuable as axes of the multipaging space. The attribute AMOUNT is not part of any key and is unlikely to be a selector (we do not anticipate requests for, say, all amounts exceeding 2.33, although they are not inconceivable). So we shall not create an axis for it. The time dimension of the relation is, of course, very important, and includes both PEREND and CHRONOL. We consider them together because it is reasonable to assume that only a limited number of corrections are made for each accounting period. Thus CHRONOL can be included by an expansion of the space allotted to each time period. The other two attributes, ACCTCR and ACCTDB, form two more axes but there is a very constrained relationship among them and time. The only transactions allowed are those specified by TRANS (Section 6.1-2), and almost all of those transactions are present in any time period.

Thus SPREAD is most clearly seen as a three-dimensional relation with two dimensions representing the fixed set of transactions between accounts for any time period (expanded to include corrections and changes) and the third dimension being time itself.

The allocation of blocks along the time axis is entirely straightforward since the data is distributed uniformly and almost deterministically along this axis. We proceed to consider the two dimensions of debit and credit accounts, initially neglecting the changes aspects of CHRONOL.

Exhibit 6.2-1 displays the projection of SPREAD onto ACCTCR and ACCTDB and Exhibit 6.2-2 shows the various consequences of choosing different blocks sizes, b, to hold the 13 tuples of the projection. The minimum number of blocks required is $f_1 \times f_2$ where f_1 and f_2 are the smallest nearly equal integers whose product is not less than $\lceil 13/b \rceil$. Thus the load factor is $\alpha = 13/bf_1f_2$. We interpret "nearly equal" to mean that f_1 and f_2 differ by, at most, one. The reason for this restriction is the symmetry of the axes: each has the same number of different accounts. Without this restriction, the required number of blocks

Exhibit 6.2-1. is a table titled at bottom:

	CREDIT									
		A	C	F	G	M	R	P	T	E	
	A					1			1		2
	C						1				1
	F							1			1
D / E / B / I / T	G	1									1
	M							1			1
	R				1				1		2
	P		1								1
	T		1								1
	E			1				1	1		3
		1	2	1	1	1	1	3	1	2	

Exhibit 6.2-1. SPREAD [ACCTCR, ACCTDB] with totals of tuples.

Exhibit 6.2-2. Block size, b, and dependent quantities: $(i,j \in \{1,2\}; i \neq j)$

b	1	2	3	4	5	6	7	8	9	10	11	12	13
$\lceil 13/b \rceil$	13	7	5	4	3	3	2	2	2	2	2	2	1
f_i	4	3	3	2	2	2	2	2	2	2	2	2	1
f_j	4	3	2	2	2	2	1	1	1	1	1	1	1
	.81	.72	.72	.81	.65	.54	.93	.81	.72	.65	.59	.54	1.0
α	$\dfrac{13}{16}$	$\dfrac{13}{18}$	$\dfrac{13}{18}$	$\dfrac{13}{16}$	$\dfrac{13}{20}$	$\dfrac{13}{24}$	$\dfrac{13}{14}$	$\dfrac{13}{16}$	$\dfrac{13}{18}$	$\dfrac{13}{20}$	$\dfrac{13}{22}$	$\dfrac{13}{24}$	$\dfrac{13}{13}$

would be $\lceil 13/b \rceil$, but with it we must increase $\lceil 13/b \rceil$ to an integer that factors correctly.

The first step in multipaging the two-dimensional projection is to choose a value for b. Ordinarily this would be selected from a range of values limited by practical considerations. We take the range to be all but the uninteresting choice of b = 13 (i.e., all tuples fit onto one block and we select the value which gives the largest load factor, α. This is b = 7 and requires two blocks, with either $f_1 = 1$ and $f_2 = 2$ or $f_1 = 2$ and $f_2 = 1$.

The second step is to use the axis distributions (shown along the outside of the box in Exhibit 6.2-1) to find candidate boundaries for the axis which is to be split into two segments. Since there are 13 tuples and two segments, there will be 6.5 tuples per segment on the average. We place one candidate boundary as close as possible on either side of this value. For instance, for the credit axis, we have a cumulative number of tuples, counting left to right, as shown in Exhibit 6.2-3. Candidate boundaries are placed just after the cumulative value 6 and just after 7 for the credit axis—i.e., between accounts M and R and accounts R and P in Exhibit 6.2-1. Similarly, candidate boundaries for the debit axis are placed just after counts 5 and 7 (counting from the bottom of the vertical axis in Exhibit 6.2-1).

Exhibit   6.2-3.   Accumulated tuples from the axis distributions showing candidate boundary positions (↑)

	Credit									Debit								
Axis distribution	1	2	1	1	1	1	3	1	2	3	1	1	2	1	1	1	1	2
Accumulated tuples	1	3	4	5	6	7	10	11	13	3	4	5	7	8	9	10	11	13
Aggregated distribution	6					1		6		5			2		6			

↑ ↑   ↑ ↑
a b   a b

The third step is to use the axis distributions again to estimate which candidate boundary gives the fewest overflows. We aggregate the axis distributions by summing counts in each of the three regions demarcated by the candidate boundaries (third line of Exhibit 6.2-3). Suppose we decide to partition the debit axis. We chose a blocksize of 7 and so 7 or fewer tuples in a segment causes no trouble. If we choose candidate (a) as boundary, the left (lower) segment will have 5 tuples and the right (higher) segment will have 8, causing an overflow. On the other hand, candidate (b) causes no overflow and so should be chosen. If, on the other hand, we partition the credit axis, no candidate gives rise to more than 7 tuples per segment and so either one is a suitable boundary.

In summary, to use a blocksize of 7, we can partition the debit axis between accounts M and R (shown as a dashed line in Exhibit 6.2-1) or we can partition the credit axis either between R and P or between M and R. In the latter case, we might choose R and P because this is also the boundary between asset and other accounts.

Exercise 6.2-1: Suppose other considerations restricted us to blocksizes of 6 or less. What multipage partition of the relation of Exhibit 6.2-1 would minimize the overflows subject to maximizing the load factor?

If we did not need to consider the facility for recording corrections and updates to the transactions, we would now have a straightforward multipage representation of SPREAD in three dimensions (Exhibit 6.2-4). Along the time axis, each accounting period has its own segment of two blocks. The credit account axis forms a single segment and the debit account axis has two segments. The blocksize is seven.

We can either accommodate corrections by a slight expansion of this multipage representation or else we can take an entirely different approach, discussed in the next section. Here we consider briefly expanding the representation to handle up to five corrections per time period. We suppose that any correction applies, with equal probability, to any of the 13 transactions in each period. We expand the capacity of each block by $5/13 : (5/13) \times 7 \simeq 3$ so each block will now hold $7 + 3 = 10$ tuples. Now we have room within the multipage representation for up to five corrections per accounting period.

These five corrections may all land on one block, increasing the number of overflows from 0 to 2. Or less than five corrections may be needed, resulting in unused space: if the average was only three corrections per period, the load factor would be degraded from $\alpha = .93$ to $\alpha = 16/20 = .8$ (13 + 3 tuples occupying 2 blocks with a capacity of 10 each).

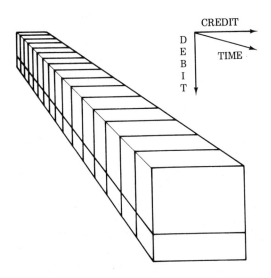

Exhibit 6.2-4. Multipaging the Spread Sheet

Exercise 6.2-2:   This section considers a very small accounting application, with about 10 accounts, and a rather academic blocksize of 7 tuples. Approximately how many segments would each accounting axis (credit, debit) have in the following case? There are 10,000 accounts (including subaccounts, lines, etc.) with about $10,000 \times (13/9)$ transactions (i.e., the same proportion as in the example in the text). Each tuple requires 12 bytes and the blocksize is 256 bytes.

6.2-2   The Differential Files

Multipaging provides a good physical representation for general query handling, and for the algebraic operations (such as equivalence reduction) needed in processing the spread sheet. Unfortunately it has poor dynamic properties in that file growth and change are restricted to limits that must be set at implementation time, just as we imposed a maximum of five corrections per time period in the last section. The spread sheet grows continually if we keep a complete historical record, and it is subject to frequent corrections, at least for the current time period.

This section describes the use of a differential file for the dynamic portion of the spread sheet, in conjunction with the multipaged representation discussed in Section 6.2-1. On the differential file we will store data for the current accounting period, as it is generated in Section 6.1-3, together with all corrections that are required as a result of trial balances and other checks. We will also store recent corrections to previous periods of the spread sheet on the differential file, supposing that they are permitted. This differential file records all current activity on the spread sheet. We call it the *differential post-file* because it reflects changes subsequent to the last reorganization of the main file.

The main file is the multipaged representation of the spread sheet, without corrections, discussed in the last section. It contains all the final entries for each accounting period up to and including the last. It is static and organized optimally for processing, such as that required to give comparative figures on the current report, and for arbitrary queries that might be made by auditors.

A second differential file, called the *differential ante-file,* is used to keep the historical record of all the corrections that were made to past time periods. This must be organized so that it grows easily (although no other kind of update is needed) and so that the earliest portions of it can be dumped easily to a cheaper level of secondary storage or, ultimately, even discarded. It is a differential file so that it can be used to "downdate" (as opposed to update) the spread sheet to an earlier stage of its history, if necessary, in the same way that the differential post-file is used to update. This process will be discussed in Section 6.2-3. The corrections on the differential ante-file are in fact anti-corrections, in that they are changes from the most recent (and presumably correct) data to earlier (and presumably incorrect) entries, as would be necessary if it is desired to restore the spread sheet to some earlier state.

(As an example of this ante-anti approach, consider a sequence of values for a single quantity, x, with 4 the first value, then subsequent corrections until the final value of 6 is arrived at: 4, 7, 5, 6. Suppose that at first 4 is on the main file and the subsequent corrections are recorded as relative changes on the differential post-file: $+3$, -2, $+1$. Thus $4 + 3 = 7$, $7 - 2 = 5$, $5 + 1 = 6$. Now suppose we do a reorganization which clears the differential post-file and puts 6 as the entry on the main file. The differential ante-file will contain the anti-corrections -1, $+2$, -3 : $6 - 1 = 5$, $5 + 2 = 7$, $7 - 3 = 4$. More of this when we discuss the differential post-file.)

The main file

The main file is multipaged in three dimensions as described in Section 6.2-1 (see Exhibit 6.2-4) with one segment per accounting period along the time axis, one segment for all credit accounts along the credit axis and two segments for all debit accounts along the debit axis. We use the addressing formula

$$block = debit + 2 \times period$$

where *debit* has the value 0 if the debit account is A, C, F, G, M or R and value 1 for debit accounts P, T or E; and where *period* is 0 for the earliest time period recorded, 1 for the next, and so on up to the present. If the record started in 1980, the value for *period* would be

$$period = month - 1 + 12 \times (year - 1980).$$

Since the absolute block address may be calculated directly from the key of the tuple sought, there is no need for a supplementary index to this file. The worst cost is one access per tuple.

A major use of the main file will be to extract comparative transactions and account totals. Thus we need to be able to select a period and to do equivalence reductions along either accounting axis quickly. This multipage representation will permit this operation with one access of each of the blocks for the time period and no more. This is true not only for the small firm of our examples, with 9 accounts and 2 blocks per period, but also for the large firm of Exercise 6.2-2, with 10,000 accounts and 702 blocks per period; since each segment holds transactions for no more than about 400 credit (or debit) accounts, the equivalence reduction can be calculated with about 400 accumulators in fast memory, as we shall see.

Once we have found *period* for the time period of interest, we perform the equivalence reduction as follows. Suppose we wish to find the totals for each debit account

let TOTIN be equiv + of AMOUNT by ACCTDB.

Here is the method.

Algorithm E:

For each segment along the debit axis:

> Set up an accumulator in fast memory, initialized to zero, for each account in the segment.
> For each block in the segment:
>> For each tuple in the block:
>>> Add AMOUNT to the accumulator for ACCTDB.
> Output the accumulators and clear them for reuse in the next segment.

Exercise 6.2-3:   Multipage the spread sheet of Section 6.1-2 for the time period considered, according to Section 6.2-1, and compute the equivalence reductions for both debit and credit accounts using Algorithm E.

Exercise 6.2-4:   If there is room in fast memory for 1000 accumulators at most, what is the largest blocksize (assumed a power of 2) for the system of Exercise 6.2-2 which will allow us to use Algorithm E?

The differential post-file

The differential post-file must be able to accommodate all transactions for the spread sheet of one period, an arbitrary number of corrections to these transactions, and an arbitrary number (presumed small) of corrections to earlier time periods. It must also support equivalence reductions on the most up-to-date versions of the transactions for the current period, and a certain number of general queries. It is hard to find a better representation than multipaging for equivalence reduction in this case, especially since the allowed transactions are predetermined; but we must add flexibility for the corrections.

To allow corrections to periods other than the current one is probably unrealistic for the spread sheet application, and it complicates the differential post-file. However, it is not too difficult and gives us some additional practice. We handle it by maintaining the post-file in two parts. One part is for all transactions and corrections for the current period. It is multipaged in a specialized way. The second part holds the recent corrections to previous periods and is presumed to be small.

The multipaged part has room for one version of each of the legal transactions. Corrections for the current period are applied and previous versions are pushed down stacks maintained by pointers to supplementary data pages. To condense the space required, these versions can be stored as relative amounts. Exhibit 6.2-5 shows the result of updating the transaction G ← A from 2.53 to 2.33. Since the most recent version of any transaction is immediately available without

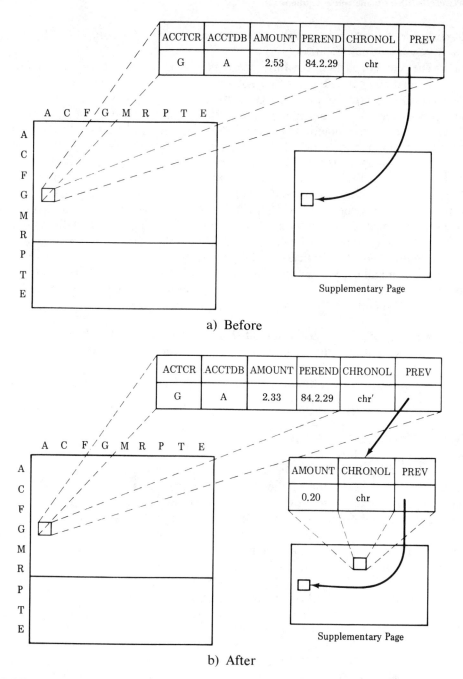

ACCTCR	ACCTDB	AMOUNT	PEREND	CHRONOL	PREV
G	A	2.53	84.2.29	chr	

a) Before

ACTCR	ACCTDB	AMOUNT	PEREND	CHRONOL	PREV
G	A	2.33	84.2.29	chr′	

AMOUNT	CHRONOL	PREV
0.20	chr	

b) After

Exhibit 6.2-5. Correcting a current transaction on the multipaged part of the differential post-file.

having to follow any pointers, the equivalence reduction is accomplished by Algorithm E without modification.

The second part of the differential post-file, for corrections to previous periods, can be scanned sequentially if small enough, or an index can be maintained on PEREND, ACCTCR, ACCTDB. Either it is always accessed prior to any processing of the main file, or else a Bloom filter can be set up. The Bloom filter requires a hash function mapping (PEREND, ACCTCR, ACCTDB) to a bit vector in main memory, such that if a correction has been made to a transaction, the corresponding bit is turned on; otherwise, it remains off. On searching for a transaction, if its bit is on we access the differential post-file first, otherwise not. Since a bit corresponds to more than one transaction in general, the search of the differential file may be fruitless. On the other hand, we never fail to search it when necessary. A well designed filter will allow us to use a quite crude data organization on the differential file itself without seriously affecting the overall average response time. For this application, since corrections are likely to be only to recent periods, we might use (current period—PEREND) **mod** (1 year) in the Bloom filter hash function instead of PEREND. Bloom filters are discussed more fully in Sections 1.2-6 and 1.3-3.

Exercise   6.2-5:   Discuss a spread sheet implementation in which there is no differential post-file. Transactions are recorded directly on the main file and corrections applied immediately and logged as anti-corrections on the differential ante-file (see next subsection).

The differential ante-file

The differential ante-file contains the inverted record of all corrections that have been made to the spread sheet. They are recorded as anti-corrections in the sense of Exhibit 6.2-5 and as discussed at the beginning of Section 6.2-2. The file changes over time only by growing each time a reorganization of the main file creates more anti-corrections to be added. We should be able to split off earlier parts of the ante-file and store them on cheaper media—including the extreme case of discarding the earliest parts. We also need to be able to access specific anti-corrections using (PEREND, ACCTCR, ACCTDB), but this need is infrequent and the access can be relatively inefficient.

A good way of meeting these requirements is to multipage the differential ante-file on CHRONOL and maintain a Bloom filter on (PEREND, ACCTCR, ACCTDB). All corrections for a given period are made after the end of the previous period. The CHRONOL of the last correction made is recorded in the main file. Thus a sequential search of the differential ante-file, starting at that CHRONOL and working backwards to the month before PEREND will include all possible anti-corrections in order, and can be stopped at whatever point of time the user wishes to restore the spread sheet. A search for anti-corrections to several or all entries for an accounting period follows the same logic. Since corrections for a given period are not likely to be made long after the period, and usually during it, this search will usually be short. The Bloom filter can be used to eliminate it altogether in those cases where the filter bit is (bits are) not set.

Since the block addresses are in order of CHRONOL in a file multipaged on CHRONOL, it is easy to add more recent anti-corrections to the file and it is easy to dump to cheaper storage those blocks referring to earlier times.

Exercise   6.2-6:   How can a Bloom filter be used with a file whose earliest entries are periodically removed?

6.2-3   The Monthly Reorganization

Periodically the differential post-file must be used to bring the main file and the differential ante-file up to date. The appropriate period coincides with the accounting period, so that the processing for reorganization can be combined with that for generating reports, and because once the reports are made, the spread sheet should be more or less in final form. Thus we will reorganize our spread sheet once a month.

Step 1. The differential post-file is in two parts, as discussed in the last section. The part which contains transactions and corrections for the current period is already multipaged, although in a specialized way. Including this part in the main file is straightforward: copy the latest version directly, omitting the pointers to the anti-corrections. The anti-corrections should be merged into chronological order and saved for the end of step 2.

Step 2. The second part of the differential post-file contains corrections to earlier transactions and must be used to update the main file and generate a set of anti-corrections (which will be in chronological order). This set is merged with the anti-corrections from step 1 and appended to the differential ante-file.

These two steps complete the reorganization without, in principle, accessing any data from the post-file more than once.

Exercise   6.2-7:   What is the advantage of the method discussed in the text over that of Exercise 6.2-5?

Downdating

Since we have both post-and ante- differential files, we can backtrack our reorganization process to restore an earlier state of the main file. The differential files discussed in the last section are not symmetrical and we will not bother with an exact restoration of the differential post-file. Instead we shall generate an anti-ante-file, which is a mirror image in time of the ante-file and has entries that are simply corrections to the main file.

Exhibit 6.2-6 shows the process of downdating the G ← A transaction from an initial configuration of main and ante-file at some point in time after March 7, 1984 (9:43 a.m.). The first downdate is to a time on March 6 and results in a changed main file, a smaller ante-file and a new anti-ante-file. Note that the entries on the latter are anti-ante-corrections, i.e., the original corrections. This file is a potential form for the differential post-file, except that we chose a more elaborate format in Section 6.2-2 in order to speed up trial balances. The second downdate restores the spread sheet to a point in time before the transaction was created. This empties the ante-file as far as this transaction is concerned, and moves all anti-ante-corrections to the anti-ante-file. We adopt the approach of leaving the original entry on the main file and simply ignoring all entries that were not there as of January 25, 1984—i.e., all those made after the point of time to which we have been downdated.

The process of downdating is useful for reviewing the apparent status of the spread sheet as of a given previous date. It is also useful in regenerating the file after some transactions or corrections have gone wrong due to hardware down-time or to embezzlement.

Exercise 6.2-8: Devise a post-/ante- file setup for the spread sheet that is symmetrical in time, so that downdating is the exact inverse of updating.

6.2-4   Advantages of Chronological Relations

The chief advantage of the chronological relation is that it provides a history. This is necessary for an application such as the spread sheet, where a record of financial transactions must be kept for auditing. It is also necessary for data whose consistency is important even if its history is not: the history of transactions provides a means of backing up in case of error or system failure.

On the other hand, the chronological relation is a specialization of the general concept of relation and imposes some restrictions and potentially tricky features. Keys are no longer keys and the chronology attribute is required. The idea of the *surface* of a relation and the related idea of a level—the surface at some previous time—resolve these difficulties. The usual key is still the key of the surface, and the chronological attribute can be hidden except when specifically needed. Algebraic operations can be performed on the surface of a chronological relation as if it were an ordinary relation. Thus the chronological relation can be thought of, in most contexts, as a generalization not a specialization. It provides an almost invisible way of giving a historical dimension to any relation.

Many of the other advantages of chronological relations stem from the implementation we have discussed using differential files. The most severe apparent disadvantage, the prospect of indefinite growth of data, is removed. The differen-

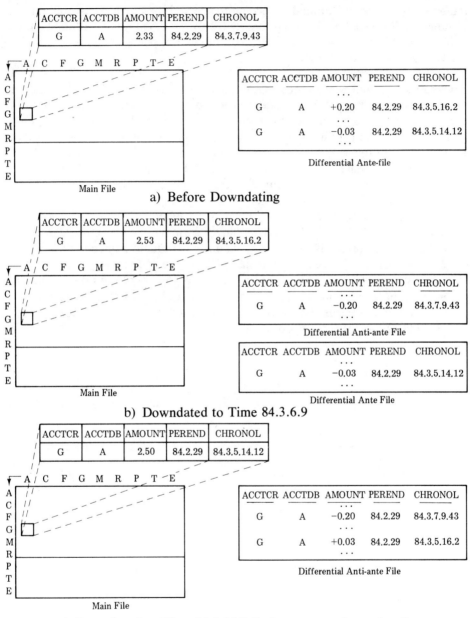

ACCTCR	ACCTDB	AMOUNT	PEREND	CHRONOL
G	A	2.33	84.2.29	84.3.7.9.43

ACCTCR	ACCTDB	AMOUNT	PEREND	CHRONOL
		. . .		
G	A	+0.20	84.2.29	84.3.5.16.2
		. . .		
G	A	−0.03	84.2.29	84.3.5.14.12
		. . .		

Differential Ante-file

Main File

a) Before Downdating

ACCTCR	ACCTDB	AMOUNT	PEREND	CHRONOL
G	A	2.53	84.2.29	84.3.5.16.2

ACCTCR	ACCTDB	AMOUNT	PEREND	CHRONOL
		. . .		
G	A	−0.20	84.2.29	84.3.7.9.43
		. . .		

Differential Anti-ante File

ACCTCR	ACCTDB	AMOUNT	PEREND	CHRONOL
		. . .		
G	A	−0.03	84.2.29	84.3.5.14.12
		. . .		

Differential Ante File

Main File

b) Downdated to Time 84.3.6.9

ACCTCR	ACCTDB	AMOUNT	PEREND	CHRONOL
G	A	2.50	84.2.29	84.3.5.14.12

ACCTCR	ACCTDB	AMOUNT	PEREND	CHRONOL
		. . .		
G	A	−0.20	84.2.29	84.3.7.9.43
		. . .		
G	A	+0.03	84.2.29	84.3.5.16.2
		. . .		

Differential Anti-ante File

Main File

c) Downdated to Time 84:1.25.9 (before transaction existed)

Exhibit 6.2-6. Downdating and the Anti-ante-file.

tial ante-file can be partitioned according to age and the partitions stored on ever cheaper media. This history is written once only, so the storage medium could be video disk, microfilm or even paper. The ultimately cheap medium is oblivion; really old data can be forgotten.

The major effect of the differential file is to *localize changes*. This leads to advantages in concurrent processing, security and efficiency. With changes confined to one small part of the file, queries to the main file can be processed at the same time. Backing out transactions after conflicts is easier. For many applications, the need for last-minute information is less important than the need to avoid file lockouts: for these, queries can be confined to the main file while the differential file is being updated. The fact that differential file updates are all additions in chronological relations further simplifies concurrent processing.

If dumps of the database must be made for security reasons, the differential file alone need not be dumped with any great frequency. The dump is faster and the database more reliable. (We have already shown that the chronological relation contains its own dumps. No more may be needed.) Finally, since the main file is not changed between reorganizations, it may be organized in a way that, while not necessarily very efficient for updates, is optimal for the queries or other processing we wish to do. For example, we used multipaging above. Freedom from update worries greatly increases the range of file organizations we can choose from. It also simplifies the software needed for the main file.

COST ANALYSIS

Exhibit 6.3-1 shows the relations discussed in the text and exercises of Chapter 6.1, and their interconnections. The sizes of the relations are given in parentheses after the relation name, in terms of the quantities a (the number of accounts), e (the number of equity accounts) and p (the number of periods).

We make the following assumptions about the allowed transactions in TRANS. Apart from transactions involving Equity accounts, each account participates in two transactions on the average. That is, a − e accounts give rise to a − e transactions (since each transaction involves two accounts). The Equities participate in the same *proportion* of transactions as E does in the example of Chapter 6.1: 5/13, with Equities debited in 2/13 and credited in 3/13 of these. Exhibit 6.3-2 shows an outline of TRANS in graphical and matrix forms. This is a crude extrapolation, but gives us a workable basis for cost estimation. It is reflected in Exhibit 6.3-1 by the fractions 13/9, (associated with TRANS and SPREAD), 2/9, 3/9 and 5/9 (associated with REVENUE, EXPENSE and INCOME respectively).

The quantities at the beginning and end of each arrow in Exhibit 6.3-1 give the number of tuples read and written, respectively, in processing the source relation and creating the target relation. These figures are discussed below.

No sizes or processing costs are given for the operational relations, CASHIN, . . . , PRODUCTION, because this would involve guessing the number of daily cash transactions, etc., quantities which would be hard to express simply in general terms. We would not learn much that has not already been covered in earlier chapters by studying these processing costs. The operations on SPREAD are the most revealing for this discussion, so we will concentrate on those.

In the following, we will estimate costs for multipaged files, for files with secondary indices and for a general implementation of the relational algebra.

6.3-1   Multipaged Files

To derive FUNDFLOW from the spread sheet requires two equivalence reductions on SPREAD and two joins. With suitable processing of the multipaged

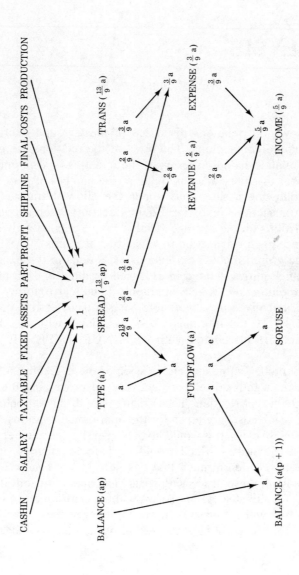

Exhibit 6.3-1.   Financial relations and some operational relations involved in computing financial statements. Parenthesis give sizes (in tuples) and figures on arrows give processing costs (see text).

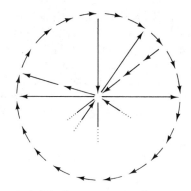

a) Graphical form (Equities at center)

Region AL	ASSETS		LIABILITIES	EQUITIES

b) Matrix form (average 1 entry per account in region AL; 5/13 of entries in region E).

Exhibit   6.3-2.   General aspects of TRANS for a large number of accounts

spread sheet, two passes of SPREAD and one of TYPE are needed with FUND-FLOW created directly in one pass. We suppose TYPE to be stored in order of ACCT, its key, and SPREAD to be multipaged as in Section 6.2-1.

Since we must do two equivalence reductions, one by debit account and one by credit account, we modify Algorithm 6.2-2E to do them alternately for the same accounts. Then we merge the sums with each other and with TYPE and write the result as FUNDFLOW.

To make this clear, suppose we have a 2 by 2 multipage segmentation of SPREAD, as in Exercise 6.2-1, shown in Exhibit 6.3-3. The figure shows the result of the equivalence reduction by debit for the first row and of the equivalence reduction by credit for the first column. The next step is to merge these accumulators and find the difference TOTIN - TOTOUT. (This could be done during the second reduction.) Then the result is merged again on account with TYPE and the sign of (TOTIN - TOTOUT) changed if the account is not an asset. This result forms the first part of FUNDFLOW. The whole process is now repeated for the next row and column of pages of SPREAD. Clearly the total cost is two accesses for each page of SPREAD (pages on the diagonal get away with one access), one pass of TYPE and one output pass to create FUNDFLOW. These costs are expressed on the arrows in Exhibit 6.3-1 from SPREAD and TYPE to FUNDFLOW.

Similar considerations give us the quantities shown in Exhibit 6.3-1 for the derivation of REVENUE and EXPENSE from SPREAD and TRANS. We assume TRANS is multipaged like SPREAD. We are interested only in equity accounts in SPREAD and TRANS: as debits for REVENUE and as credits for EXPENSE. Thus we need only scan one row of pages of SPREAD and TRANS for EXPENSE and one column for REVENUE. According to our assumptions, this gives 3a/9 and 2a/9 tuples respectively.

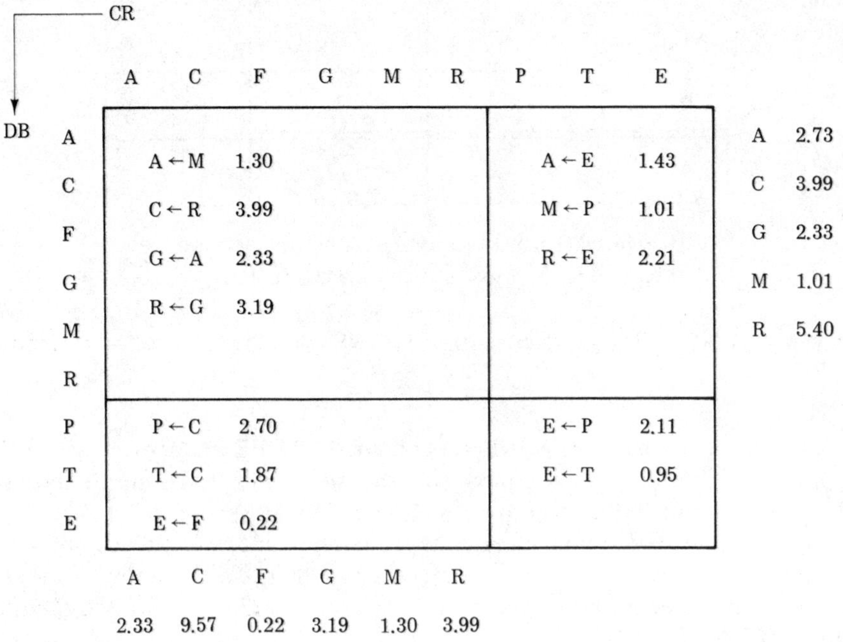
CR
A C F G M R P T E
DB
A C F G M R P T E
A←M 1.30
C←R 3.99
G←A 2.33
R←G 3.19
A←E 1.43
M←P 1.01
R←E 2.21
P←C 2.70
T←C 1.87
E←F 0.22
E←P 2.11
E←T 0.95
A 2.73
C 3.99
G 2.33
M 1.01
R 5.40
A C F G M R
2.33 9.57 0.22 3.19 1.30 3.99

Exhibit 6.3-3. SPREAD multipaged 2 by 2 showing tuples and accumulators for first row and column of pages.

Exercise   6.3-1:   Confirm the costs shown in Exhibit 6.3-1 for the derivation of INCOME from FUNDFLOW, REVENUE and EXPENSE.

6.3-2   Indexed Files

We look at the derivations again, assuming SPREAD and TRANS are not multipaged but that their tuples are distributed randomly over n blocks. (In the case of SPREAD, we will allow each accounting period to have a disjoint set of n blocks: SPREAD is multipaged on the time axis.)

To fix our ideas at first, we consider the 10000-account example of Exercise 6.2-2. TRANS and each period of SPREAD occupy n = 702 blocks. Each account is a credit in 13/9 transactions and a debit in a further 13/9 transactions, on the average. To do the equivalence reduction by debit (or by credit) requires accessing 13/9 tuples for each account. A crude guess at the number of blocks accessed uses the formula

$$n \left[1 - (1 - 1/n) \uparrow r \right] \simeq r = 1.444$$

if n = 702 and r = 13/9. To sum all accounts requires 1.4×10^4 accesses for each equivalence reduction: 2.9×10^4 all told. This is a ridiculous cost compared with multipaging.

Exercise   6.3-2:   Improve this guess by using the assumptions: each account is debited (credited) only once on the average for transactions not involving equities; 2a/9 transactions debit equities; and 3a/9 transactions credit equities.

Clearly it is impractical to compute FUNDFLOW using indexes. What about REVENUE and EXPENSE? Here the issue is to access the 2/13 of all transactions that debit equities and the 3/13 that credit equities. In the case that n = 702 blocks and the transactions of TRANS (or of the surface of SPREAD) are distributed evenly among these 702 blocks we must access 108 pages for transactions debiting equities and 162 for transactions crediting equities. This is worse than the 26 or 27 blocks needed with multipaging.

The difference between multipaging and the simple form of indexing that we have assumed is that multipaging *clusters related data* while indexing must cope with whatever data-to-storage mapping it meets. The data-to-storage mapping assumed in this section is random, and gives almost the worst behavior for our processing. Any other mapping, however, would have to be contrived. Multipaging is such a contrivance.

Exercise   6.3-3:   How expensive would sequential files be for the generation of FUNDFLOW and of REVENUE and EXPENSE?

6.3-3   Via Relational Algebra

To assess the cost of using a moderately sophisticated general implementation of the relational algebra for the spread sheet application, we must alter Exhibit 6.3-1. Exhibit 6.3-4 shows the modification. The direct step from SPREAD to FUNDFLOW is replaced by two double steps with TEMP1 and TEMP2 as intermediate results. These correspond to subexpressions in Expression 6.1-1 as follows

TEMP1 = ACCTDB, TOTIN **where** PEREND = 1984/3/30 **in** SPREAD.
TEMP2 = ACCTCR, TOTOUT **where** PEREND = 1984/3/30 **in** SPREAD.

Our assumption here is that a general implementation of the relational algebra would probably not be able to take advantage of the combined calculation of the two equivalence reductions that we used in the multipaged implementation. So we suppose that these subexpressions are computed separately, temporary results stored and then merged with TYPE to give FUNDFLOW. As Exhibit 6.3-4 suggests, the additional cost is only one read and one write of two files of a accounts each.

Apart from this, it is reasonable to assume that the relational algebra implementation can take advantage of multipaging and of existing sort orders in files. So the extra four passes of a tuples each is the only increase in cost over that of the multipaged implementation of Section 6.3-1. Inspecting the code for Exercises 6.1-2 through 6.1-5 reveals no other statements that could not be handled easily by a simple general implementation with the same cost as in Section 6.3-1. Even an implementation of the relational algebra using only sequential files would not give impossibly high costs, as Exercise 6.3-3 indicates.

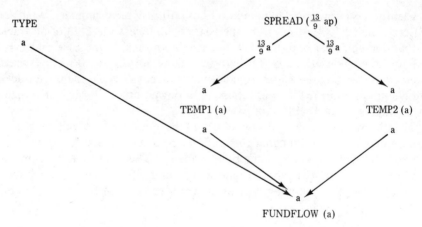

Exhibit   6.3-4.   Cost of creating FUNDFLOW using a relational algebra implementation.

Appendix

Graphs and Networks

A *graph,* G(V,E), is a set of *nodes* or *vertices,* V, together with a set, E, of *edges* or *arcs* connecting pairs of vertices. In fact, E $\subseteq$ V $\times$ V, is a binary relation with both attributes drawn from the domain V.

A *network,* N(G,A), is a graph G(V,E) together with a set of *edge-values* or *arc-values,* A, with one arc-value associated with each edge. A *multi-valued network*, N(G,A), has a set, A $\triangleq$ $\{A_1,A_2,\ldots\}$ of sets of arc-values, such that one arc-value from A_1, one arc-value from A_2, etc., is associated with each edge of G.

A graph can be *directed* or *symmetrical.* In a *directed* graph, the attributes in the binary relation E are distinguished, as in E(V_s,V_f). The first attribute describes the *start* nodes and the second describes the *finish* nodes. Thus each edge has a direction, from the start node to the finish node. Both attributes are still subsets of the domain of nodes: $V_s \subseteq$ V, $V_f \subseteq$ V. All graphs discussed in this book are directed, since this corresponds best to the definition of relations. In a *symmetrical* graph, the edges have no direction, so that e(v_1, v_2), where e ϵ E and v_1,v_2 ϵ V, could be interpreted to mean that there is both a (directed) edge from v_1 to v_2 and a (directed) edge from v_2 to v_1. For the discussion of relations in this book, it is easiest to consider a symmetrical graph as a special type of (directed) graph in which the existence of an edge e(v_1,v_2) implies the existence of an edge, e(v_2,v_1). Most mathematical texts, however, treat symmetrical graphs as a class distinct from directed graphs, and call them undirected graphs or just graphs. The edge e(v_2,v_1) is the *symmetric complement* of e(v_1,v_2).

In a *bipartite* graph the *start* nodes are distinct from the *finish* nodes, $V_s \cap V_f = \phi$. This can be used to represent a binary relation on distinct attributes.

A *root* is a node that finishes no edges. A *leaf* is a node that starts no edges. A bipartite graph has only roots and leaves.

A *path* is a sequence of edges such that the finish node of an edge is the start node of the subsequent edge, and all nodes are distinct. If the start node of the first edge is the same as the finish node of the last edge, the path is a *cycle*. A graph is *acyclic* if it contains no cycles. A bipartite graph is acyclic. An acyclic graph has at least one root and at least one leaf. Its *height* is the length of the longest path from a root to a leaf and its *width* is the number of paths from roots to leaves.

A graph is *strongly connected* if for every pair of nodes, v_1 and v_2, there is a path from v_1 to v_2. If symmetric complements of existing edges can be added to a graph so as to make it strongly connected it is *connected*. An acyclic graph may be connected but is not strongly connected.

Graphs and networks can be represented in various ways. Exhibits. A.1 and A.2 give examples, respectively, of a bipartite graph linking employees to work teams and of a flow of funds network with two cycles, CPER and CPMAGR. Note that employees and teams are distinct sets in Exhibit A.1, even though some nodes have the same label, e.g., P. Both graphs are connected. Exhibit A.2 is strongly connected. For instance, in Exhibit A.1, employee A connects with team T by the path A, AP; P, PT; T, T, where u,v indicates that e(u,v) has been used in the path and u;v indicates that the symmetric complement, e(v,u), has been used.

The matrix form in Exhibits A.1 and A.2 is known as the *adjacency* matrix in graph theory, and is the only one we shall discuss. It indicates which pairs of nodes are adjacent, i.e., connected by an edge. Strictly speaking, the matrix of Exhibit A.1 should be square, with both sets of nodes (employees and teams) along the top, heading columns, and both sets down the side, heading rows. However, all parts of the matrix are empty except that shown, and so we reduce it for convenience. In principle, an adjacency matrix, G, is square and so it is meaningful to talk of powers of G such as G^2, G^3, etc.

The square, G^2, of the adjacency matrix G of a graph is taken by ordinary matrix multiplication, but using Boolean algebra on the elements. That is,

$$(G^2)_{ik} = \sum_j G_{ij} \cdot G_{jk}$$

where $0 + 0 = 0$, $0 + 1 = 1$, $1 + 0 = 1$, $1 + 1 = 1$ and $0 \cdot 0 = 0$, $0 \cdot 1 = 0$, $1 \cdot 0 = 0$, $1 \cdot 1 = 1$. The interpretation of G^2 is that it gives all paths of length 2 in the graph, as G gives all paths of length 1 (edges). Similar interpretations of higher powers are easy to establish. Thus $G^2 = 0$ if G is a bipartite graph, and $G^n = 0$ for all integers n greater than some value h if and only if G is acyclic: h is the maximum path length, or height.

A graph can always be abstracted from a network and the above considerations applied. Interpreting powers of N, where N is the matrix form of the network, as in Exhibit A.2, depends on the network and is not always meaningful. For instance if N is the matrix of Exhibit A.2 and + and · are ordinary addition and multiplication, no useful interpretation can be made of N^2, N^3, etc. On the other hand, if N is the bill of materials network of Exhibit A.3, N^2 has a simple meaning using ordinary addition and multiplication. N shows the number of subassemblies required to make up an assembly, which in turn becomes a subassembly at the next level. Call a subassembly such as Q the child of assembly B. Then N^2 gives the

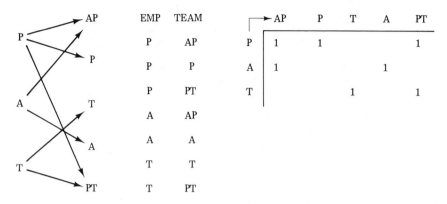

EMP	TEAM
P	AP
P	P
P	PT
A	AP
A	A
T	T
T	PT

	AP	P	T	A	PT
P	1	1			1
A	1			1	
T			1		1

Exhibit A.1. Graph, table and matrix representations of team membership graph.

grandchildren and the appropriate quantities: e.g., B has two A and four R grandchildren. (Addition is not used here, but it is in the bill of materials of Exhibit 5.1-2.)

A *subgraph* of G is a graph whose edges are a subset of the edges of G and whose nodes are those nodes of G belonging to some edge of the subgraph. A *strongly connected component* of G is a subgraph of G which is strongly connected. A *maximal strongly connected component* of G is a strongly connected component of G to which no edges of G can be added without it ceasing to be strongly connected. A strongly connected graph has one maximal strongly connected component, namely itself. Parallel definitions may be given for *connected components* and *maximal connected components*.

The *reduced graph* of G, $\rho(G)$, is the graph obtained by reducing each strongly connected component of G to a single node, s_i, and defining an edge $r(s_1, s_2)$ if G has an edge from any node in the component represented by s_1 to any node in the component represented by s_2. The reduced graph is always acyclic. The reduced graph of an acyclic graph G is G itself. The reduced graph of the graph G shown in Fig. A.2 is a single node, since C is strongly connected.

An acyclic graph represents a partial ordering, $\leq$, on the nodes: $u \leq v$ if there is a path from u to v. A *partial ordering* is *transitive* (if $u \leq v$ and $v \leq w$ then $u \leq w$), *antisymmetric* (if $u \leq v$ and $v \leq u$ then $u = v$) and *reflexive* ($u \leq u$). A *linear ordering* is a partial ordering, $\leq$, such that for every pair u,v, either $u \leq v$ or $v \leq u$.

The objective of a *topological sort* is to embed the partial order of an acyclic graph in a linear order. Graphically this means that the nodes are to be arranged in a line so that the direction of the edges is from left to right. We can speak of topologically sorting an arbitrary graph, G, whether acyclic or not, if we embed the reduced graph, $\rho(G)$, in a linear ordering. The process of topologically sorting a graph, which is discussed in Section 5.2-2, can result in a list of nodes in the

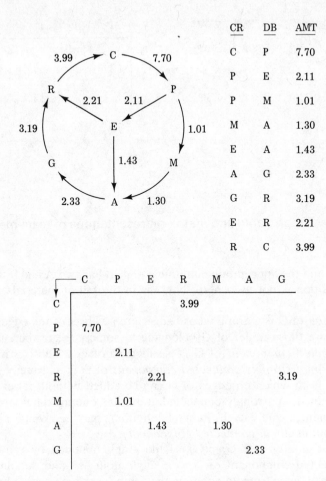

	CR	DB	AMT
	C	P	7.70
	P	E	2.11
	P	M	1.01
	M	A	1.30
	E	A	1.43
	A	G	2.33
	G	R	3.19
	E	R	2.21
	R	C	3.99

	C	P	E	R	M	A	G
C				3.99			
P	7.70						
E		2.11					
R			2.21				3.19
M		1.01					
A			1.43		1.30		
G						2.33	

Exhibit A.2. Graph, table and matrix representations of funds flow network.

required order or in ordering the whole graph, as given for example by a list of edges with starting (or finishing) nodes in the required order. The effect on the matrix form of topologically sorting the nodes of an acyclic graph or network is to triangularize the matrix: either no entries will appear above or no entries will appear below the diagonal. Exhibit A.3 is an example.

The *transitive* closure $\tau(G)$, of a graph G is a graph which has an edge, e(u,v), wherever there is a path in G from u to v. The transitive closure of an acyclic graph is acyclic. The transitive closure of a path of $n = |V|$ nodes is a graph of $n(n-1)/2$ edges. The transitive closure of a cycle of $|V|$ nodes with, in addition, a reflexive edge from each node to itself, is the *complete graph* on $|V|$ nodes, containing $|V|^2$ edges, one from each node to each other or to itself.

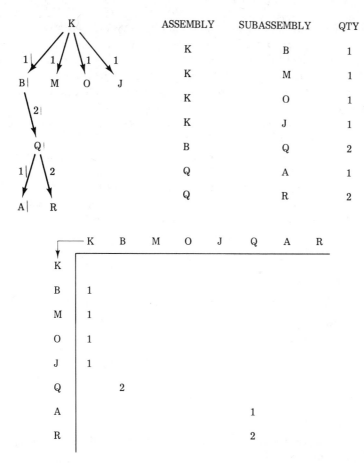

ASSEMBLY	SUBASSEMBLY	QTY
K	B	1
K	M	1
K	O	1
K	J	1
B	Q	2
Q	A	1
Q	R	2

	K	B	M	O	J	Q	A	R
K								
B	1							
M	1							
O	1							
J	1							
Q		2						
A						1		
R						2		

Exhibit A.3. Graph, table and matrix representations of bill of materials.

Trees and Forests

A *tree* is a graph, T, which satisfies the following equivalent definitions.

1a) There is one special node, called the *root*; 1b) the remaining nodes are partitioned into disjoint sets, each of which is in turn a tree, called a *subtree*.

2a) T is connected and acyclic; 2b) each node is the finish of at most one edge; and exactly one node, called the *root*, is the finish of no edges.

3a) T is connected and has $|V| - 1$ edges; and (2b).

4a) T is acyclic and has $|V| - 1$ edges; and (2b).

The bill of materials in Exhibit A.3 is a tree (although that in Exhibit 5.1-2 is not).

A *forest* is a graph, each of whose maximal connected components is a tree. A forest of t trees on $|V|$ nodes has $|V| - t$ edges.

The *root* of a tree has been defined. A *leaf* of a tree is a node that starts no edge. An *internal* node is any node that is not a leaf. The *internal path length* of a tree is the sum of all path lengths from the root to an internal node. The *external path length* is the sum of all path lengths from the root to a leaf.

An *m-ary tree* is a tree in which each internal node starts m edges. The *fanout* of an m-ary tree is m. An m-ary tree with $|I|$ internal nodes has $|L| = (m - 1) |I| + 1$ leaves or $m |I| + 1$ nodes in all (it has $|I| + |L| - 1$ edges because of the $|I| + |L|$ nodes; it has $m|I|$ edges because there are m per internal node).

A *complete* m-ary tree has a maximum path length of h and has all leaves either h or $h - 1$ edges from the root. If the root node is at level 0 and the leaves at level $h - 1$ and h, the following formulas hold at level ℓ.

	$\ell < h$	$\ell = h$
Number of nodes	m^ℓ	k
Total nodes, levels 0 to ℓ	$(m^{\ell+1} - 1)/(m - 1)$	$k + (m^h - 1)/(m - 1)$
Sum of path lengths from root to level ℓ	ℓm^ℓ	kh
Total path length, levels 0 to ℓ	$\sigma(\ell)$	$\sigma(h - 1) + kh$

where $\sigma(\ell) = 0 + m + 2m^2 + \ldots + \ell m^\ell = m(m^{\ell+1} - (\ell + 1)m^\ell + 1)/(m - 1)$.

The number, k, of leaves at level h, is a multiple of m determined by the total number, $|I|$, of internal nodes:

Total nodes $= |V| = m|I| + 1 = k + (m^h - 1)/(m - 1)$

The *height*, h, of the tree is given in terms of the number of leaves, $|L| = (m - 1) |I| + 1$

$$h = \log_m |L|$$

since $(m^{h-1} - 1)/(m - 1) < |I| \le (m^h - 1)/(m - 1)$. The external path length is $(h - 1) |L| + k$ and the internal path length is $\sigma(h - 2) + (h - 1)k/m$.

Complete m-ary trees are too regular and simple to arise very often in practice. We have given all the above formulas because they can be used to deal approximately with less regular but more realistic trees, such as B-trees. The *fanout*, ϕ, of a general tree can be defined as the number of edges, $|E|$, divided by the number of internal nodes, $|I|$. This gives $\phi = m$ for an m-ary tree on one hand and, on the other, even gives a useful characteristic of an acyclic graph that is almost a tree, but has a few nodes that finish more than one edge (so that the number of edges exceeds $|V| - 1$ where there are $|V|$ nodes). In Section 5.3-2 we make use of some of the m-ary tree formulas with ϕ replacing m : ϕ need not even be an integer.

We can even get away with using some of the above formulas for graphs that are "almost trees." A tree on $|V|$ nodes is characterized by having a single root, no cycles and $|E| = |V| - 1$ edges. We can define an *almost tree* as a connected graph with one root, no cycles and $|E| \gtrsim |V| - 1$ edges: a few nodes (relative to $|V|$) finish more than one edge. A tree is an almost tree. The Bill of Materials of Exhibit 5.1-2 is almost a tree, and this is exploited in the analyses of Sections 5.3-2 and 5.3.3.

Answers

Answers for Exercises in Sections 1.1-1 and 1.1-2, Chapter 1.1.

1.1-2

None, as it happens.

1.1-3

All three: Hannah Trainman would give rise to 3 × 3 tuples in the reconstruction, Eric Brakeman to 3 × 2 and Natacha Engineer to 2 × 2: a total of 19 tuples where there are really only 8.

1.1-4

{ORD#,ASSEMBLY}.

1.1-5

Exhibit 5.2-6 shows ORDERBOOK and more.

1.1-6

Exhibit 1.1-9 can be expanded to show all the consequences of the three functional dependences given. Using abbreviations O for ORD# and for {ORD#}, OA or $\frac{O}{A}$ for {ORD#,ASSEMBLY}, etc., and ϕ for the set of no attributes (see table on page 380).

If you did not get all of these, do not be distressed: they are of mainly theoretical interest and are easily found using the axioms of Section 1.4-2. Thinking about it a little is the main benefit for your understanding of functional dependence. What is the meaning of $\phi \rightarrow X$ for attribute X? The italic entries are called *non-trivial*: in what sense are the others trivial?

Further dependences which hold for ORDERBOOK are {ORD#,QTY} $\rightarrow$ ASSEMBLY and {ASSEMBLY,QTY} $\rightarrow$ ORD#, as can be seen by inspecting Exhibit 1.1-3a. It is hard to attach significance to these, since QTY could be anything, and we term these *accidental* or *non-essential* dependences. There are some other close calls: a change of one value of

QTY from 37 to, say, 38, would give two more accidental dependences QTY → ORD# and QTY → ASSEMBLY (which we could write QTY → {ORD#,ASSEMBLY}); if Hannah Trainman and Natacha Engineer did not both have orders with New York Central, we would have CUSTOMER → SALESMAN and if Eric Brakeman did not have two orders with Great North of Scotland then {CUSTOMER,SALESMAN} → ORD# (Exhibit 1.1-4b). These almost-dependences have no significance, but finding them is good exercise.

	φ	O	C	S	A	Q	OC	OS	OA	OQ	CS	CA	CQ	SA	SQ	AQ	OCS	OCA	OCQ	OSA	OSQ	OAQ	CSA	CSQ	CAQ	SAQ	OCSA	OCSQ	OCAQ	OSAQ	CSAQ	OCSAQ
φ	1																															
O	1	1	1	1			1	1			1						1															
C	1		1																													
S	1			1																												
A	1				1																											
Q	1					1																										
OC	1	1	1	1			1	1			1						1															
OS	1	1	1	1			1	1			1						1															
OA	1	1	1	1	1	1	1	1	1	1	1	1	1	1	1	1	1	1	1	1	1	1	1	1	1	1	1	1	1	1	1	1
OQ	1	1	1	1		1	1	1		1	1		1		1		1		1		1			1				1				
CS	1		1	1							1																					
CA	1		1		1							1																				
CQ	1		1			1							1																			
SA	1			1	1									1																		
SQ	1			1		1									1																	
AQ	1				1	1										1																
OCS	1	1	1	1			1	1			1						1															
OCA	1	1	1	1	1	1	1	1	1	1	1	1	1	1	1	1	1	1	1	1	1	1	1	1	1	1	1	1	1	1	1	1
OCQ	1	1	1	1		1	1	1		1	1		1		1		1		1		1			1				1				
OSA	1	1	1	1	1	1	1	1	1	1	1	1	1	1	1	1	1	1	1	1	1	1	1	1	1	1	1	1	1	1	1	1
OSQ	1	1	1	1		1	1	1		1	1		1		1		1		1		1			1				1				
OAQ	1	1	1	1	1	1	1	1	1	1	1	1	1	1	1	1	1	1	1	1	1	1	1	1	1	1	1	1	1	1	1	1
CSA	1		1	1	1						1	1		1									1									
CSQ	1		1	1		1					1		1		1									1								
CAQ	1		1		1	1						1	1			1									1							
SAQ	1			1	1	1								1	1	1										1						
OCSA	1	1	1	1	1	1	1	1	1	1	1	1	1	1	1	1	1	1	1	1	1	1	1	1	1	1	1	1	1	1	1	1
OCSQ	1	1	1	1		1	1	1		1	1		1		1		1		1		1			1				1				
OCAQ	1	1	1	1	1	1	1	1	1	1	1	1	1	1	1	1	1	1	1	1	1	1	1	1	1	1	1	1	1	1	1	1
OSAQ	1	1	1	1	1	1	1	1	1	1	1	1	1	1	1	1	1	1	1	1	1	1	1	1	1	1	1	1	1	1	1	1
CSAQ	1		1	1	1	1					1	1	1	1	1	1							1	1	1	1					1	
OCSAQ	1	1	1	1	1	1	1	1	1	1	1	1	1	1	1	1	1	1	1	1	1	1	1	1	1	1	1	1	1	1	1	1

1.1-8

See Secton 5.1-2.

1.1-10

$$\text{SIN} \ (\ \underset{\pi/4}{\underline{X}} \quad \underset{1/\sqrt{2}}{\underline{\text{SINX}}} \ )$$
$$\vdots \qquad \vdots$$

1.1-11

NETWORK 1

(LINE	PT1	PT2)
A	1	3
:	:	:

or

NETWORK 2

(LINE	POINT)
A	1
A	3
:	:

LINE

	A	B	C	D	E	F	G
1	1	1					
2		1		1	1		
3	1		1				
POINT 4						1	1
5			1	1		1	
6						1	1

1.1-12

MANAGES (BOSS	WORKER)
E8	E4
E8	E7
E4	E1
:	:

E1 E2 E3 E4 E5 E6 E7 E8

E1 E2 E3 E4 E5 E6 E7 E8

1.1-13

a) Two ways: (STUDENT, OFFICE) and (OFFICE, TELE-PHONE);
(STUDENT, OFFICE) and (STUDENT, TELEPHONE).

Note that STUDENT is the key and that there is a *transitive* functional dependence STUDENT → OFFICE → TELEPHONE.

b) Two ways: (STUDENT, OFFICE) and (OFFICE, BLACKBOARD);
(STUDENT, OFFICE) and (STUDENT, BLACKBOARD).

Note that {STUDENT, BLACKBOARD} is the key, and there is a functional dependence STUDENT → OFFICE.

c) Two ways: (A,B) and (A,C); (B,C) and (A,C). Note that A and C are keys. The splits and their recombinations are shown below for this example:

```
( A  B  )  ( B  C  )   ( A  C )   ( A  B      )
  A1 B1       B1 C1       A1 C1    (    B  C )
  A2 B1       B1 C2       A2 C2      A1 B1 C1
  A3 B2       B2 C3       A3 C3      A1 B1 C2
                                     A2 B1 C1
( A  B      )  (    B  C  )          A2 B1 C2
( A     C )    ( A     C  )          A3 B2 C3
  A1 B1 C1       A1 B1 C1
  A2 B1 C2       A2 B1 C2
  A3 B2 C3       A3 B2 C3
```

1.1-14

A relation with the functional dependence $M_1 \cdots M_\ell \rightarrow O_1 \cdots O_k$. Note, however, the possibility that the set of member tuples for a given owner is empty.

1.1-15

F(X,Y) with the functional dependence $X \rightarrow Y$. Strictly speaking X and Y in $F: X \rightarrow Y$ are *domains* while X and Y in F(X,Y) are *attributes*.

1.1-16

[Fagin, Mendelzon and Ullman, 1982]

a. PROFESSOR teaches COURSE, COURSE meets in ROOM at WHEN, STUDENT gets GRADE in COURSE. This is not the only answer.
b. COURSE $\rightarrow$ PROFESSOR (if only one section) $\therefore$ CP (COURSE, PROFESSOR)
WHEN, ROOM $\rightarrow$ COURSE
(If course meets several
times)
COURSE, WHEN $\rightarrow$ ROOM $\Big\}$ $\therefore$ CWR (COURSE, WHEN, ROOM)
(If > 1 room, else COURSE
$\rightarrow$ ROOM)
COURSE, STUDENT $\rightarrow$ GRADE $\therefore$ CSG COURSE, STUDENT, GRADE)
These depend on interpretation.
Extra-relation FDs: PROFESSOR, WHEN $\rightarrow$ ROOM; STUDENT, WHEN $\rightarrow$ ROOM (cannot be 2 places at once)

1.1-17

[Imielinski and Lipski, 1982]
a. PRODUCT costs PRICE, COMPANY has AGENT representing PROD-

UCT **or** PRODUCT represented by AGENT, PRODUCT produced by COMPANY, (COMPANY has AGENT).

b. Various answers are possible:

i.   (PRODUCT, PRICE)   (AGENT, PRODUCT, COMPANY)

ii. (AGENT, PRODUCT)   (PRODUCT, PRICE, COMPANY)
     or (PRODUCT, PRICE), (PRODUCT, COMPANY)

iii. (PRODUCT, PRICE) (AGENT, PRODUCT) (PRODUCT, COMPANY) (AGENT, COMPANY)

iv. (AGENT, COMPANY) (AGENT, PRODUCT, PRICE) (COMPANY, PRODUCT)

1.1-18

[Fagin, Mendelzon and Ullman, 1982]

a. CUSTOMER has ACCOUNT at BANK with BALANCE, CUSTOMER has LOAN at BANK with AMOUNT, CUSTOMER lives at ADDRESS.

b. ACCOUNT, BANK → CUSTOMER, BALANCE (accounts unique only within bank)
   ∴ CAB (CUSTOMER, ACCOUNT, BANK, BALANCE)
   LOAN, BANK → CUSTOMER, AMOUNT ∴ CLB (CUSTOMER, LOAN, BANK, AMOUNT)
   CUSTOMER → ADDRESS ∴ CA (CUSTOMER, ADDRESS)

Extra-relation constraint: suppose we require that the sum of BALANCEs exceeds the sum of AMOUNTs.

1.1-19

[Imielinski and Lipski, 1982]

a. SUPPLIER is in CITY, SUPPLIER supplies PRODUCT, PRODUCT costs PRICE.

b. (SUPPLIER, CITY) **or** (SUPPLIER, CITY), (SUPPLIER, PRODUCT), (PRODUCT, PRICE)

Answers

Answers for Exercises in Section 1.2-1, Chapter 1.2.

1.2-1

Average latency is the time required for half a revolution: the constants convert from minutes to milliseconds. Transfer time is the inverse of the number of bytes that are transferred per microsecond: $\sigma\beta/60$ gives the transfer rate in bytes/sec. Access/transfer ratio is total access time (latency + arm movement) divided by transfer time: note that the access time could be spent transferring 14100 bytes and so we often measure this ratio in terms · of *equivalent bytes*.

1.2-2

Simple-mindedly, capacity = $\beta\gamma\nu$, so RISDISK = 100 M and RISFLOPPY = 0.6 M. However in practice β gives only an upper limit to the capacity of a track, which is reduced by blocking, sectoring and space reserved for administrative data.

1.2-3

Average latency is the time required to read half the tape: the 12 converts from feet to inches. Transfer time is the inverse of density × speed, the number of bytes transferred per microsecond. Access/transfer ratio is the average latency divided by the transfer time per byte, or it is half the capacity of the tape.

1.2-4

Simple-mindedly, capacity = $12\phi\delta$ = 180 M. In practice, blocking cuts this down as noted: the inter-block gap is equivalent to 3750 bytes.

1.2-5

Ignoring sectoring or administrative data needs, we have: blocksize = 41 × 80 = 3280 bytes, i.e., 2 per track on RISFLOPPY or 3 per track on RISDISK; $\lceil 1250/41 \rceil$ = 31 blocks, i.e., 16 tracks on RISFLOPPY or 11 tracks on RISDISK.

1.2-6

$1000\lambda/\tau$ or $\beta/2$, $10^6\lambda/\tau$, $1000\mu/\tau$.

1.2-7

Algorithm LI: (Hash Insert with Linear Probing.) Insert one record with hash key k.

LI1   (Hash) $a \leftarrow h(k) = k \bmod n$

LI2   (Search Block) $\ell \leftarrow b - 1$

Repeat until $\ell < 0$:

   If location ℓ is empty, goto LI4

   If record at location ℓ of block a matches new record then terminate (already present).

   $\ell \leftarrow \ell - 1$

End repeat

LI3   (Overflow) $a \leftarrow a - 1$. If $a < 0$ then $a \leftarrow a + n$. If $a = h(k)$ then terminate (file full). Goto LI2

LI4   (Insert) Insert new record at location ℓ of block a.

1.2-8

Algorithm LS. (Hash Search with Linear Probing.) All records with hash key k are to be found.

LS1   (Hash) $a \leftarrow h(k) = k \bmod n$

LS2   (Search block) $\ell \leftarrow b - 1$

Repeat until $\ell < 0$:

   If location ℓ is empty, terminate: successful if output not empty.

   If $key(\ell) = k$, add record at location ℓ of block a to output.

   $\ell \leftarrow \ell - 1$

End repeat

LS3   (Overflow) $a \leftarrow a - 1$. If $a < 0$ then $a \leftarrow a + n$.

   If $a = h(k)$, terminate: successful if output not empty. Goto LS2.

1.2-9

Algorithm SS. (Hash Search with Separate Chaining.) All records with hash key h are to be found.

SS1   (Hash) $a \leftarrow h(k) = k \bmod n$

SS2   (Search block) $\ell \leftarrow b - 1$

Repeat until $\ell < 0$:

   If location ℓ is empty, terminate: successful if output not empty.

   If $key(\ell) = k$, add record at location ℓ of block a to output.

   $\ell \leftarrow \ell - 1$

End repeat

SS3   (Overflow) $p \leftarrow$ pointer on block a

While $p \neq$ null

   $r \leftarrow$ record pointed to by p

   If $key(r) = k$, add r to output

   $p \leftarrow$ pointer at record r

End while

Terminate: successful if output not empty.

1.2-10

Algorithm SD. (Hash Delete with Separate Chaining.) Delete a record hashed by separate chaining to location r. If the record is normal, $r = ab + 1$. Otherwise r is the address of the record in the overflow area and p is the address of its predecessor (which is either another overflow record or a normal record). The address of the first location in the list of free space is q. Other addresses are given by pointer: $ptr(p) = r$, $ptr(r) =$ address of successor of r.

SD1 (Overflow?) If r is an overflow, goto SD5.

SD2 (Successor?) If $ptr(r) \neq$ null goto SD4.

SD3 (Delete.) Mark r empty and terminate.

SD4 (Move up overflow chain.) $t \leftarrow ptr(r)$.
   Copy record from location t to location r.
   $r \leftarrow t$. Goto SD6.

SD5 (Remove from overflow chain.) $ptr(p) \leftarrow ptr(r)$.

SD6 (Garbage collection.) $ptr(r) \leftarrow q$. $q \leftarrow r$. Terminate.

1.2-11

k	p	j	α	a = 0	1	2	3	4	5	6	7	8	9	10
0	0	0	.5	0										
1			1.0	0,1										
2		1	.75	0,2	1									
4	0	2	.67	0,4	1	2								
5	1		.83	0,4	1,5	2								
6			1.0	0,4	1,5	2,6								
8			.88	0,4	1,5	2,6	,8							

←(block 1 split, nothing hashed to 3 but $k = 8$ overflows to 3.)

k	p	j	α	a = 0	1	2	3	4	5	6	7	8	9	10
9	0	3	.8	0,8	1,5	2,6		4,9						
10	1		.75	0,8	1,9	2,6		4	5,10					
12	2		.83	0,8	1,9	2,6		4,12	5,10					
13			.79	0,8	1,9	2,10		4,12	5,13	6				
14	3		.86	0,8	1,9	2,10		4,12	5,13	6,14				
16			.81	0,8	1,9	2,10		4,12	5,13	6,14	,16			

←($k = 9$ overflows to block 4)

k	p	j	α	a = 0	1	2	3	4	5	6	7	8	9	10
17	0	4	.78	0,16	1,9	2,10		4,12	5,13	6,14		8,17		
18	1		.75	0,16	1,17	2,10		4,12	5,13	6,14		8	9,18	
20	2		.73	0,16	1,17	2,18	,20	4,12	5,13	6,14		8	9	10
:		3												

The underlined rows show the fullest occupation of $2^j \nu$ blocks, states in which h_j is the unique hash function. The same states occur in virtual hashing. Note that linear probing stores overflows in blocks cyclically before the home block.

1.2-13

Calculate the hash address of each search key and sort the requests on this address. Then the requests can be processed by merging them with the file in a single pass. Overflows degrade the performance badly, however, because they are out of order. For single-record hashing, we can define the *record probe factor* as $\pi \overset{\Delta}{=} 1 +$ (number of tuples which overflow)$/N$. For high-activity hashing we have the *block probe factor,* $\pi' \overset{\Delta}{=} 1 +$ (number of blocks with tuples which overflow)$/n$. These factors exceed 1 by an amount which increases with overflows, and are crude measures of the cost of hashing in these two cases. Since about 20% of the records are likely to collide (see Section 1.3-3a) and there are probably at least 50 records per block, every block will undoubtedly overflow. Thus $\pi = 1.2$ but $\pi' = 2$. This rough assessment assumes the best possible treatment of overflows, in particular that only one extra access is required to capture all the overflows from any one block. Usually the degradation is much worse.

1.2-14

Roughly, $n \uparrow (1-k/m)$ accesses. If we knew more, say $n = f_1 \times \ldots \times f_m$, so that the m-dimensional space of records is partitioned into f_i segments of n/f_i blocks each along the ith axis (attribute), and, say, the search specified attributed $i_1, \ldots, i_k$, then the cost is exactly $n/(f_{i_1} \times \ldots \times f_{i_k})$ accesses. For ORDERS $n = f_1 \times f_2 = 2 \times 2 = 4$ and the cost is

k attributes specified	0	1	2
cost = 4 $\uparrow$ (1−k/2)	4	2	1

1.2-15

Remove the boundary between Fischerman and General Toy Corp, add a boundary between Mettal Toys and Noisy Toys on the MAKER axis; shift the boundary between Locomotive and Toy Train to a new position between Toy Train and Tractor on the TOY axis. Now only 8 tuples overflow from 5 blocks if the blocksize is 2 and only 3 from 3 blocks if it is 3. This can be summarized, using the *load factor* $\alpha \overset{\Delta}{=}$ (number of tuples)/(capacity of storage) and the *probe factor* $\pi \overset{\Delta}{=} 1 +$ (number of tuples which overflow)/(total number of tuples):

α	.5	.67	1
π	1.06	1.16	1.28

from Exhibit 1.2-11

α	.5	.67	1
π	1.0	1.09	1.25

best partitioning

1.2-16

α	.67	1
π	1.0	1.25

1.2-17

Algorithm H.   (Create Order-Preserving Hash Function for Given File.) We use

$$t_{part}^{(guess)}(a) \overset{\Delta}{=} b_{part} + \lfloor (a - a_{part})/w_{part}^{(guess)} \rfloor$$

where part is the current partition (i in text) varying from 1 to a value p which this algorithm attempts to minimize as discussed in the text; guess is one of g guesses (0 to $g - 1$), g being predetermined; b_{part}, a_{part} and $w_{part}^{(guess)}$ appear in the text as b_i, a_i and $w_i^{(j)}$ respectively. Records are counted from 0 to $N - 1$ by recd, and a_{recd} is the search key of the record.

H1 (Initialize.) Set part $\leftarrow$ 1, recd $\leftarrow$ 0, block $\leftarrow$ 1. Read record (recd).

H2 (Parameters.) $a_{part} \leftarrow a_{recd}$, $b_{part} \leftarrow t_{part}^{(0)}(a_{part})$

H3 (Guess.) All g guesses are valid. For each guess, set $oflo_{guess} \leftarrow 0$, $block_{guess} \leftarrow block$, $w_{part}^{(guess)} \leftarrow (a_{recd+2^j b} - a_{recd})/2^j$. (The last requires looking ahead in the file.)

H4 (Read record.) Set recd $\leftarrow$ recd + 1. Read next record (recd). If no more records, p $\leftarrow$ part and terminate: hash parameters are w_i, a_i, b_i, i = 1, .., p.

H5 (Evaluate.)

For each valid guess:

   If $t_{part}^{(guess)}(a_{recd})$ gives a new block, check last block:

      Set $\alpha \leftarrow recd/(b \times block_{guess})$, $\pi \leftarrow 1 + oflo_{guess}/N$.
      If $\alpha < \alpha_0$ or $\pi > \pi_0$, guess becomes invalid.
      If all guesses are now invalid, close the partition by selecting one of the guesses just invalidated, namely the one with the largest value of α among those with the smallest value of π: $w_{part} \leftarrow w_{part}^{(guess)}$, part $\leftarrow$ part + 1, block $\leftarrow block_{guess} + 1$ and goto step H2.
      Set $block_{guess} \leftarrow block_{guess} + 1$

   Else if the number of previous records mapping to $block_{guess}$ with $t_{part}^{(guess)}$ exceeds b, $oflo_{guess} \leftarrow oflo_{guess} + 1$.

Goto step H4.

1.2-18

Tidy functions were introduced to preserve order and the motive for preserving order is to improve response to high-activity queries such as range queries. Thus overflows should be placed in their correct order in the file, as in the case of the CUSTOMER example. This can be done by loading the file sequentially. The problem is to *find* them in a direct search. Clearly a variant on linear probing is needed. If a collision occurs at t(a), *absolute linear probing* tests locations t(a) ± 1, t(a) ± 2, and so on until the values at the "+" locations exceed or the values at the "−" locations are less than the search key or until both ends of the file have been reached.

1.2-19

They terminate as soon as they pass a record with a search key too large (going forward) or too small (going backward): as for an ordered sequential file, unsuccessful searches do not cost more than successful searches.

1.2-20

a) $m \times \sqrt[m]{n}$ entries.

n \ m	2	5	10	20
10^2	20	13	16	25
10^5	632	50	32	36
10^8	20000	199	63	50

b) n entries: the same as for a standard index—unless this can be reduced by a C-directory approach or other approximation to the distribution function.

1.2-21

Use the usual formula for m-dimensional array addressing. If the block coordinates are $(i_1, \ldots, i_m)$ in an $f_1 \times \ldots \times f_m$ partitioning ($i_j = 0, \ldots, f_j - 1$ for $j = 1, \ldots, m$) the address is

$$i = i_1 + i_2 f_1 + i_3 f_1 f_2 + \ldots + i_m (f_1 \times \ldots \times f_{m-1}) \text{ (row major form)}$$

or

$$i = i_m + i_{m-1} f_m + i_{m-2} f_m f_{m-1} + \ldots$$
$$+ i_1 (f_m \times \ldots \times f_2) \text{ (column major form).}$$

The example of Exhibit 1.2-11 is (in row major form): $i = i_1 + 4 i_2$.

1.2-22

This requires trial and error. Try $n = \lceil 10000 / (55 \times .8) \rceil = 227$. This is prime, so we hunt for smaller values of n with nearly equal factors: $n = 216 = 6 \times 6 \times 6$ is nice, giving $b_0 = 47$, $b \in [47, 57]$ and $\alpha \in [.81, .99]$. Alternatively, $n = 225 = 5 \times 5 \times 9$, giving $b \in [45, 55]$ and $\alpha \in [.81, .99]$; or $n = 220 = 4 \times 5 \times 11$, giving $b \in [46, 56]$ and $\alpha \in [.81, .99]$.

1.2-23

$n \, 2^m / n \uparrow (1/m)$, shown below for various n and m.

n \ m	2	5	10	20
10^2	40	1274	6.5×10^4	8.3×10^7
10^5	1265	3.2×10^5	3.2×10^7	5.9×10^{10}
10^8	4×10^4	8.0×10^7	1.6×10^{10}	4.2×10^{13}

1.2-24

The recursive procedure Loop The Loop (m) implements the m nested loops shown.

For $i_m \leftarrow a_m$ to z_m by s_m

    .

      .

        .

    For $i_1 \leftarrow a_1$ to z_1 by s_1

        Statement

Loop The Loop(ℓ)

For $i_\ell \leftarrow a_\ell$ to z_ℓ by s_ℓ

if $\ell = 1$ then Statement

else Loop The Loop $(\ell - 1)$

Be careful using it!

1.2-25

$$\Pi\, 2^{(f_i - 1)} = 2^{(\Sigma f_i) - m}.$$

1.2-26

ASSEMBLY	1	2	3	4	5	6	7	8
Caboose		(PR,H,37)	L&S,E,3				GTRC,N,43	
Car		(NYC,N,1)	L&S,E,23		NYC,H,31	B&O,H,17	GTRC,N,139	
Locomotive	GNS,E,2		L&S,E,5		NYC,H,13		GTRC,N,47	
Toy Train	GNS,E,7			PR,H,11				GNS,E,37
	2	1	3	2	2	1	3	1

The attributes CUSTOMER, SALESMAN and QTY are shown explicitly. Ordinarily ORD# and ASSEMBLY would also appear explicitly, but to save space are here indicated by the positions of the tuples. Overflow tuples that have been moved to block (0,0) are shown in parentheses with arrows from their home blocks. The axial distributions and candidate boundaries are shown. The three candidate partitionings passed to the last step of Algorithm MP, and the results, are

TOTAL SEGMENT O'FLOW	CANDIDATE PARTITIONING	TUPLE DISTRIBUTION HISTOGRAM	π for $b = 3$ $a = 0.63$	$b = 2$ $\alpha = 0.94$
1	1 0 1 1 0	0 3 2 2	1	1.13
		3 2 1 2		
	1 1 0 1 0	0 2 3 2	1	1.13
		3 1 2 2		
2	0 1 1 1 0	2 1 2 2	1.07	1.13
		4 1 1 2		

It is clear that there is not much of a choice on the ASSEMBLY axis.

1.2-28

Exhibit 1.2-17b is a slight improvement over partitioning aC in Exhibit 1.2-16. The dynamic result is not as good as the best static result, but it is pretty good. For the specified blocksize, $(\pi, \alpha) = (1.25, 1)$ is the best that can be done.

1.2-29

Each plane is an $(m-1)$-dimensional array, which can be addressed in row-major or column-major order (see Ex. 1.2-19). Either of these addressing methods needs $m-1$ parameters, the dimensions of the array. These $m-1$ numbers must be recorded, as the "size" of the plane, in the entry of the axial array corresponding to the plane. The product of these $m-1$ numbers and the index of the plane (*i.e.*, of the entry in the axial array) give the starting block number for the plane.

1.2-30

If $m \times row(m) > t \times col(t)$ then location number is $m \times row(m) + t$

else location number is $t \times col(t) + m$.

1.2-31

The axial array elements

$$\underline{axial}_i(j) \qquad 1 \le i \le m, 0 \le j < f_i$$
where f_i is the number of segments on the ith axis

are vectors of length $m-1$, as in Ex. 1.2-24, with components

$$axial_i(j)_k \qquad 1 \le k \le m-1$$

To find the location number of block $(j_1, \ldots, j_m)$, find

$$\max_i \ (s_i \overset{\Delta}{=} j_i \times \prod_k axial_i(j_i)_k).$$ Then, with this value of i,

$$location\ number \leftarrow s_i + address\ (j_1, \ldots, j_{i-1}, j_{i+1}, \ldots, j_m:$$
$$f_1, \ldots, f_{i-1}, f_{i+1}, \ldots, f_m)$$

where address gives the usual row-major or column major $(m-1)$-dimensional address of an $f_1 \times \ldots \times f_{i-1} \times f_{i+1} \times \ldots \times f_m$-dimensional array.

1.2-33

Simply remove them. The segments may be coalesced on the basis of one of two criteria. In one case, if α goes below a given threshold, combining two neighboring segments would be required. In the other case, neighboring segments would be recombined whenever this did not push π above a given upper limit. The latter is more in keeping with the way we have used to build the file up. If recombining is impossible, it may be possible to reduce π by shifting a boundary after deletion.

For example, deleting G Tri from Exhibit 1.2-20 makes recombination of the Tricycle segment of TOYS possible with either the Tractor segment or the ∞ segment.

1.2-34

Algorithm BS.   (Prefix B-tree search for search key sk.)
BS1   Set p to address of root node. Set s ← null.
BS2   Read node p.
BS3   If p is a leaf, if sk is there then access main file else fail.
BS4   Set s ← p. Find i such that $k_i \le sk < k_{i+1}$.
Set p ← p_i. Goto BS2.

1.2-35

In step BS4, if sk = k_i for some i, terminate successfully. Note that if sk is not a key, as in Exhibit 1.2-5, the subtrees left and right of k_i must be searched. Remove step BS3 and add step BS1a after BS1:
If p = null then fail.

1.2-36

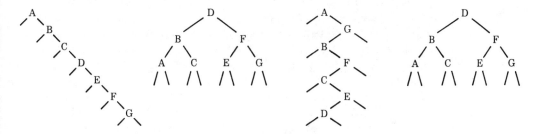

1.2-37

B1:   The root node is created (when the tree is not empty) by splitting nodes below it: step BI3 creates a root of two subtrees, and entries can only be added (by step BI4).

B2:   Step BI5 produces two nodes satisfying the lower bound, and entries are added until the upper bound is reached.

B3:   By induction: the root is a leaf initially and new levels are added by producing new roots so all leaves change level simultaneously. (The growth is more that of a carrot than a tree.)

1.2-39

Leaf nodes. If root, f entries are to be placed in two blocks: [f/2] on first, [f/2] on second. Otherwise, 2f − 1 entries are to be placed in three blocks: [(2f−2)/3] + 1, [(2f−1)/3], [2f/3].

Internal nodes. If root, b′ > b bytes are to be placed in two blocks: place the separator occupying byte [b′/2] and nearby bytes in a new root, the entries before this in the first block and the entries after in the second. Otherwise, b″ > 2b bytes are to be placed in three blocks: place the separators at bytes [b″/3], [2b″/3] in the parent node (this may cause the parent node to split, and even further splits as far as the root), and the remaining entries in the three blocks in the obvious way.

1.2-40

In the algorithm that follows, steps $1.5 - 1.8$ and $2.3 - 2.6$ generate a configuration, config, which has the form either (separator) or (separator, pointer, separator) which later replaces the separator k_{pos} in the parent node. Note that we cannot simply replace one separator by another when an overflow of a descendant node causes a rotation, because separators are variable length and the replacement might cause an overflow. Where we split a pair of blocks a new pointer and two separators are generated. This is the reason for using the notation config and pos.

Note that right splits may occasionally affect the *grandparent* node, since this may contain k_{pos} (used in P*I2).

Algorithm P*I   (Insert search key sk into Prefix B*-tree.)

P*I1.   (Insert in leaf.)

    1.1   (Search.) If sk found: terminate successfully. (If the search key is not a key, the match must occur on sufficient attributes to form a key or all matching records must be found.)

    1.2   (Empty.) If s = null (see search algorithm BS): create root node with sk and pointer to main file; terminate.

    1.3   (Block has room.) If node s has room: insert sk and pointer; terminate.

    1.4   (Split root.) If s is root node: insert sk to give f entries; find minimum-length separator, k', within the split interval around $[f/2]$; q ← pointer to new leaf node; place entries in the two nodes and make root (s, k', q); terminate.

    1.5   (Overflow right.) If node s has a neighbor to the right which has room: insert sk to give $f' > f$ entries in the two nodes and find a minimum-length separator, k', within the split interval around $[f'/2]$; place entries in the two nodes; config ← k'; pos ← (index of s in parent) + 1; goto P*I2.

    1.6   (Overflow left.) If node s has a neighbor to the left which has room: insert sk to give $f' > f$ entries in the two nodes and find a minimum-length separator, k', within the split interval around $[f'/2]$; place entries in the two nodes; config ← k'; pos ← (index of s in parent); goto P*I2.

    1.7   (Split right.) If node s has a neighbor to the right: insert sk to give $2f-1$ entries in the two nodes; find minimum-length separators k'_1 and k'_2, within the split interval around $[(2f-2)/3] + 1$ and $[(2f-2)/3] + 1 \div [(2f-1)/3]$; q ← pointer to new (middle) leaf node; place entries in the three nodes; config ← $k'_1 q k'_2$; pos ⇌ (index of s in parent) + 1; goto P*I2.

    1.8   (Split left.) Insert sk to give $2f-1$ entries in node s and its left neighbor; find minimum-length separators, k'_1 and $\hat{k}$, within the split interval around $[(2f-2)/3] + 1$ and $[(2f-2)/3] + 1 + [(2f-1)/3]$; q ← pointer to new (middle) leaf node; place entries in the three nodes; config $\leftarrow k_1' qk_2'$; pos $\leftarrow$ index of s in parent; goto P*I2.

P*I2.　(Insert in internal node.) s $\leftarrow$ parent of s.

　2.1　(Block has room.) If node s has room: $k_{pos} \leftarrow$ config; terminate.

　2.2　(Split root.) If s is root node: $k_{pos} \leftarrow$ config to give $b' > b$ bytes; find a minimum-length separator, k', within the split interval around $[b'/2]$; q $\leftarrow$ pointer to new sibling node; place entries in the two nodes and make root (s, k', q); terminate.

　2.3　(Overflow right.) If node s has a neighbor to the right which has room: $k_{pos} \leftarrow$ config to give $b' > b$ bytes in the two nodes (including their separator in the parent node); find a minimum-length separator, k', within the split interval around $[b'/2]$; place entries in the two nodes; config $\leftarrow k'$; pos $\leftarrow$ (index of s in parent) $+ 1$; goto P*I2.

　2.4　(Overflow left.) If node s has a neighbor to the left which has room: $k_{pos} \leftarrow$ config to give $b' > b$ bytes in the two nodes (including their separator in the parent node); find a minimum-length-separator, k', within the split interval around $[b'/2]$; place entries in the two nodes; config $\leftarrow k'$; pos $\leftarrow$ index of s in parent; goto P*I2.

　2.5　(Split right.) If node s has a neighbor to the right: $k_{pos} \leftarrow$ config to give $b'' > 2b$ bytes in the two nodes (including their separator in the parent node); find minimum-length separators, k_1' and k_2', within the split interval around $[b''/3]$, $[2b''/3]$; q $\leftarrow$ pointer to new (middle) sibling node; place entries in the three nodes; config $\leftarrow k_1'qk_2'$; pos $\leftarrow$ (index of s in parent) $+ 1$; goto P*I2.

　2.6　(Split left.) $k_{pos} \leftarrow$ config to give $b'' > 2b$ bytes in node s and its left neighbor (including their separator in the parent node); find minimum-length separators, k_1' and k_2', within the split interval around $[b''/3]$, $[2b''/3]$; q $\leftarrow$ pointer to new (middle) sibling node; place entries in the three nodes; config $\leftarrow k_1'qk_2'$; pos $\leftarrow$ index of s in parent; goto P*I2.

1.2-42

If sk is found, delete it from the leaf node. If the block is now $< 2/3$ full, concatenate it with its left and right neighbors to form two blocks. If this is impossible, "underflow" the right or left neighbor so that each block is $\geq 2/3$ full, rotating the parent node separator appropriately. In the cases of concatenation or underflow, the parent node will be altered and may cause its neighbors to concatenate or underflow. The detailed algorithm is in two parts, like Algorithm P*I, with similar individual steps.

1.2-43

(Lomet [1979].) Use fixed-length tables, one for each length of separator, and do binary searches on each one (see Knuth [1973] §6.2.1). The justification for this approach is that there are few tables because the expected separator length is short: $E(\text{separator length}) = \sum_{k=0}^{\infty} (1 - (1 - 1/|\alpha|^k)^N) \simeq \log_{|\alpha|}^N$ for N words from an alphabet of $|\alpha|$ symbols.

$$E(L) = \sum_{k=0}^{\infty} \text{prob}(L > k)$$

$$= \sum_{k=0}^{\infty} \text{prob (at least one of the N words has } x_i = x_2 = \ldots = x_k = \flat)$$

$$= \sum_{k=0}^{\infty} (1 - (1 - 1/|\alpha|^k)^N)$$

where x_i is the ith symbol of a word and $\flat$ is the blank symbol in the alphabet. This derivation, due to Luc Devroye, is for the length of the first separator, which is taken (for the purpose of the derivation) to be $\flat\,\flat\,\ldots\,\flat\,x_L$ where there are $L - 1$ blanks and $x_L \neq \flat$. Since all separator lengths have the same distribution, the derivation gives the expected length of all separators.

$|\alpha|$ \ N	10^5	10^6	10^7	10^8
10	5.71	6.71	7.71	8.71
26	4.20	4.97	5.60	6.28
36	3.94	4.47	5.15	5.85
256	2.01	3.06	3.45	4.02

The expected length of a separator for N words in an $|\alpha|$-symbol alphabet is just the expected depth of a trie (Fredkin [1960]; Knuth [1973] §6.3) of N items from the same alphabet. This makes it apparent that $\log_{|\alpha|} N$ is a lower bound for the average separator length, and it can be shown that $\log_{|\alpha|} N + \gamma/\log|\alpha| \le E(L) \le \log_{|\alpha|} N + 1 + (\gamma + 1/2N)/\log|\alpha|$ (Devroye [1980]), where $\gamma = 0.5772156649..$ is Euler's constant.

1.2-44

There are $N - 1$ consecutive pairs ($N - p + 1$ consecutive p-plets). The expected number of same-block pairs is $(N - 1) \times$ (probability a given consecutive pair falls into the same block). Given the location of the first record of a pair, there are $nb - 1$ remaining locations for the second, $b - 1$ of which are in the same block as the first: the probability is $(b - 1)/(nb - 1)$. Hence the expected number of same-block pairs is

$$\frac{(N - 1)(b - 1)}{(nb - 1)} \xrightarrow[b \to \infty]{} \frac{N - 1}{n}$$

Similarly, the expected number of same-block p-plets is

$$(N - p + 1) \frac{(b - 1)(b - 2)}{(nb - 1)(nb - 2)} \cdot \cdot \frac{(b - p + 1)}{(nb - p + 1)} \xrightarrow[b \to \infty]{} \frac{N - p + 1}{n^{p-1}}$$

1.2-46

Algorithm KDBI

KDBI1. If tree empty, create a leaf containing the tuple. (This leaf is the root.) Terminate.

KDBI2. Search tree for tuple: if found, report and terminate.

KDBI3. If leaf node has room, add tuple and terminate. Otherwise set p → leaf node.

KDBI4. Choose discriminator attribute and value and split node p. Set l → left, r → right node. (This step is ambiguous. Policies for choosing discriminator include: ensure node r has no fewer tuples than node l; alternate discriminating attributes cyclically unless the choice is forced; etc.)

KDBI5. If p is not the root node, set oldp to p and p → parent of p; if node p has room, replace the pointer to oldp in p by the configuration (ℓ, new discriminator pair, r) and terminate, otherwise go to KDBI4 (to split p).

KDBI6. Create a new internal node as root containing (ℓ, new discriminator pair, r).

Algorithm KDBS

KDBS1. (Split a leaf.) Create two new leaves: left node contains all tuples with discriminator attribute less than the discriminator value; right node contains those greater than or equal.

KDBS2. (Split an internal node.) Create two new internal nodes: left node contains all regions with discriminator attribute less than the discriminator value; right node contains those greater or equal. Furthermore, if any region contains values both less and greater or equal to the discriminator value, that region is split into two, part for left node and part for right node.

1.2-47

The K-D-B-Tree of Exhibit 1.2-27 results if the following choices of discriminator are made. On insertion of 3Q3 use ORD# 2 (instead of ORD# 3 or ASSY Q). For 3L5 use ASSY Q (not ORD# 3). 5L13 → ORD# 3 (no option). 6C17 → ASSY L (ORD# 5, ORD# 6) at the leaf level then ORD# 3 (ASSY Q) to split the root. 5C31 → ORD# 5 (ORD# 6). 8T37 (added after 4C37) →

ORD# 4 then ASSY Q (ASSY L) to split the internal node. 7Q43 → ORD#
7 (ASSY T). 7L47 → ORD# 5 (ORD# 7). 7C139 → ORD# 6 (ORD# 7) then
ORD# 6 (ASSY L). Of course, there are plenty of alternative routes, indicated in parenthesis in the above list, not to mention the further choices
available if any of these alternatives is followed.

1.2-48

Algorithm TSI (Trie Search and Insert). In this algorithm the *terminator* is the
latter part of the search key bit sequence starting from the bit that dis-
tinguishes it from any other search key. The whole search key is designated
bit $[1 \cdot \cdot h - 1]$. Leaf nodes differ from internal nodes only in that they hold
the terminator and the other values from the tuple, while internal nodes hold
pointers to right and left sons.

TSI1   (Empty trie?   If trie is empty, create root with terminator ← se-
                    quence, and quit.

TSI2   (Initialize.)   i ← 1; p ← root.

TSI3   (Search.)   If p is a leaf then go to step TSI4.
        If bit [i] = 0 then p ← left son of p else p ← right son of p. i ← i +
        1. If i ≥ h then fail else repeat step TSI3.

TSI4   (Found?)   j ← first bit at which bit $[i \cdot \cdot h - 1]$ differs from termi-
                    nator in node p, or h if all bits match.
        If j ≥ h then quit: the search key is found.

TSI5   (Extend trie.)   If bit [i] = 0 then create left son of p; p ← left
                                    else create right son of p;p ← right.
        i ← i + 1. If i < j then repeat step TSI5.

TSI6   (Insert.)   If bit [i] = 0
        then create left son of p with terminator ← bit $[j + 1 \cdot \cdot h - 1]$;
            create right son of p with
                        terminator ← last h − j − 1 bits of old terminator
        else ditto, swapping left ↔ right. □

1.2-49

Replace the binary comparison "if bit [i] = 0" by a loop through the $|\alpha|$
symbols of the alphabet.

1.2-50

Reverse steps TSI6 and TSI5, removing any internal nodes that no longer
discriminate different entries.

1.2-51

With 15 data items, a binary tree could have a height of from 4 to 15 levels
(with an average over all possible tries of 2 ln 15 = 5.4 − see Knuth [1973]
§6.2.2). The trie for this data ranges from 10 to 16 levels in height. However
the trie can be represented more compactly, indeed as a bit string with only
two bits per node (see Orenstein [1982]). Furthermore, as we add data to this

space, the trie will not exceed 17 levels in height, while the tree will require $\lceil \log_2 (N + 1) \rceil$ levels at best (see Appendix) and N at worst, where N is limited to the size of the space, $N \leq 2^{16}$.

1.2-52

$00110001 \leq$ ORD# ≤ 00110111 divides into 3 ranges of ASSEMBLY: 01000011 to 01000111, 01001000 to 01001111 and 01010000 to 01010100.

1.2-54

See Merrett and Orenstein [1982].

1.2-55

Build a "Huffman Tree", as follows. Create $(1 - r)$ mod $(f - 1)$ "dummy runs" of length zero, so that all merges will have degree f. Merge the runs, f at a time, in ascending order of their length, adding the run resulting from each merge to the remaining runs, at the right place in the sequence.

1.2-56

a)   1.33
b)   1.08

1.2-57

Sort the relevant requests and the contents of each block and do a merge for each block addressed directly or by overflow pointers. Process the blocks in ascending order of block address if the collision resolution goes from a block to its successor; otherwise it goes from a block to its predecessor and the blocks should be processed in descending order.

1.2-58

Secondary storage has a high access/transfer ratio, is permanent and is cheaper than RAM.

1.2-59

Blocking.

1.2-60

Equivalent bytes: number of bytes that could have been transferred instead of seek.

1.2-65

A prime, $p \geq 1000$, e.g., 1009, 1013, 1019, 1021, 1031.

1.2-66

1024; $h(k) = (158k$ **mod** $256) | 10$ on an 8-bit machine $(w = 2^8)$.

1.2-68

Where to put new blocks resulting when a block is split so that the same access method applies.

1.2-71

a_i, $(0 \le i < p)$, w, N_i, $(1 \le i < p)$

1.2-72

Keep g small enough that 2^{g-1} search keys can fit into RAM.

1.2-73

Face:volume and surface:volume of a hypercube of volume n in m dimensions.

1.2-74

Addressing need be done along the axes only.

1.2-75

Advantage: better fit to the distribution of tuples.
Disadvantage: the index size must be proportional to the size of the file.

1.2-76

a − e : 4, 2, 4, 1, 1
z − w : 3, 5, 2, 2,
1 − 5 : 4, 3, 2, 2, 1

1.2-77

a)   4 , 2 │ 4 , 1 , 1 ; 3 , 5 │ 2 , 2 ; 4 , 3 │ 2 , 2 , 1
b)   4 │ 2 │ 4 │ 1 , 1 ; 3 │ 5 │ 2 , 2 : 4 │ 3 │ 2 │ 4 , 1

1.2-78

a)   Since the two-segment partitionings in Ex. 1.2-77 are a subset of the three-segment partitionings, we need only consider the latter. These give us $4 \times 3 \times 4 = 48$ cells in the histogram. If we use the three-segment partitioning for (a − e), we must use a two-segment partitioning either for (z − w) or for (1 − 5) but not both, to give n = 6 blocks. Thus there are two choices, and for each of these we can choose one of two locations for the second boundary for (a − e). Similarly, there are four possibilities if we use the three-segment partitioning of (1 − 5). There are only two possibilities if we partition (z − w) into three, since all boundaries are unambiguous. This gives $4 + 2 + 4 = 10$ combinations.

b)   Imposing V/f = constant (as nearly as possible) with n = 6 blocks forces us to do a one-segment partitioning on (z − w), which has the fewest values (i.e., not to partition it), and two-segment and three-segment partitionings on the others. This reduces the histogram to $4 \times 4 = 16$ cells and the number of combinations to 4.

1.2-79

a b │ c d e ; z y x w ; 1 │ 2 │ 3 4 5. This gives

α	1	0.67
π	1.08	1

1.2-80

a − e would get an additional segment: a | b | c d e. This gives

$$\frac{\alpha \quad 13/18 \qquad 13/27}{\pi \quad 1 + 1/13 \qquad 1} .$$

1.2-81

1.2-82

Advantage: only one index entry per block instead of per record.
Disadvantage: hard to modify (add, change, delete).

1.2-84

When splitting, always combine ℓ blocks and split into $\ell + 1$.

1.2-86

High activity and high query complexity.

1.2-88

Sort it: cost is 1 pass for initial runs, 1 pass to merge, 1 pass to search. (The merge and search passes could be combined in a specialized merge-and-search algorithm: just do a four-way merge instead of the three-way merge required by the sort. Of course, the search on the unordered file could be done in one pass in this case, by storing the items in an array in RAM and checking each one against each tuple of the file. But this method does not generalize to handle searches for more items than can fit into RAM.)

1.2-90

Direct: fast on average. Logarithmic: fast worst case.
Sequential: simple.

1.2-91

a. b = 3   n = 6 $V_{P/3} = 2.3$ $V_{S/2} = 2.5$ $\alpha = 15/18 = 0.83$

b. P 1   2 3 4 5 6 7   S   a   b   c   d
    2 3 | 3 1   1 | 3 2   3   4 ⊦ | 2   2

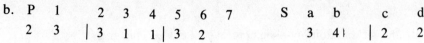

c. S

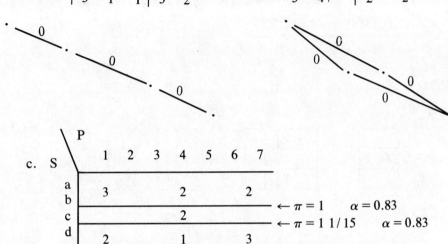

$\leftarrow \pi = 1$ $\alpha = 0.83$

$\leftarrow \pi = 1\,1/15$ $\alpha = 0.83$

NB alternatives (do not result from following Algorithm MP)

$- b = 2$ $f_S = 2$ $f_P = 4 \Rightarrow V_S/f_S = 2.5$ $V_P/f_P = 1.75$ $\pi = 1\,2/15$

$\alpha = 15/16 = .93$

$- b = 4$ $f_S = 2 = f_P \Rightarrow V_S/f_S = 2.5$ $V_P/f_P = 3.5$ $\pi = 1$ $\alpha = .93$

1.2-92

a. $b = 4$ $n = 3$ $V_{P/3} = 2.3$ $V_{S/1} = 3$

b. P 1   2   3   4   5   6   7
     1   1 | 3 |1 | 1 | 2   1

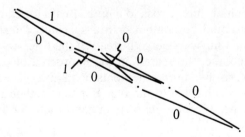

c. Graph gives exact answer, since S has only one segment: $\pi = 1$, $\alpha = 0.83$.

1.2-93

	τ	ρ	σ	λ	μ	β	γ	ν	capacity	cost
Video disk	3.8 μsec.	34406	960 rpm	31.25 ms.	100 ms.	16384	40000	2	$1.3_{10}9$ bytes	$2.4_{10}{}^{-7}$ ¢/bit

Answers

Answers for Exercises in Sections 1.3-1 and 1.3-3, Chapter 1.3.

1.3-1

Assuming a sector size of 512 bytes, we get five records per block, a block access time of $323 + 100$ ms and a transfer time of 500×30 μsec : about 440 ms total or 88 ms per record. For O(N log N) we use 3, the recommended order of merge for a micro, as base:

# records processed	in 1 sec	in 1 min	in 1 hour	in 1 day	in 1 month	in 1 year
1	∞	∞	∞	∞	∞	∞
$\log_2 N$	$2.6_{10}3$	(200)	$(4.9_{10}3)$	$(1.2_{10}5)$	$(3.5_{10}6)$	$(4.3_{10}7)$
N	11	680	$4.1_{10}4$	$9.8_{10}5$	$2.9_{10}7$	$3.6_{10}8$
$N \log_3 N$	6.6	150	$5.8_{10}3$	$1.1_{10}5$	$2.3_{10}6$	$2.3_{10}7$
N^2	3.4	26	200	990	$5.4_{10}3$	$1.9_{10}4$
N^3	2.2	8.8	34	99	310	710
2^N	3.5	9.4	15	20	25	28
10^N	1.1	2.8	4.6	6.0	7.5	8.6

1.3-2

$$\pi_s - 1 \simeq \frac{1}{\alpha b} \sum_{k > b} \left(\substack{k - b + 1 \\ 2}\right) e^{-\alpha b} \frac{(\alpha b)^k}{k!} \simeq \frac{1}{2}(\alpha b - b + 1)\omega + \frac{1}{2}\sigma$$

$$\text{where } \sigma \stackrel{\Delta}{=} \sum_{j \geq b} e^{-\alpha b} \frac{(\alpha b)^j}{j!} \simeq \frac{\alpha}{\alpha - 1}\omega - \frac{e^{-\alpha b}}{\alpha - 1} \frac{(\alpha b)^b}{b!}$$

$$\textit{i.e., } \omega \doteq \frac{\alpha - 1}{\alpha}\sigma + \frac{e^{-\alpha b}}{\alpha} \frac{(\alpha b)^b}{b!}.$$

We can follow Knuth [1973] Ex. 6.4.49 and write

$$\sigma = e^{-\alpha b} \frac{(\alpha b)^b}{b!} (1 + \alpha R(\alpha, b))$$

where $R(\alpha, b) \overset{\triangle}{=} \dfrac{b}{b+1} + \dfrac{b^2 \alpha}{(b+1)(b+2)} + \dfrac{b^2 \alpha^2}{(b+1)(b+2)(b+3)} - \cdots$

getting $\pi_s - 1 \simeq \dfrac{e^{-\alpha b}}{2} \dfrac{(\alpha b)^b}{b!} [(\alpha^2 b - (2\alpha - 1)(b - 1)) R(\alpha, b)$

$+ \alpha b - b + 2]$.

Knuth uses the function $R(\alpha, b)$ to evaluate π for both separate chaining and linear probing for $c = 1$.

π_s' and μ are straightforward.

1.3-3

As $c \to \infty$, $k_1 \to 0$, $k_2 \to k - b$, $k_3 \to 1$. The results follow.

1.3-4

One extra probe is required for all those blocks of size b that overflow, two extra probes are needed for all adjacent pairs of blocks (effectively blocks of size 2b) that overflow, and so on. This argument depends on a theorem which proves that the cost of linear probing is independent of the order of insertion of records into the hash table. See Knuth [1973] §6.4.

1.3-5

To answer this question precisely we should compute numerical values for π_s (Equations 1.3-9 and 1.3-10) and compare with those computed for π_L and shown in Exhibits 1.3-4, 1.3-5 and 1.3-6 (formula in Ex. 1.3-4). Instead, we will use the approximation $\pi_s \simeq 1 + \omega$, noting from Exhibit 1.3-8 that it is not far wrong. We consider $\alpha = .85$.

a)   In RAM, use b = 1.

	Successful	Unsuccessful
Linear Probing	3.8	22.7
Separate Chaining	~1.4	a little less than 1.4

b)   On secondary storage, say b= 50

	Successful	Unsuccessful
Linear Probing	1.015	?
Separate Chaining	~1.01	~1.5

(The results of Ex. 1.3-2 were used to estimate unsuccessful separate chaining.) Separate chaining is always better. Linear probing in the worst case runs the risk of accessing every block, especially at high α. Separate chaining localizes the overflows: it costs O(n) accesses only if every record hashes to the same location. Linear probing, however, is a very good method for secondary storage. It catches up rapidly to separate chaining as the blocksize increases, and it is a simpler method to implement.

1.3-6

Choose j records from a block of b and $r - j$ from the remaining $N - b$ records, out of a possible $\binom{nb}{r}$ ways of choosing r of nb records. This is the result for *selection without replacement* (no record is accessed more than once). The limit as $b \to \infty$ gives *selection with replacement,* i.e., $(1 - 1/n)^r$. Numerical comparison (Yao [1977b]) of these two cases shows that selection with replacement is a close approximation for selection without replacement for quite small b — e.g., within 2% for b = 15.

1.3-8

Write a small computer program to find the minimum of Eq. 1.3-35 with respect to ϕ by fitting successive parabolas to it, each one positioned at the minimum predicted by extrapolating its predecessor. The result depends on α, R and N. For $N = 10, 10^2, \ldots, 10^{10}$ find the average value of the minimum cost/$\log_{10} N$ and tabulate as a function of α and R.

1.3-9

$a = \ln(N/2F) = \ln(N_b/2F_b)$ and $c = \rho/F_b$ where $N_b = 10^5, 10^8, 10^{11}$ bytes respectively in Exhibit 1.3-13, $F_b = 10^4, 10^5, 10^6$ bytes respectively for micro, mini and mainframes. To minimize, set $0 = d[(1 + cf)(1 + a/\ln f)]/df$ i.e., $0 = cf(\ln f)^2 + acf(\ln f - 1) - a$. This can be solved on a programmable calculator or one which finds zeros of functions. The resulting values of f are

	MAIN	MINI	MICRO
$F_b = 10^5$			2.46
10^8	22.0	6.72	3.18
10^{11}	29.2	7.52	3.34

1.3-10

Sequential file: 1 pass = NR bytes transferred.
Direct file: r accesses = $(R + \rho)r$ bytes effectively transferred.

$$\text{Breakeven } r/N = R/(R + \rho).$$

1.3-11

We give values for contributions to $NR\omega$, measured in bytes (equivalent to the number of bytes that could have been transferred while time was being spent in activity other than data transfer), for 1) transmission time, 2) discontinuities due to computations after every j^{th} block of the n blocks, 3) delays between cylinders, 4) wastage due to tracks not being fully occupied by B-byte blocks.

$$\omega = \omega_1 + \omega_2 + \omega_3 + \omega_4$$

The initial search time is, of course, ρ equivalent bytes, by definition of ρ, the access/transfer ratio.

$NR\omega_1 = NR$ bytes transferred: $\omega_1 = 1$

$$NR\omega_2 = \left(\left\lceil \frac{n}{j} \right\rceil - 1\right)(L_2 + CC) \text{ where } L_2 = 10^3 \lambda/\tau = \beta/2, \text{ the average}$$

latency, and CC is the computation time (measured in equivalent bytes) and usually $L_2 + CC = \beta$, the maximum latency time. That is, we assume it does not take more than one extra revolution of the disk to do the computation. This may be worse, or better if there is only one block per track and $CC \le$

$\beta - b$.

$$NR\omega_3 = \left(\left\lceil \frac{n}{\gamma t} \right\rceil - 1\right)(A_3 + L_3) \text{ where } t = \left\lceil \frac{\beta}{B} \right\rceil, \text{ the number of blocks}$$

per track, A_3 and L_3 are the average arm movement and latency, respectively, $A_3 = 10^3 \mu/\tau$, $L_3 = \beta/2$, and $A_3 + L_3 = \rho$ in a multitasking environment or one in which we do not know how the data is distributed across cylinders. If the file is on *contiguous* cylinders, $L_3 = 0$ and $A_3 =$ the minimum arm delay, which is not given in Exhibit 1.2-2.

$$NR\omega_4 = \left\lceil \frac{n}{t} \right\rceil \beta - NR.$$

Answers

Answers for Exercises in Sections 2.1-2 through 2.1-3, Chapter 2.1.

2.1-1

ORDLINE contains the key, {ORD#, ASSEMBLY}, of ORDERBOOK.

2.1-2

The join attribute, ORD#, is the key of ORDERS, the other component of ORDLINE. (Note the different answer to apparently the same question as Ex. 2.1-1.)

2.1-3

$10 = 2 \times 2 + 3 \times 2$. (First term due to floor 1, second due to floor 2.)

2.1-4

0 to $|R| \times |S|$ where R contains $|R|$ tuples and S contains $|S|$ tuples.

2.1-5

(Informally, in terms of rectangular patterns in the matrix form of R). Think of R represented as a set of B-C planes, one for each value of A. $A \rightarrow B$ means that at most one value of B can occur on each plane, so the 1s on the plane, if any, must form a rectangle of width 1.

2.1-6

R cannot contain any tuple (a,b,c) not in the natural join, since (a,b) ϵ (A,B **in** R) and (a,c) ϵ (A,C **in** R).

2.1-7

$R^\ell = \phi$, the empty relation, for $\ell > 3$, because R contains no paths longer than 3.

2.1-8

a) If the null value, *DC,* appears in the join attribute A, we suppose the comparison $DC = DC$ is **true** and $DC = x$ is **false** for any x other than *DC*. With this supposition the relationship is valid. (Note that GAIN is not a projection of GAIN **ujoin** LOSS since the tuple (F,*DC*) is missing.)

b) $R \subseteq$ (A,B **in** *R*) **ijoin** (A,C **in** R) = (A,B **in** R) **ujoin** (A,C **in** R)

2.1-9

The regions labelled A,B,C,D in the Venn diagram shown are the only disjoint regions that can arise from two sets R_w, S in a universe U. We have the following equivalences

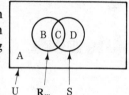

$R_w \supseteq S$	$R_w \uplus S$	$R_w \subseteq S$	$R_w \cap S$
$D = \phi$	$A = \phi$	$B = \phi$	$C = \phi$

so that the emptiness or not of any of the regions can be expressed by a logical combination of set comparisons.

2.1-10

For each value, z, of Z in S, let S_z be Y **where** Z = z **in** S: then

$$R[X \, \sigma \, Y] S \overset{\Delta}{=} \{w,z) \mid z \, \epsilon \, S[Z] \textbf{ and } w \, \epsilon \, R[X \, \sigma \, Y] \, S_z\}.$$

2.1-11

$R[X \textbf{ not } \cap Y] \, S \equiv R[X \textbf{ icomp } Y] \, S.$

2.1-12

$R \, [X \textbf{ lojoin } Y] S \overset{\Delta}{=} \{(w,x,y,z) \mid (w,x) \, \epsilon \, R \textbf{ and } (y,z) \, \epsilon \, S \textbf{ and } x \geq y$
           and $\forall \, y\,'[(y\,' \, \epsilon \, S[Y] \textbf{ and } x \geq y\,') \textbf{ implies } y \geq y\,']\}$
$R \, [X \textbf{ hijoin } Y] S \overset{\Delta}{=} \{(w,x,y,z) \mid (w,x) \, \epsilon \, R \textbf{ and } (y,z) \, \epsilon \, S \textbf{ and } x \leq y$
           and $\forall \, y\,'[(y\,' \, \epsilon \, S[Y] \textbf{ and } x \leq y\,') \textbf{ implies } y \leq y\,']\}$

2.1-13

FAMILY1 = (PARENT, WEDDING **in** FAMILY1) **ijoin** (WEDDING, CHILDBIRTH **in** FAMILY1) But this is an accidental decomposition because many couples may get married on the same day. The decomposition on SURNAME into FAMILY3A and FAMILY3B is also accidental but we assume that families with the same surname can and will be distinguished somehow. Real databases are always built on such little inconsistencies. . . .

2.1-16

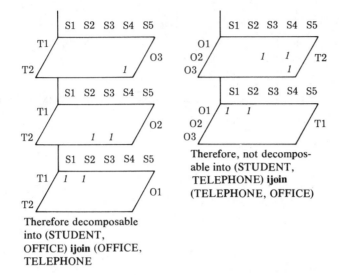

Therefore decomposable
into (STUDENT,
OFFICE) **ijoin** (OFFICE,
TELEPHONE

Therefore, not decompos-
able into (STUDENT,
TELEPHONE) **ijoin**
(TELEPHONE, OFFICE)

2.1-18

GRANDPARENT ← PARENT [JUNIOR **icomp** SENIOR] PARENT.

2.1-19

MIDTERM **ujoin** FINAL. The union join is necessary in case a student was
ill for one exam but sat the other.

2.1-20

a)   PC ⊇ {blue, yellow, red}   or   PC **sup** {blue, yellow, red}   or
PC **divide** {blue, yellow, red} .

b)   PC ⋒ {P1, P2}   or   PC **sep** {*P1, P2*} .

c)   PC ⊉ {P1, P2}   or   PC **not sup** {P1, P2} .

2.1-21

a)   ITEM, FLOOR **in** INVENTORY **ijoin** (**where** STOCKMAN =
'Joe' **in** WAREHOUSEMAN).

b)   STOCKMAN **in** WAREHOUSEMAN **ijoin** (INVENTORY ⊇
{Tractor, Computer})-

2.1-22

FINAL [FIMARK **lojoin** MARK]MG .

2.1-26

a.   COULD ⊇ SUPPLIER, PART **in** SUPPLY;
NEEDS ⊆ PROJECT, PART **in** SUPPLY

b.   COULD **ijoin** NEEDS ⊇ SUPPLY

2.1-27

[Imielinski and Lipski, 1982]

Four: BANK, CUSTOMER **in** R1;   BANK, CUSTOMER **in** R2;
BANK, CUSTOMER **in** R1 **ijoin** R2;
BANK, CUSTOMER **in** R1 **ujoin** R2.

(Customers with accounts at bank, with loans, with accounts and loans, with accounts or loans.)

2.1-28

RESULTS decomposes into RES, ULTS

RES(STUDENT	COURSE	MARK)	ULTS(BASE	GRADE)
a	1	80	80	A
a	2	79	65	B
b	1	65	55	C
b	3	64	0	F
c	2	55		
c	3	54		

RESULTS = STUDENT, COURSE, MARK, GRADE **in**

RES [MARK **lojoin** BASE]ULTS

2.1-29

a.   **let** MDIV **be** DIVISION; UDIV **be** DIVISION

DIVPRED ← (MDIV, PART **in** MAKES) **icomp** (UDIV, PART **in** USES)

MDIV makes some parts used by UDIV

let UPART **be** PART;   MPART **be** PART
PARTPRED ← (UPART, DIVISION **in** USES) **icomp** (MPART, DIVISION **in** MAKES)
UPART is used by some divisions to make MPART.

b.   An infinite number.

MDIV **where** UDIV = x **in** DIVPRED, divisions making parts used by DIVISION x

MDIV **where** UDIV = x **in** DIVPRED [UDIV **icomp** MDIV]
DIVPRED, divisions making parts used by some division making parts used by DIVISION x.

2.1-30

a. The μ-joins are constructed according to Section 2.1-3 using the following *left wing, right wing,* and *centre.*

left wing

(AGENT	ITEMS	FLOOR)
Smith	V.C.R.s	DC

right wing

(AGENT	ITEMS	FLOOR)
DC	Videodisks	2

centre

(AGENT	ITEMS	FLOOR)
Raman	Micros	1
Hung	Micros	1
Raman	Terminals	1
Raman	Terminals	2

The σ-joins are either empty or as follows:

$\supseteq$, $=$

(AGENT	FLOOR)
Raman	1

$\not\ni$

(AGENT	FLOOR)
Raman	2

$\ni$

(AGENT	FLOOR)
Smith	1
Smith	2
Hung	2

$\subseteq$, $\subset$

(AGENT	FLOOR)
Hung	1

b. The μ-join predicates are formed as shown from the following three primitive predicates.
1) AGENT is responsible for ITEMS
2) AGENT is responsible for ITEMS and these are located on floor FLOOR
3) ITEMS are located on floor FLOOR

ijoin   (2)

ujoin   (2) **or** (**not** (2) **implies** ((1) **or** (3) but not both)

ljoin   (2) **or** (**not** (2) **implies** (1))

rjoin   (2) **or** (**not** (2) **implies** (3))

sjoin   (1) **or** (3) but not both

dljoin   (1) **and** no FLOOR has been assigned

drjoin   (3) **and** no AGENT has been assigned

The σ-join predicates are as follows.
$\supseteq$ AGENT is responsible for all ITEMS on floor FLOOR
$\subseteq$ Floor FLOOR is the location of all ITEMS under AGENT
$\ni$ AGENT is responsible for some ITEMS on floor FLOOR
$\not\ni$ AGENT is responsible for no ITEMS on floor FLOOR
$=$ AGENT is responsible for exactly those ITEMS on floor FLOOR

Answers

Answers for Exercises in Sections 2.2-1 through 2.2-4, Chapter 2.2.

2.2-4

Selecting tuples for which an attribute has a predetermined constant value, such as X = x **in** R can be implemented by **ijoin** if there is a facility for defining a *constant relation* on X with the single value, x. Then

$$X = x \textbf{ in } R \qquad \equiv \qquad R[X \textbf{ ijoin } X]\{(x)\}.$$

This is very inefficient, however,

2.2-10

Let the threshold activity be a: the percentage of tuples accessed in R and S such that if more than a tuples per hundred are required, sort-merge techniques become cheaper. Then the following are all necessary for **R ijoin** S, to be a low-activity process on R(X,Y), S(Y,Z).

1) There is a selection of not more than b tuples per hundred.
2) If the selection is on Y, the mapping cardinality (see Section 1.1-2) from Y to X in R and from Y to Z in S must be not more than 1 to c, where bc = a.
3) If the selection is on X (or, by symmetry, on Z), the mapping cardinalities from X to Y in R (Y in S) and from Y to Z in S (Y to X in R) must not exceed 1 to c and 1 to d respectively, where bcd = a.

2.2-13

It would reduce by 1, since the intersection join would no longer require a sort. In the multipage version, a secondary index on G would speed things up.

2.2-14

The selection of both values of Z can be done as early as during the evaluation of D, greatly reducing the sizes of F and H.

2.2-20

Two passes

2.2-21

400×8000 by $250 \times 8000 = 3.2 \times 10^6$ by 2×10^6 values

Answers

Answers for Exercises in Section 2.3-1, Chapter 2.3.

2.3-1

(V. Chvatal, Y. Kambayashi) See Merrett, Kambayashi & Yasuura [1981].

2.3-2

With more than two buffers, the page-pair graph remains the same, but much more variety is possible in the "paths" through it. This greater flexibility can lead to a cheaper join, but complicates even more the problem of finding the optimum path. Each "edge" of the "path" consists of a set of up to k nodes, where k is the number of buffers permitted in RAM. The set is constrained to span only k_r different blocks of relation R and k_s different blocks of relation S, where $k = k_r + k_s$.

Can we get significantly cheaper joins in return for the added complication of using more than two buffers? Probably not. First, if there is room in RAM for k buffers, we can use the same space for two big buffers. Second, if the cost is measured in terms of accesses, the more buffers, the more accesses. Third, if cost is measured (on the other hand) using the plausible assumption that reading k_r (k_s) consecutive blocks of R (S) costs only one access, since most of the cost is finding the first block in the sequence, the k-buffer method seems to be competitive with using two big buffers, but not significantly superior. Here are some examples supporting this third point. In Example 1, the two-buffer case is an improvement over k = 5 (cost: 7 accesses compared with 9) because of the extra accesses required to span the gaps in the columns s_i. Suppose that the relations in this example were mutually clustered so that the 11 nodes shown in the case k = 5 is the minimum possible number. If mutual clustering had been achieved by sorting, the r_i would be arranged in order of i and the k = 5 cost would reduce to 6 accesses. But the two-buffer cost would reduce to 5 accesses. Sorted mutual clustering is preferable for k > 2 because it maximizes the number of consecutive blocks to be read and so reduces the cost when we use the second cost measure above.

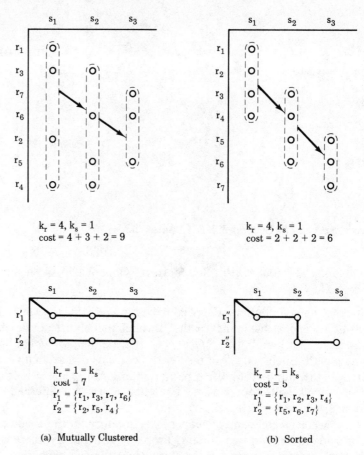

(a) Mutually Clustered   (b) Sorted

Example 1. Sorting favors k > 2 but k = 2 is better.

Example 2 shows a sorted case where k = 3 is better than two buffers (cost: 7 accesses compared with 8). This is because the double-sized block, r_3', is half wasted as a representation of r_5. This situation arises only at the outer edges of the page-pair graph, a region negligible in area compared with the interior.

We can use this weakness to make two buffers look bad in Example 1a by setting $k_r = 2 = k_s$ and comparing with two buffers when the block is similarly proportioned. This is shown in Example 3, where two buffers are still no worse than k = 4.

Further study of this problem might be useful. Or it might not.

2.3-3

Yes, if we are prepared to trust guesswork. If inspection of the first 100 (or 1000 or some small number) of tuples reveals that they are in order, it is pretty likely that somebody sorted them, since the probability of the order

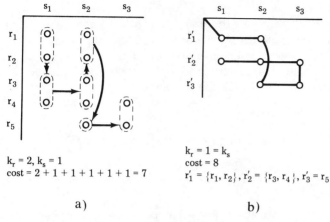

$k_r = 2, k_s = 1$
cost $= 2 + 1 + 1 + 1 + 1 + 1 = 7$

a)

$k_r = 1 = k_s$
cost $= 8$
$r'_1 = \{r_1, r_2\}, r'_2 = \{r_3, r_4\}, r'_3 = r_5$

b)

Example 2. Two buffers are worse.

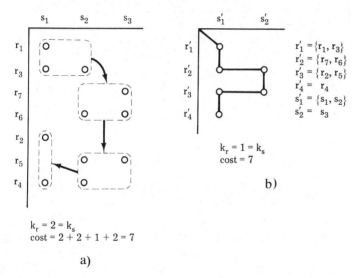

$r'_1 = \{r_1, r_3\}$
$r'_2 = \{r_7, r_6\}$
$r'_3 = \{r_2, r_5\}$
$r'_4 = r_4$
$s'_1 = \{s_1, s_2\}$
$s'_2 = s_3$

$k_r = 1 = k_s$
cost $= 7$

b)

$k_r = 2 = k_s$
cost $= 2 + 2 + 1 + 2 = 7$

a)

Example 3. Bad proportions have no serious effect.

occurring spontaneously can be made arbitrarily small for a big enough run. However, the file may have been sorted but new records added, out of order, at the end. It is hard to make a rigorous analysis of this sampling method, however, it is quite unlike sampling a population of assembly-line products to test for defects or a population of a country to test political opinions. It is rather a matter of inferring a property of a single complexly structured object by inspecting part of it—like passing an aircraft for safety by looking at its turbofans and tailplanes.

2.3-4

Build the page-pair graph for the first 10 (or other small number) pages of each relation. If there are nearer 10 nodes than 10×10, we can surmise that somebody must have done something to make the relations mutually clustered throughout. This is imprecise, will not always work, and is subject to our remarks (Exercise 2.3-3) about sampling.

2.3-5

$R = Cb$ and $N = C2^b$ so we can solve $N/R = 2^b/b$ for b:

N/R	10	10^2	10^3	10^4	10^5	10^6
b	6	10	14	17	21	24

The number of values per axis of each cell is approximately $\ell = 2^s \uparrow (1/m) = 2^{s/m}$.

N/R m	10	10^2	10^3	10^4	10^5	10^6
1	64	1024				
2	8	32	128	362.0	1448.2	4096
3	4	10.1	25.4	50.8	128	256
4	2.8	5.7	11.3	19.0	38.1	64
5	2.3	4	7.0	10.6	18.4	27.9
10	1.5	2	2.6	3.2	4.3	5.3
20	1.2	1.4	1.6	1.8	2.1	2.3

2.3-6

a) $C_i = [C \uparrow (1/m)]$

b) $C_i = \left[V_i \left(C / \prod_{j=1}^{m} V_j \right) \uparrow (1/m) \right]$

Of course, $\prod_{i=1}^{m} C_i$ would be less than C in general under either of these strategies. If we defined (for the second strategy) $\underline{C}_i \stackrel{\Delta}{=} \left[V_i \left(C / \prod_{j=1}^{m} V_j \right) \uparrow (1/m) \right]$ and $\overline{C}_i \stackrel{\Delta}{=} \left[V_i \left(C / \prod_{j=1}^{m} V_j \right) \uparrow (1/m) \right]$ we could search for the best combination of $\underline{C}_i$ and $\overline{C}_i$ whose product does not exceed C. An exhaustive search would compare 2^m alternative combinations, but heuristics which investigate only m different combinations—or m^2, or m^3, etc.—can be devised to improve but not necessarily optimize the fit. The first strategy is easier: with $\underline{C} \stackrel{\Delta}{=} [C \uparrow (1/m)]$ and $\overline{C} \stackrel{\Delta}{=} [C \uparrow (1/m)]$ it is easy to show that

using $\overline{C}$ segments on $[\log (C/\underline{C}^m)/\log (\overline{C}/\underline{C})]$ of the m axes and $\underline{C}$ segments on the remaining most fully utilizes the C cells available in RAM.

2.3-7

Segment z spans ℓ different Z-values in R. Consider one of them. The projection, z in R, will have no tuples for this value if R has no tuples for each of the m possible values of Y at this value of Z. Assuming uniformity within the sectors, we can use standard arguments to derive the probability, P_j, that R has j tuples at this value of Z:

$$P_j = \binom{k}{j} \binom{k\ell - k}{c_z - j} / \binom{k\ell}{c_z}$$

Thus in particular:

$$P_0 = \binom{k\ell - k}{c_z} / \binom{k\ell}{c_z} \quad \underset{k \to \infty}{\longrightarrow} \quad ((\ell - 1)/\ell) \uparrow c_z$$

The probability that there is at least one tuple in R for this value of A is $1 - P_0$. Because of uniformity, this probability applies to each of the n different values of Z in the segment and the expected value is thus $\ell(1 - P_0)$ or Eq. 2.3-1.

2.3-8

The variance is $\ell\{(1 - P_0)[1 - (1 - P_0)^2] + P_0[0 - (1 - P_0)]^2\} = \ell(1 - P_0)P_0$ where P_0 is defined in Exercise 2.3-7.

2.3-9

Suppose that for the ith of the n values of Z in cell (z,y) for R there are r_{zi} tuples, and that there are s_{zi} tuples for this value in cell (z,x) of S. Then the number of tuples for this value in cell (z,y,x) of the join will be $r_{zi} s_{zi}$. The number of tuples in the whole cell (z,y,x) for all n values of Z is thus

$\sum_{i=1}^{n} r_{zi} s_{zi}$. The value of c_{xyz}^{XYZ} (R **ijoin** S) is defined to be the expected value

$$E(\Sigma\, r_{zi} s_{zi}) = \Sigma\, E(r_{zi} s_{zi}) = \Sigma\, E(r_{zi})\, E(s_{zi})$$

where the last equality holds because the tuples in R and S are assumed to be arranged independently.

By uniformity[1] r_{zi} is independent of i, as is s_{zi}. We now write them r_z, s_z.

Then $E(r_z) = \sum_{j=0}^{k_1} j\, P_j$ where k_1 is the number of Y-values in cell (z,y) of R

---

[1] (It has been shown that the same result can be derived using a weaker assumption than uniformity of distribution: see Rosenthal [1981].)

and where P_j is the probability, encountered in Exercise 2.3-7, that there are j tuples of the possible k_1 for a given value of Z in cell (z,y). Thus

$$E(r_z) = \sum_j j \binom{k_1}{j} \binom{k_1 \ell - k_1}{d_{zy} - j} / \binom{k_1 \ell}{d_{zy}} = c^{ZY}_{zy}(R)/\ell$$

Similarly

$$E(s_z) = c^{ZX}_{zx}(S)/\ell$$

Eq. (3) follows:

$$\sum E(r_z)\, E(s_z) = c^{ZY}_{zy}(R) \times c^{ZX}_{zx}(S)/\ell.$$

2.3-10

The alternatives are (R **ijoin** S) **ijoin** T or (R **ijoin** T) **ijoin** S: other possibilities are excluded by absence of common attributes. Using Equation 2.3-3 and Equation 2.3-5 for R **ijoin** T, we get an expected size of 23 ± 3.1 (25.3 ± 7.6 if we had used single cells; the true size is 23). Thus we expect R **ijoin** T to be bigger than R **ijoin** S, so we should use (R **ijoin** S) **ijoin** T.

2.3-11

Let $z_{i_1..i_k} \overset{\Delta}{=} z_{i_1} \cap .. \cap z_{i_k}$, $k \le j$ and let $\ell_{i_1..i_k}$ be the number of different Z-values in $z_{i_1..i_k}$. Consider for instance the evaluation $(.. (R_1 \text{ ijoin } R_2) \text{ ijoin } .. \text{ ijoin } R_j)$ of $\overset{j}{\bowtie} R_i$. Then we show

$$c^{Z \quad Y_1..Y_j}_{z_{1..j}\, y_1..y_j} = \frac{\ell_{1..j}}{\ell_{1..j-1}\ell_j}\, c^{Z \quad Y_1..Y_{j-1}}_{z_{1..j-1}\, y_1..y_{j-1}}\, c^{Z\ Y_j}_{z_j\, y_j}$$

$$= \frac{\ell_{1..j}}{\ell_{1..j-1}\ell_j} \left(\frac{\ell_{1..j-1}}{\ell_{1..j-2}\ell_{j-1}}\, c^{Z \quad Y_1..Y_{j-2}}_{z_{1..j-2}\, y_1..y_{j-2}}\, c^{Z \quad Y_{j-1}}_{z_{j-1}\, y_{j-1}} \right) c^{Z\ Y_j}_{z_j\, y_j}$$

$$= ... = \frac{\ell_{1..j}}{\ell_{1..}\ell_j}\, c^{Z\ Y_1}_{z_1\, y_1} ... c^{Z\ Y_j}_{z_j\, y_j}$$

The demonstration for Equation 2.3-7 is similar. Note that *this is not a derivation* of Equations 2.3-6 and 2.3-7. To show that Equations 2.3-6 and 2.3-7 give the expected number of tuples in the cell in each case requires a statistical derivation not given here. The extension of Equations 2.3-6 and

2.3-7 to the conjecture that repeated application of Equation 2.3-4 gives the expected number of tuples in a cell after an arbitrary sequence of natural joins is an open question which has not been proved.

2.3-12

The right wing of the union join contains tuples corresponding to tuples of S which do not match any tuple of R on Z. Using r_{zi}, s_{zi}, ℓ and k_1 as defined in Exercise 2.3-9 we have the expected number of tuples in cell (z,x) of the left wing

$$E\left(\sum_i r_{zi}\,(\text{if } r_{zi} = 0 \text{ then } 1 \text{ else } 0)\right) = \sum_i E(r_{zi})\,E(\text{if } r_{zi} = 0 \text{ then } 1 \text{ else } 0)$$

The second term resembles projection and can be evaluated in terms of P_0 (Exercise 2.3-7).

$$E(\text{if } r_{zi} = 0 \text{ then } 1 \text{ else } 0) = 1 \times \text{prob}(s_{zi} = 0) + 0 \times \text{prob}(s_{zi} \neq 0)$$

$$= P_0$$

$$= \binom{k_1\ell - k_1}{c_z(R)} \Big/ \binom{k_1\ell}{c_z(R)} \xrightarrow[k_1 \to \infty]{} (1 - 1/\ell) \uparrow c_z(R)$$

We have again the limiting case of selection with replacement to use as an approximation.

2.3-13

Consider first two sets A and B with a and b elements respectively and a possible maximum of n elements in each case. We will find the *a priori* probability that $A \supseteq B$ given that we know only a, b and n. There are $\binom{n}{b}$ arrangements of the b elements of B and for *any* arrangement of the a elements of A, $\binom{a}{b}$ of the arrangements for B are subsets of the arrangement for A. So prob $(A \supseteq B) = \binom{a}{b} / \binom{n}{b}$.

Now consider the m × n cell for R, containing c_{xy} tuples and the n × p cell for T, containing c_{yw} tuples. Suppose the m values of x in cell (x,y) for R are $x_1, \ldots, x_m$ and that the p values for w in cell (y,w) for S are $w_1, \ldots, w_p$. Suppose there are j tuples in cell (x,y) for value x_1 and k tuples for value w_1 in cell (y,w). Then the probability that the set $Y(x_1, y)$ of y-values associated with x_1 in R contains the set $Y(w_1,y)$ of y-values associated with w_1 in T is $\binom{j}{k} / \binom{n}{k}$.

Given that there are c_{xy} tuples in cell (x,y), the probability that exactly j are associated with x_1 in R is $\binom{n}{j}\binom{mn-n}{c_{xy}-j} / \binom{mn}{c_{xy}}$. Similarly, the probability that exactly k tuples of the c_{yw} in cell (y,w) of T are associated with w_1 is $\binom{n}{k}\binom{np-n}{c_{yw}-k} / \binom{np}{c_{yw}}$. Thus the *a priori* probability that $Y(x_1,y) \supseteq Y(w_1,y)$, if we know c_{xy} and c_{yz} but not j or k, is

$$\sum_k \left[\sum_j \binom{n}{j}\binom{mn-n}{c_{xy}-j}\binom{j}{k} \right] \binom{np-n}{c_{yw}-k} / \binom{mn}{c_{xy}}\binom{np}{c_{yw}}$$

$$= \sum_k \binom{mn-k}{c_{xy}-k}\binom{n}{k}\binom{np-n}{c_{yw}-k} / \binom{mn}{c_{xy}}\binom{np}{c_{yw}}$$

There is more than one cell in both R and T containing tuples for x_1 and w_1 respectively — $|Y|/n$, to be exact. Since the set of y-values for x_1 in R contains that for w_1 in T if and only if $Y(x_1,y) \supseteq Y(w_1,y)$ for each $y = 1, \ldots,$ $|Y|/n$, we must take the product of the above probabilities for $y = 1, \ldots,$ $|Y|/n$. Finally, by uniformity, the argument of the last two paragraphs applies equally to all pairs of values, (x_i,w_h), $i = 1, \ldots, m$, $h = 1, \ldots, p$, so the expected number of values of cell (x,w) of R sup T is

$$mp \prod_{y=1}^{|Y|/n} \sum_k \binom{mn-k}{c_{xy}-k}\binom{n}{k}\binom{np-n}{c_{yw}-k} / \binom{mn}{c_{xy}}\binom{np}{c_{yw}}.$$

2.3-14

$$c_x^X (R = V) = m \prod_y \binom{mn-n}{c_{xy}-c_y} / \binom{mn}{c_{xy}}$$

$$c_x^X (R \neq V) = m \left[1 - \prod_y \binom{mn-n}{c_{xy}-c_y} / \binom{mn}{c_{xy}} \right]$$

$$c_x^X (R \supset V) = c_x^X (R \supseteq V) - c_x^X (R = V) \quad (\supseteq \text{ is } \mathbf{sup})$$

$$c_x^X (R \subset V) = c_x^X (R \subseteq V) - c_x^X (R = V) \quad (\subseteq \text{ is } \mathbf{sub})$$

2.3-15

We examine the split step, MSI3, of Algorithm MSI. If we do a constant number of accesses for each new block, then we can combine this information with the knowledge that we do at most πb accesses per block in step MSI1, inserting tuples into existing blocks, to conclude that the number of accesses is proportional to the number of blocks. In step MSI3, the dominant criterion, the size of V_i / f_i, $i = 1, \ldots, m$, can be found from information in RAM, so as long as this is the only criterion used, the result follows.

However, if we must compare values of π for different axes, we may need to do $O\left(\sum n/f_i\right)$ accesses, as in Expression 2.3-20, to create $O(n/f_i)$ blocks for some i, as in Expression 2.3-18. In this case *the result does not follow*, although the cost is unlikely to be significantly worse than linear. If we allow shifting, as in step MSI2, we do $O\left(\sum n/f_i\right)$ accesses each shift for a possibly large number of shifts each time we create $O(n/f_i)$ blocks for some axis i.

This argument also supposes that in practice we have an overflow method good enough to keep the true probe factor to π.

Answers

Answers for Exercises in Section 3.1-2, Chapter 3.1.

3.1-1

let   TOTQY **be red** + **of** QTY
TOTQTY **in** ORDERBOOK (TOTQTY)
$$416$$

3.1-2

let   TOTQTY **be red** + **of** QTY
TOTQTY **in** (**where** ASSEMBLY = 'Car' **in** ORDERBOOK) (TOTQTY)
$$247$$

3.1-4

let   QTYASM **be equiv** + **of** QTY **by** ASSEMBLY
ASSEMBLY, QTYASM **in** ORDERBOOK (<u>ASSEMBLY QTYASM</u>)

ASSEMBLY	QTYASM
Car	247
Locomotive	68
Caboose	46
Toy Train	55

3.1-5

let   QTYORD **be equiv** + **of** QTY **by** ORD#
ORD#, QTYORD **in** ORDERBOOK (<u>ORD#</u>   <u>QTYORD</u>)

ORD#	QTYORD
1	9
2	1
3	31
4	48
5	44
6	17
7	229
8	37

3.1-6

let #YEAR be red max of (fcn + of 1 order YEAR)
let #YEARD be equiv max of (par + of 1 order YEAR by DIV) by DIV

3.1-7

let TOTMARK be .2 × MTMARK + .8 × FIMARK.

3.1-8

let TOTVAL be equiv + of QTY × UNIT VALUE by DEPT SHIPSUM ←
DEPT, TOTVAL in SHIPPED.

3.1-9

let COURSEAVG be (equiv + of MARK by COURSE)/(equiv + of 1 by
COURSE)
iet STUDAVG be (equiv + of MARK by STUDENT)/(equiv + of 1 by
COURSE)
COURSES ← COURSE, COURSEAVG in STUDRECORD
STUDENTS ← STUDENT, STUDAVG in STUDRECORD.

3.1-10

let COURSEMAX be equiv max of MARK by COURSE
BESTUDENT ← COURSE, STUDENT where MARK = COURSEMAX in
STUDRECORD.

3.1-11

let COURSECT be equiv + of 1 by STUDENT
COURSELOAD ← STUDENT, COURSECT in STUDRECORD.

3.1-12

let JUNIOR1 be JUNIOR; SENIOR1 be SENIOR
GRANDPARENT ← SENIOR, JUNIOR in ((SENIOR, JUNIOR1 in
PARENT)
[JUNIOR1   ijoin   SENIOR1]   (SENIOR1,   JUNIOR   in
PARENT)).

3.1-13

let VALUEAB be equiv + of VALUEA × VALUEB by I,K
AB ← VALUEAB, I, K in (A ijoin B).

Answers

Answers for Exercises in Section 3.2-1, Chapter 3.2.

3.2-1

S1.   For each tuple in:
S1.1   Set tuple out $\leftarrow$ (X,Y,X $<$op$>$ Y)

3.2-2

R1.   Set (ACCUM) $\leftarrow$ first tuple in.
R2.   While more tuples in:
R2.1   Set (X) $\leftarrow$ next tuple in, ACCUM $\leftarrow$ ACCUM $<$op$>$ X.
R3.   Set tuple out $\leftarrow$ (ACCUM).

3.2-3

E1.   Sort R on X.
E2.   Set (X,ACCUM) $\leftarrow$ first tuple in.
E3.   While more tuples in:
E3.1   Set (X',Y) $\leftarrow$ next tuple in.
E3.2   If X = X' then set ACCUM $\leftarrow$ ACCUM $<$op$>$ Y
                  else set tuple out $\leftarrow$ (X,ACCUM); (X,ACCUM) $\leftarrow$ (X',Y).
E4.   Set tuple out $\leftarrow$ (X,ACCUM).

3.2-4

F1.   Sort R on X.
F2.   Set (X,Y) $\leftarrow$ first tuple in; Z $\leftarrow$ Y.
F3.   While more tuples in:
F3.1   Set (X',Y') $\leftarrow$ next tuple in.
F3.2   If X $\neq$ X' then:
F3.2.1   Set tuple out $\leftarrow$ (X,Y,Z); (X,Y) $\leftarrow$ (X',Y');
                  Z $\leftarrow$ Z $<$op$>$ Y.
F4.   Set tuple out $\leftarrow$ (X,Y,Z).

3.2-5

P1.   Sort R on X within W.

P2.   Set W,X,Y ← first tuple in; Z ← Y.

P3.   While more tuples in:

P3.1   Set (W',X',Y') ← next tuple in.

P3.2   If W ≠ W' then:

P3.2.1   Set tuple out ← (W,X,Y,Z); (W,X,Y) ← (W',X',Y');
                   Z ← Y.

P3.3   else if X ≠ X' then:

P3.3.1   Set tuple out ← (W,X,Y,Z); (W,X,Y) ← (W',X',Y');
                   Z ← Z <op> Y.

P4.   Set tuple out ← (W,X,Y,Z).

Answers

Answers for Exercises in Section 4.1-1 and Review Questions and Exercises, Chapter 4.1.

4.1-1

See Section 4.2-1.

4.1-2

a) Find items supplied to more than two departments:
let COUNT **be equiv** + **of** 1 **by** ITEM
ITEM **where** COUNT > 2 **in** (ITEM, DEPT **in** SUPPLY)

b) Find all items except those supplied in volumes of less than 10.
(ITEM **in** SUPPLY) **djoin** (ITEM **where** VOL < 10 **in** SUPPLY)

c) Find items supplied by at least two companies to more than one department.
let COUNTC **be equiv** + **of** 1 **by** ITEM
let COUNTD **be equiv** + **of** 1 **by** ITEM, COMP
ITEM **where** COUNTC ≥ 2 **in** (ITEM, COMP **where** COUNTD > 1 **in**
(ITEM, COMP, DEPT **in** SUPPLY))

4.1-4

a) ITEM **where** (. < 1) DEPT **in** SUPPLY
b) ITEM **where** (. > .5) COMP **in** SUPPLY
c) ITEM **where** (# ≥ 2) COMP, (. > .5) DEPT **in** SUPPLY
d) ITEM **where** (# ≥ 2 **and** . < .75) COMP **in** SUPPLY.

4.1-5

a) COMP **in** ((SUPPLY **ijoin where** FLOOR = 2 **in** LOC) **sup** (**where** TYPE = A **in** CLASS))
b) COMP **where** (# = 0) ITEM, ITEM = 'Ball' **in** SUPPLY
c) DEPT **where** (# = 0) ITEM, TYPE = 'B' **in** (SALES **ijoin** CLASS)

d)   Let DEPT1 be DEPT; FLOOR1 be FLOOR; ITEM1 be ITEM
let COUNT be equiv max of (par + of 1 order ITEM by FLOOR) by
FLOOR
DEPT where (# = COUNT) ITEM1, ITEM = ITEM1 in ((SALES
ijoin LOC) ijoin
((ITEM1, DEPT1 in SUPPLY) ijoin (DEPT1, FLOOR in LOC)))

4.1-6

a)   SNO in SHIPMENT ijoin (where PRICE > 25 in PART)
b)   SNAME in SUPPLIER ijoin (SHIPMENT ⊇ PNO where COLOR =
'Red and PRICE > 25 in PART)

4.1-7

a)   let MPNO be red max of PNO
PNO where PNO = MPNO in (where PRICE > 25 in PART)
b)   let MNPO be red max of PNO
SNO in SHIPMENT ijoin (PNO where PNO = MPNO in (where
JLOC = 'New York' in PROJECT))

4.1-8

a)   R2 icomp R3
b)   R1 ijoin (R2 icomp R3)

4.1-9

a)   let EMPCT be equiv + of 1 by DEPARTMENT
(DEPARTMENT where DIVISION = 'Marketing' in DEPT) ijoin
(DEPARTMENT, EMPCT in EMP)
b)   let SALSUM be equiv + of SALARY by DEPARTMENT
let SALAVG be (equiv + of SALSUM by DIVISION)/(equiv + of 1
by DIVISION)
DIVISION, SALAVG in (DEPT ijoin (DEPARTMENT, SALSUM in
EMP))

Answers

Answers for Exercises in Sections 4.4-4 and 4.4-5, Chapter 4.1.

4.4-4

Any two-dimensional projection of the progress space must be serializable. That is, the path of the transactions must lie outside the envelope containing all potential conflicts. This envelope is contained in a hyper-rectangle which parallels the axes of the program space. Up to the point where the first potential conflict for every transaction has been passed, the envelope coincides with this hyper-rectangle.

4.4-7

See Shakespeare [1589].

4.4-8

a)   [Scheuler, 1977] An Aton Update: this is a massive compensating transaction. It might also be called a 1984 Update in view of the tendency to rewrite history described in Orwell's novel.

b)   [Gray, 1981] A log, unfortunately susceptible to hard crash. The bird was a catastrophe.

c)   A Daniel Update, Type I. This is an addition, a writing where no writing was before. It brings no danger. A Daniel Update, Type II, is a write to protected storage, as attempted by the lions' den. Daniel Updates are the only safe kind.

Answers

Answers for Exercises in Sections 5.1-1 and 5.1-2, Chapter 5.1.

5.1-2

The answer is not unique and space limits details here, but one solution, using the following lists of raw materials and operations, has a BOM of 30 assemblies and subassemblies (35 tuples) and a routing of 25 tuples.

PARTS LIST		OPERATIONS
$1\frac{1}{2}''$ Dowel (Boiler, Small Wheels)	#16 Wire (Axles)	Assembling (Wheels)
3/4″ Dowel (Funnel, Small Wheels)	#18 Rivet, 3″	Gluing
1/2″ × 2″ (Burner)	Glue	Lathing (Funnel)
$1\frac{1}{2}''$ × 2″ (Cab)	String	Shearing (Wire)
2 × 2 Nominal (Block)	Staple	Cutting (Wood)
3/4″ × 2″ Moulding (Roofs)	Black Paint	Riveting (Funnel)
1 × 2 Nominal (Cabin)	Red Paint	Snipping (String)
	Yellow Paint	Stapling
		Knotting
		Painting

(See page 434 for Answer 5.1-3.)

5.1-4

```
<<LABCOST>>
let LAB$ be equiv + of WAGE × HOURS by ASSEMBLY
LABCOST ← ASSEMBLY, LAB$ in (ROUTING ijoin TEAMS ijoin
          SALARY)
```

5.1-3

TIMECARD	(DATE	EMP	ASSEMBLY	EQUIP	JOB	HOURS)
	1984/3/12	Andrea Porter	Car	Gluset	Glue Car	5
	1984/3/12	Andrea Porter	Caboose	Gluset	Glue Caboose	1
	1984/3/12	Andrea Porter	Body	Gluset	Glue Base	2
	1984/3/13	Andrea Porter	Car	Gluset	Glue Car	4
	1984/3/13	Andrea Porter	Caboose	Gluset	Glue Caboose	3
	1984/3/13	Andrea Porter	Body	Gluset	Glue Base	1
. .	. .	. .	. .	. .	. .	. .

Split into teams on basis of job and credit each team with the maximum of total hours worked for each employee.

<<EQUIPCOST>>
let PROPOR **be** HOURS/(**equiv** + **of** HOURS **by** EQUIP)
let DEPR **be** (EQCOST − SALVAGE)/LIFE
let EQUIP$ **be equiv** + **of** DEPR × PROPOR **by** ASSEMBLY
EQUIPCOST ← ASSEMBLY, EQUIP$ **in** ((EQUIP, DEPR **in** FIXED
ASSETS) **ijoin** (EQUIP, ASSEMBLY, TEAM,
PROPOR **in** ROUTING))

Note that DEPR should be evaluated on FIXED ASSETS only and PROPOR must be evaluated on ROUTING only.

5.1-5

let LABPRICE **be** LAB$/QTY; EQUIPPRICE **be** EQUIP$/QTY
let PART **be** ASSEMBLY
BASICCOSTS ← RMCOST **ujoin** (PART, LABPRICE, EQUIPPRICE
in (PRODUCTION **ijoin** (LABCOST **ujoin** EQUIPCOST)))

5.1-7

let QTY1 **be** 1
CONSTITUENTS ←+ CONSTITUENTS [ASSEMBLY, SUBAS-
SEMBLY, QTY **ujoin** ASSEMBLY, ASSEMBLY,
QTY1] (ASSEMBLY, ASSEMBLY, QTY1 **in** CON-
STITUENTS)
let FGCOST **be equiv** + **of** QTY × (RMPRICE + LABPRICE +
EQUIPPRICE) **by** ASSEMBLY
FINALCOSTS ← ASSEMBLY, FGCOST **in** (CONSTITUENTS
[SUBASSEMBLY **ijoin** PART] BASICCOSTS)

Note that we must add to CONSTITUENTS the information that each assembly contains itself once or else the labor and equipment cost of the last stage of production will not be included in the calculation.
FINAL COSTS derived here will contain, in addition to the four tuples shown in the text, the information that a BODY costs $6.52, a BIG costs 7¢, a SMALL costs 5¢ and a BASE costs $1.82.

5.1-8

Replace the derivation of FGCOST:
let RMCOST **be equiv** + **of** QTY × RMPRICE **by** ASSEMBLY
let LABCOST **be equiv** + **of** QTY × LABPRICE **by** ASSEMBLY
let EQCOST **be equiv** + **of** QTY × EQUIPPRICE **by** ASSEMBLY
let FGCOST **be** RMCOST + LABCOST + EQCOST

Include the three new attributes in FINALCOSTS.

5.1-9

let PPROFIT **be** FGPRICE − FGCOST
PARTPROFIT ← ASSEMBLY, PPROFIT **in** (FINALCOSTS **ijoin**
PRICE)

5.1-10

let FGPRICE be $(1.0 + PR\% / 100.0) \times$ FGCOST
PRICE ← ASSEMBLY, FGPRICE in (FINALCOSTS ijoin
    PROFIT%)

5.1-11

<<ORDERANAL>>
let OSALES be equiv + of FGPRICE × QTY by ORD#
let OPROFIT be equiv + of PPROFIT × QTY by ORD#
let OPS% be 100 × OPROFIT / OSALES
ORDERANAL ← ORD#, OSALES, OPROFIT, OPS% in (PRICE
        ijoin PARTPROFIT ijoin ORDLINE)

<<CUSTANAL>>
let CSALES be equiv + of OSALES by CUSTOMER
let CPROFIT be equiv + of OPROFIT by CUSTOMER
let CPS% be 100 × CPROFIT / CSALES
CUSTANAL ← CUSTOMER, CSALES, CPROFIT, CPS% in
        (ORDERANAL ijoin ORDERS)

<<SALESANAL>>
let SSALES be equiv + of OSALES by SALESMAN
let SPROFIT be equiv + of OPROFIT by SALESMAN
let SPS% be 100 × SPROFIT / SSALES
SALESANAL ← SALESMAN, SSALES, SPROFIT, SPS% in
        (ORDERANAL ijoin SALESMAN)

5.1-12

Use relation RETURN (ORD#, ASSEMBLY, RQTY) and substitute NET-
LINE for ORDLINE:

let NQTY be QTY − RQTY
NETLINE ← ORD#, ASSEMBLY, NQTY in (ORDLINE ijoin
        RETURN)

5.1-13

Statements: 10 (relational algebra) + 17 (domain algebra) + 18 (relational
            declarations) + 32 (attribute declarations) = 77, or two
            pages of code.

Answers

Answers for Exercises in Sections 5.2-1 and 5.2-2, Chapter 5.2.

5.2-1

The transitive closure of PERT [SEVENT, FEVENT] will contain an edge for each possible path of PERT: parallel paths will be represented by only one edge, however. The duration associated with an edge of the closure must be the duration of the set of parallel paths. That is, the value of DURATION is added to other values along a path of connected edges and the maximum value is taken when paths meet.

5.2-3

PATHS ← **closure** PERT (SEVENT, FEVENT, + **of** DURATION **meet max**)

5.2-4

A	0	1	1	1	0
B	0	0	1	0	0
L	0	0	0	0	0
S	0	0	1	0	0
W	0	1	1	0	0

5.2-5

for i ← 2 **to** n **do for** j ← 1 **to** i−1 **do if** g(i,j) = 1 **then**
        for k ← 1 **to** n **do** g(i,k) ← g(i,k) **or** g(j,k)
for i ← 1 **to** n−1 **do for** j ← i+1 **to** n **do if** g(i,j) = 1 **then**
        for k ← 1 **to** n **do** g(i,k) ← g(i,k) **or** g(j,k)

5.2-6

L	0	0	0	0	0
B	1	0	0	0	0
S	1	0	0	0	0
W	0	1	0	0	0
A	0	1	1	0	0

(See Page 439 for Answer 5.2-7.)

5.2-8

They never arise because each node in T_i terminates a path of length $< 2^i$ and each path of length $< 2^i$ is terminated by some node in T_i. Thus if "$P_i{}^s$ is low" then T_i has a matching value, i.e., "$P_i{}^s = T_i$ and low". Also "$P_i{}^f = T_i$ and low" implies a contradiction, since "$P_i{}^f$ is low" $=> P_i{}^f$ [FINISH] terminates a path of length 2^i, while "T_i is low" $=> T_i$ [NODE] terminates a path of length $< 2^i$. The remaining case is the three-way match, which is eliminated by the last argument.

It also follows from this reasoning that the loop in Algorithm T can be terminated as soon as $P_i{}^s$ is exhausted.

5.2-9

Exhibit 5.2-2 shows the result: row and column labels have the same alphabetical ordering as the assemblies, subassemblies and parts of Exhibit 5.1-2.

5.2-10

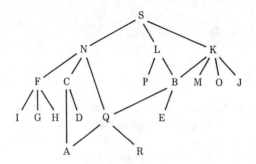

5.2-7

P_0^f	P_0^s	T_1^+	P_1	T_1	P_1^f	P_1^s	T_2^+	P_2	T_2	$P_0^f * T_2$
B A 1	B A	L 0	L A	B 1	L A	L A	A 2	ϕ	A 2	B A 1 2
S A 1	B W	B 1	L W	L 0	L W	L W	W 2		B 1	S A 1 2
L B 2	L B	S 1	L A	S 1					L 0	L B 2 1
L S 1	L S								S 1	L S 1 1
B W 2	S A								W 2	B W 2 2

T_2 is the topologically ordered set of nodes; $P_0^f * T_2$ is the topologically ordered set of original tuples

5.2-11

{(K,B), (L,B), (S,B), (N,C), (S,C), (N,F), (S,F), (K,J), (S,J), (K,M), (S,M), (K,O), (S,O), (L,P), (N,P), (S,P)}. {(B,E), (B,Q), (C,D), (F,G), (F,H), (F,I)} = {(K,E), (K,Q), (L,E), (L,Q), (S,E), (S,Q), (N,D), (S,D), (N,G), (N,H), (N,I), (S,G), (S,H), (S,I)}.

5.2-12

Step 3 is executed for $\ell = 2,3,4$. The successive outputs are shown opposite, in the form OUP (START, FINISH, Q).

5.2-13

Matrix multiplication of the submatrices incorporates both the natural composition required for the transitive closure and the quantitative component $\times$ of QTY meet $+$.

5.2-14

In step 3.1 replace $\times$ by $+$ in $Q \leftarrow$ (Q from OUP) $\times$ (Q from INP_ℓ). In steps 3.2, 3.4 replace "sum" by "maximum" in "... whose Q value is the sum of the Qs from all tuples ..."

5.2-16

R_{rc} is the duration of the activity starting at event r and finishing at event c.

For each row, r, from the first to the last
    For each c, $T_c \leftarrow T_c$ **max** $(T_c + R_{rc})$

ℓ = 1

S K 1		
S L 3		
S N 1		

ℓ = 2

K B 1	
L B 1	
S B 4	
N C 2	
S C 2	
N F 1	
S F 1	
K J 1	
S J 1	
S K 1	
S L 3	
K M 1	
S M 1	
S N 1	
K O 1	
S O 1	
L P 1	
S P 3	

ℓ = 3

K B 1	F I 1
L B 1	N I 1
S B 4	S I 1
N C 2	K J 1
S C 2	S J 1
C D 2	S K 1
N D 4	S L 3
S D 4	K M 1
B E 1	S M 1
K E 1	S N 1
L E 1	K O 1
S E 4	S O 1
N F 1	L P 1
S F 1	S P 3
F G 1	B Q 2
N G 1	K Q 2
S G 1	L Q 2
F H 1	N Q 1
N H 1	S Q 9
S H 1	

ℓ = 4

B A 2	S E 4	S N 1
C A 1	N F 1	K O 1
K A 2	S F 1	S O 1
L A 2	F G 1	L P 1
N A 3	N G 1	S P 3
Q A 1	S G 1	B Q 2
S A 1	F H 1	K Q 2
K B 1	N H 1	L Q 2
L B 1	S H 1	N Q 1
S B 4	F I 1	S Q 9
N C 2	N I 1	B R 4
S C 2	S I 1	K R 4
C D 2	K J 1	L R 4
N D 4	S J 1	N R 2
S D 4	S K 1	Q R 2
B E 1	S L 3	S R 18
K E 1	K M 1	
L E 1	S M 1	

Answers

Answers for Exercises in Sections 5.3-1 and 5.3-2, Chapter 5.3.

5.3-1

Using the node abbreviations of Chapter 5.2, the input (C,A), (Q,A), (K,B), (L,B), (N,C), (C,D), (B,E), (N,F), (F,G), (F,H), (F,I), (K,J), (S,K), (S,L), (K,M), (S,N), (K,O), (L,P), (B,Q), (N,Q), (Q,R), gives

COUNT	2	2	1	1	1	1	1	1	1	1	1	1	1	1	1	1	2	1	0
HEAD	A	B	C	D	E	F	G	H	I	J	K	L	M	N	O	P	Q	R	S
SUCCS		E	A			G					B	B		C				A	K
		Q	D			H					J	P		F				R	L
						I					M			Q					N
											O								

5.3-2

$\phi = |E|/|I| = 21/8$ from the definition in the Appendix; h follows from Equation 5.3-2.

5.3-3

h = 7.65, 14.8 and 22.0.

5.3-4

$\phi = 7.03$, 45.7 and 306.

5.3-5

$$P_\ell = |E| - t\sum_{i=1}^{\ell-1} \phi^i = |V| - t(\phi^\ell - 1)/(\phi - 1) \text{ since } |E| = |V| - t. \text{ For an}$$

"almost forest", replace $|V|$ by $|E| + t$.

5.3-6

ℓ	1	2	3	4
P_ℓ	21	18.4	11.5	-6.6 i.e., 0
true # of paths	21	20	13	2

5.3-7

$|E| = 10^3$ l o j w l ʦ

i	0	1	2	4
X_i	1000	997.4	972.4	0
Y_i		3.63	25.0	876
Z_i		3.63	28.6	905

$|E| = 10^6$ records

i	0	1	2	4	8
X_i	10^6	10^6	10^6	9.99×10^5	0
Y_i		3.63	25.0	1358	9.03×10^5
Z_i		3.63	28.6	1386	9.05×10^5

$|E| = 10^9$ records

i	0	1	2	4	8	16
X_i	10^9	10^9	10^9	10^9	9.97×10^8	0
Y_i		3.63	25.0	1358	3.13×10^6	9.02×10^8
Z_i		3.63	28.6	1386	3.13×10^6	9.05×10^8

5.3-8

$|E| = 10^3$ records

i	0	1	2	4
X_i	1000	993.0	596.3	0
Y_i		8.03	396.7	500.0
Z_i		8.03	404.7	904.8

$|E| = 10^6$ records

i	0	1	2	4
X_i	10^6	10^6	9.03×10^5	0
Y_i		46.7	9.75×10^4	8.07×10^5
Z_i		46.7	9.75×10^4	9.05×10^5

$|E| = 10^9$ records

i	0	1	2	4
X_i	10^9	10^9	9.71×10^8	0
Y_i		307.3	2.88×10^7	8.76×10^8
Z_i		307.3	2.88×10^7	9.05×10^8

5.3-10

Inspecting Exhibit 5.3-3b and generalizing from 3 to ϕ shows that the "triangle" of ϕs is made up of rectangular blocks of sizes $\phi \times 1$, $\phi \times (1 + \phi)$, ..., $\phi \times (1 + (h - 2)\phi)$, summing to $(n - \phi - 1)(n - 2\phi + 1)/2$. The total number of new edges added is ϕ times this or 1 plus an overlap of $\phi - 1$ times it.

5.3-11

$$0 = \frac{d}{d\phi} (\phi-1)(n-\phi-1)(n-2\phi+1)/2 = 3\phi^2 - (3n+1)\phi + (n^2+3n-2)/2,$$

so $\phi \simeq .21n$.

5.3-12

The graph which is already the transitive closure of a path of length $n-1$

requires $\sum_{i=1}^{n} (i-1)(n-i) = 0(n^3)$ overlaps in finding closure (which of course

turns out to be itself.)

5.3-14

SALESMAN and CUSTOMER nodes are roots and so have participation 1. ORDER nodes each have one SALESMAN and one CUSTOMER as predecessor and so have participation 2. BOM nodes are more complicated: part(S) = 6, part(N) = 16, part(L) = 10, part(K) = 10, etc. Eventually we reach the leaf nodes RMPRICE (Σ part = 222), FGPRICE (Σ part = 58), QTY and hours (Σ part = 100 each), WAGE, EQ COST, SALVAGE and LIFE (Σ part = 132 each).

Answers

Answers for Exercises in Section 6.1-2, Chapter 6.1

6.1-2

in SPREAD			in SPREAD	
ACCTDB	TOTIN		ACCTCR	TOTOUT
A	2.73		A	2.33
C	3.99		C	9.57
E	3.28		E	3.64
G	2.33		F	0.22
M	1.01		G	3.19
P	7.70		M	1.30
R	5.40		P	3.12
T	1.87		R	3.99
			T	0.95

FUNDFLOW

(ACCT	ADESCR	ACTYPE	FF)
A	Goods in assembly	Asset	0.40
C	Cash	Asset	−5.58
E	Stockholders'	Equity	0.36
F	Fixed Assets	Asset	−0.22
G	Finished Goods	Asset	−0.86
M	Raw materials	Asset	−0.29
P	Accounts payable	Liability	−4.58
R	Accounts receivable	Asset	1.41
T	Taxes payable	Liability	−0.92

6.1-3

let SUAMT **be** abs (FF)
let SU **be** if ACTYPE = 'Asset' **and** FF ≤ 0
      or ACTYPE ≠ 'Asset' **and** FF > 0 **then** 'Source' **else** 'Use'
SORUSE ← ACCT, ADESCR, SUAMT, SU **in** FUNDFLOW

6.1-4

let TODAY be 1984/3/30; NEWBAL be BAL + FF
BALANCE ←+ TODAY, ACCT, NEWBAL in
    ((where DATE = 1984/2/29 in BALANCE)[ACCT ujoin ACCT]
    FUNDFLOW)

6.1-5

REVENUE ← (ACCTDB, AMOUNT where ACCTCR='E' and
            PEREND > 1984/3/0 in SPREAD)
            ijoin (where ACCTCR = 'E' in TRANS)
EXPENSE ← (ACCTCR, AMOUNT where ACCTDB='E' and
            PEREND > 1984/3/0 in SPREAD)
            ijoin (where ACCTDB = 'E' in TRANS)
let REV be 'Revenue'; EXP be 'Expense'
let PL be if FF ≥ 0 then 'Profit' else 'Loss'
let PLDESCR be 'Net'||PL||'after tax'
<<|| means concatenate strings>>
let PLAMT be abs (FF)
INCOME ←(REVENUE[ACCTDB,TDESCR,AMOUNT,REV ujoin
        ACCTCR,TDESCR,AMOUNT,EXP]EXPENSE)
        [ACCTCR,TDESCR,AMOUNT,EXP ujoin
        ACCT, PLDESCR,PLAMT,PL]
        (ACCT,PLDESCR,PLAMT,PL where ACCT = 'E' in
        FUNDFLOW)

6.1-6

let THISAMT be if PEREND = 1984/3/30 then AMOUNT else 0
let TOTIN be equiv + of THISAMT by ACCTDB
let TOTOUT be equiv + of THISAMT by ACCTCR
let FF be if ACTYPE='Asset' then TOTIN-TOTOUT else TOTOUT−
    TOTIN
let LASTAMT be if PEREND = 1984/2/29 then AMOUNT else 0
let LASTIN be equiv + of LASTAMT by ACCTDB
let LASTOUT be equiv + of LASTAMT by ACCTCR
let LASTFF be if ACTYPE='Asset' then LASTIN − LASTOUT else
    LASTOUT − LASTIN
let YAGOAMT be if PEREND = 1983/3/31 then AMOUNT else 0
let YAGOIN be equiv + of YAGOAMT by ACCTDB
let YAGOUT be equiv + of YAGOAMT by ACCTCR
let YAGOFF be if ACTYPE='Asset' then YAGOIN − YAGOUT else

YAGOUT − YAGOIN
let YTDAMT **be if** PEREND ≥ 1984/1/31 **then** AMOUNT **else** 0
let YTDIN **be equiv** + **of** YTDAMT **by** ACCTDB
let YTDOUT **be equiv** + **of** YTDAMT **by** ACCTCR
let YTDFF **be if** ACTYPE='Asset' **then** YTDIN − YTDOUT **else**
    YTDOUT − YTDIN
FUNDFLOW ← ACCT,ADESCR,ACTYPE,FF,LASTFF,YAGOFF,
YTDFF **in** (TYPE[ACCT **ijoin** ACCTCR])
((ACCTDB,TOTIN,LASTIN,YAGOIN,YTDIN **in** SPREAD)
    [ACCTDB **ujoin** ACCTCR])
(ACCTCR,TOTOUT,LASTOUT,YAGOUT,YTDOUT **in** SPREAD))

6.1-7

let TODAY **be** 1984/3/30; NEWBAL **be** BAL + FF
let BALAS **be if** ACTYPE = 'Asset' **then** NEWBAL **else** 0
let PERAS **be** NEWBAL × 100/(**red** + **of** BALAS)
BALANCE ↤ TODAY,ACCT,NEWBAL,PERAS **in** ((**where**
DATE=1984/2/29 **in** BALANCE) **ujoin** FUNDFLOW)

6.1-8

let TODAY **be** 1984/3/30; ACCTC **be** 'F'; ACCTD **be** 'E'
let SUM **be red** + **of** ((EQCOST − SALVAGE)/LIFE)
SPREAD ↤ TODAY,ACCTC,ACCTD, SUM **in** FIXED ASSETS

6.1-9

let TODAY **be** 1984/3/30; ACCTC **be** 'E'; ACCTD **be** 'R'
let QSUM **be equiv** + **of** QTY **by** ASSEMBLY
let SUM **be red** + **of** QSUM × PPROFIT
SPREAD ↤ TODAY,ACCTC,ACCTD,SUM **in** ((ASSEMBLY,
QSUM **where** 1984/2/29 < DATE **and** DATE ≤ TODAY **in**
SHIPLINE) **ijoin** PARTPROFIT)

6.1-10

let TODAY **be** 1984/3/30; ACCTC **be** 'E'; ACCTD **be** 'A'
let QSUM **be equiv** + **of** QTY **by** ASSEMBLY
let SUM **be red** + **of** QSUM × (LABCOST + EQCOST)
SPREAD ↤ TODAY,ACCTC,ACCTD, SUM **in** ((ASSEMBLY,
QSUM **where** 1984/2/29 < DATE **and** DATE ≤ TODAY **in**
PRODUCTION) **ijoin** FINAL COSTS)

Answers

Answers for Exercises in Sections 6.2-1 and 6.2-2, Chapter 6.2.

6.2-1

$b = 4$, $f_1 = 2$, $f_2 = 2$. Boundaries can be either of the candidate boundaries given in the text for each axis. Total overflows $= 0$. (Remember that each segment contains two blocks so $b = 4$ implies a segment size of 8. Thus the vertical axis, too, has no overflows for either boundary choice. However, just considering the axis distributions, as in the example in the text, is not enough to minimize the overflows in this case where *both* axes are segmented. We must do an exhaustive search over the four possible partitions $\begin{matrix} 3 & 5 \\ 3 & 2 \end{matrix}$, $\begin{matrix} 2 & 4 \\ 4 & 3 \end{matrix}$, $\begin{matrix} 4 & 4 \\ 3 & 2 \end{matrix}$ and $\begin{matrix} 3 & 3 \\ 4 & 3 \end{matrix}$.

These all, however, give the same result: no overflows. (Note that in general, exhaustive searches are (exponentially) expensive and that the data to do them is not usually available.)

6.2-2

$\lfloor 256/12 \rfloor = 21$ tuples/block; $\lceil 14445 \text{ tuples}/21 \rceil = 688$ blocks; $\lfloor \sqrt{688} \rfloor = 26$, $\lceil \sqrt{688} \rceil = 27$; therefore 26 segments along one axis, 27 along the other, giving 702 blocks and a load factor $\alpha = 14445/(702 \times 21) = .98$. This does not attempt to minimize overflows, which requires knowledge of the tuple distribution and will presumably reduce α. Note that each segment will hold transactions for $(10^4/26) = 385$ or $(10^4/27) = 370$ accounts on the average.

6.2-4

1024, since $\lfloor 2048/12 \rfloor = 170$; $\lceil 14445/170 \rceil = 85$; $\lfloor \sqrt{85} \rfloor = 9$, $\lceil \sqrt{85} \rceil = 10$; $10^4/9 > 1000$.

6.2-5

This suggestion is preferable to using the post-file discussed in the text in terms of simplicity. It is as good for doing equivalence reductions on the latest version. It costs more in storage since pointers are not used and gives slower response to queries about earlier versions (see next subsection on the differential ante-file). The method in the text *does not update the main or post-files*.

6.2-6

The problem concerns turning off the on-bits in the filter: since a bit does not determine a transaction (only the converse is true), removing the transaction from the differential file does not entitle us to turn off the bit in the filter. One possibility is to multipage the Bloom filter on CHRONOL (which is not stored explicitly in the filter) so that a block or subfilter, is stored for each portion of the file. A whole portion is discarded when it becomes old enough, and so is the corresponding subfilter.

6.2-7

The implementation with no post-file never needs reorganizing. However, each update can potentially lock the spread and all its history against any other concurrent processing. The method of the text never locks more than the differential post-file.

6.2-8

A simple setup is to make the differential post-file just the anti-ante-file of Exhibit 6.2-6, with an additional entry (e.g., G, A, 2.50, . . .) for the original appearance of the transaction and the convention that a ''change'' to a non-existent transaction (i.e., one with no matching key in the main file) creates the transaction. This is not quite symmetric because transactions are never deleted and the main file always grows. More elaborately, we could cut off the main file before a certain date—say a year ago—and dump all its data to the ante-file. Then the ''deletions'' of transactions—i.e., their removal from the main file to the ante-file—would appear, inverted, as additions on the ante-file and be represented by the same convention as additions on the post-file, above. This symmetrical approach does not give such rapid trial balance or historical comparison calculations as the method of the text.

Answers

Answers for Exercises in Sections 6.3-1 and 6.3-2, Chapter 6.3.

6.3-1

We may assume that the procedures in the text create FUNDFLOW, REVENUE and EXPENSE sorted by account, their key. We can further assume that FUNDFLOW has an index enabling us to find the changes in equity accounts without scanning all of FUNDFLOW. The code to produce INCOME (see Exercise 6.1-5) simply merges REVENUE, EXPENSE and the profit/loss (from the change in equities) from FUNDFLOW. So one pass of REVENUE, EXPENSE and INCOME and a few accesses at most to FUNDFLOW suffice.

6.3-2

By debit.   a-e non-equities: $n'[1-(1-1/n')\uparrow r'] \simeq r' = 10/8$
            e equities: $n''[1-(1-1/n'')\uparrow r''] \simeq n'' = 3 \times 702/13 = 162$
            Mean no. accesses *per account* = $((a-e)10/8 + 162e)/a$.

By credit. a-e non-equities: $n'[1-(1-1/n')\uparrow r'] \simeq r' = 11/8$
            e equities: $n''[1-(1-1/n'')\uparrow r''] \simeq n'' = 2 \times 702/13 = 108$
            Mean no. accesses *per account* = $((a-e)11/8 + 108e)/a$

If $e=a/9$ and $a=10^4$, this gives $(19.1 + 13.2) \times 10^4 = 3.2 \times 10^5$ accesses for the equivalence reductions.

6.3-3

FUNDFLOW. For each equivalence reduction, the surface of SPREAD must be sorted. For 10,000 accounts, this is a file of 702 256-byte pages or 1.8×10^5 bytes, which is at the small end of the range discussed in Section 1.3-5 on sorting analysis: say two or three passes on a minicomputer. Once this is done, assuming TYPE is already sorted on account, the rest of the process is as described in Section 6.3-1. Thus two or three additional passes of the surface of SPREAD are needed beyond the processing for multipaged files.

REVENUE and EXPENSE. A small sort is needed after selecting transactions debiting (or crediting) equities so that the join can be implemented by merging. The files are 2.8×10^4 and 4.1×10^4 bytes for 10,000-account example, so sorting involves negligible additional file accesses.

Bibliography

This bibliography contains a selection of research papers and a few books referred to mainly in the "Advanced Topics" chapters of each part of the book. In choosing papers for inclusion I have sought relevance to the theme of this book, namely state-of-the-art contributions that are readily applicable to relational information systems, and classical works that give insight into the history of the field. Where possible, for series of related papers by an author, I have selected seminal publications and descriptions of the latest work, rather than list all papers in the middle of the series. I have tried to cite papers that are readily accessible, rather than technical reports and the like, which are not. This is not always possible and occasionally this list contains related works by an author which are more accessible even though they have not been cited in the text.

For many papers, abbreviations have been used for the sources. These are expanded below, together with indications of where to obtain the publications. Appearance here does not guarantee that the sources are still available.

An extensive bibliography on database research has been compiled by Kambayashi [1981]. Wiederhold [1977] also lists more than 1,000 references.

ACM (Association for Computing Machinery; 11 West 42nd St., New York, N.Y. 10036):

    CACM (Communications of the ACM)

    Comp. Surv. (ACM Computing Surveys)

    JACM (Journal of the ACM)

Pacific 75: Data: Its Use, Organization and Management (San Francisco, 17-18 April, 1975). (Mail Room, Boole and Babbage, Inc., 850 Stewart Dr., Sunnyvale, CA 94086)

SIGMOD (Special Interest Group on Management of Data; formerly SICFIDET, SIGFIDET.):

SIGMOD Record (formerly FDT)

ACM SIGMOD International Conference on Management of Data (so called from 1975 on):

SICFIDET 70: Record of the 1970 ACM SICFIDET Workshop on Data Description and Access, (Houston, 15-16 Nov., 1970)

SIGFIDET 71: Proc. of 1971 ACM-SIGFIDET Workshop Data Description, Access and Control, E.F. Codd & A.L. Dean, *eds.* (San Diego, 11-12 Nov. 1971).

SIGFIDET 72: Proc. of 1972 ACM-SIGFIDET Workshop Data Description, Access and Control, A.L. Dean *ed.* (Denver, 29 Nov.-1 Dec., 1972).

SIGMOD 74: ACM SIGMOD Workshop on Data Description, Access and Control, R. Rustin *ed.* (Ann Arbor, 1-3 May, 1974) (Proceedings and Supplement in separate volumes.)

SIGMOD 75: W.F. King *ed.* (San Jose, 14-16 May, 1975).

SIGMOD 76: J.B. Rothnie *ed.* (Washington, 2-4 June, 1976).

SIGMOD 77: D.C.P. Smith *ed.* (Toronto, 3-5 Aug., 1977).

SIGMOD 78: E. Lowenthal & N.B. Dale *eds.* (Austin, 31 May-2 June, 1978).

SIGMOD 79: P.A. Bernstein *ed.* (Boston, 30 May-1 June, 1979).

SIGMOD 80: P.P. Chen & R.C. Sprowls *eds.* (Santa Monica, 14-16 May, 1980).

SIGMOD 81: Y.E. Lien *ed.* (Ann Arbor, 29 April-1 May, 1981).

SIGMOD 82: M. Schkolnick *ed.* (Orlando, 2-4 June, 1982).

PODS (Proceedings of the ACM Symposium on Principles of Database Systems).

PODS 82: (Los Angeles, 29-31 March, 1982).

TODS (ACM Transactions on Database Systems.)

CACM (see ACM)

Comp. Surv. (see ACM)

CSRG (Computer Systems Research Group, University of Toronto, Toronto, Ontario, Canada M5S 1A1)

ERL (Electronics Research Laboratory, College of Engineering, University of California, Berkeley)

FDT (see ACM)

IBM J. Res. & Devel. (IBM Journal of Research and Development)

IBM Syst. J. (IBM Systems Journal)

ICMOD: International Conference on Data Base Management Systems (Milano, 29-30 June, 1978)

IFIP (International Federation for Information Processing)

> IFIP 74: Information Processing 74, Proceedings of IFIP Congress 74, J.L. Rosenfeld *ed.* (Stockholm, 5-10 Aug., 1974)

> IFIP 77: Information Processing 77, Proceedings of IFIP Congress 77, B. Gilchrist *ed.* (Toronto, 8-12 Aug., 1977)

> IFIP TC-2 (IFIP Technical Committee 2, Programming):

>> Nijssen 76: Modelling in Data Base Management Systems, G.M. Nijssen *ed.* (Freudenstadt, 5-8 Jan., 1976). North Holland Publishing Co., Amsterdam

>> Nijssen 77: Architecture and Models in Data Base Management Systems, G.M. Nijssen *ed.* (Nice, 3-7 Jan., 1977) North Holland Publishing Co., Amsterdam.

Info. Proc. Lett. (Information Processing Letters, North Holland Publishing Co., Amsterdam)

INFOR (Canadian Journal of Operational Research and Information Processing. Canadian Operational Research Society; Canadian Information Processing Society)

Info. Syst. (Information Systems, Pergamon Press, Oxford)

JACM (see ACM)

J. Comptr. Syst. Sci. (Journal of Computer and System Science, Academic Press, New York)

NCC (National Computer Conference)

Nijssen 76, Nijssen 77 (see IFIP)

N.T.I.S. (National Technical Information Service, U.S. Dept. of Commerce, Springfield, VA)

Pacific 75 (see ACM)

Scheuermann: Improving Database Usability and Responsiveness, P. Scheuermann *ed.* (Jerusalem, 22-4 June, 1982) Academic Press, New York.

Shneiderman: Databases: Improving Usability and Responsiveness, B. Shneiderman *ed.* (Haifa, 2-4 Aug., 1978) Academic Press, New York.

SIGMOD, SIGFIDET, SICFIDET (see ACM)

SOCS (School of Computer Science, McGill University, 805 Sherbrooke St. W., Montréal, Québec, Canada, H3A 2K6)

VLDB (International Conference on Very Large Databases, Proceedings available from IEEE Computer Society, P.O. Box 80452, Worldway Postal Center, Los Angeles, CA 90080 from VLDB3 to VLDB7.)

VLDB1: D.S. Kerr *ed.* (Framingham, Mass., 22-24 Sept., 1975)

VLDB2: Systems for Large Data Bases, P.C. Lockemann & E.J. Neuhold *eds.* (Brussels, 8-10 Sept. 1976).

VLDB3: A.G. Merten *ed.* (Tokyo, 6-8 Oct., 1977)

VLDB4: S.B. Yao *ed.* (West-Berlin, 13-15 Sept. 1978)

VLDB5: A.L. Furtado & H.L. Morgan *eds.* (Rio de Janeiro, 3-5 Oct., 1979)

VLDB6: F.H. Lochovsky & R.W. Taylor *eds.* (Montréal, 1-3 Oct., 1980).

VLDB7: C. Zaniolo & C. Delobel *eds.* (Cannes, 9-11 Sept., 1981)

UKSC (U.K. Scientific Centre, IBM (U.K.) Ltd., Neville Rd., Peterlee, County Durham, U.K.)

Utah 76: Proceedings of Conference on Data: Abstraction, Definition and Structure (Salt Lake City, 22-4 March, 1976). FDT *8* 2; SIGPLAN Notices *11* (1976 Special Issue).

A

J.R. Abrial, 1974. "Data semantics" *in* J.W. Klimbie & K.L. Koffeman *eds.*, **Data Base Management.** (Corsica, 1-5 April, 1974) North Holland Publishing Co., Amsterdam.

M. Adiba & C. Delobel, 1976. **Les Modèles Relationnels de Bases de Données,** IRIA, April, 1976. (Now INRIA, Institute Nationale de Recherche d'Informatique et d'Automatique, Le Chesnay, France).

A.V. Aho, J.E. Hopcroft & J.D. Ullman, 1974. **The Design and Analysis of Computer Algorithms,** Addison-Wesley Publishing Co., Reading, MA.

T. Amble, K. Bratbergsengen & O. Risnes, 1979. "ASTRAL—a structured and unified approach to database design and manipulation" *in* G. Bracchi & G.M. Nijssen *eds.* **IFIP TC-2 Working Conference on Data Base Architecture** (Venice, 26-9 June, 1979) 240-57.

ANSI, 1975. "Interim report of the ANSI/X3/SPARC Study Group on Data Base Management Systems." **FDT** *7* 2 (1975) 3-139.

W.W. Armstrong, 1974. "Dependency structures of database relationships. **IFIP 74,** 580-3.

W.W. Armstrong & C. Delobel, 1977. "Decompositions and functional dependencies in relations." **TODS** *5* 4 (Dec., 1980) 404-30.

W. Ash & E.H. Sibley, 1968. "TRAMP: an interpretive associative processor with deductive capabilities." **Proc. ACM 23rd Nat. Conf.** (27-9 Aug., 1968) 143-56.

M.M. Astrahan *et al.,* 1976. "System R: relational approach to database management." **TODS** *1* 2 (June, 1976) 97-137.

M.P. Atkinson, K.J. Chisholm & W.P. Cockshott, 1981. "The design of an algorithmic language that conveniently accommodates persistent data." University of Edinburgh, Dept. of Computer Science (12 March 1981).

B

F. Bancilhon & N. Spyratos, 1981. "Update semantics of relational views." **TODS** *6* 4 (Dec., 1981) 557-75.

D.S. Batory, 1981. "An analytical model of physical databases." CSRG-124 (Jan., 1981). See also Batory [1982].

D.S. Batory, 1982. "Optimal file designs and reorganization points." **TODS** *7* 1 (March, 1982) 60-81.

R. Bayer & E.M. McCreight, 1970. "Organization and maintenance of large ordered indices." **Acta Informatica** *1* 3 (1972) 173-89.

R. Bayer & K. Unterauer, 1977. "Prefix B-trees." **TODS** *2* 1 (March, 1977) 11-26.

C. Beeri, R. Fagin & J.H. Howard, 1977. "A complete axiomatization for functional and multivalued dependencies." **SIGMOD 77,** 47-61.

J.L. Bentley, 1975. "Multidimensional binary search trees used for associative searching." **CACM** *18* 9 (Sept., 1975) 509-17.

J.L. Bentley, 1979. "Data structures for range searching." **Comp. Surv.** *11* 4 (Dec., 1979) 397-409.

P.A. Bernstein, 1975. "Normalization and functional dependencies in the relational database model." CSRG-60 (Oct., 1975).

P.A. Bernstein, 1976. "Synthesizing third normal form relations from functional dependencies." **TODS** *1* 4 (Dec. 1976) 277-98.

P.A. Bernstein & N. Goodman, 1980. "What does Boyce-Codd normal form do?" **VLDB6,** 245-59.

P.A. Bernstein, B.T. Blaustein & E.M. Clark, 1980. "Fast maintenance of semantic integrity assertions using redundant aggregate data." **VLDB6,** 126-36.

P.A. Bernstein *et al.,* 1981. "Query processing in a system for distributed databases (SDD-1)." **TODS** *6* 4 (Dec. 1981) 602-25.

J.H. le Bihan *et al.,* 1980. "SIRIUS: a French nationwide project on distributed data bases." **VLDB6,** 75-85.

H. Biller, W. Glatthaar, E.J. Neuhold, 1976. "On the semantics of data bases: the semantics of data manipulation languages," Nijssen 76, 239-67.

M.W. Blasgen & K.P. Eswaran, 1977. "Storage and access in relational databases." **IBM Syst. J.** *16* 4 (1977) 363-77.

B.T. Blaustein, 1981. "Enforcing database assertions: techniques and applications." Aiken Computation Laboratory, Harvard University, report TR-21-81 (Aug., 1981).

B.H. Bloom, 1970. "Space/time trade-offs in hash coding with allowable errors." **CACM** *13* 7 (July, 1970) 422-6.

R. Bosak *et al.,* 1962. "An information algebra. Phase I report—language structure group of the CODASYL development committee." **CACM** *5* 4 (April, 1962) 190-204.

G. Bracchi, A. Fedeli & P. Paolini, 1972. "A language for a relational data base management system." **Proc. Sixth Annual Princeton Conf. on Information Sciences and Systems,** Dept. Electrical Engineering, Princeton University, 84-92.

M.L. Brodie, 1978. "Specification and verification of database semantic integrity." CSRG-91 (April, 1978).

M.L. Brodie & J.W. Schmidt, 1981 *eds.* "Final report of the ANSI/X3/ SPARC DBS-SG Relational Database Task group." **SIGMOD Record** *12* 4 (July, 1982) 1-62.

M.L. Brodie & S.N. Zilles, 1980. **Proceedings of the Workshop on Data Abstraction, Databases and Conceptual Modelling.** (Pingree Park, Colo., June 23-6, 1980). SIGART Newsletter #74 (Jan. 1981); SIGMOD Record *11* 2 (Feb., 1981); SIGPLAN Notices *16* 1 (Jan., 1981).

O.P. Buneman & E.K. Clemons, 1979. "Efficiently monitoring relational databases." **TODS** *4* 3 (Sept., 1979) 368-82.

W.A. Burkhard, 1982. "Advances in interpolation-based index maintenance." CISC 1982 Princeton Conference.

C

C.R. Carlson & R.S. Kaplan, 1976. "A generalized access path model and its application to a relational data base system." **SIGMOD 76** 143-54.

J.L. Carter & M.N. Wegman, 1977. "Universal classes of hash functions." **J. Comptr. Syst. Sci.** *18* (1979) 143-54.

D.D. Chamberlin & R.F. Boyce, 1974. "SEQUEL: a structured English query language." **SIGMOD 74** 249-64.

D.D. Chamberlin *et al.*, 1981. "A history and evaluation of System R." **CACM** *24* 10 (Oct., 1981) 632-46.

J.M. Chang & K.S. Fu, 1980. "A dynamic clustering technique for physical database design." **SIGMOD 80** 188-99.

P.P.S. Chen, 1976. "The entity-relationship model—toward a unified view of data." **TODS** *1* 1 (March, 1976) 9-36.

G. K.-W. Chiu, 1982. **MRDSA User's Manual.** SOCS-82-9 (May, 1982).

S. Christodoulakis, 1981. "Estimating selectivities in data bases." CSRG-136 (Dec., 1981).

CODASYL, 1971. **Report of the Data Base Task Group of the CODASYL Programming Language Committee** (April, 1971) (COnference on DAta SYstems Languages.)

E.F. Codd, 1970. "A relational model of data for large shared data banks." **CACM** *13* 6 (June, 1970) 377-87.

E.F. Codd, 1971a. "Further normalization of the data base relational model" *in* R. Rustin *ed.* **Data Base Systems,** Prentice-Hall, Englewood Cliffs, N.J. (1972) 34-64.

E.F. Codd, 1971b. "Relational completeness of data base sublanguages" *in* R. Rustin (see Codd [1971a]) 65-98.

E.F. Codd, 1971c. "A data base sublanguage founded on the relational calculus." **SIGFIDET 71,** 35-68.

E.F. Codd, 1974. "Recent investigations in relational data base systems." **IFIP 74,** 1017-1021.

E.F. Codd, 1975. "Understanding relations" (installment #7). **FDT** *7* 3-4 (1975) 23-8.

E.F. Codd, 1978. "How about recently? (English dialog with relational data bases using RENDEZVOUS Version I)." Shneiderman 3-28.

E.F. Codd, 1979. "Extending the database relational model to capture more meaning." **TODS** *4* 4 (Dec., 1979) 397-434.

E.F. Codd, 1981. "Relational databases: a practical foundation for productivity." **CACM** *25* 2 (Feb., 1982) 109-17.

D. Comer, 1978. "The difficulty of optimum index selection." **TODS** *3* 4 (Dec., 1978) 440-5.

D. Comer, 1979. "The ubiquitous B-tree." **Comp. Surv.** *11* 2 (June, 1979) 121-37.

D

C.J. Date, 1979. "Locking and recovery in a shared database system: an application programming tutorial." **VLDB5,** 1-15.

U. Dayal & P.A. Bernstein, 1978. "On the updatability of relational views." **VLDB4,** 368-77.

A. De Morgan, 1859. "On the syllogism no. IV, and on the logic of relations." **Cambridge Philosophical Transactions** *10* (1864) 331-58.

C. Deheneffe, H. Hennebert & W. Paulus, 1974. "Relational model for a data base." **IFIP 74,** 1022-5.

C. Delobel, 1972. "A theory about data in an information system." Report R J 964, IBM Research Laboratory, San Jose, CA. (28 Jan., 1972).

C. Delobel & R.G. Casey, 1973. "Decomposition of a data base and the theory of Boolean switching functions." **IBM J. Res. & Devel.** *17* 5 (Sept., 1973) 374-86.

C. Delobel & M. Léonard, 1974. "The decomposition process in a relational model." **Proc. Internat. Workshop on Data Structure Models for Information Systems,** Presses U. de Namur, Namur, Belgium (May, 1974) 57-80.

C. Delobel & D.S. Parker, 1978. "Functional and multivalued dependencies in a relational database and the theory of Boolean switching functions." Tech. Rept. 142, Dept. of Math. Appl. et Informatique, Université de Grenoble I (Nov., 1978).

R. Demolombe, 1980. "Estimation of the number of tuples satisfying a query expressed in predicate calculus language," **VLDB6** 55-63.

R. Devillers, 1977. "Game interpretation of the deadlock avoidance problem." **CACM** *20* 10 (Oct., 1977) 741-5.

L. Devroye, 1980. "A note on the average depth of trees." **Computing** *28* (1982) 367-71.

E

A.L. Eliason & K.D. Kitts, 1974. **Business Computer Systems and Applications.** Science Research Associates Inc., Chicago.

D.W. Embley, 1982. "A natural forms query language—an introduction to basic retrieval and update operations." Scheuermann 121-45.

K.P. Eswaran & D.D. Chamberlin, 1975. "Functional specifications of a subsystem for data base integrity." **VLDB1** 48-68.

K.P. Eswaran, J.N. Gray, R.A. Lorie & I.L. Traiger, 1976. "The notions of consistency and predicate locks in a database system." **CACM** *19* 11 (Nov., 1976) 624-33.

F

R.Y. Fadous & J.J. Forsyth, 1975. "Finding candidate keys for relational databases." **SIGMOD 75,** 203-10.

R. Fagin, 1976. "Dependency in a relational database and propositional logic." IBM J. Res. & Devel. *21* 6 (Nov., 1977) 534-44.

R. Fagin, 1977. "Multivalued dependencies and a new normal form for relational databases." **TODS** *2* 3 (Sept., 1977) 262-78.

R. Fagin, J. Nievergelt, N. Pippenger & H.R. Strong, 1979. "Extendible hashing—a fast access method for dynamic files." **TODS** *4* 3 (Sept., 1979) 315-44.

R. Fagin, 1981. "A normal form for relational databases that is based on domains and keys." **TODS** *6* 3 (Sept., 1981) 387-415.

R. Fagin, A.O. Mendelzon & J.D. Ullman, 1982. "A simplified universal relation assumption and its properties." **TODS** *7* 3 (Sept., 1982) 343-60.

J.A. Feldman & P.D. Rovner, 1969. "An Algol-based associative language." **CACM** *12* 8 (Aug., 1969) 439-49.

E.B. Fernandez, 1980. **Comp. Surv.** *12* 1 (March, 1980) 111-2.

M.J. Fischer & A. Michael, 1982. "Sacrificing serializability to attain high availability of data in an unreliable network." **PODS** 82, 70-5.

E.H. Fredkin, 1960. "Trie memory." **CACM** *3* 9 (Sept., 1960) 490-9.

J.P. Fry & T.J. Teory, 1978. "Design and performance tools for improving database usability and responsiveness." **Schneiderman** 151-89.

J.P. Fry, T.J. Teory, D.A. De Smith & L.B. Oberlander, 1978. "Survey of state-of-the-art database administration tools: survey results and evaluation." DSRG Tech. Rept. 78 DE 14-2, The University of Michigan.

A. Fung, 1978. "Distribution of data." School of Computer Science, McGill University, M.Sc. project report (Sept., 1978).

A.L. Furtado & L. Kerschberg, 1977. "An algebra of quotient relations." **SIGMOD 77,** 1-8.

A.L. Furtado, K.C. Sevcik & C.S. dos Santos, 1979. "Permitting updates through views of data bases." **Info. Syst.** *4* 4 (1979) 269-83.

G

G. Gardarin & M. Melkanoff, 1979. "Proving consistency of database transactions." **VLDB5** 291-8.

K. Gödel, 1931. "On formally undecidable propositions." Basic Books, New York (1962) (Translation).

J. Goldman, 1973. "Use of computed relations in a set theoretic data base." Dept. Electrical Engineering, M.I.T. (June, 1973).

R.C. Goldstein & A.J. Strnad, 1970. "The MacAIMS data management system." **SICFIDET 70,** 201-29.

L.R. Gotlieb, 1975. "Computing joins of relations." **SIGMOD 75,** 55-63.

J.N. Gray, 1981. "The transaction concept: virtues and limitations." **VLDB7,** 144-54.

P.M.D. Gray & R. Bell, 1979. "Use of simulators to help the inexpert in automatic program generation" *in* P.A. Samet *ed.* **EURO IFIP '79,** North-Holland Publishing Co., Amsterdam.

D. Greenblatt & J. Waxman, 1978. "A study of three database query languages," Shneiderman 77-97.

J. Guttag, 1976. "Abstract data types and the development of data structures." **CACM** *20* 6 (June, 1976) 396-404.

H

V. Hadzilacos, 1982. "An algorithm for minimizing roll back and cost." **PODS 82,** 93-7.

J.-L. Hainault & B. Lecharlier, 1974. "An extensible semantic model of data base and its data language." **IFIP 74,** 1026-30.

P.A.V. Hall, 1974. "Common subexpression identification in general algebraic systems." UKSC-0060 (Nov., 1974).

P.A.V. Hall & S.J.P. Todd, 1974. "Factorizations of algebraic expressions." UKSC-0055 (April, 1974).

P.A.V. Hall, P. Hitchcock & S.J.P. Todd, 1975. "An algebra of relations for machine computation." **Proc. 23rd ACM Symp. on Principles of Programming Languages,** Palo Alto (20-22 Jan., 1975) 225-32.

M.M. Hammer & D.J. McLeod, 1975. "Semantic integrity in a relational data base system." **VLDB1,** 25-47.

M.M. Hammer & S.K. Sarin, 1978. "Efficient monitoring of database assertions." **SIGMOD 78,** Supplement 38-49.

W.P. Heising, 1963. "Note on random addressing techniques." **IBM Syst. J.** *2* 2 (June, 1963) 112-6.

G.D. Held, 1975. "Storage structures for relational data base management systems." ERL-M533 (Aug., 1975).

G.D. Held, M.R. Stonebraker & E. Wong, 1975. "INGRES—a relational data base system." **Proc. AFIPS NCC** *44* (Anaheim, 19-22 May, 1975) 409-16.

L. Henkin & A. Tarski, 1961. "Cylindric algebras" *in* R.P. Dilworth *ed.* **Lattice Theory,** Proc. Symp. Pure Math. *2,* American Mathematical Society, Providence, R.I. 83-113.

H.C. Ho, 1982. "Integrity control in a relational database." SOCS-82-8 (March, 1982).

C.A.R. Hoare, 1969. "An axiomatic basis for computer programming." **CACM** *12* 10 (Oct., 1969) 576-80, 583.

Y.C. Hong & S.Y.W. Su, 1981. "Associative hardware and software techniques for integrity control." **TODS** 6 3 (Sept., 1981) 416-40.

D. Hsiao & F. Harary, 1970. "A formal system for information retrieval from files." **CACM** *13* 2 (Feb., 1970) 67-73 and *13* 4 (April, 1970) 266.

H.B. Hunt & D.J. Rosenkrantz, 1979. "The complexity of testing predicate locks." **SIGMOD 79,** 127-33.

I

T. Imielinski & W. Lipski, Jr., 1981a. "The relational model of data and cylindric algebras." Polish Academy of Sciences, ICS PAS Report 446 (Aug., 1981) (Presented at **PODS** 82).

T. Imielinski & W. Lipski, Jr., 1981b. "On representing incomplete information in a relational database." **VLDB7,** 388-97.

T. Imielinski & W. Lipski, Jr., 1982. "A systematic approach to relational database theory." **SIGMOD 82,** 8-14.

T. Imielinski & W. Lipski, Jr., "Incomplete information in a relational database." Polish Academy of Sciences, ICS PAS Report 475 (May, 1982).

J

G. Jaeschke & H.-J. Schek, 1982. "Remarks on the algebra of non first normal form relations." **PODS,** 124-38.

J.R. Jordan, J. Banerjee & R.B. Batman, 1981. "Precision locks." **SIGMOD 81,** 143-7.

K

Y. Kambayashi, 1981. **Database: a Bibliography.** Computer Science Press, Inc., Rockville, Maryland.

Y. Kambayashi, K. Tanaka & S. Yajima, 1981. "Problems of relational database design" *in* S.B. Yao & T.L. Kunii *eds.* **Database Design.** Lecture Notes in Computer Science, Springer-Verlag.

R.F. Kamel, 1980. "The information processing language Aldat: design and implementation." SOCS-80-14 (Aug., 1980).

W. Kent, 1981. "Consequences of assuming a universal relation." **TODS** 6 4 (Dec., 1981) 539-56.

L. Kerschberg, E. A. Ozkarahan & J.E.S. Pacheco, 1976. "A synthetic English query language for a relational associative processor." CSRG-68 (April, 1976).

L. Kerschberg, P.D. Ting & S.B. Yao, 1980. "Query optimization in star computer networks." Bell Laboratories. Database Research Report No. 2 (21 March, 1980).

C.Y. Kim, 1976. "Implementation and comparison of key-finding algorithms. School of Computer Science, McGill University, M.Sc. thesis (23 Aug., 1976).

W. Kim, 1979. "Relational database systems." **Comp. Surv.** *11* 3 (Sept., 1979) 185-211.

D.E. Knuth, 1968. Fundamental Algorithms. Vol. I of **The Art of Computer Programming.** Addison-Wesley Publishing Co., Reading, Mass.

D.E. Knuth, 1973. Sorting and Searching. Vol. III of **The Art of Computer Programming.** Addison-Wesley Publishing Co., Reading, Mass.

L.A. Kraning & A.I. Fillat, 1970. "Generalized organization of large databases; a set-theoretic approach to relations." Dept. Electrical Engineering, M.I.T. (June, 1970).

H.T. Kung & C.H. Papadimitriou, 1979. "An optimality theory of concurrency control for databases." **SIGMOD 79,** 116-28.

H.T. Kung & J.T. Robinson, 1981. "On optimistic methods for concurrency control." **TODS** *6* 2 (June, 1981) 213-26.

L

M. Lacroix & A. Pirotte, 1976a. "Example queries in relational languages." M.B.L.E. Research Laboratory (now Philips Research Laboratory) Technical Note No. 7 (Jan., 1976; revised April, 1978).

M. Lacroix & A. Pirotte, 1976b. "Generalized joins." **SIGMOD Record** *8* 3 (Sept., 1976) 14-15.

M. Lacroix & A. Pirotte, 1977. "ILL: an English structured query language for relational data bases," **Nijssen 77,** 237-60.

B.W. Lampson *et al.,* 1977. "Report on the programming language EUCLID." **ACM SIGPLAN Notices** *12* 2 (Feb., 1977) 1-79.

P.-A. Larson, 1980. "Linear hashing with partial expansions." **VLDB6,** 224-32.

P.-A. Larson, 1982. Performance analysis of linear hashing with partial expansions. **TODS** *7* 4 (Dec., 1982) 566-87.

R.E. Levein & M.E. Maron, 1967. "A computer system for inference execution and data retrieval." **CACM** *10* 11 (Nov., 1967) 715-21.

T.A. Linden, 1976. "The use of abstract data types to simplify program verifications." **Utah 76,** 12-23.

W. Lipski, Jr., 1979. "On semantic issues connected with incomplete information databases." **TODS** *4* 3 (Sept. 1979) 262-96.

W. Litwin, 1980. "Linear hashing: a new tool for file and table addressing." **VLDB6,** 212-23.

F.H. Lochovsky, 1978. "Data base management system user performance." CSRG-90 (April, 1978).

D.B. Lomet, 1979. "Multi-table search for B-tree files." **SIGMOD 79,** 35-42.

V.Y. Lum *et al.,* 1979. "The 1978 New Orleans data base design workshop report." **VLDB5,** 328-39. A summary of IBM Tech. Rept. RJ 2554, IBM Research Laboratory, San Jose, Ca.

N.A. Lynch, 1982. "Multilevel atomicity." **PODS 82,** 63-9.

M

G.C. Magalhaes, 1981. "Improving the performance of data base systems." CSRG-138 (Dec., 1981).

D. Maier, D. Rozenshtein, S. Salveter, J. Stein, D.S. Warren, 1982. "Toward logical data independence: a relational query language without relations." **SIGMOD 82,** 51-60.

G. McLean, Jr., 1981. "Comments on SDD-1 concurrency control mechanisms." **TODS** *6* 2 (June, 1981) 247-50.

D.J. McLeod, 1976. "High level domain definition in a relational data base system." **Utah 76,** 47-57.

T.H. Merrett, 1976. "MRDS—an algebraic relational database system." **Proc. Canadian Computer Conf. Session '76** (Montréal, 17-19 May, 1976) 102-24.

T.H. Merrett, 1977a. "Database cost analysis: a top-down approach." **SIGMOD 77,** 135-43.

T.H. Merrett, 1977b. "Aldat—augmenting the relational algebra for programmers." SOCS-78.1 (Nov., 1977).

T.H. Merrett, 1978a. "Multidimensional paging for efficient data base querying." **ICMOD 78,** 277-90.

T.H. Merrett, 1978b. "The extended relational algebra, a basis for query languages." Shneiderman, 99-128.

T.H. Merrett & E.J. Otoo, 1979. "Distribution models of relations." **VLDB5,** 418-25.

T.H. Merrett & S.H.K. Zaidi, 1981. **MRDSP User's Manual.** SOCS-81-27 (Aug., 1981).

T.H. Merrett, Y. Kambayashi & H. Yasuura, 1981. "Scheduling of page fetches in join operations." **VLDB7,** 488-98.

T.H. Merrett & E.J. Otoo, 1982. "Dynamic multipaging: a storage structure for large shared data banks." Scheuermann, 237-56.

S. Miranda & R. Demolombe, 1983. **Proceedings, Conference on Design, Implementation and Use of Relational D.B.M.S. on Microcomputers.** Toulouse, 14-15 Feb., 1983.

C. Mohan, D. Fussell & A. Silberschatz, 1982. "A biased non-two-phase locking protocol." Scheuermann, 337-61.

R. Morrison, 1979. "S-Algol reference manual." St. Andrews University, Scotland (June, 1979).

J. Mylopoulos, P.A. Bernstein & H.K.T. Wong, 1978. "A language facility for designing database-intensive applications." **TODS** 5 2 (June, 1980) 185-207.

N

K.K. Nambiar, 1980. "Some analytic tools for the design of relational database systems." **VLDB6,** 417-28.

J.M. Nicolas & K. Yazdanian, 1977. "Integrity checking in deductive data bases" *in* H. Gallaire & J. Minker *eds.* **Logic and Data Bases** (Toulouse, 16-18 Nov., 1977) Plenum Publ. Co., New York (1978) 325-44.

M.G. Notley, 1972. "The Peterlee IS/1 system." UKSC-0018 (March, 1972).

O

J.A. Orenstein, 1982. "Multidimensional tries used for associative searching." **Info. Proc. Lett.** *14* 4 (13 June, 1982) 150-7.

J.A. Orenstein, T.H. Merrett & L. Devroye, 1982. "A class of data structures for associative searching." BIT *23* 2 (June, 1983) 170-80.

S.L. Osborn, 1978. "Normal forms for relational data bases." University of Waterloo, Dept. Computer Science Research Report CS-78-06 (Jan., 1978).

S.L. Osborn, 1979. "Towards a universal relation interface." **VLDB5,** 52-60.

P

F.P. Palermo, 1972. "A data base search problem." **Proc. 4th Internat. Symp. on Computer and Info. Sciences** (Miami Beach, Dec., 1972), Plenum Publ. Co., New York (1973) 67-101.

D.S. Parker & K. Parsaye-Ghomi, 1980. "Inferences involving embedded multivalued dependencies and transitive dependencies." **SIGMOD 80,** 52-7.

F.D. Parker, 1960. "Matrices, relations and graphs." **Math. Mag.** *34* (1960) 5-9.

R.M. Pecherer, 1975. "Efficient evaluation of expressions in a relational algebra." Pacific 75, 44-9.

C.S. Peirce, 1870. "Description of a notation for the logic of relatives, resulting from an amplification of the conception of Boole's calculus of logic." **Memoirs of the American Academy** 9 (1870) 317-78.

C.S. Peirce, 1882. "Brief description of the algebra of relatives" *in* C. Hartshorne & P. Weiss *eds.* **Collected Papers of Charles Sanders Peirce,** Vol. III Exact Logic, Harvard University Press, Cambridge, 1933, 180-6.

A. Pirotte, 1977. "High level data base query languages" *in* H. Gallaire & J. Minker *eds.* **Logic and Data Bases** (Toulouse, 16-18 Nov., 1977) Plenum Publ. Co., New York (1978) 409-36.

R

M. Regnier, 1982. "Linear hashing with groups of reorganization: an algorithm for files without history." Scheuermann, 257-72.

P. Reisner, 1981. "Human factors studies of database query languages: a survey and assessment." **Comp. Surv.** 13 1 (March, 1981) 13-32.

P. Reisner, R.F. Boyce & D.D. Chamberlin, 1975. "Human factors evaluation of two data base query languages: SQUARE and SEQUEL." **Proc. AFIPS NCC** 44 (Anaheim, 19-22 May, 1975) 447-52.

P. Richard, 1981. "Evaluation of the size of a query expressed in relational algebra." **SIGMOD 81,** 155-63.

D.R. Ries & M. Stonebraker, 1977. "Effects of locking granularity in a database management system." **TODS** 2 3 (Sept., 1977) 233-46.

D.R. Ries & M. Stonebraker, 1979. "Locking granularity revisited." **TODS** 4 2 (June, 1979) 210-27.

D.M. Ritchie & K. Thompson, 1974. "The UNIX time sharing system." **CACM** 17 7 (July, 1974) 365-75.

R.L. Rivest, 1974. "Analysis of associative retrieval algorithms." Stanford University, Computer Science Dept., Tech. Rept. STAN-CS-74-415.

J.T. Robinson, 1981. "The K-D-B-Tree: a search structure for large multidimensional dynamic indexes." **SIGMOD 81,** 10-18.

D.J. Rosenkrantz, R.E. Stearns & P.M. Lewis II, 1978. "System level concurrency control for distributed database systems." **TODS** 3 2 (June, 1978) 178-98.

D.J. Rosenkrantz, R.E. Stearns & P.M. Lewis II, 1980. "Consistency and serializability in concurrent database systems." Dept. Computer Science, SUNY at Albany Tech. Rept. 80-12.

A.S. Rosenthal, 1981. "Note on the expected size of a join." **SIGMOD Record** 11 4 (July, 1981) 19-25.

J.B. Rothnie & T. Lozano, 1974. "Attribute file organization in a paged memory environment." **CACM** *17* 2 (Feb., 1976) 63-9.

N.D. Roussopoulos, 1977. "A semantic network model of databases." Dept. Computer Science, University of Toronto Tech. Rept. 104 (April, 1977).

L.A. Rowe & K.A. Shoens, 1979. "Data abstraction, views and updates in RIGEL." **SIGMOD 79,** 71-81.

B. Russell, 1908. "Mathematical logic as based on the theory of types." **Am. J. Math.** *30* (1908) 222-62.

R. Rustin, 1974. **Data Models: Data-Structure-Set** *versus* **Relational.** Supplement to **SIGMOD 74.**

S

B.-M. Scheuler, 1977. "Update reconsidered." Nijssen 77, 149-64.

M. Schkolnick, 1978. "A survey of physical database design methodology and techniques." **VLDB 4,** 474-87.

H.A. Schmid & J.R. Swenson, 1975. "On the semantics of the relational model." **SIGMOD 75,** 211-33.

J.W. Schmidt, 1977. "Some high level language constructs for data of type relation." **TODS** *2* 3 (Sept., 1977) 247-61.

K.C. Sevcik, 1981. "Data base system performance prediction using an analytical model." **VLDB7,** 182-98.

D.G. Severance, 1975. "A parametric model of alternative file structures." **Info. Syst.** *1* 2 (1975) 51-5.

D.G. Severance & G.M. Lohman, 1976. "Differential files: their application to the maintenance of large databases." **TODS** *1* 3 (Sept., 1976) 256-67.

D.G. Severance & J.V. Carlis, 1977. "A practical approach to selecting record access paths." **Comp. Surv.** *9* 4 (Dec., 1977) 259-72.

W. Shakespeare, 1589. "The comedy of errors" *in* C.J. Sisson *ed.* **William Shakespeare The Complete Works,** Odhams Press Ltd., London (1954) 122-42.

J.E. Shapiro, 1979. "Theseus—a programming language for relational databases." **TODS** *4* 4 (Dec., 1979) 493-517.

J.M. Smith & P.Y.T. Chang, 1975. "Optimizing the performance of a relational algebra database interface." **CACM** *18* 10 (Oct., 1975) 568-79.

J.M. Smith & D.C.P. Smith, 1977a. "Database abstractions: aggregation." **CACM** *20* 6 (June, 1977) 405-13.

J.M. Smith & D.C.P. Smith, 1977b. "Database abstractions: aggregation and generalization." **TODS** *2* 2 (June, 1977) 105-33.

E. Soisalon-Soininen & D. Wood, 1982. "An optimal algorithm for testing for safety and detecting deadlocks in a locked transaction system." **PODS 82,** 108-16.

P.G. Sorenson, J.P. Tremblay & R.F. Deutscher, 1978. "Key-to-address transformation techniques." **INFOR** *16* 1 (Feb., 1978) 1-34.

R.E. Stearns & D.J. Rosencrantz, 1981. "Distributed database concurrency controls using before-values." **SIGMOD 81,** 74-83.

J. Steuert & J. Goldman, 1974. "The relational data management system: a perspective." **SIGMOD 74,** 295-320.

M. Stonebraker, 1975. "Implementation of integrity constraints and views by query modification." **SIGMOD 75,** 65-78.

M. Stonebraker, E. Wong & P. Kreps, 1976. "The design and implementation of INGRES." **TODS** *1* 3 (Sept., 1976) 189-222.

M. Stonebraker, 1980. "Retrospection on a database system." **TODS** *5* 2 (June, 1980) 225-40.

J.E. Stoy, 1977. **Denotational Semantics: The Scott-Strachey Approach to Programming Language Theory.** The M.I.T. Press, Cambridge, Mass. (1977).

A.J. Strnad, 1971. "The relational approach to management of data bases." Project MAC Tech. Memorandum 23 (April, 1971). Available from **N.T.I.S.**

R.C. Summers, C.D. Coleman & E.B. Fernandez, 1975. "A programming language extension for access to a shared data base." **Pacific 75,** 114-8.

P. Suppes, 1957. **Introduction to Logic.** D. van Nostrand Co., Princeton, N.J.

T

M. Tamminen, 1982. "Efficient spatial access to a data base." **SIGMOD 82,** 200-6.

T.J. Teory & K.S. Das, 1976. "Application of an analytic model to evaluate storage structures." **SIGMOD 76,** 9-19.

T.J. Teory & J.P. Fry, 1980. "The logical record access approach to database design." **Comp. Surv.** *12* 2 (June, 1980) 179-212.

J.C. Thomas & J.D. Gould, 1975. "A psychological study of query by example." **Proc. AFIPS NCC** *44* (Anaheim, 19-22 May, 1975) 439-45.

S.J.P. Todd, 1974. "Implementation of join operator in relational data bases." IBM UK Scientific Centre Technical Note 15, Peterlee, U.K. (Nov., 1974).

S.J.P. Todd, 1976. "The Peterlee Relational Test Vehicle—a system overview." **IBM Syst. J.** *15* 4 (1976) 285-308.

S.J.P. Todd, 1977a. "Automatic constraint maintenance and updating defined relations." **IFIP 77,** 145-8.

S.J.P. Todd, 1977b. "Relational database research at the IBM U.K. Scientific Centre, Peterlee, a survey 1970-1977." UKSC-93 (Dec., 1977).

C.J.C. Tsao, 1979. "Heuristic detection of extrinsic functional dependencies." School of Computer Science, McGill University M.Sc. Thesis (20 Aug., 1979).

U

J.D. Ullman, 1982. "The U.R. strikes back." **PODS 82,** 10-22.

V

Y. Vassiliou, 1979. "Null values in database management: a denotational semantics approach." **SIGMOD 79,** 162-9.

J.S.M. Verhofstad, 1978. "Recovery techniques for database systems." **Comp. Surv.** *10* 2 (June, 1978) 167-95.

W

W.A. Walker, 1982. Private communication (25 June, 1982).

H.S. Warren, 1975. "A modification of Warshall's algorithm for the transitive closure of binary relations." **CACM** *18* 4 (April, 1975) 218-20.

S. Warshall, 1962. "A theorem on Boolean matrices." **JACM** *9* 1 (June, 1962) 11-12.

A.I. Wasserman, 1976. "PLAIN: reliable interactive software and programming language design." University of California San Francisco Laboratory of Medical Information Science Tech. Rept. #20 (April, 1976).

A.I. Wasserman, 1979. "The data management facilities of PLAIN." **SIGMOD 79,** 60-70.

H. Weber, 1976. "A semantic model of integrity constraints on a relational data base." Nijssen 76, 269-92.

C. Welty & D.W. Stemple, 1981. "Human factors comparison of a procedural and a nonprocedural query language." **TODS** *6* 4 (Dec., 1981) 626-49.

V.K.M. Whitney, 1974. "Relational data management implementation techniques." **SIGMOD 74,** 321-50.

G. Wiederhold, 1977. **Database Design.** McGraw-Hill Book Co., New York.

N. Wirth, 1971. "The programming language PASCAL." **Acta Informatica** *1* 1 (May, 1971) 35-63.

N. Wirth, 1977. "Modula: a language for modular multiprogramming." **Software—Practice and Experience** *7* (1977) 3-35.

E. Wong & K. Youssefi, 1976. "Decomposition—a strategy for query processing." **TODS** *1* 3 (Sept., 1976) 223-41.

K.C. Wong & M. Edelberg, 1977. "Interval hierarchies and their application to predicate files." **TODS** *2* 3 (Sept., 1977) 223-32.

Y

S.B. Yao, 1977a. "An attribute based model for database cost analysis." **TODS** *2* 1 (March, 1977) 45-67.

S.B. Yao, 1977b. "Approximating block accesses in database organizations." **CACM** *20* 4 (April, 1977) 266.

S.B. Yao & D. De Jong, 1978. "Evaluation of access paths in a relational database system." **SIGMOD 78,** 66-77.

Z

C. Zaniolo, 1976. "Analysis and design of relational schemata for database systems." Tech. Rept. UCLA-ENG-7669 (July, 1979).

M.M. Zloof, 1975. "Query by example." **Proc. AFIPS NCC** *44* (Anaheim, 19-22 May, 1975) 431-8.

M.M. Zloof, 1978. "Design aspects of the query-by-example data base management language," Shneiderman, 29-55.

W. Zook *et al.*, 1976. **INGRES Reference Manual—Version 6.** ERL-M579 (6 April, 1976).

Glossary

TERM	MEANING	SECTION USED IN
a	(local) loc. of recd. in block	1.2-3a
	value of attrib. A	1.2-3b, 1.2-4, 2.1-5
	(local) 1n r	1.3-5
	threshold activity	2.2-3
	set element	2.3-1
	(local)	2.3-2
	no. accounts	6.3, 6.3-1, 6.3-2, 6.3-3
a_i	first value of attrib. A in interval i $0 \le i < p$	1.2-3b
A	(local) odd integer	1.2-3a
	attribute	1.2-3b, 1.4-3, 2.1-1, 2.1-5, 2.4-2, 4.2-1, 4.2-2
	accumulator (multipage axis partition)	1.2-3b
	(local) relation	2.2-4
b	blocksize	1.2-3a, 1.3-3, 1.3-4, 1.3-5, 6.2-1
	value of attrib. B	2.1-5
	set element	2.3-1
	(local)	2.3-2

TERM	MEANING	SECTION USED IN
b, b', b''	no. bytes to be placed in node of prefix B-tree	1.2-4
b_0	lower threshold for b : $b \geq b_0$	1.2-3b (Exercise 1.2-22)
B	attribute	2.1-1, 2.1-5, 2.4-2, 4.1, 4.2-1, 4.2-2
	relation	2.2-4
	binary relation	1.4-3
	(local)	1.3-3
B_i	(local) $1 \leq i \leq k$	1.3-3
c	value of attribute CUSTOMER	1.2-3b
	normalization const. for usage distrib.	1.3-3
	(local) F / F_b	1.3-5
	value of attrib.	2.2-4
	set element	2.3-1
	blocksize for o'flow area	1.3-3
	column of matrix R_r	5.2-4
	tuple count in tuple-density histo.	2.3-2
C	Attribute	2.1-1, 2.1-5, 2.4-2, 4.2-1, 4.2-2
	relations	2.2-4
	no. cells in histogram	2.3-2
d	set element	2.3-1
D	domain	1.1-1, 1.4-3
	relation	2.2-4
	attribute	2.1-1, 2.1-5, 2.4-2, 4.2-1 4.2-2
D_i	domain	1.1-1
D_A	cum. distrib. fcn. for attrib. A	1.2-3b

TERM	MEANING	SECTION USED IN
DC	don't care null value	2.1-3, 2.1-4, 2.4-3
DK	don't know null value	2.1-4, 2.4-3
e	set element	2.3-1
	edge in graph	Appendix
	no. equity accounts	6.3, 6.3-3
E	attrib.	2.1-1, 2.1-5
	set of edges in graph	Appendix
	no. edges in graph	1.3-1
	(local) relation	2.2-4
$|E|$	no. edges in tree	5.3-2, 5.3-3, Appendix
f	f_j for some j if unambiguous	1.2-3b, 2.2-2
	degree of tree	1.2-2
	fanout for node of B-tree	1.2-4
	degree of merge in sorting	1.2-5, 1.3-5
	(local) # tuples in P_i^f	5.2-2
	set element	2.3-1
f_j	the factor of n, $1 \leq j \leq m$	1.2-3b, 2.3-3, 6.2-1
f'	fanout for node of B-tree	1.2-4
$f(x)$	alphabetic pos. of 1st letter in x	1.2-2
F	abbrev. for Father's Age attrib.	1.2-6
	RAM capacity (records)	1.3-5, 1.4-2
	(local) relation	2.2-4
F_b	RAM capacity (bytes)	1.3-5
g	(local) no. guesses in Alg. H	1.2-3b
	(local) fcn. relating x,z in partial expansion anal.	1.3-3
	set element	2.3-1

TERM	MEANING	SECTION USED IN
G	(local) relation	2.2-4
	graph	Appendix
h	hash function	1.2-2, 1.2-3a
	height of tree	1.2-4, 1.3-4, 5.3-2, 5.3-3, 5.3-4, Appendix
h_j	hash function, linear hashing	1.2-3a
H	# hash fcns. to Bloom filter	1.3-3
	(local) relation	2.2-4
	equivocation	2.4-6
i	used locally extensively	
I	(local) relation	2.2-4
j	used locally extensively	
k	hash key	1.2-3a
	tree key	1.2-4
	degree of merge in sorting	1.2-5
	no. attrib. specified in a multidim. query	1.2-3, 2.3-3, 4.2-1
	no. diff. values of attrib. in a histo. cell	2.3-2
	no. buffers in RAM for join rels. $k = k_r = k_s$	2.3-1
	(local)	1.3-3
k_i	$1 \le i < f$ key in B-tree	1.2-4
k_p	key in node p of tree	1.2-4
k_q	key in node q of tree	1.2-4
k'	min-length separator in prefix B-tree	1.2-4
k'_1	min-length separator in prefix B-tree	1.2-4
k'_2	min-length separator in prefix B-tree	1.2-4

TERM	MEANING	SECTION USED IN
k_{pos}	separator in prefix B-tree	1.2-4
k_1	no. diff. values of attrib. in a histo. cell	2.3-2
k_2	no. diff. values of attrib. in a histo. cell	2.3-2
k_3	no. diff. values of attrib. in a histo. cell	2.3-2
k_{13}	no. diff. values of attrib. in a histo. cell	2.3-2
k_r	no. buffers in RAM for join rels.	2.3-1
k_s	no. buffers in RAM for join rels.	2.3-1
K	(local) integer	1.2-3a
	key	1.1-1, 1.4-3
ℓ	location of recd. in block	1.2-3a
	location of block	1.3-3
	no. diff. values of attribute in histo. cell	2.3-2
	max. path length of network	5.2-2
	pointer left node in KDB tree	1.2-4
	level in a tree	5.3-2
	level in topologically sorted graph	5.2-3
ℓ_p	left subtree pointer, binary tree	1.2-4
ℓ_q	left subtree pointer, binary tree	1.2-4
ℓ_1	no. diff. values of attribute in histo. cell	2.3-2
ℓ_2	no. diff. values of attribute in histo. cell	2.3-2
ℓ_{12}	no. diff. values of attribute in histo. cell	2.3-2
ℓ_3	no. diff. values of attribute in histo. cell	2.3-2
L	location of record	1.3-3
	$L \log_{10} N$ is no. eff. passes to retrieve every record in B-tree	1.3-4
$|L|$	no. leaf nodes in tree	5.3-2, Appendix
m	degree of rel = dim. of tuple space	1.1-1, 1.2-3b, 1.2-4, 1.2-6, 1.3-1, 1.4-2, 2.3-2, 2.3-3, 5.2

TERM	MEANING	SECTION USED IN
	(local) $n = 2^m$	1.2-3a
	(local) value of attrib. MAKER	1.2-3b
	(local)	1.3-3
	(local)	2.3-2
	fanout of tree	Appendix
M	(local) avg. space alloc./block	1.3-3
	(local) abbrev. for Mother's Age attrib.	1.2-6
n	no. blocks = no. nodes in tree	1.2-3a, 1.2-3b, 1.2-4, 1.3-3, 1.3-4, 1.3-5, 2.2-2, 2.3-1, 2.3-3, 2.3-4, 5.2-2, 5.3-4, 6.3-2, Appendix
	(local)	2.3-2
n_*	no. blocks in result of μjoin	2.3-4
N_*	no. tuples in result of μjoin	2.3-4
N	no. records in file = no. tuples in rel.	1.2-2, 1.2-3b, 1.2-4, 1.3-1, 1.3-3, 1.3-4, 1.3-5, 1.4-3, 1.4-4, 2.3-4, 2.4-4
	network	Appendix
N_b	file size (bytes)	1.3-5
p	(local) pointer to next block to be split	1.2-3a
	number of tidy function intervals	1.2-3b
	pointer to node of binary tree	1.2-4
	pointer to node of B-tree	1.2-4
	no. records in "p-plet"	1.2-4 (Exercise 1.2-44)

TERM	MEANING	SECTION USED IN
	record location in Alg. SD	1.2-3
	pointer to node in KDB tree	1.2-4
	pointer to node of tree	1.2-4
	no. blocks in group in partial expansion	1.3-3
	no. accounting periods	6.3
	(local)	2.3-2
p'	(local) pointer to next block to be split	1.2-3a
p_i	descendent pointer in B-tree $0 \le i < f$	1.2-4
	set of paths of length 2^i (also p_i^f, p_i^s)	5.2-2
p_f	prob. of filtering error	1.3-3
p_j	prob. that j requests out of r are on same block	1.3-3, 2.3-2
P	no. effective passes	1.3-3, 5.3-1
	(local)	1.3-3
q	pointer to node of binary tree	1.2-4
	pointer to node of B-tree	1.2-4
	record location, Alg. SD	1.2-3
q_p	expansion factor in partial expansion anal.	1.3-3
Q	query	2.4-3
$\|Q\|^*$	set of objects which certainly satisfy Q	2.4-3
$\|Q\|_*$	set of objects which may satisfy Q	2.4-3
Q_i	quantifier predicate $1 \le i \le k$	4.2-1, 4.2-2
r	record (tuple)	1.2-3a
	(local)	1.2-3a
	no. search requests in a batch	1.2-3a, 1.3-3, 6.3-2
	no. initial runs in sort	1.2-5, 1.3-5
	record location Alg. SD	1.2-3
	pointer to right node in KDB tree	1.2-4
	row of matrix R_{rc}	5.2-4
	edge of reduced graph	Appendix

TERM	MEANING	SECTION USED IN
r_p	right subtree pointer, binary tree	1.2-4
r_q	right subtree pointer, binary tree	1.2-4
r_i	block of relation R (also r'_i)	2.3-1
R	relation	1.1-1, 1.1-2, 1.4-3, 2.1-1, 2.1-3, 2.1-5, 2.2-1, 2.2-2, 2.2-3, 2.3-1, 2.3-2, 2.4-1, 2.4-2, 2.4-5, 2.4-6, 3.2-1, 4.1, 4.1-1, 4.1-2, 4.2-1, 4.2-2, 4.4-2
	# bytes/record	1.3-3, 1.3-4
	no. bits of RAM avail. for histogram	2.3-2, (Exercises 2.3-5 and 2.3-6)
R'	# bytes/record	1.3-3, 1.3-4
R_{rc}	matrix holding BOM for closure join in RAM	2.3-1
s	pointer to node of B-tree	1.2-4
	(local) no. tuples in P_i^s	5.2-2
s_i	block of relation S (also s'_i)	2.3-1
	strongly connected component of graph	Appendix
S	relation	2.1-1, 2.1-3, 2.1-5, 2.2-1, 2.2-2, 2.2-3, 2.3-1, 2.3-2, 2.4-5, 2.4-6, 4.1, 4.1-1, 4.1-2, 4.4-2
S_j	sum used in evaluating QT-expressions	4.2-1, 4.2-2
S_k	sum used in evaluating QT-expressions	4.2-1, 4.2-2

TERM	MEANING	SECTION USED IN
t	(local) value of attribute TOY	1.2-3b
	no. ϕ-ary trees in forest	5.3-2
	no. 1s terminating binary rep. of attrib. value in Z-order	1.2-4
t_A	tidy function for attribute A	1.2-3b
T	relation	2.1-1, 2.3-2, 4.1, 4.1-2
	attribute	2.2-4
	tuple predicate	4.2-1, 4.2-2
T_i	set of nodes within dist. 2^i from a root	5.2-2
T_c	vector holding BASIC COSTS / FINAL COSTS for closure join	5.2-4
u	usage distribution	1.3-3
	vertex	Appendix
u_r	distrib. of depths	1.3-5
U	prob. fcn. related to usage distrib.	1.3-5
	(local) attribute	2.2-4
	set of all attrib. of a rel. ("universe")	2.4-2
U_r	prob. fcn. related to distrib. of depths	1.3-5
v	# values of attributes	1.3-1
	vertex (also v_i)	Appendix
v_ℓ	no. nodes at level ℓ of tree	5.3-2
V	# vertices in graph	1.3-1
	no. pairs of tuples violating an FD	1.4-2
	attribute	2.2-4
	relation	2.3-2
	no. values of an attribute (also V_i)	1.2-3b, 2.3-3
	set of vertices in a graph	Appendix
$|V|$	no. vertices in a tree	5.3-2, 5.3-3, 5.3-4

TERM	MEANING	SECTION USED IN
w	computer word size (e.g., 2^8, 2^{16}, 2^{32})	1.2-3a
	no. values in tidy function interval	1.2-3b
	value of attrib. set	2.1-3, 2.2-1, 2.3-2, 2.4-1
W	set of attributes	1.4-2, 2.1-3, 2.2-1, 2.3-2, 2.4-1, 2.4-2, 2.4-5, 3.2-2, 4.1-2
	attribute	2.2-4
x	value of attrib.-set	1.1-2, 1.4-2, 2.1-3, 2.1-4, 2.2-2, 2.3-2, 2.4-1
	(local)	2.1-3
	proportion of partial expansion completed	1.3-3
X	set of attributes (also X_i)	1.1-1, 1.4-2, 2.1-3, 2.2-1, 2.2-2, 2.2-3, 2.3-1, 2.3-2, 2.4-1, 2.4-2, 2.4-5, 2.4-6, 3.2-1, 3.2-2, 4.1, 4.1-1, 4.1-2, 4.1-3, 4.4-2
	attribute	2.2-4
X_ℓ	(local) random variable on 0,1	1.3-3
$\overline{X}_\ell$	expected value of x_ℓ	1.3-3
$\overline{\overline{X}}_\ell$	expected value of x_ℓ with uniform usage	1.3-3
X_i	no. paths of length 2^i in network in Hardy topological sort	5.3-3
y	value of attrib. set	1.1-2, 1.4-2, 2.1-3, 2.1-4,

TERM	MEANING	SECTION USED IN
	(local)	2.2-2, 2.3-2, 2.4-1 3.1-3
Y	set of attributes	1.1-2, 1.4-2, 2.1-3, 2.2-1, 2.2-2, 2.2-3, 2.3-1, 2.3-2, 2.4-1, 2.4-5, 2.4-6, 3.2-1, 3.2-2, 4.1, 4.1-1, 4.1-2, 4.1-3, 4.4-2
	attribute	2.2-4
Y_{i+1}	used in Hardy topological sort anal.	5.3-3
z	load factor (partial expansion) value of attrib. set	1.3-3 2.1-3, 2.2-1, 2.3-2, 2.4-1
Z	set of attributes	1.4-2, 2.1-3, 2.2-1, 2.2-3, 2.3-1, 2.3-2,. 2.4-1, 2.4-5, 3.2-1, 3.2-2, 4.1, 4.1-2
	attribute	2.2-4
Z_i	used in Hardy topological sort anal.	5.2-3
α	load factor $\overset{\Delta}{=}$ (no. tuples)/(cap. of storage)	1.2-3a, 1.2-3b, (Exercise 1.2-15), 1.2-4, 1.3-3, 1.3-4
α'	load factor after deleting o'flow area load factor (also α'')	1.2-3a 1.3-3
α_0	threshold load factor, $\alpha \geq \alpha_0$	1.2-3a, 1.2-3b, (Exercise 1.2-17)

TERM	MEANING	SECTION USED IN
$|\alpha|$	no. symbols in alphabet (trees)	1.2-4
β	bytes / track (disk) (local)	1.2-1, 1.3-5 3.1-3
γ	tracks / cycl. (disk)	1.2-1, 1.3-5
Δ	increase in $\lfloor$value of attribute A$\rfloor$	1.2-3b
δ	recording density, bits per inch (tape)	1.2-1
ϵ	set membership e.g., a ϵ A	Used throughout text.
θ	parameter for 80-20 family of usage distrib. don't know null value	1.3-3 2.4-3
ι	interblock gap (tape)	1.2-1
λ	avg. latency (disk)	1.2-1
μ	avg. arm delay (disk) inverse of load factor for hashed file with sep. o'flow	1.2-1 1.3-3
ν	cyl. / unit (disk) no. blocks initially in dynamic file	1.2-1 1.2-3a
π	probe factor $\overset{\Delta}{=}$ $1 + $ (no. tuples which o'flow)/(total no. tuples)	1.2-3b, (Exercise 1.2-15), 1.3-3, 2.3-3
π_0	threshold for probe factor, $\pi \leq \pi_0$	1.2-3b, (Exercise 1.2-17)
π_L	probe factor for successful search with linear probing	1.3-3
π'_L	probe factor for unsuccessful search with linear probing	1.3-3
π_s	probe factor for successful search with separate chaining	1.3-3
π'_s	probe factor for unsuccessful search with separate chaining	1.3-3

TERM	MEANING	SECTION USED IN
ρ	access/transfer ratio	1.2-1, 1.3-3, 1.3-4, 1.3-5
$\rho(G)$	reduced graph of G	Appendix
σ	rotation speed (disk)	1.2-1
	tape speed	1.2-1
τ	transfer time/byte (disk, tape)	1.2-1, 1.3-3
$\tau(G)$	transitive closure of G	Appendix
ϕ	tape length	1.2-1
	fanout of ϕ-ary tree	1.3-4, 5.3-2, 5.3-3, 5.3-4, Appendix
ω	no. o'flows/record	1.3-3
	overhead ratio, sequential access	1.3-5
	don't care null value	2.4-3
Ω	(local) $= \alpha \, b \, \omega$	1.3-3
@	don't know null value	2.4-3
$\#_j$	cardinality of attrib. B_j in R (QT-expression)	4.2-1
$\rightarrow$	functional dependence	Used throughout text.
$\ell \atop {\overrightarrow{} \atop s}$	mapping cardinality	1.1-1, 1.4-3
$\leftarrow$	assignment	Used throughout text.
$\leftarrow +$	incremental assignment	Used throughout text.
$\supseteq$	superset	Used throughout text.
	σ-join operator **sup** or **divide**	2.1-3

TERM	MEANING	SECTION USED IN
$\subseteq$	subset	Used throughout text.
	σ-join operator **sub**	2.1-3
$\cap$	empty intersection of sets	2.1-3
	σ-join operator **sep**	2.1-3
$\cup$	complementary sets	2.1-3
	σ-join operation **span**	2.1-3

Index